Trading & Valuing Agency CMO Derivatives

An Execution Trader's Reference Guide

Part Art & Part Science

Ezekiel 25:17

"And I will execute great vengeance upon them with furious rebukes; and they shall know that I am the LORD, when I shall lay my vengeance upon them."

By Udoma A. Onwuachi, MBA

ISBN: 1452832943
ISBN-13: 9781452832944

FORWARD

I began my career in allocating Default Losses and, today, I allocate prepayment speeds to Mortgage Derivatives. When it comes to allocating prepayment, it is all about analyzing the collateral. In this book, I am going to walk you, step-by-step, through setting up a fund, from the documents that the Broker Dealer will need from you, to hiring your employees, to choosing third-party vendors, measuring the performances of your third party vendors, how to trade Agency CMO Derivatives and managing your Broker Dealer. Always remember you can fire your Broker Dealer or request to have a different Sales Trader, if you think your calls are not been returned promptly. Or your Sales Trader is regurgitating what he/she read in the *Wall Street Journal* or better yet, each time you visits your Broker Dealer you wind up in their Derivatives Department and they keep trying to sell you a financial product you don't need or have no idea about how the payoffs work.

In this book, I left out back-of-the-envelope math in arriving at the value of IIO and INV.

I have an example of a $5 million account that generates $330,000 annually. Yes, there are U.S. Government CMO Agency Bonds that appreciate with inflation as well as pay you interest; hence, you can live off your income. It makes me sick to read about professional athletes and Hollywood entertainers going broke. No man or woman should go broke after you have made it big. Long end PAC, SEQ, and Z Bonds continue to be a solid source of income. The key here is to have an expert on your side. Don't go in there by yourself trying to pay for bond; you will have your eye gouge out period.

I emphasized the need to have an active account when it comes to trading IIO. Begin your valuation by looking at the CAP/Floor levels. Look at the forward rates established or get a sense of how long you want to be in the market; that is, hold on to the bond. If you have an Asset Under Management(AUM) of $5 million, some Broker Dealers will not pick up the phone when you call and if your AUM is $50 million, some will be glad to sell you plain vanilla. And if you want to actively trade Agency CMO Derivatives, some Broker Dealers need a minimum of $100 million. Now, this is not to say some Broker Dealer out there may not waive this requirement; it is just that the Security and Exchange Commission (SEC) has a law that says the amount an asset management needs to have in order to buy Government Backed Derivatives.

I believe the Agency CMO Derivative is the hidden gem of the bond business. The media erroneously write about them, hence, the bad name. The bottom line is, hire a seasoned professional to run your account. This book should serve as a reference manual for any individual or commercial institution with more than $5 million to invest.

Udoma A. Onwuachi, MBA
Agency CMO Derivatives Specialist

TABLE OF CONTENT

Send your comments, negative or positive to:
Email: cmotrading@gmail.com

I wrote this reference guide to solve these following problems:

Problem 1:

Pension shortfall (Government, Corporations, Individuals, and Foundations)

Solution:

Buy MBS FIXED, MBS ARMS, and Long Lockout Paper (Zs, PAC, SEQ, etc.)

Problem 2:

You have $5 million and you want to sit back for the rest of your life. How can you make sure you do not have to work anymore? How can you live off your income?

Solution:

Buy Lockout Long End SEQ and PAC Bonds.

Problem 3:

A company has interest rate exposures; the cost of hedging your Portfolio and the margin call is costing you an arm and a leg.

Solution:

IIO and Inverse Floaters backed by 4.5 percent

Problem 4:

You are looking for double-digit yield.

Solution:

Buy Support Bonds and IIO.

Just like you say telephone in any language, there are liabilities to match, money to put to work, and numerous challenges to deal with at the end of the day, including being able to identify the problem and come up with solutions. You want to be receiving good news not bad news.

QUESTIONS EVERY AGENCY CMO DERIVATIVES TRADER SHOULD ASK

How can I trade Inverse IO/IO/PO/INV?
Can I use MBS as collateral?
Which Broker Dealer should I use?
I saw a similar IIO trade higher than what I paid for it.
I want to increase my position size.
How do I go about it?
Can I trade IIO/IO/PO using inventory financing?
How long should I hold on to an IIO/IO before I sell.
Why are most boutique firms based in Boca Raton, Florida?
I don't have \$100 million, but I have \$10 million.
Can I still trade IIO/IO Bonds?
I want to actively trade Mortgage Derivatives.
What I need to know?
I am not allowed to trade Mortgage Derivatives because of my benchmark restrictions.
What can I do?
Can I take the bond to the issuer for them to buy it back from me?
How much sales coverage do I need?
How can I manage the expectation of my sales coverage?

CASE STUDY:

A multi-billionaire industrialist is considering buying 16 percent stake in English Premier League Club, Arsenal. The stake is said to be worth £96 million as the battle for the takeover of the elite football club appears set for a grand finale. The millionaire confirmed to his friend last night that he was "seriously considering" investing in the club. He has already registered his interest with Blackstone, the American finance house contracted by Lady Nina Bracewell-Smith, Arsenal's fourth-largest shareholder who wants to sell her stake, worth about £96 million. She expects the sale will fetch her around £160 million.

The millionaire's interest had been in the making for a while, while his relationship and support for Arsenal dates back "a long time." "It started in 1980 when I forged a relationship with Mr. David Dein, former vice-chairman of the board of Arsenal," he said, explaining that Dein sold him his first consignment of sugar at the time. He began watching Arsenal's matches as Dein's guest and remained a firm supporter of the club. "That is when I developed an interest in Arsenal, and when the opportunity presented itself to acquire a stake in the club, I went for it," he said.

If the millionaire's bid is successful, he could become a major factor in the cold takeover war between American billionaire, Stan Kroenke, and Uzbek Oligarch and Alisher Usmanov—the two biggest investors in the company.

Kroenke currently owns 29.9 percent of the club, while Usmanov owns 26 percent. Under UK rules, any investor who hits the 29.99 percent threshold will be obliged to launch a formal takeover bid and buy out the other shareholders.

Kroenke is yet to declare a takeover intent, but Usmanov has not hidden his interest in owning a majority stake in the club. Usmanov, who is in the steel business, started investing in Arsenal three years ago through Red & White Holdings, after Dein sold his 14.58 percent stake to the Uzbek.

Arsenal stock currently trades for £10,000 per share while the company's overall market value is estimated at £606 million. Apart from the millionaire, Kroenke and Usmanov are also said to be interested in buying Bracewell-Smith's share in what would be the mother of all fights to take full control of the club. Kroenke is just a few shares away from hitting the threshold, and is said to enjoy the trust of other members of the board who had initially resisted his interest until Usmanov showed up. In a twist, board members are now friendly with him and antagonistic of Usmanov who, despite being the second largest shareholder in the club, has not been offered a seat on the board.

Dein, acrimoniously left his Arsenal position in August 2007 to become chairman of Usmanov's special purpose vehicle, Red & White, which was set up to bid for the controlling stake in Arsenal. Dein left as chairperson of the outfit a year later, reportedly to improve relations between Usmanov and the Arsenal board.

Bracewell-Smith, the lady whose stake is up for sale, is believed to want to do business quickly before the new UK Government announces its emergency budget in four weeks which it is expected that capital gains tax will be significantly increased. If she does not by the following month, she could lose millions of pounds if she still sells under a new capital gains tax regime.

"A Long end PAC or SEQ bond is better than this investment."

Kroenke, who owns the NBA's Denver Nuggets and the Colorado Rapids, an MLS football team, both in the US, was reported by Times of London summer 2010 as the favorite to buy Bracewell-Smith's shares. This will increase his stake to over 45 percent and automatically trigger the takeover clause.

Under UK rules, once a shareholder reaches a 30 percent shareholding, he/she is deemed by the takeover panel to have "effective control" of the firm and must then make an offer for the remaining shares.

If, after the offer has been made, the "offerer" has more than 50 percent of the shares, he/she is deemed to have been successful in the takeover and legally in control.

If an offer is unsuccessful and the 50 percent shareholding level is not breached, then the "offerer" cannot come back with another takeover attempt for twelve months, unless invited to do so by the company.

AGENCY CMO MORTGAGE DERIVATIVES FUND SET UP

1. Raise cash
2. Write up your investment policy
3. You need a Tax ID
4. Background information of principle, where the trader went to school, how long the trader has been in the industry, and the trader's work experience
5. Recruit your board of directors
6. Document the ultimate Beneficial Owner/ Principal of the asset management document
7. Prepare your Limited Partnership Agreement
8. Recent financial statement showing current cash under management
9. Most firms have a cut off point AUM wise, that is, if your AUM is less than $5 million, the Broker Dealer will not offer or sell any private placement products.

- Investment Management: Establishing investment strategy, trading, Portfolio modeling, compliance monitoring and periodic reporting

- Risk Assessment and Management: Measuring all forms of risk and establishing risk controls and mitigates, benchmark comparisons, and periodic reporting

- Transaction and Data Management: Trade ticketing and income processing leading to timely settlement and accounting of investment account activities by custodian, and accounting

All securities should be held in a custodian accounts for the company's benefit. All investment Portfolio transactions should be delivered to the chosen custodian, who then settles, clears, and processes trade and income transactions.

AGENCY CMO DERIVATIVES FINANCIAL TECHNOLOGY

You should have your custodian perform the following tasks:

- Electronic receipt of trade instructions—the automated pre-matching of instruction and swift resolution of discrepancies, and the final exchange of payments for securities
- Safekeeping of assets and corporate action processing, income collection, proxy voting, and tax services
- Evaluations given that they are battle tested and have seasoned top notch structured products evaluators (The Company's investment Portfolio should be evaluated twice a month.)

Independent bond pricing is like raising a child. Once you have a child, you have to send him/her to school, help the child with his/her home work, feed him/her the right food, and go to the parent-teacher association meetings.

Know what's going on in the market; this way, you can keep up with your NAV. Do remember that you have to work with various financial vendors.

Support the Bonds in your Portfolio by providing your third party vendors with the market colors that you get from various Broker Dealers.

Make sure to read the methodology page of your chosen vendor. Please set up a meeting with your Account Manager and have all your questions ready, this way you understand how the vendors systems works.

I recommend that you send market color, such as the types of trade that you get from your Broker Dealer, for it will help to understand why you may say you saw a bond at XY dollars and your pricing vendor have it at XPY dollars. The best thing to do is to get to know the evaluators. Your pricing vendors are here to help you achieve your objective by providing you with daily market levels.

REPORTS THAT EVERY AGENCY CMO DERIVATIVES TRADER NEEDS

Exposure Report: should be generated in Excel using data from a Portfolio analytic platform in combination with the static guideline limits. This should be delivered to the Portfolio Manager. Your hedge fund should use the report to measure the available room per specific guidelines, in conjunction with similar information produced by your trading platform.

Portfolio Analytic Platform Guideline Report: should be delivered automatically to a pre-established list, including parties outside of your fund. This report should display the results of testing all investment rules run on a trade-date.

Portfolio Appraisal Report: should be delivered to your fund's Portfolio Manager. This report should display security-specific details about each holding in various client accounts. You should use this report as a reference in determining investment strategy.

Finance Portfolio Summary Report: should be generated with a custom reporting tool and should be augmented, as appropriate, to adhere to finance requirements. The report should produce an Excel spreadsheet compatible file that should include a variety of descriptive summaries and risk-related measures of the Portfolios.

Portfolio Report: should be delivered to the Portfolio Managers. This report should display Portfolio-level summary statistics. This report should be used as a reference in determining investment strategy and as an additional indication of guideline compliance.

Compliance Report:_should be generated automatically within the compliance manager function within your trading platform of choice upon the breech of an investment guideline due to a trade execution. This alert will then be delivered automatically to a pre-established mailing list of recipients, including parties outside of the company. The alerts should include information about the breech, including the trade date, CUSIP, par amount, and so on.

Additionally, compliance function within your trading platform provides users with on-line queries of previously alerted compliance breeches.

Lastly, compliance reports are available within your trading platform to indicate the current status of the Portfolio in relation to rules established within the system.

Cash Report: should be generated in Excel by combining output from the trading system with adjustments made after daily cash reconciliation is complete. Capital flows are ticketed in your trading platform of choice and should automatically update the cash positions. The report should indicate available cash, on both a trade-date and settlement-date basis, for the ensuing twenty-five days. This is what you will use to determine cash availability with respect to trading.

The Duties of an Agency CMO Derivatives Portfolio Manager and a CMO Derivatives Trader

- To manage all assets classes within the investment Portfolio
- Maintain the company's aim
- Strict adherence to internal/external investment rules
- To work synergistically with other departments within your fund, by providing them with market color which, hopefully, allows them do a better job in revenue generation.
- To leverage the systems in place to generate revenues for your clients_

- Asset management/trading
- Strict adherence to diversification rules and policies
- A complete understanding and awareness of the impact of trading, and the aggregate exposure of holdings
- Reassess importance/diversification of holdings

The Battalion

Agency CMO Portfolio Manager:

Determines macro view of markets and asset allocation strategy for all Portfolios
A process needs to be in place so that the PM's market view is clearly relayed to Traders for execution and implementation
Determines which new U.S Government Agency CMO strategies should be pursued

Agency CMO Trader:

Determines relative value, executes trades, and helps to form the PM's Portfolio strategy. Responsible for vetting and modeling strategies

Administrative Manager:

Responsible for obtaining third party performance measurement system
Responsible for vetting and modeling new revenue generating strategies within the firm and should help educate the desk with respect to U.S Government Agency CMO market strategies being applied in the tax exempt markets. Continue to work with other groups internally to assess the various asset classes overall risk.

AGENCY CMO DERIVATIVES FUND WORKFLOW

The Trader should contact one or more dealers with the amount of Bonds and CUSIP that his/her fund is offering. The negotiated selling process should be employed at the discretion of the Trader. Typically, negotiation occurs when the bond to be sold has characteristics that limit its liquidity or when there is a desire to maintain a greater degree of anonymity.

Ticketing Your Trade

The custodian accepts and processes transactions based on instruction received from the company. The custodian should verify the trade instructions conform to the Investor Service Agreement signed between the custodian and your firm, and you should verify that the transaction is from an authorized source. If the transaction is authorized, then on settlement date, the custodian should either take the security into custody and pay for the security based on the agreed price or should deliver the security sold and receive payment for the security based on the agreed sale price. The custodian should record all transaction action activity into its system. In addition, the custodian should:

1. Record interest and principle received
2. Ensure that securities are properly valued in accordance with client instructions.
3. Ensure that net asset values are properly calculated.
4. Ensure that cash is invested in accurately and timely in accordance with client instructions.

5. Ensure transaction files submitted to Accounting, the accounting service providers, are complete, accurate, and sent timely.
6. The physical trade ticket should be retained and made available for review as necessary

Trade Confirmation

Market practice dictates that all completed trades are checked out between trading and Portfolio Assistants of the executing broker and buy-side firm, respectively.

The Portfolio Assistant should affirm the following with the executing broker and remediate as appropriate:

1. Trade details CUSIP, par amount, price/yield, net money, and settlement date
2. Settlement location DTC number
3. Any other unique transaction specific details
4. Trade instructions

Releasing the trade for settlement accomplishes several critical tasks in the trade life cycle.

It makes the custodian department aware that there should be an item that must be settled in the market for the company's investment Portfolio. Then custodian enters the trade into their system, the information is conveyed to the custodian bank accounting department, which then forwards the trade to your accounting system.

Money flows

Accurate tracking of capital inflows results in more efficient investment of the incoming cash. Likewise, adequate cash availability for outflows prevents unnecessary shortfalls. The treasury team should deliver all capital adjustments, inflows, and outflows by email. The email should include dollar amount and expected/required timing of the flow.

Money Management

Your hedge fund is responsible for managing the cash flows of the investment Portfolios to ensure timely settlement of trades, adequate provision of liquidity, and optimization of Portfolio returns. Cash flows into the Portfolio arise from a number of sources including capital inflows, coupon payments, settlement proceeds of securities sold, and proceeds due to redemption call or maturity of a security. Cash flows out of the Portfolio should include capital withdrawals and payment on settlement of securities bought.

Use a spreadsheet-based report to displays the next fifteen business days' cash balances based upon information generated in Portfolio analytic platform and received from the treasury. The report should include both the trade- and settlement-date cash balances.

Trade Settlements

After successfully reviewing submitted trades on-line within the custodian's report, company personnel should monitor the trade until it shows settled in the system. If for some reason an item appears unsettled after noon on the scheduled settlement date, your hedge fund should contact custodian to ascertain the status of the trade.

When purchasing securities, accurate tracking of required trade settlement cash is a must. You should avoid unnecessary trade failures. A mistake like this could easily ruin your relationship with your counterparties. Likewise, accurate tracking of proceeds from selling securities results in more efficient reinvestment of the cash. Each trade ticket produced by your trading platform of choice includes net money, which is the sum of the transaction value of the security and accrued interest, if any.

COUPON PAYMENTS

Accurate tracking of future coupon payments results in more efficient investment of the cash flows. Expected cash flows resulting from coupon payments should be automatically calculated by both your trading platform of choice and Portfolio analytic platform.

Redemption of Securities

Accurate tracking of redemptions results in more efficient reinvestment of the cash flows. Maturity dates are part of a security's description, as are call features. When a bond matures, your trading platform of choice automatically incorporates the cash flow in its cash report. Most calls, at the option of the issuer, can be for only part of a position, and are typically announced twenty-five plus days prior to the call date and are reported to the custodian. Operations should review daily basis to track all new notices of calls.

Performance Measurement

Your firm should measure the performance of the Portfolios using the Portfolio analytic platform system. Portfolio analytic platform calculates the total rate of return using the daily method, time-weighted approach that is consistent with the rules outlined.

Your clients must review your Portfolio on a periodic basis; document in a client's memorandum that they did and that they understand what you bought.

The investment team should have a daily discussion of current and expected market conditions. While various members of your hedge fund produce the reports, this should be the responsibility of the Portfolio Manager to ensure their accuracy.

If issues, concerns, and/or discrepancies are noted, they should be followed up with the Trader in writing. A list of items pending resolution is maintained and reviewed by the Finance Officers to ensure that issues are being addressed in a timely manner.

Your hedge fund should generate reports that include a listing of holdings with both descriptive and risk-related information as well as Portfolio-level descriptive information and risk measures. In addition, the reports include comparable data for the appropriate benchmarks.

Transactions for the Period

Your hedge fund is responsible for reporting all transactions, purchases, and sales for the current reporting period. The report should include both descriptive security information as well trade specifics, including trade date, par amount, and price.

The Portfolio Manager should convey trades to the Trader via email. These instructions should usually be in the form of general parameters. When parameters are provided, they should typically include coupon range, par amount or percentage of Portfolio, maturity and/or duration range, and call structure or sector.

If you put Traders from Broker Dealer A, Broker Dealer B, and Broker Dealer C in a room and give them one IIO SUP or IIO PAC bond, I guarantee you they will all come out with a different price. It does not mean that they are all wrong;

it is called prepayment speed. If we all could predict prepayment, we would all be very rich. Hence, the reason why you should never say your price is right and the other one is wrong.

The Trader must confirm, independently, that all potential trades meet client Portfolio guideline requirements. In the case of potential sell trades, the Trader is expected to determine whether the potential GAAP and tax impact of the trade conforms to Finance department directives.

It is the Trader's responsibility to determine the fair market value of securities that may be traded. Your Trader's judgments should be based upon his/her knowledge gained through experience, current market information acquired in course of communicating with the Street, and by the use of various databases, tools, and models designed to aid in the valuation of securities.

The firm should to be responsible for identifying, discussing, and addressing key risk issues. The following two main committees should be responsible for the provide oversight and guidance for management of the investment Portfolio are the Investment Policy and Executive Asset Allocation Committee:

The primary objectives of these committees are as follows:

- To define appropriate policies and procedures to ensure that the risks associated with the management of the Portfolio are identified and addressed. To provide a forum for the senior officers of your fund to discuss current Portfolio issues, remedies, and mitigates.
- To review the business climate and to provide guidance and direction to the PM.

New Asset Acquisition

This capability should be required to update Portfolios and instruct the custodian bank for new issue securities that are not yet established in the pricing vendor or security master databases. For most Bonds, the new security should be setup by your pricing vendor.

Your fund staff is authorized to create new securities. New security setups are typically modeled on descriptive information provided during the transaction. Typically, a new security is setup by either the Trader or the Portfolio Assistant. Operations should confirm the setup for accuracy independently. Note that your Portfolio analytic platforms are data providers and should provide most of the information required to populate a new security record.

This is accomplished by performing an inquiry on the similar security and then selecting the add function.

Setting Up Your Broker Dealers of Choice

Consistent with the best practices of most investment operations, you should have access to establish new Broker Dealer and related settlement instructions. Access should be controlled by who is anticipated to be a resource within the firm. However, once established, your fund should review a report to ensure accurate entry within your trading platform of choice.

Brokers Dealers should be required to issue instructions on their letterhead for entry into the system.

Abiding by the Law

Your hedge fund is responsible for reporting on the compliance status of the Portfolios. This includes an affirmation that the Portfolios are in compliance and/or there is a disclosure of non-compliance over the reporting period. When a violation occurs, a violation disclosure report is generated and distributed to the Financing Group. Therefore, a quarter-ending violation report summarizes previously conveyed information.

Making Sure Your Portfolio Is in Compliance with SEC

Both your trading platform of choice and Portfolio analytic platform should be used for ensuring the investment Portfolios comply with the company's rules for the investment Portfolio. Your hedge fund should encode the compliance rules into your trading platform of choice and Portfolio analytic platform compliance modules.

Investment guideline compliance is primarily verified using compliance systems embedded within the trading system and the Portfolio management system, Portfolio analytic platform. Your hedge fund should encode the investment rules into the compliance module, which operates on a pre-trade basis and runs each time a trade is entered. Portfolio analytic platform is coded for rules as well, but runs on a next day or trade-date plus one basis, and runs daily. Several compliance rules cannot be measured in either or both systems. These tests are performed manually by either the Trader as appropriate, using Excel spreadsheets. The results of all tests are delivered to the PM and individuals outside of the company, and stored both electronically and in paper copy form.

All trades are modeled against investment rules/mandates before being implemented. The report and other compliance reports are generated to ensure the investment rules have been adhered to.

Your hedge fund should defined the following approach for reviewing and establishing the rules into your trading platform of choice

1. Active warning/violation – due to a trade
2. Passive warning/violation – due to an event other than a trade, such as a change in market values

Caution

This is a break through tolerance level that is set near the hedge fund's guideline limit. Building on the example above, a warning tolerance level could be at 3 percent. When an exposure exceeds 6.5 percent, a warning is delivered that an absolute guideline limit is being approached. Tolerance levels should be set based on factors such as total asset size and the practical size of individual bond positions.

Detection

Active: Your trading platform of choice should immediately produce a notice at the point of trade entry. In addition, the post-trade compliance feature of Portfolio analytic platform should also indicate that a breach has occurred. Both systems should automatically deliver notices to all appropriate parties.

Passive: By its nature, this event should typically be detected by the Portfolio analytic platform post-trade compliance system, on a next day basis.

Reporting of Test Results

Trading platform should automatically produce a report upon the occurrence of an active warning or violation. This report should be distributed by the system automatically to the Trader, the PM, Financing Group, and Legal. Your hedge fund should follow up with a report that explains the non-compliance.

The trading platform should generate and deliver both passive and active and warning and violation reports.

In addition to the automatic creation of warning and violation reports, the Trader should follow up immediately with the PM regarding a breach. Corrective action should then be discussed. Depending on the nature and severity of the breach, the Office of the Chief Finance Officer should be included in this conversation. Within a designated period of time, an error report should be generated that includes the nature of the error, the reason for its occurrence, the action taken to correct the error, and an estimate, if applicable, of the cost of the error.

Corrective Action

Passive: Correction of a passive violation is dependent upon the circumstances that led to the failure. The PM should confer with the treasurer, or the appropriate senior officer, to determine the best course of action.

Active: In most cases, a trade that results in a violation should be immediately reversed. In some situations, the PM should confer with the treasurer as to whether the failure should be corrected in a different manner or treated as an exception. When the Portfolio is in violation, the Trader should be required to pre-clear all trades until the failure is corrected.

Rules Generation

Compliance rules are entered both into your trading platform of choice and Portfolio analytic platform. Your trading platform of choice is the one currently used to monitor all rules except those that measure calculated fields against a designated benchmark.

On-going Monitoring

It should be important for the company's group to generate reports that identify remaining capacity to own a position before it exceeds a guideline limit. The report, Current Exposure Report, should provide current exposures and remaining room relative to a specific guideline. Data should be from your trading platform or Portfolio analytic platform.

However, as a final alert, once the Trader is ticketing a trade within the Portfolio analytic platform, he/she should be alerted if that specific trade triggers any violations, and must be manually overridden to continue. However, the trade may already be committed and, thus, an override is required to settle the commitment.

Rules and Regulators Report

The system should automatically notify specified company personnel whenever a violation has been identified within the system. The current delivery mechanism for this message should be via an e-mail.

A historical reporting engine is available to you via the other department function, which can query violations over a specified period.

Asset Servicing

Once the purchase of an instrument has been successfully settled, the on-going activity of asset servicing begins. Below are the on-going activities that are part of the maintenance of your fund

Reporting

For the company's investment Portfolio, custodian bank is the custodian and is responsible for the above stated services. This requires them to deliver accurate and timely information to various parties including the company, Financing and Accounting, and your firm's trading counterparts. This information is used to update and reconcile internal records and applicable components of the technology platform.

Income Processing

Forecasting future coupons and maturities should be critical for effectively managing the cash flow of Portfolios. This is accomplished by utilizing various tools available on the company's platform.

Making Sure Company Rules Are Enforced

Oversight and control of the company's group should be accomplished through existing account defined investment rules, organizational controls, and best practices that exist in the investment management business. More specifically, the following should exist:

Investment rules: General rules are approved by the client while more specific rules are been established by the investment committee. The rules include the investment objective, investment limits, and benchmark for the Portfolios. At least quarterly, Portfolio-specific investment rules should be reviewed by the clients to ensure they are consistent with the overall investment strategy.

Each member of the company's professional staff should affirm his/her receipt and understanding of the investment rules.

Your hedge fund senior management and clients must review the Portfolio on a periodic basis.

Once the vendors have been selected, the negotiation of the contract terms and service level agreements is managed by your hedge fund in coordination with other groups, as appropriate. Each vendor should be provided with appropriate company processing instructions, such as investment rules, custodian instructions, and accounting policies, systems protocols, and so on, as appropriate. Prior to signing the contract, The company's legal representative must review the contract for the appropriateness of terms, enforceability, jurisdiction issues, compliance with established policy, and other pertinent matters.

Once contracts between your hedge fund and the third party investment management services provider have been signed, your hedge fund should provide a listing of authorized individuals who can instruct the vendors on related investment and Portfolio activities. Any changes to these authorized individuals or their authorization level must be communicated in writing to the appropriate company in a timely manner.

The Trader should be provided with the client's specific investment rules that they input into their systems. All changes and/or modification to general and specific investment rules must be in writing and communicated and verified on a timely basis by an authorized individual. At least on an annual basis, the company's officers review account instructions to ensure accuracy with the company's directives. This should be documented via a positive confirmation of the account setup instruction with each Investment Manager.

On a monthly basis, the Finance department should receive invoices from each of the investment service providers. The Finance department confirms that the terms of the invoice are per the contract. If there are questions or concerns with the bill, the Finance department should resolve prior to authorizing payment. The invoices are signed to document the Finance department's authorization to pay.

MANAGING INSTITUTIONAL AGENCY CMO DERIVATIVES ACCOUNTS

Your overall investment strategy and goals should be reviewed and approved by the clients; yes, the clients have to be comfortable with how you are going to help maintain their fortune. Then the Investment Committee will draft and approved Portfolio-specific investment rules within the scope of your fund's investment policy and rules for each Portfolio. These rules should be more specific than the board approved investment rules, detailing specific Portfolio objectives, indices, security, and diversity limitations. Your fund investment rules are approved only by the Investment Committee. Where applicable, these rules are appended to the investment management agreements between your fund and each investment management firm.

The Portfolio Manager should be responsible for the oversight of both internal and external investment activities. In monitoring the internal investment management process, the PM reviews the daily trading log, the daily Portfolio summary report, and quarterly broker volume reports. In addition, the entire fund staff receives system-generated notices when a compliance violation occurs. Your fund typically confirms trades with the custodian by accessing custodian's platform.

The Portfolio Manager is also responsible for reviewing the existing investment rules, in the context of market developments, to ensure that they continue to achieve the company's investment objectives. Any proposed modifications to the specific rules are presented by the Portfolio Manager to the Investment

Committee along with documentation and/or research supporting the change. If a change was needed in the board approved investment rules, the proposed change would be submitted to the board for its approval.

The Investment Committee, as appropriate, reviews the proposed changes and makes necessary additions. The directors should approve the company's investment policy and rules and documents.

At least on an annual basis, both the board approved investment policy and rules, and the specific investment rules are formally reviewed and approved by the Investment Committee.

On an as needed basis, the trading department should receive a capital flow notice from the capital introduction department. There are two types of notices, an inflow notice and an outflow notice. An inflow notice indicates that money available for investment should be transferred into the investment Portfolio. An outflow notice indicates that money is required and must be transferred out of the investment Portfolio. All notices, which should normally be delivered by email, should also indicate the size and timing of the capital flow.

An inflow requires investment of the newly available cash. The Portfolio Manager should apply this cash within the framework of the existing investment management strategy. Then transferred cash should be temporarily invested in cash equivalent securities, including money market funds.

An outflow should be funded through the liquidation of cash equivalents and the borrowing against, or the sale of, longer term securities vis-à-vis Repo. In the latter scenario, the Portfolio Manager and other fund officer should identify the securities that should be sold or utilized for Repo after taking into account the overall investment strategy and the potential impact, if any, on the investment Portfolio's expected after-tax performance. Your hedge fund should provide notice, via email, to the finance team as to when the cash would be available for transfer.

The Portfolio Manager should be responsible for establishing the appropriate asset allocation mix relative to the investment strategy and other factors.

The Trader's daily functions should be parsed into two sub-functions: asset allocation and trading. Your hedge fund should be under the supervision of the

Portfolio Manager; this way, he/she will have full authority to carry out its responsibilities with respect to the management of the Portfolio.

Trading Agency CMO Derivatives

Your Trader should be responsible for understanding current market conditions and the relative value of the specific bond that may be traded by the company's group. The Trader has access to a broad range of resources to accomplish this task including systems, models, and databases that are either developed internally or available from external sources.

Asset Allocation

The Portfolio Manager should model and maintain an asset allocation strategy that incorporates multiple factors, which may include

1. Duration targets
2. Current structure vs. the benchmark
3. Tax impact, sector weightings/risk distribution

MAKING SURE YOU DON'T LOSE YOUR CLIENT'S MONEY

The fund working in close coordination should employ several tactics to measure and Report market, credit, and operational risks inherent to the investment management process.

Your funds should be responsible for identifying, quantifying, and, when necessary, mitigating the various forms of risk that the investment Portfolios may encounter, including, but not limited to, interest rate, call, reinvestment, credit, and operational risk.

Risk management should begin with the investment rules, which define the Portfolios' duration as a measure of interest rate risk targets and ranges, credit quality, and sector and security exposures. Your fund should then uses a range of tools to identify and quantify risk, including Portfolio analytic platform, your trading platform of choice, and other functionality, spreadsheet models, external research. Severity and/or probability, when measurable or estimate able, are taken into account when quantifying risk.

Portfolio reports that include Portfolio-level risk information should be delivered to the Financing Group. In addition, Portfolio reporting is made available to the Financing Group as requested. Violations of investment rules limits should automatically reported to members of the finance department as well.

The PM should be responsible for assessing the level of risk in the Portfolios and determining whether mitigation actions should be taken. Depending on the nature of the perceived risk, mitigation may be achieved through either the trading of Bonds or the use of Derivative hedge instruments.

Yes, you are in Government Backed space, but that does not mean you should not be concerned with the credit quality of the economy, corporations, vis-a-vis your vendor, because if your vendor goes under, you are in trouble. Check, on a quarterly basis, the credit of your counterparts by way of surveillance.

MAKING SURE THE AGENCY CMO DERIVATIVES YOU PAID FOR IS WHAT GETS DELIVERED

Trades are used to change in the security composition of a Portfolio and, therefore, potentially change in the income, return, and risk of the Portfolio. Trading is the primary tool in actively managing a Portfolio.

Each member of your fund's professional staff should affirm the reading of the company's trading procedures. The trading procedures should describe each aspect of the trading process, including required pre-trade procedures, modes of trading telephonic or electronic execution, separation of duties; trade related reporting, and oversight. Only approved personnel in your fund may execute a trade. This approved list should be sent to your trading counterparty. Likewise, only approved personnel in your fund have access to your trading platform, which is used to generate trade tickets.

The terms of a trade which include the CUSIP, par amount, price, net money, and settlement date, should be checked five times. After you have agreed to a trade's terms check, typically verbally, a trade ticket will then be entered into your trading platform.

Check with the back office of the executing broker from the details of the ticket and releases the ticket to custodian for electronic trade matching and settlement via your trading platform screen.

For your fund, Portfolio Manager must ensure that approval is granted by the clients for certain types of investment activities. This way, no client will come back to accuse you of buying an asset that is too risky for their taste.

TOOLS OF THE TRADE

1. Custodian account
2. An OAS platform
3. Trading Platform
4. Portfolio analytic platform
5. A bond analytics application
6. Broker dealer research

Side Chat:

I have been an institutional CMO Trader for over twenty years, and I wonder where some of these so-called broker/investors come up with these requests. People do not deliver free unless it is to a primary dealer. For sure, an investor is not buying from a brokerage house delivered free. I have traded in excess of $8 billion dollars in MBS paper over the last seven years. Not 8 B. This is a dead giveaway that this is a mystery deal. If you are not registered with FSA or FINRA you cannot collect money for the transfer of securities (CMOs). If you have any questions regarding the purchase and sale of roundlots, I would be happy to assist in the understanding. We are a registered BD.

So here we go again....When you borrow against a security (Government or private label), you are subject to the margin requirements of an opened margin account at a Broker Dealer or bank. The Federal Reserve Board (FRB) REG T, NYSE rules, and FINRA mandates that on margin accounts, money is loaned against the purchase of a security. FRB dictates the amount of credit margin a brokerage or bank may lend to its customers. REG T defines the minimum amount of margin required. Brokerage and bank internal policy may have more stringent rules. Reg T requires 50 percent of the cost of the transaction up front, and on options, you cannot margin that product. This is called the initial margin. Then there is a maintenance margin requirement; this is the requirement of maintaining at least a 25 percent equity in that margin account. If your margin account drops below that 25 percent requirement, you should receive a margin call, which can be met by either depositing cash or securities in that account. If you cannot deposit cash or securities, the whole account is liquidated and you are charged any shortage.

I have heard of some cases where Derivatives were margined. I do not believe an Interest Only Strip or INVIO should be margined. You are already buying a leveraged instrument; when borrowing you multiply the leverage. Two good examples of this trade going bad are Askin Capital Management and Long Term Capital Management. Self liquidating loans on securities accounts are scams. Loans against face value of Derivatives are scams. This is why investors need to have a professional on their side when investing in any type of Derivative.

Run, do not walk, away from anyone marketing a (MTN) Medium Term Note Program involving $50 billion dollars. There is no such animal. These supposed trading programs are the biggest scams in the securities business. Go to the

SEC enforcement Web page and type in MTN Trading program. You should get eighty-two enforcement actions. Here is the Web page related to this type of fraud:

http://www.sec.gov/divisions/enforce/primebank/howtheywork.shtml.

If you are choosing an investment, make sure it comes from a registered representative who is FINRA registered, and investigate the firm. You can check out the brokerage house and broker via broker check on their Web site.

OK, time to pan up? Let's take a poll. Raise your hand if you've ever traded over a billion dollars in cash Bonds in your life.

Not that I expect an honest answer (raising my hand), I came on here to lend my twenty-two years experience in CMO and Derivatives and am now being bombarded with BS. If you are not FINRA or FSA licensed you cannot take a fee for transacting in registered securities. And you can't have a client. If I get one more phone call or email stating, "I have a client...," I am gonna puke. Please get a job. If you want to transact bond trades, get licensed and work for a legit firm.

Done with the message; time to educate the new hire.

AGENCY CMO DERIVATIVES BROKEN BAND ANALYSIS

This is what you need to known about Agency CMO Structures: the number of tranche depends on demand and supply. From a microeconomics point of view, the marginal revenue has to be higher than the marginal cost. The goal of every Broker Dealer is to optimize their revenue either by cutting their fixed or variable cost.

The other thing to remember is in the PAC tranche, you will see or hear dealers say the upper or lower band is broken. This means is that if the PAC was structured and based on the assumptive data, the PAC would not go below 250, and given the economic events like the one we are now experiencing, the PAC is 150; the lower band is broken. The reverse would be true for the upper band.

Once a PAC is broken, chances are the companion tranche has taken a life of its own, meaning it might have paid off. The value of each tranche changes automatically.

As a Trader, you are valuing the structured risk, and your opinion may not be shared by all.

Types of Agency CMO Structures

Planned Amortization Class (PAC) Tranche

Sequential

Targeted Amortization Class (TAC) Tranche

Companion Tranches

Z-Tranches

Principal-Only (PO) Securities

Interest-Only (IO) Securities

Floating-Rate Tranche

Inverse Floater

Residuals

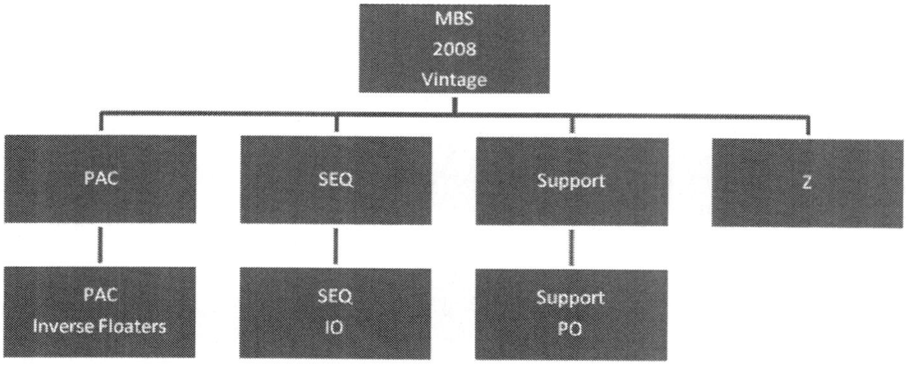

U.S GOVERNMENT AGENCY CMO TRADING STEP-BY-STEP

Below are the various components that you need to know as you embark on your trading career. Please do remember there could be other things that are not mentioned here; however, with this information, you will be able to buy and sell Bonds comfortably.

Sample of a Bond Liquidation Announcement

Auction will be structured as a sealed bid auction, whereby each bidder will submit its best bid by 10:00 a.m., New York City time, on June 30, 2010.

- Submit bids by emailing this form and a signed copy of the Bid Sheet (Annex 1 to the Investor Representations and Confidentiality Agreement (Exhibit A) in the Bid Package)

- Each submitted bid is subject to the terms and conditions of the Term Sheet and the Bid Sheet.

- In order to receive deal documents on underlying positions, please sign and return the Investor Representations and Confidentiality Agreement.

- Enter clean prices below—in terms of percentage of par, please change all ticks to decimals; all Bonds trade with accrued interest unless specified in the asset detail.

- Partial Bids will not be accepted.

- Bids may be submitted by Bucket or on a Lot basis (for each Transferable Sub-Lot); no bids on individual securities will be accepted.

- Bids may be submitted on a Lot basis only for Stub Piece Sub-Lots; no bids on individual Buckets in the Stub Piece Sub-Lots or on individual securities will be accepted.

- Any bidder who submits a bid on a Bucket Basis for a Bucket of a Sale Lot will be deemed to have submitted a bid of $1.00 on all of the other Buckets within such Sale Lot.

- Any cash bidder who submits a bid (either on a Bucket Basis or on a Portfolio Basis) for any Sale Lot other than the Schedule 1 Sale Lot must submit a bid (either on a Bucket Basis or on a Portfolio Basis) on the Schedule 1 Sale Lot.

- Winning bidders for the Stub Piece Sub-Lots will be awarded an interest in a securities maintenance account administered by Deutsche Bank or an affiliate, instead of receiving actual securities.

- Bids must be firm and actionable until 2:00 p.m.

- NO RESERVES—ALL LISTS WILL TRADE.

Pricing Agency CMO Derivatives

Pricing is a significant contributor to the Portfolio management and accounting process. As it relates to the accounting process, you should authorized your pricing vendor to deliver month-end prices to custodian accounting and those prices should then be used as necessary for GAAP purposes.

You should select your pricing vendor as your company's official source for all Portfolio security evolutions pricing.

For the Portfolio management function, daily prices should be procured and used to recalculate update risk measures including current yield, durations, compliance adherence, and other market sensitivities. Have the Trader/Portfolio Manager review and approve the updated price and reconcile prices between and pricing vendors. But be mindful because here is where, if the bond was not or is not performing well, it winds up being a back and forth with the pricing group and the pricing vendor.

For the trading process, price yield analysis can be performed utilizing your trading platform of choice's tools to assist in the rich/cheap analysis.

Selling IIO and IO Bonds

Bid Wanted

In a bid wanted situation, a finite list of brokers is notified—via your trading platform of choice's bid wanted system—of a specific list of Bonds that are out for the bid, the time that the bids are due, the bid time, the length of time that the bidder is committed to the bid (the firm time), and any other special terms. At the bid time, interested brokers should submit their bids. Prior to the end of the firm time, your fund must confirm the sale of the targeted Bonds to lock in the high bid price.

Bid lists should be sent out with a sufficient amount of time prior to the bid time to provide the Broker Dealers with sample opportunity to develop a bid. The length of notice time should depend on the number of items for the bid and the nature of the Bonds. Firm time length should vary with the size of the bid list and should be sufficient enough to allow for an orderly confirmation time.

Normal procedure in the bid wanted process is that Bonds to be traded should be confirmed to the highest bidder during the firm time. Your fund reserves the right, in all cases, not to trade a bond out for the bid.

On occasion, Bonds should not be confirmed to the highest bidder due to an error in the bid on the part of the broker, or for other reasons. Instead, the Bonds may be confirmed to the second highest bidder. This override must be approved by the PM. The Trader should document why the high bid was not valid and maintain a file.

The Trader is responsible for execution. If a trade requires any deviation from these written procedures, the Trader must seek prior approval from the PM. The trade should be documented as to reasons why procedures were modified.

At the Trader's discretion, a limited participant bid wanted process may be employed that uses your trading platform of choice's automated system. The

Trader should typically contact a limited number of dealers—usually less than six Broker Dealers—informing them that they are invited to bid. The bid process is essentially the same, but typically completed in a more compressed period of time. Bids from the participating dealers should be delivered via a message from your trading platform of choice. In most cases, this process should occur when there is more than one bond to sell and the Trader fully expects to sell the bond in question. It is anticipated, though, that most Bonds should be sold in competition via your trading platform of choice's bid wanted mechanism.

Now, be careful if you just want market color; say so, because no Mortgage Derivatives Trader likes to waste his/her time on a trade that will not be executed.

Selling IIO/IO

Confirm that the trade that you are about to do complies with the firm's rules.

Confirm the trade complies with tax and accounting directives.

Verify position in your trading platform of choice, and that it matches position at the custodian bank prior to trade.

Confirm securities are not used as collateral

Buying IIO/IO

Confirm that the trade that you are about to do complies with the firm's rules.

Confirm the amount of room available in any proposed buy candidate by checking with the Exposure Report.

Upon the selection of a bond, but prior to confirming the bond with the broker or placing an order with the salesperson, the Trader must run a compliance test in your trading platform of choice to confirm the bond doesn't violate any internal rules.

Below are the steps that you will need to follow when executing a trade:

- Type CUSIP of bond in your trading platform of choice to bring up description.
- Type in BO A Tax (amount of purchase) (price).
- When the security purchase screen appears, type in the broker code with whom you are doing the trade in the "broker" field.

If the amount, price, and broker fields are filled in, the compliance window should flash on the screen and disappear if there aren't any guideline violations. If a compliance violation/warning appears on the screen and asks you to OK the purchase, select Cancel since the purchase would violate the company's internal rules.

The Trader must now select a different bond that conforms to the purchase request from the Portfolio Manager and continue the process above to confirm that the selected security meets internal rules.

- Confirm that the cash position is sufficient to pay for the Bonds being purchased by delivering a message to the Portfolio Assistant regarding the liquidity need on the specific settlement date.
- Review the Cash Flow report. Add the trade amount and settlement date to the calendar of cash flows.

IIO/IO Trade Execution

Select security that fits the Portfolio Manager's stated criteria and comply with both the Portfolio rules and the firm's investment requirements. In the event that a bond must be sold, sale candidates should be identified by CUSIP. The Trader and/or the Portfolio Manager must provide to Finance Group a listing of all Bonds that are considered to be for sale as soon as the decision is made to sell.

Before executing a trade, the Trader must confirm that the Broker Dealer is listed as counterparty in desktop or the trading platform of choice.

Buying IIO and IO

It is the Trader's responsibility to advise the PM of all prospective purchases and to provide Finance with access to all necessary, available documentation. The Trader should provide an opinion on whether the prospective bond holding is acceptable and, if so, to provide an assessment of its credit quality. Your hedge fund may not purchase securities identified as rejected by Finance. The Trader is responsible for determining if a bond's offering price reflects Finance's credit assessment. While prospective purchases must be approved prior to purchase, a Trader may submit a subject order to secure potential access to an offered bond. When a subject order is given, the Trader must advise your hedge fund Finance department and provide the Broker Dealer with the conditions upon which the order is placed.

Secondary Market: Buying Previously Issued IO/IIO

Information on Bonds in the secondary market may be gathered from a number of sources, including a specific dealer's inventory, a bid wanted list, your trading platform of choice's Pick system, and in situations when customers are seeking buyers through the negotiation process.

Ticketing an IIO/IO Trade

Under normal operating conditions, the PM and Trader should enter tickets in your trading platform of choice's system. However, your back office should have the authority to enter and modify tickets in the event of an error. Trades should be ticketed in a reasonable time period after execution, and should always be written on the same day as the ticket written by the counterparty.

Confirm par amount, settle date, dollar price, and total money with the dealer. Every trade that is executed should have an electronic ticket sent to the Trader and Trader Assistant via your trading platform of choice by the counterparty. In addition, every trade should be printed out. The Trading Assistant should then confirm that the two tickets match. The Portfolio Assistant should initial both the company's ticket and the dealer's printed ticket, staple the two together, and file in the appropriate cabinet. Any discrepancies between the two tickets should generate a phone call to the salesperson to remedy the error.

Settlement

IO trades executed in the secondary market typically settle the regular way, which means money and Bonds should be delivered in three days from the trade date. Most IO Bonds settle through DTC—Depository Trust Company—which is an electronic clearinghouse that only settles trades if the money and the Bonds match exactly.

If Bonds are purchased in the primary market, settlement usually occurs within four weeks. Some new issue deals settle months, or even a full year, in the future in what is called a forward delivery. These types of purchases may call for collateral securities to be set aside until settlement date.

With forward delivery, please take into account that your accounting methods, by the time the securities are delivered, might have changed, hence, your firm needs to report a loss instead of a gain. Oops...do I hear buyer's remorse!

Side Talk:

Let me begin by saying thank you for stopping by CMO Derivatives.

My job here is to create a community of Mortgage Derivatives experts where we get to talk about the next stages of structured Mortgage Derivatives.

Let me give you some general understanding of the IO/IIO sectors.

There are two types of interest only sectors. We have the Trust and we have the Structure. Both sectors have an IO and IIO. When you say "Reverse IO—Floaters," I take it you mean IIO. Reverse IO coupon payment is mathematically calculated base on TSY/CMT/COFI or 3MLIBOR, depending on the one that was use. Therefore, your major risk here is interest rate risk. For as rates go down, it favors you; but when rates go up, you lose value.

The next risk is that of collateral risk. As rates go down, the 10TYS is probably following suit as well, which leads to a lower mortgage rates. Now, I am not going to go into seasoning, burnout, and loan size here, but customers tend to refinance whenever the rate is palatable to them, and if they have no pre-payment penalties. With a Reverse IO, you want a slow payer, that is, people who cannot refinance for reasons best know to them and collateral with high pre-payment penalty. Bear in mind when you look at this Reverse IO, know when to use PSA or CPR given the vintage.

The next risk is what I called perceptions of other PM's. Most, if not all, PM's look at the economic data in making investment decisions. They look at the PPI/CPI/RETAIL, SALES/UNEMPLOYMENT, and so on. If any of these economic data begin to show trends of being bullish, the PM may decide to act on it, which should affect the 10TSY, which then ultimately affects the thirty-year mortgage rate, which in turn affects the consumers ability to refinance or not and, hence, your Reverse IO.

The risk this instrument hedge is your loan and cash flow. For example, a mortgage company or bank that loaned out money when rates were at 5 percent and the rate are now at 2 percent with Reverse IO, is fully protected. Furthermore, asset management firms can use it to manage their Portfolio's duration as well as generate an alpha return if the right Reverse IO is bought. But, like I asserted earlier in my comment, not all Reverse IO are equal. They all behave differently based on a whole host of factors. It is imperative to have a well seasoned person look at these instruments to avoid having yours eye ripped out.

AGENCY CMO DERIVATIVES RELATIVE VALUE

Here are the variables that affect the value of your Agency CMO Derivatives.

- The ten year treasury
- Forward curve
- LIBOR
- Prepayment
- Settlement date/waterfall
- Tranche size
- The ability of the other parties to quantify the risk
- Portfolio Managers who must buy no matter what comes, rain or sunshine; they have to put money to work with a particular coupon/ tranche size

As you can see, as a tranche matures, the way each one of the above variable affects it is different than when it is a young tranche. You should be able to look at Bonds individually and collectively, arriving at a sound relative valuation; thus, when I wake you up at any given time of day, you should be able to tell your investors the value of the Bonds in their Portfolio.

There are so many moving parts to an Agency Derivatives that very rarely is it static. It is very vital that we don't take the approach of something is wrong with a model, for Derivatives are affected by the following variables:

- Prepayment
- Forward curve

- LIBOR
- Cash flow distribution/settlement date
- TSY
- PM view of rates
- Size

A LITTLE HISTORY FOLKS!

Since 1990, the securitization of Mortgage Derivatives has taken different shape. There are so many IO that look so identical, but when one looks at the structure, it is already busted. For example, some structure may have one Z bond and two Support Bonds while another may have only one support bond. Now, bear in mind that these two IO could have the same exact WAM, WAC, and Coupon. When it boils down to distribution on income and the pre-tax yield, it is never the same.

The only Derivatives that can be grouped are your STRIPS IO/PO; the very moment the investor moves in structure Derivatives, all bets are off.

Furthermore, the idea of going by the label is wrong. For example, a bond may begin as a PAC, but once broken, it becomes a SEQ. I saw a bond a few months ago that started out as a Floater but is now an IO.

In a nutshell, people change, Bonds also changes. The best analogy here is because two children are identical twin does not mean they will turn out the same way.

All Derivatives are not equal.

It is what it is, and that's it.

CMO PO BOND TRADING

Question:

My Traders continue to overpay for PO Bonds. Could you please let me know the variables to use when pricing and trading a PO bond?

Answer:

There are different types of PO Bonds, such as PAC, TAC, SC, SEQ, PT, STP SUP, PO, or Remics, and so on. You must take the following factors into consideration before submitting a bid or asking for a PO bond:

- The uncertainty of loan payments due to poor documentation and human error
- Proper hedging instrument
- The number of hedging contracts that you need
- Costs of hedging
- Option
- Past cash flow
- Scaling up prepayment models vectoring out the PSA/CPR with emphasis on key attributes, modified duration, effective duration, average life, and convexity using your trading platform of choice
- Forecasting payments given inflation, mortgage services fees, and loan balances

- Is the collateral backed by GNMA, FNMA, FHLMC, or a private label (whole loan CMO)?

PO(A) PO(B) PO(C)

PSA: 90 percent Base 110 percent

Coupon and Average live: 5.94 8.9 5.60

Coupon and Standard Deviation: 0.12 0.10 0.11

WAM: 307 311 300

PO (A) PO(B) PO(C)

Effective Duration: 11.4 20.0 10.50

The PO with a 20.0 effective duration is the most volatile, so when you bid/ask, you need to know the correct OAS and the forward yields curve, as you can see from above. The correct way to look at this PO is that as a prop Trader, this PO asset class should appreciate or lose 11 to 20 percent in the event of a 100bps in yield change.

As a prop Trader you want to shock the cash flow and duration; this gives you an idea of where to bid. The goal is to avoid overpaying for a bond and to avoid losing out on a bid.

PO(A) PO(B) PO(C)

Duration: 4.0 8.6 3.49

A prop Trader should quantify the exposure of the prepayment models risk with emphasis on the PSA if the deal is new, and CPR if the deal is a seasoned one. Bear in mind that major Broker Dealers have their own matrix; it is imperative that you use public information in analyzing the price that you want to pay for a bond. After all, Long Term Capital Management had its own matrix and the model failed.

The transparency and flexibility of your prepayment model should allow the Trader to modify the parameters to reflect your PSA/CPR expectations.

In trading Agency CMO PO, you should remember that the PO depreciates in a rising rates environment and appreciates in a low rate environment. You goal is to be able to tell when to bid either using OAS or a forward yield curve. When bidding for a new issue, it is imperative to remember that the value of your PO should depreciate due to amortization and discount value factors because the original principle decreases every month. I have priced over a thousand of PO (SUP, TAC, PT, STP, PAC, SEQ, and REMICS); these Bonds are not all equal. Remember that the OAS is not the be all and end all variable; other variables such as the effective duration, LTV, FICO scores and geographic analysis are as vital.

The best thing for a Hedge Fund Manager to do is visit an underwriter with his/her own coupon formula. Place an order instead of waiting for the underwriter to sell you some PO nobody wants to buy, and then get a promise that the value of your PO will not go down. I know of, and have seen, structures that were extremely profitable and remained so! The game of PO trading is like Las Vegas—the house never loses. You just need a seasoned Trader who can go toe-to-toe with the house and come out on top.

Always remember there are times to buy and sell PO. The question is, do you know the right time? And, can you value PO within minutes and place a bid/ask price if you have to?

In conclusion, an Agency CMO prop Trader needs to have an assumption based on the historical volatility vis-à-vis forward rates, option markets, effective duration, modified duration, and so on.

INVERSE FLOATER ANALYSIS

Question:

I am a Portfolio Manager with equity trading experience and not U.S Government CMO Agency Bonds Derivatives. How can I include Inverse Floating Bonds without destroying my P & L?

Answer:

Poor P & L is as a result of a badly negotiated coupon formula and the lack of an understanding on how to analyze the collateral and the structure.

My goal is to give you a worthwhile explanation of how to value and trade Inverse Floating Bonds in order to avoid heavy losses.

These are some of the variables you should look at when deciding to bid/ask for an Inverse Floater:

- Collateral: WAC, WALA, CPN, SPEED
- Coupon Structure: Bond Type, Lever, CPN, DM, CAP, YLD FWD and the effective duration
- Hedging: A Portfolio of Inverse Floating Bonds should be hedge with an option contract.

In buying an option contract, you should ask yourself these following questions:

1. Which option contract should be used for the hedge?
2. Which month?

3. Which strike price?
4. How many contracts should be used?

The first CMO was created by Credit First Boston in 1983. Some of today's Traders were still in elementary school when the first CMO was structured, so they were not trading CMO during the President Carter's double digit inflationary rate or President Regan's double digit interest rates. Thus, they won't know how Inverse Floating Bonds should react in a double digit inflation or interest rate environment.

Not all Inverses are equal. Most are volatile, while some are not. Also consider that you could be looking at PAC Inverse, SEQ Inverse, PT Inverse, SUP Inverse, Remic Inverse, and so on.

In a structure of two tranches in comparison to an Inverse with five structures, I do not recommend you use recombination in valuing the Inverse. In addition, the effective duration signals the change in cash flows due to a change in prepayment speeds and interest rate changes, that is, for those Bonds that are linked to the 1M Libor, COFI or T12. A Trader should know the collateral prepayment speed, inflation, interest swaptions, convexity, and forward yield curve.

The Inverse bond reset margin is vital. What is driving the index levels, in some cases the currency market, does play a role on most indexes like the Libor. Why? Foreign investors in pursuit of a better return on their investment might buy other currency instead of the dollar; this way, they get a better interest income on their currency, hence forcing the Fed to choose to save the dollar or the housing market.

For a Trader who pays 64¢ on a dollar in the primary market, if the index hits the strike, it is customary for the Inverse Floater to trade around 63¢ on a dollar to 65¢ on a dollar. In this case, the option is what the street is looking at, and predicting the index should decrease by 25bps. However, if the index does not equal the value of your Inverse, the outcome could be anyone's call.

As someone who has seen the Inverse Floating universe and the mistakes Traders make, it is no surprise that most proprietary trading desk Portfolio Managers are having sleepless nights while the Hedge Fund star Traders sleep like babies.

Now, with all this talk about option this and option that, don't underestimate the power of the collateral prepayment speed. If a good number of people walk away from their mortgage payment, you can forget the high lever, for you won't have enough cash to meet employee retirements or any other obligations for that matter.

In modeling deals, you probably subscribe to an analytics platform meaning that you have to wait around for a third party entity to send you the cash flow. Now, If you have not modeled the deal and you cannot wait, the programmers on your trading desk should know what to do. I recommend you sit down with your C++ developers and I tell them the variables that you need in other to arrive at the bid/ask price for the Inverse Floater.

In order to trade profitably, an Inverse Floater bond Trader must understand what is vital and what's not vital about the Inverse Floating bond asset class, such as, margin reset, forward curve, swap, the PSA/CPR at which the mortgage borrower is paying back the loan, the OAS level, and so on. For example, I pointed a proprietary Trader in the right direction.

This Trader was going to sell 1,000,000 shares of Bonds at $75.00 each, and I told him to sell it for $88.50/32 base on my algorithmic calculations. In the end, the Trader was paid $88.50/32 for the bond. The major factor here was the CPR speed—the rate at which people are paying back the loans they borrowed to buy their first house—in the case of default, puts the investor in trouble. The lesson learned here is the need for a Trader to have a solid evaluation skill set, like mine. My experience and abilities allowed me to value the bond and arrive at a bid/ask price.

The question is, does your Trader know when to buy and when to sell? Some Inverse Floating Bonds are linked to the real estate business cycles. As someone who has seen thousands of Inverses and valued them given the interest rate environment, your fortune should take off. The company's sentimental issue is the structure and cash flow.

The major loss that the U.S Government CMO Agency Bonds Derivative asset class has seen in the past years has to do with Traders who did understand that the LIBOR index and the Inverse is linked to the prepayment speed. These Traders buy into strength and then turn around to sell weakness. Most of the time, the Trader does not have an exit strategy.

As the Hedge Fund industry becomes a full grown adult, investment banks are jumping into the game, which means the lack of the required specialist skill sets to look at various Agency CMO asset classes. However, the good news here is the volume of illiquid property that should turn into cash is very huge, hence, creating the opportunity for great wealth creation. While Wall Street is the capital market center of the world, and a most innovative one at that, I expect China, Japan, and India to follow suit in the creation of Collateral Mortgage Obligations, hence calling for the demand for a hands-on, seasoned Agency CMO specialist. As someone who has seen the whole universe of Agency CMO Inverse Floaters, I know of, and have seen, Inverse Floaters and the struggles Hedge Fund Managers and commercial bank trading desks have in arriving at a bid/ask price due lack of trading experience.

In conclusion, the paramount issue here is been able to submit a bid/ask in the primary or secondary market of Inverse Floaters. In addition, making sure to have an entry and exit strategy. Your goal as a proprietary Portfolio Manager is to make sure that your Traders submit the right bid/ask price when selling Inverse Floaters.

Agency CMO Inverse Floaters is a very volatile asset class. If you structure a solid Inverse Floater, you should be rewarded. If you buy an Inverse Floater backed with poor quality collateral, you should bleed to death, money wise. Your Agency CMO Inverse Floater is only as good as the collateral backing it.

Inverse Floater Bond Cash Flow Mechanics:_

New-Issue CMO Bond:

Customer buys $100m 6/20

CMO closing date

(also settlement date) 6/25

Ginnie Mae releases August pool factors.

Updated bond factor for 7/5

June cash flows paid to investors 7/16

Settlement Date

In secondary trading of CMO classes, the settlement is **T+3**, or three business days after the trade date. The **accrual date** for Agency CMOs—the date from which interest starts to accrue on the Bonds—is, as with Agency pass-through, the first of each month.

Expected Income Flow Math

Because this is a new issue, the current **bond factor** is 1.0, so the current face is equal to the original face of $50 million. Since the accrual date is June 1, 2010, the accrued interest is:

Accrued Interest = Current Face * Coupon Rate * (Day of Month - 1)/360

= $50,000,000 * 12% * (30-1)/360 = $483,333.33

Hence, the total amount due from the investor is:

Total Amount Due = Current Face * (Price / 100) + Accrued Interest

= $50,000,000 * (95 / 100) + $483,333.33

= $47,983,333.33

Agency CMO Monthly Cash Flow Income

Payment dates for Agency CMO usually correspond to the payment dates for the underlying pass-through. For Ginnie Mae's, the payment date is the fifteenth of the month. The investor receives the June principal and interest on July 2010. The interest paid is:

Monthly Interest Payment You will receive = Face Amount (as of June 1, 2010) * Coupon Rate / 12

= $100,000,000 * 6.5% / 12 = $541,666.67

The key here is to search for a bond with a lockout window.

Payments

Accrued Interest = Current Face (Notional) * Coupon Rate * 155/360

= $100,000,000 * 6.5% * 155/360

= $2,798,611.11

Total Amount Due = Current Face * (Price / 100) + Accrued Interest

= $100,000,000 * (105 / 100)

= $107,798,611.11

Amount of Money to Expect:

Normal Interest Payment = Current Face * Coupon Rate / 12

= $100,000,000 *6. 5% / 12 = $541,666.67

Pool Factor Release Prediction

Statistical modeling shows there are IO/IIO that swing tremendously around this date, so it is imperative to know the type of IO/IIO structure to buy given the health of the economy, looking at the CPI, PPI, and unemployment and inflationary data points, or you can simply use a technical trend indicator and to hell with fundamentals.

In a nutshell, you can have a strategy were by you position a trade based on where you see or think factors will fall vis-a-vis prepayments.

Fannie Mae's Purchases of Delinquent Loans from MBS Trusts

In order to help Fannie Mae preserve capital by reducing net funding costs and, thereby, reduce the amount of additional draws from the U.S. Department of Finance, on February 10, 2010, Fannie Mae announced that it intends to increase significantly its purchases of delinquent loans—loans that are delinquent as to four or more full consecutive monthly payments—from its single-family MBS trusts.

The delinquent loan removals or reclassifications should generally comply with the provisions set forth in Fannie Mae's trust documents and published servicing rules.

At a high level, on approximately the fourteenth business day of each month, Fannie Mae instructs servicers who qualify delinquent loans to remove them from specific pools.

Reclassifications generally occur by the last business day of the month. In both Fannie Mae's systems and through servicers' operational processes, once the loan has been removed from the pool, the loan's payment cycle is changed from a scheduled/scheduled to an actual/actual cycle. If the servicer is unable to reclassify the loan from the servicer's system in the initial given month, the loan follows an exception process by which the loan should be addressed in the next month.

Prior to the removal of the loan from the MBS pool, the servicer should remit scheduled principal and scheduled interest. However, after the loan is removed from the MBS pool, the servicer should remit actual principal and actual interest.

For investors, it is important to note that a prepayment of the loan is reflected in the month immediately following removal. Fannie Mae publishes the Factors File on the fourth business day of the month and the principal and interest remittance to certificate holders is made on the twenty-fifth day of the month. If the twenty-fifth day is not a business day, payment should be made on the next business day. The following timeline summarizes the reclassification process at a high level.

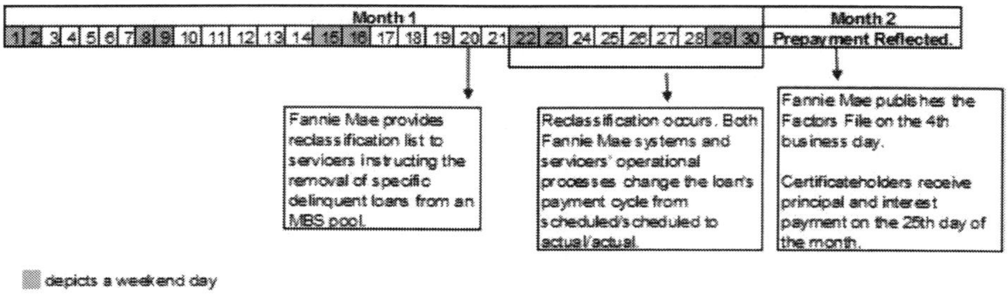

Pool Factor Dates

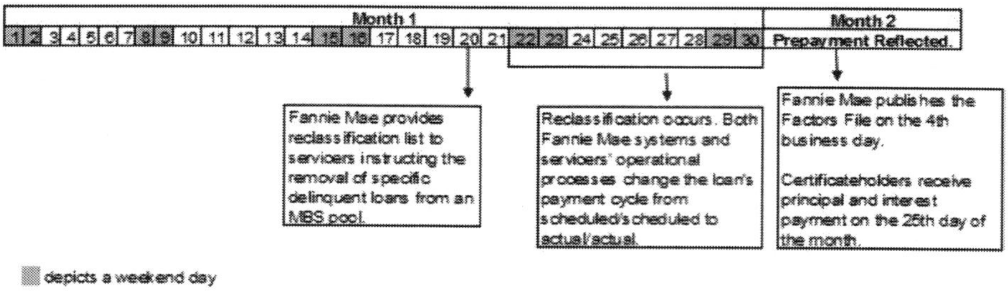

Source: Fannie Mae

Calculation:

$$\text{Pool Factor} = \frac{\text{Outstanding principle balance}}{\text{Original principle balance}}$$

Freddie Mac:

Factor: a truncated eight-digit decimal that Freddie Mac calculates each month for each PC that, when multiplied by its original principal balance, equals its remaining principal balance. The Pool Factor for any month reflects the principal balance that remains after the payment to the holder of the PC is made on the payment date:

- In the same month, for Gold PCs
- In the following month, for ARM PCs

Factor Date: The date corresponding factor is effective, which is first day of the month for all PCs.

Ginnie Mae: Certificate Factor Date

With respect to each distribution date, the seventh business day (for each Ginnie Mae I certificate) or the eighth business day (for each Ginnie Mae II certificate) of the month in which such distribution date occurs.

CALCULATING MACAULAY'S DURATION

$$\text{Par Value Bond Duration} = \frac{\left(1+\frac{\text{YTM}}{2}\right)}{\text{YTM}}\left[1-\frac{1}{\left(1+\frac{\text{YTM}}{2}\right)^{2M}}\right]$$

This is how Macaulay's duration for a par value bond is modeled in any static or OAS model:

Duration Math

$$\text{MD} = \frac{1+\frac{\text{YTM}}{2}}{\text{YTM}} - \frac{\left(1+\frac{\text{YTM}}{2}\right)+M(C-\text{YTM})}{\text{YTM}+C\left[\left(1+\frac{\text{YTM}}{2}\right)^{2M}-1\right]}$$

Know your benchmark inside and out. You should consider matching the duration and call it a day. Or, you can actively trade daily or weekly, look at the historical data, do your backward testing, and then trade.

TOTAL RETURN SWAP IO/PO MECHANICS (DELTA ONE TRADING)

Here are some basic mechanics of how a TRS would work.

You and your Broker Dealer should work through the mechanics and in terms of risk, you also need an offsetting risks to any of these exposures.

Mechanics

- Total Return Payer (Short): Pays cash flow off of Reference Obligation + MTM change (if positive)
- Total Return Receiver (Long): Pays (LIBOR + spread) financing + MTM change (if negative)
- TRS Notional: For P&I bond, notional of Reference Obligation; if IO/PO notional for the purposes of calculating the LIBOR leg should be the market value.
- MTM: Monthly, determined by your Broker Dealer
- Tenor: TBD
- <u>IO:</u> Total Return Payer pays the interest off the IO which is partially offset by the MTM decrease over time; LIBOR leg based off of market value
- <u>PO:</u> Total Return Payer pays generally no ongoing cash flow off the PO, but generally pays the accretion in the MTM; LIBOR leg based off of market value

SIMPLE AGENCY CMO DERIVATIVES QUANTITATIVE METHODS

The price of the bond is

$$V = \sum_{i=1}^{n} c_i P(t_i)$$

The yield on the bond, which we should call $\overline{r}$, is the unique number that satisfies the equation

$$V = \sum_{i=1}^{n} c_i e^{-\overline{r} t_i}$$

$$V = ce^{-\overline{r}t}$$

$$\overline{r} = \frac{1}{t} \; -\ln(V / c) \; .$$

$$\overline{r} = \frac{1}{t} \; -\ln(P(t)) \; .$$

Yield curve

$$\boxed{\overline{r}(t) = \frac{1}{t} \; -\ln(P(t))}$$

Forward Interest Rates

$$r(t) = \frac{D'(t)}{D(t)}. \tag{0.1}$$

Since P(t) = 1/D(t), it's not too hard to convert this to

$$r(t) = -\frac{P'(t)}{P(t)}. \tag{0.2}$$

Converting r, $\bar{r}$, P(t), D(t)

r(t) = -P'(t) / P(t) = - d/dt (ln P(t))

$\bar{r}$ (t) = (1/t) (-ln P(t))

From r to $\bar{r}$

$\bar{r}(t) = \left(\frac{1}{t}\right)\int_0^t r(s)ds$ (that is, $\bar{r}$(t) is the average value of r(s) on the interval [0, t])

r(t) = $\bar{r}$(t) + t$\bar{r}$'(t)

From r and $\bar{r}$ to P

$$\text{P(t)} = \exp\left(-\int_0^t r(s)ds\right)$$

$$\text{P(t)} = \exp\left(-t\bar{r}(t)\right)$$

COMMON SENSE MORTGAGE DERIVATIVES TRADING

No one person has all the answers. You will make mistakes because you are human. Learn from your mistakes and move on; the key is to fix your mistake. Furthermore, at the end of the day, trading Agency CMO Derivatives is like a poker game; either you are wining or the house is winning. In addition, you are betting against other investors, Governments, and God's plans for the future.

Tricks of the trade:

Cap = Believes rates will get that high, say 7.5 percent

Floor = Believes rates will get this low, say 0.25 percent

Swap = I have $500 million coming in the next six months, and I am scared the value of the dollar may not hold, or I have to give my subsidiary $1 billion, but I have Yen and I don't want to use more Yen to buy the dollar.

Understand liquidity. What I am saying to you here is if your bond is one of a kind, then the value could be peanuts or the whole peanut farm. So please don't be a tourist in the bond market.

If the Government issues thirty-year bond you should short thirty year and go long ten year. This way you can dabble in spread trading. But be careful, for this trade may or may not work due to the demand for the thirty-year paper.

Trading in fraction form can be profitable.

If a major Broker Dealer refuses to do business with you, you can deal with Broker Dealers in Boca Raton or Memphis, TN. These bond daddies may cut you some slack. Positive carry means the cost of borrowing is lesser than the profit.

Negative carry cost of borrowing is greater than the profit.

Trivia: In 1981, the fund rate was a whopping 21 percent.

REPO

As an MBS Trader/Portfolio Manager, you need to get your Repo on.

Here are the things you need to know about Repo application:

There were twenty-two dealers in the U.S. as of the time I dealt in Repos, but after the credit debacle, it should be less now.

Repo is a one-day transaction because of the constant turn over in inventory.

Repo's Profile:

- High interest rate
- Cash balance been invested
- Sell today buy back tomorrow

Special lending at an advantageous rate, as a buy Side Trader/Portfolio Manager you can double your return by using this free money.

Now, there is this thing called open-ended Repo; this means it is subject to negotiation. The Fed uses Repo as a part of their monetary tool to increase money for holiday spending. The Fed will use matchbook operations, and this is possible because of credit risk. Deutsche Bank is the highest rated bank in the U.S., and the largest matchbook player in the great U.S.

Creating more of the same bond creates liquidity. A new deal is about to come to the market. What bid to pay? Where should it trade?

Look at previous deals.

New three months, look at current trading three months.

The direction of the market

Demand from the market; do I see liquidity: customers demand.

Current inventory

Do not do too much business with one Broker Dealer. The key here is relationship and services. Watch out for trade activities before settlement date because lots of Hedge Funds love this kind of trade, because it is free cash flow.

Not every deal is the same, no matter what you may have read or what you were told. Same ratings or credit enhancement are not equal due to events, for example, MBIA, Katrina. Other insurers were not exposed.

Questions to Ask Yourself

When would I want volatility in my Portfolio?

For me I wanted it when rates were going down. I increased my durations by buying long WAL Bonds. Be mindful of lower coupons Bonds because of the higher volatility.

Lower CPI may lead to higher bond prices. I simply built a duration neutral Portfolio.

Positive convexity simply means the price will go up a lot higher than how sharply it will fall. The reverse is true for negative convexity bond. Prepayment risk leads to negative convexity, which is like a callable bond, hence, if your Portfolio is negatively convex, expect lost of value depreciation.

How can you use negative convexity to your advantage?

Buy all high negatively convexity Bonds and store them away.

The three-month T-bill is what is used to introduce money into the system. Look at the three- month bill trend. An increase in three month T-bill interest rate will or can be seen as an indicator of a continuing rise in interest rate.

Spread trading is for Broker Dealers and Hedge Funds.

Duration trading is for Insurance and Pension Funds.

If you have never traded in a sector before, make sure you have room for errors.

A $1 billion PAC bond buyer and $2 million PAC bond buyer will never get the same attention or information for that matter!

Here is a $100 million tranche: if you buy $2 million and some other fund buys $98 million, mark my words, you both will not get the same price quote!

Right or wrong depends if you are a buy and hold account or a buy and sell account!

Since the capital market crash, many investors have found a new investment haven in the U.S Government CMO Agency Bonds market. And as of now, the market players say that the equity market has shrunk so much that it has reduced to just a mere fraction of the existing bond market in the country.

It is not that capital preservation is so much bigger that there is so much money for the ordinary investors, who consider IIO and INV markets, especially the Hedge Fund, looking for double-digit yields. Right now, after the credit melee, IIO and INV is pointing to only one direction. There is an overwhelming switchover from the equity market, which has ballooned to an oversubscription, particularly for Agency CMO Bonds. But, as they say, one man's gain is another man's loss; the latest development tends to be choking out other instruments in the non-fixed income market, as my findings reveal.

Recovering from the price meltdown at the stock market, small investors should shift their attention to the Agency CMO bond market. This marks the era of steady profits for the foreseeable future. But despite the oversubscriptions that have trailed the Agency CMO Bonds in the primary U.S Government CMO Agency Bonds market, the secondary segment, particularly the private, continue to lack that type of depth. As for the on-going appetite for Agency CMO Derivatives Bonds and the increased activities in the Agency CMO Derivative market, I will say there is nothing but happy times ahead for now.

OAS

Here are some of the component that goes into making an OAS model. Think of the OAS as a big entity with various moving parts. These moving parts need raw materials, which are your data, and these data must be accurate. Analyze all you want; at the end of the day, it is all about experience and timing.

Below are some of the components of an OAS model

- Interest rate path
- Volatility
- HPA
- Geography
- Option market
- Forward curve
- Stochastic

In addition, you have these to comprehend: market-implied-volatility, fixed-volatility OAS, setting your parameters, long-run mean OAS, and implied-volatility OAS. The gist of the story is all about the darn averages, my friend. Oh, by the way, remember that volatility is an asset class; there are banks that trade volatility now. Be on the lookout for faulty errors in judgments, which could lead to bad OAS—not to mention all sorts of parameters and mean revisions.

SPREADS

Thou must know thy spreads, sayeth the Lord of mortgage Bonds (what it is and isn't)—spread over TSY, spread over LIBOR, spread over Munis, new issues spread compared to secondary market spreads, the historical spread of a practical bond since issuance compared to the bond's comparable, yada, yada, yada.

The starting point is USTSY; then, begin to add points based on your risk analysis ability. Remember one fund's liability is another fund's assets. So if you have focused on cutting your liability, you are destroying the other guy's assets—vis-à-vis the asset is being hammered.

Z spread, Nominal Yield spread, and SWAP spreads, and a couple of others are not mentioned here.

The ten-year TSY is the benchmark used to encourage consumer borrowing, and the three month TSY is the Government instrument for controlling money supply, hence, monetary policy.

YIELD

This is the cost of borrowing money in the borrower's eyes and how much someone is willing to lend in the investors' lenders point of view.

To some people, yield means return, and to others it means cost of capital; get the definition down before you engage in a conversation with the other party. In this book, yield means the cost of capital. Hence, you can do lots of carry trade.

Commercial banks give their consumers a 2 percent CD and invest the money in a PAC bond that pay 5 percent, clearing at 3 percent! Not bad for zero risk Government Backed paper. Or you buy an Inverse Floater that pay 12 percent monthly, and you give your investors an 8 percent return—not bad either. Slow and steady is the name of the game; don't try to get rich quick now.

Hierarchy ofYield, That Is, the Cost of Borrowing

- Government TSY: 3 percent (e.g., U.S., Government ten-year TSY)
- Government agencies: 4 percent (e.g., Fannie Mae, Freddie Mac and Ginne Mae)
- AAA Corporation : 5.5 percent (e.g., Microsoft, etc.)
- Consumers: 6 percent and up (home equity tends to be a lot higher)

Remember, the above is just to give you an idea, because some smart people in Government, CFO, and in the community do have good credit and can borrow at a lower rate than I have just mentioned above.

VOLATILITY

Different models will distribute weight or probability of an event on the different components that go into the value of Mortgage Derivatives in the OAS model, such as the collateral component, the option market components, the interest rate component, the economy component and housing price appreciation, and so on.

The major mathematical tool used to do this distribution is called log-normal. This tool is assuming the future value of your IIO, IO, PO, or INV is based on random events, basically with each event not correlated to the other.

Implied volatility means expectation about the future. If it is high that means a big pay day, which backwards means you could lose big time.

In looking at volatility, think of future value, value at the market, and the time value. All these will affect the value of your Mortgage Derivatives. If time is not on your side, then it will not hit the strike, hence, you are not getting that 7 percent coupon that you paid for that has a notion of $500 million.

When you think of Mortgage Derivative volatility, just remember if two IIO with the same collateral structure volatility deviate, it is a buying opportunity.

The major driver here is time and the volatile nature of interest rate. Do not concern yourself with the direction of the move, whether it is IIO or INV, the key is to trade the volatility, hence, you are a volatility Trader in a sense.

PREPAYMENT

Prepayment is simply how we pay our mortgage debt. As a Fund Manager/ Trader, you will have an opinion has to were or which direction prepayments will go. You should begin this analysis with the macro economic factors: CPI, PPI, employment, durable goods, ISM report, and new building permits.

Next, you can then look at the various interest rate products, with their maturity and structure risk, and how these products will behave in different scenarios. Mind you, there are people out there you may not agree with; that is why it is called a market. And because majority of the people agree or share the same sentiments does not necessary mean they are right.

SELL SIDE RELATIONSHIP MANAGEMENT

Relationship is everything; say the wrong thing and your Broker Dealer will lose respect for you. Your calls will no longer be returned; you will become the laughing stock of every trading desk, not to mention, your reputation is on the line.

The Trader's behavior and trading style should, at all times, reflect the company's corporate values and adhere to the firm's standard of conduct. You and your Traders must know your product and know when you are being taken for a ride. Do not loss your cool; maintain your composure at all times.

Breath of coverage: trading relationships should be maintained with the appropriate number of dealers to optimize trade execution by asset type.

Dealer trading volume should be tracked and reported to the PM

A strategy you can use is to target trading volume to compensate dealers for research resources that are made available; meaning, increase your trade base on the quality of research and market colors you get from the Broker Dealer. It makes no sense dealing with Broker Dealers with a weak research department.

Finding out what the delay is for your MBS trading platform, for it will make the difference between a winning and losing trade. Not all systems are fast. Some are behind from one to two hours, so when you are quoting or valuing, make sure your information is correct. Remember, with cross platform trading, in one platform a bond can be offered cheaper compared to another. You should deal with your Broker Dealer from an arm's length. They don't talk to you because they like it; it is because they have to make money and you have liabilities to match. Remember, ones man's or woman's assets is another's liability.

Next, I am going to show you how to let your money work for you. It is a crime to go broke after making millions of dollars. I read about millionaires going broke and it makes me sick in the stomach. Once you make your millions, you should stay rich for life.

Be mindful of the communication between you and your Broker Dealer: email, text, bb, im, and what have you.

Intend to maintain relationships with eight to ten large and small Broker Dealers to take advantage of their respective strengths, regional expertise, retail distribution, new issue underwriting capability, research department-technical/ fundamental skills, trading, and innovative products/ideas.

LIVING OFF A $5 MILLION FORTUNE

Below is what the monthly cash flow will look like with a $5 million income fund (pre-tax of cause).

Make sure that your Trader knows the right product for each client. Different U.S Government CMO Agency Bonds will achieve different objectives. You, the investment advisor, ought to design a product after talking to your clients, not a product you think your clients will like.

I recommend you buy a lockout PAC or SEQ paper as it gets close to paying principle or prepayment begins to snap trade the bond in for another lockout paper.

Below is a generic living expense of Client A:

Mortgage: $2,500.00

Cable: $200.00

Electricity: $150.00

Water Bill: $500.00

Groceries: $700.00

Medical Insurance: $1,000.00

Car Insurance: $450.00

Car Note: $2,000.00

Up Keep: $2,000.00

Entertainment: $500.00

Emergency fund: $5,000.00

Total Expenses: $15,000.00

Money is not finite; if not manage properly it will disappear—easy come, easy go.

Get a good tax expert to make sure the Government does not shake you down.

Dates	Principle	Coupon	Pre-Tax Monthly Income	
6/25/2010	**$5,000,000.00**	**6%**	$25,000.00	
7/25/2010	**$5,000,000.00**		$25,000.00	
8/25/2010	**$5,000,000.00**		$25,000.00	
9/25/2010	**$5,000,000.00**		$25,000.00	
10/25/2010	**$5,000,000.00**		$25,000.00	
11/25/2010	**$5,000,000.00**		$25,000.00	
12/27/2010	**$5,000,000.00**		$25,000.00	
			$175,000.00	**Annual Pre-Tax Income**
1/25/2011	**$5,000,000.00**		$25,000.00	
2/25/2011	**$5,000,000.00**		$25,000.00	
3/25/2011	**$5,000,000.00**		$25,000.00	
4/25/2011	**$5,000,000.00**		$25,000.00	
5/25/2011	**$5,000,000.00**		$25,000.00	
6/25/2011	**$5,000,000.00**		$25,000.00	
7/25/2011	**$5,000,000.00**		$25,000.00	
8/25/2011	**$5,000,000.00**		$25,000.00	
9/25/2011	**$5,000,000.00**		$25,000.00	
10/25/2011	**$5,000,000.00**		$25,000.00	
11/25/2011	**$5,000,000.00**		$25,000.00	
12/27/2011	**$5,000,000.00**		$25,000.00	
			$300,000.00	**Annual Pre-Tax Income**
1/25/2012	**$5,000,000.00**		$25,000.00	
2/25/2012	**$5,000,000.00**		$25,000.00	
3/25/2012	**$5,000,000.00**		$25,000.00	

4/25/2012	**$5,000,000.00**	$25,000.00	
5/25/2012	**$5,000,000.00**	$25,000.00	
6/25/2012	**$5,000,000.00**	$25,000.00	
7/25/2012	**$5,000,000.00**	$25,000.00	
8/25/2012	**$5,000,000.00**	$25,000.00	
9/25/2012	**$5,000,000.00**	$25,000.00	
10/25/2012	**$5,000,000.00**	$25,000.00	
11/25/2012	**$5,000,000.00**	$25,000.00	
12/27/2012	**$5,000,000.00**	$25,000.00	
		$300,000.00	**Annual Pre-Tax Income**
1/25/2013	**$5,000,000.00**	$25,000.00	
2/25/2013	**$5,000,000.00**	$25,000.00	
3/25/2013	**$5,000,000.00**	$25,000.00	
4/25/2013	**$5,000,000.00**	$25,000.00	
5/25/2013	**$5,000,000.00**	$25,000.00	
6/25/2013	**$5,000,000.00**	$25,000.00	
7/25/2013	**$5,000,000.00**	$25,000.00	
8/25/2013	**$5,000,000.00**	$25,000.00	
9/25/2013	**$5,000,000.00**	$25,000.00	
10/25/2013	**$5,000,000.00**	$25,000.00	
11/25/2013	**$5,000,000.00**	$25,000.00	
12/27/2013	**$5,000,000.00**	$25,000.00	
		$300,000.00	**Annual Pre-Tax Income**
1/25/2014	**$5,000,000.00**	$25,000.00	
2/25/2014	**$5,000,000.00**	$25,000.00	
3/25/2014	**$5,000,000.00**	$25,000.00	
4/25/2014	**$5,000,000.00**	$25,000.00	

5/25/2014	**$5,000,000.00**	$25,000.00	
6/25/2014	**$5,000,000.00**	$25,000.00	
7/25/2014	**$5,000,000.00**	$25,000.00	
8/25/2014	**$5,000,000.00**	$25,000.00	
9/25/2014	**$5,000,000.00**	$25,000.00	
10/25/2014	**$5,000,000.00**	$25,000.00	
11/25/2014	**$5,000,000.00**	$25,000.00	
12/27/2014	**$5,000,000.00**	$25,000.00	
		$300,000.00	**Annual Pre-Tax Income**
1/25/2015	**$5,000,000.00**	$25,000.00	
2/25/2015	**$5,000,000.00**	$25,000.00	
3/25/2015	**$5,000,000.00**	$25,000.00	
4/25/2015	**$5,000,000.00**	$25,000.00	
5/25/2015	**$5,000,000.00**	$25,000.00	
6/25/2015	**$5,000,000.00**	$25,000.00	
7/25/2015	**$5,000,000.00**	$25,000.00	
8/25/2015	**$5,000,000.00**	$25,000.00	
9/25/2015	**$5,000,000.00**	$25,000.00	
10/25/2015	**$5,000,000.00**	$25,000.00	
11/25/2015	**$5,000,000.00**	$25,000.00	
12/27/2015	**$5,000,000.00**	$25,000.00	
		$300,000.00	**Annual Pre-Tax Income**
1/25/2016	**$5,000,000.00**	$25,000.00	
2/25/2016	**$5,000,000.00**	$25,000.00	
3/25/2016	**$5,000,000.00**	$25,000.00	
4/25/2016	**$5,000,000.00**	$25,000.00	
5/25/2016	**$5,000,000.00**	$25,000.00	

6/25/2016	**$5,000,000.00**	$25,000.00	
7/25/2016	**$5,000,000.00**	$25,000.00	
8/25/2016	**$5,000,000.00**	$25,000.00	
9/25/2016	**$5,000,000.00**	$25,000.00	
10/25/2016	**$5,000,000.00**	$25,000.00	
11/25/2016	**$5,000,000.00**	$25,000.00	
12/27/2016	**$5,000,000.00**	$25,000.00	
		$300,000.00	**Annual Pre-Tax Income**
1/25/2017	**$5,000,000.00**	$25,000.00	
2/25/2017	**$5,000,000.00**	$25,000.00	
3/25/2017	**$5,000,000.00**	$25,000.00	
4/25/2017	**$5,000,000.00**	$25,000.00	
5/25/2017	**$5,000,000.00**	$25,000.00	
6/25/2017	**$5,000,000.00**	$25,000.00	
7/25/2017	**$5,000,000.00**	$25,000.00	
8/25/2017	**$5,000,000.00**	$25,000.00	
9/25/2017	**$5,000,000.00**	$25,000.00	
10/25/2017	**$5,000,000.00**	$25,000.00	
11/25/2017	**$5,000,000.00**	$25,000.00	
12/27/2017	**$5,000,000.00**	$25,000.00	
		$300,000.00	**Annual Pre-Tax Income**
1/25/2018	**$5,000,000.00**	$25,000.00	
2/25/2018	**$5,000,000.00**	$25,000.00	
3/25/2018	**$5,000,000.00**	$25,000.00	
4/25/2018	**$5,000,000.00**	$25,000.00	
5/25/2018	**$5,000,000.00**	$25,000.00	
6/25/2018	**$5,000,000.00**	$25,000.00	
7/25/2018	**$5,000,000.00**	$25,000.00	
8/25/2018	**$5,000,000.00**	$25,000.00	
9/25/2018	**$5,000,000.00**	$25,000.00	
10/25/2018	**$5,000,000.00**	$25,000.00	
11/25/2018	**$5,000,000.00**	$25,000.00	
12/27/2018	**$5,000,000.00**	$25,000.00	
		$300,000.00	**Annual Pre-Tax Income**

Here Is another Living-off-Your-Income Idea

I will suggest you sell the entire tranche before you start receiving the principles because in Agency CMO land, you don't get your principle in a lump sum payment; it trickles in bit by bit.

Dates	Principle	Coupon	Pre-Tax Monthly Income	
6/25/2010	**$7,062,000.00**	**5%**	$29,425.00	
7/25/2010	**$7,062,000.00**		$29,425.00	
8/25/2010	**$7,062,000.00**		$29,425.00	
9/25/2010	**$7,062,000.00**		$29,425.00	
10/25/2010	**$7,062,000.00**		$29,425.00	
11/25/2010	**$7,062,000.00**		$29,425.00	
12/27/2010	**$7,062,000.00**		$29,425.00	
			$205,975.00	**Annual Pre-Tax Income**
1/25/2011	**$7,062,000.00**		$29,425.00	
2/25/2011	**$7,062,000.00**		$29,425.00	
3/25/2011	**$7,062,000.00**		$29,425.00	
4/25/2011	**$7,062,000.00**		$29,425.00	
5/25/2011	**$7,062,000.00**		$29,425.00	
6/25/2011	**$7,062,000.00**		$29,425.00	
7/25/2011	**$7,062,000.00**		$29,425.00	
8/25/2011	**$7,062,000.00**		$29,425.00	
9/25/2011	**$7,062,000.00**		$29,425.00	
10/25/2011	**$7,062,000.00**		$29,425.00	
11/25/2011	**$7,062,000.00**		$29,425.00	
12/27/2011	**$7,062,000.00**		$29,425.00	
			$353,100.00	**Annual Pre-Tax Income**
1/25/2012	**$7,062,000.00**		$29,425.00	

2/25/2012	**$7,062,000.00**	$29,425.00	
3/25/2012	**$7,062,000.00**	$29,425.00	
4/25/2012	**$7,062,000.00**	$29,425.00	
5/25/2012	**$7,062,000.00**	$29,425.00	
6/25/2012	**$7,062,000.00**	$29,425.00	
7/25/2012	**$7,062,000.00**	$29,425.00	
8/25/2012	**$7,062,000.00**	$29,425.00	
9/25/2012	**$7,062,000.00**	$29,425.00	
10/25/2012	**$7,062,000.00**	$29,425.00	
11/25/2012	**$7,062,000.00**	$29,425.00	
12/27/2012	**$7,062,000.00**	$29,425.00	
		$353,100.00	**Annual Pre-Tax Income**
1/25/2013	**$7,062,000.00**	$29,425.00	
2/25/2013	**$7,062,000.00**	$29,425.00	
3/25/2013	**$7,062,000.00**	$29,425.00	
4/25/2013	**$7,062,000.00**	$29,425.00	
5/25/2013	**$7,062,000.00**	$29,425.00	
6/25/2013	**$7,062,000.00**	$29,425.00	
7/25/2013	**$7,062,000.00**	$29,425.00	
8/25/2013	**$7,062,000.00**	$29,425.00	
9/25/2013	**$7,062,000.00**	$29,425.00	
10/25/2013	**$7,062,000.00**	$29,425.00	
11/25/2013	**$7,062,000.00**	$29,425.00	
12/27/2013	**$7,062,000.00**	$29,425.00	
		$353,100.00	**Annual Pre-Tax Income**
1/25/2014	**$7,062,000.00**	$29,425.00	
2/25/2014	**$7,062,000.00**	$29,425.00	

3/25/2014	**$7,062,000.00**	$29,425.00	
4/25/2014	**$7,062,000.00**	$29,425.00	
5/25/2014	**$7,062,000.00**	$29,425.00	
6/25/2014	**$7,062,000.00**	$29,425.00	
7/25/2014	**$7,062,000.00**	$29,425.00	
8/25/2014	**$7,062,000.00**	$29,425.00	
9/25/2014	**$7,062,000.00**	$29,425.00	
10/25/2014	**$7,062,000.00**	$29,425.00	
11/25/2014	**$7,062,000.00**	$29,425.00	
12/27/2014	**$7,062,000.00**	$29,425.00	
		$353,100.00	**Annual Pre-Tax Income**
1/25/2015	**$7,062,000.00**	$29,425.00	
2/25/2015	**$7,062,000.00**	$29,425.00	
3/25/2015	**$7,062,000.00**	$29,425.00	
4/25/2015	**$7,062,000.00**	$29,425.00	
5/25/2015	**$7,062,000.00**	$29,425.00	
6/25/2015	**$7,062,000.00**	$29,425.00	
7/25/2015	**$7,062,000.00**	$29,425.00	
8/25/2015	**$7,062,000.00**	$29,425.00	
9/25/2015	**$7,062,000.00**	$29,425.00	
10/25/2015	**$7,062,000.00**	$29,425.00	
11/25/2015	**$7,062,000.00**	$29,425.00	
12/27/2015	**$7,062,000.00**	$29,425.00	
		$353,100.00	**Annual Pre-Tax Income**
1/25/2016	**$7,062,000.00**	$29,425.00	
2/25/2016	**$7,062,000.00**	$29,425.00	
3/25/2016	**$7,062,000.00**	$29,425.00	

4/25/2016	**$7,062,000.00**	$29,425.00	
5/25/2016	**$7,062,000.00**	$29,425.00	
6/25/2016	**$7,062,000.00**	$29,425.00	
7/25/2016	**$7,062,000.00**	$29,425.00	
8/25/2016	**$7,062,000.00**	$29,425.00	
9/25/2016	**$7,062,000.00**	$29,425.00	
10/25/2016	**$7,062,000.00**	$29,425.00	
11/25/2016	**$7,062,000.00**	$29,425.00	
12/27/2016	**$7,062,000.00**	$29,425.00	
		$353,100.00	**Annual Pre-Tax Income**
1/25/2017	**$7,062,000.00**	$29,425.00	
2/25/2017	**$7,062,000.00**	$29,425.00	
3/25/2017	**$7,062,000.00**	$29,425.00	
4/25/2017	**$7,062,000.00**	$29,425.00	
5/25/2017	**$7,062,000.00**	$29,425.00	
6/25/2017	**$7,062,000.00**	$29,425.00	
7/25/2017	**$7,062,000.00**	$29,425.00	
8/25/2017	**$7,062,000.00**	$29,425.00	
9/25/2017	**$7,062,000.00**	$29,425.00	
10/25/2017	**$7,062,000.00**	$29,425.00	
11/25/2017	**$7,062,000.00**	$29,425.00	
12/27/2017	**$7,062,000.00**	$29,425.00	
		$353,100.00	**Annual Pre-Tax Income**
1/25/2018	**$7,062,000.00**	$29,425.00	
2/25/2018	**$7,062,000.00**	$29,425.00	
3/25/2018	**$7,062,000.00**	$29,425.00	
4/25/2018	**$7,062,000.00**	$29,425.00	
5/25/2018	**$7,062,000.00**	$29,425.00	
6/25/2018	**$7,062,000.00**	$29,425.00	
7/25/2018	**$7,062,000.00**	$29,425.00	
8/25/2018	**$7,062,000.00**	$29,425.00	
9/25/2018	**$7,062,000.00**	$29,425.00	
10/25/2018	**$7,062,000.00**	$29,425.00	
11/25/2018	**$7,062,000.00**	$29,425.00	
12/27/2018	**$7,062,000.00**	$29,425.00	
		$353,100.00	**Annual Pre-Tax Income**

INDEX

8197010R0

Made in the USA
Lexington, KY
14 January 2011

Short Stories by Keith Abbott

Harum Scarum

ILLUSTRATIONS BY GAYLORD SCHANILEC

Coffee House Press :: Saint Paul, Minnesota

Acknowledgements: "Logger Linkhorn's 1928 Buick" appeared in German in a different version in *Sweet Little Sixteen* (Rowohlt). "Harum Scarum" appeared in German in *Ein Johnny Weismüller Parkplatz* (Marburg). Many thanks to Gunter Ohnemus and Jurger Schoenich, editors and translators.

The publishers wish to thank the National Endowment for the Arts, a federal agency, for a Small Press Assistance Grant that aided in the production of this book.

Designed by Allan Kornblum. Typesetting and layout by Annie Graham, Iowa City, Iowa.

Coffee House Press books are distributed by:
Bookslinger
213 East Fourth Street
St. Paul, MN 55101

Library of Congress Cataloging in Publication Data

Abbott, Keith, 1944-
Harum Scarum.

Contents: Harum scarum—Logger Linkhorn's 1928 Buick —A 50-50 marriage—[etc.]
I. Title.
PS3551.B26H3 1984 813'.54 84-15003
ISBN 0-918273-00-5 (pbk.)

Contents

I think what I was interested in in high school
was what every adolescent is interested in,
in proving himself to be a man.

—NELSON ALGREN

Harum Scarum

Harum Scarum :: Douf Kyllo was a big tall rawboned Swede, about 6 foot 3 and 210 pounds, with blond crewcut hair. Douf played tackle, number 76. The other guys on the team had a joke about that. "Kyllo wears his IQ on his football uniform." But they only made that joke when Douf wasn't around.

By September Pete Dwyer and Douf were both regular second string varsity football players. Douf was a Junior and Pete a Sophomore. Because they were both on the second string team, Douf thought he was Pete's friend. Pete had other ideas but kept them to himself.

When Douf called Pete one Saturday in October and asked him if he was busy, Pete said no. Then Douf said he wanted Pete to go out on a triple blind date with him. Pete didn't have to hear any more than that. Dating with Douf was not Pete's idea of a good time.

Douf said that he had to go.

"Why?" Pete said.

"Because Jackie and Roberta have a cousin in town and Mrs. Knepper won't let them go out unless they take their cousin," Douf said.

"Great," Pete told Douf, "but I can't do it, Douf."

"You're not doing nothing tonight, are you? That's what you said," Douf said.

"No blind dates, Douf," Pete told him.

"I'll pay for everything," Douf said, "honest."

"The last blind date I went on was a *dog,"* Pete said. "I said then, *no more."*

"But I *gotta* see Roberta tonight," Douf said. "You don't know what it's like. I gotta."

"So, see her without me along. See her alone, Douf, you might do better."

"Dwyser," Douf said, "I *said* I'd pay for everything. All you gotta do is sit in the back seat with her cousin."

"I don't *want* to sit in the back seat with someone I don't know," Pete snapped. "No, goddamnit Douf, no." There was a silence at the other end of the line.

"Pete, I don't wanta haveta start ragging you," Douf said.

Pete didn't want Douf to "rag" him either. Pete always was matched across from Douf in the football drills. Douf was not aware of his own strength. Ragging started with arm punches and worked its way up. Bruises didn't mean much to Douf, whether he dealt them out or got them.

"You know what I mean, Dwyser?" Douf asked.

"Stop calling me Dwyser," Pete said. "Okay, but you pay to get *both* of us in the movie, and the food."

"Right," Douf said, "pick you up at 7:30. Hey, thanks a lot, Dwyser babe."

"Wait a minute," Pete said, "what's this girl's name?"

"I don't know."

"What's she look like?"

"Got me, I've never seen her before."

"Great," Pete said, "what movie are we seeing?"

"Whatever Roberta wants to see."

Pete hung up. Douf was in love with one Knepper sister one week, the other the next. They looked close enough to be twins, but they were one year apart. The youngest, Roberta, was the best. With a face like Tuesday Weld, she was stacked and had great hips. Her older sister Jackie was slimmer, had the same bust line, but not the teen starlet face of Roberta. Pete had dated each once and never got to first base with either. As far as Pete was concerned,

Jackie and Roberta were both boring, total duds. Everybody said that they had great bodies but no guy had got any farther than just sitting next to those great bodies. At dances Jackie and Roberta flirted like crazy and danced real close, but once alone in the car, it was eyes straight ahead and hands off.

Pete assumed the cousin would be another Knepper ice queen. He went up to his room and changed his clothes. He hoped none of his friends called. Pete didn't like the idea of telling them that he had a triple blind date with Douf and the Knepper sisters.

A car drove in the driveway. Pete went downstairs and out the back door. Douf was behind the wheel of his father's big 1960 four-door Ford. Sitting next to him in the front seat were Roberta and Jackie. "Hey," Douf said, "thanks a lot, Dwyser."

Pete got in the back seat. Roberta turned and gave Pete her best Tuesday Weld profile. "Edna's at a Young Life meeting," she said. "We have to pick her up."

"Great," Pete said. "Edna, terrific." No one said anything in the front seat. Young Life was the Christian youth organization. "Young Life," Pete said, "she go to Young Life meetings regular?"

"She didn't know if Douf could get her a date, so she went to the meeting just in case."

Just in case of what? Pete thought. "She likes to talk about God, huh?" Pete muttered.

"What?" Jackie said, turning to Pete.

"Never mind," Pete said. "Who's your date?"

"Whitey," Jackie said.

Pete slumped down in the back seat. Whitey was the

biggest hambone Pete knew, a totally obnoxious big mouth. "Great, what movie are we seeing?"

"Roberta wants to see *Harum Scarum,"* Douf said, turning to smile at her.

She would, Pete thought. He was furious. He was going to be trapped in the back seat with some Christian watching a dumbbutt Elvis Presley film *and* with Whitey yapping next to him.

"Great, Douf," Pete said.

Douf stopped the Ford at the local Young Life leader's house on Pacific Avenue. Pete got out of the car with Jackie. He looked back and saw that Douf had put his arm in back of Roberta. *Jesus,* Pete thought, *I hope I don't have to sit in the back seat and watch Douf try to kiss her.* He followed Jackie into the house. The meeting was just breaking up. He looked for the ugliest, fattest stranger there but he didn't see anyone like that, only the local Lutheran types. "Pete," Jackie said, touching his arm, "here comes Edna."

Pete turned and saw a freckle-faced brunette coming towards them. She had an easy swinging walk. "Edna, I'd like you to meet Pete Dwyer, he's your date."

Edna smiled at Pete. She had a small gap in her front teeth. Pete could not believe it. She was hot. "Hello," Pete said, "how'd you like the meeting?"

"Oh," she said, "it was really boring. There's sure a lot of Scandinavians around here. Hold my coat?" She handed him her coat and stepped back to bend down and get her purse on the hallway floor. Her hip leaned into Pete's leg. She straightened up and Pete held up her coat for her. She slipped her arms into it and her right hand brushed Pete's hand as she adjusted the collar. She looked up at him.

"Well," Pete said. He leaned forward so he could smell her perfume. "That's nice."

She took his arm. "You like it?" she said. She leaned in and gave him another whiff.

"Yeah," Pete said, "wow, that's really nice."

"Edna doesn't go to these back home in Idaho," Jackie said as they went out the door, "but then she's Catholic."

Pete could not believe his luck. He'd *heard* about Catholic girls but he had never dated one. "Oh yeah," he said. She was holding his arm close.

"I was hoping we would be going out," Edna said to Jackie. "I don't think I could have stood another minute in there." Then, to Pete, "Do you go?"

"Uh, go?" Pete paused. "Me? To these? Naw. Guys only go to Young Life to pick up girls."

"There weren't any of them here tonight," Edna said. She opened the back door and climbed into the car.

"Let's get going," Pete said to Douf, "let's get to the show."

"We gotta pick up Whitey first," Douf said.

Harum Scarum was on a double bill with a Beach Blanket movie at the Starlite Drivein. Douf pulled into a Union station a block away from the theater. He got out of the car. "Hey, guys," he said, "give me a hand, will ya?" Both Whitey and Pete were sitting on the outside of the back seat with Jackie and Edna between them. Edna's leg was tight against Pete's leg. Pete looked at Whitey. Douf walked around to the back of the Ford and opened the trunk. Whitey shrugged. They both got out of the Ford.

Pete wondered what was up. Douf didn't drink, so it couldn't be beer or anything.

Douf was staring into the trunk. It was empty except for a spare tire and an Army blanket. "Get in," he whispered.

"WHAT?" Pete said.

"SHH," Douf whispered, "come on."

"You said you were going to pay," Pete hissed.

"Yeah," Whitey seconded. "You said."

"I don't have enough money," Douf said. "Get in."

"We gotta sneak in?" Pete was outraged.

"Dwyser, just get in," Douf said.

"I'll pay," Pete said. He wanted to get back in there up next to Edna. He'd been looking at her lips and thinking of what it was going to be like.

"You gonna pay for me?" Whitey said. "I'm broke."

Pete felt Douf's big paw on his neck. "Don't embarrass me in front of Roberta," Douf said.

"What about *me?*" Pete said.

Douf gave his neck a gentle push. "I'll get you guys right out," he said. "Soon as we get inside the drivein."

"Yeah, but what're they gonna think when they see *you* driving in there with three girls?" Pete said.

Douf took Whitey's arm with his other hand and lifted Whitey up a bit to help him into the trunk. Whitey put one foot in the trunk to get the pressure off his arm.

"Ow, let go," Whitey said. He stood up in the trunk.

"Dwyser," Douf said. "You're next." His fingers tightened around Pete's neck.

"What are you guys doing?" Edna said, looking back at them through the rear window.

Whitey lay down in the trunk.

"There's not enough room," Pete said, his neck bending under Douf's fingers.

"In," Douf said, "I'll get you right out, promise."

Pete lay in the trunk looking at Whitey's shoes. He could hear the girls giggling as the Ford inched towards the ticket booth. Douf was laughing too, but telling them to shut up.

"You know we're going to get caught, don't you?" Pete said to Whitey.

"Shutup," Whitey said.

Pete thought of all the ways he could revenge himself on Douf without Douf getting mad.

"I didn't want to go on this, either," Whitey said. "I was planning to go get drunk with Logger and the boys tonight. Douf said he would get me at Monday football practice if I didn't come."

"Join the club," Pete said.

Then they both stayed quiet as Douf paid for four admissions and drove out of the ticket booth area. Pete began banging on the back seat as soon as they were clear. "Lemme out of here!"

"HEY," Douf yelled, "SHUTUP. There's an attendant standing right there, man."

Pete and Whitey lay quiet until Douf parked the Ford. "Okay, get us out of here," Pete said.

"Gotta wait til it's dark," Douf said.

"WHAT!" Pete screamed. "Hit the back of the seat with your heel," he said to Whitey.

"Douf'll get mad," Whitey said.

"You yellow prick," Pete hissed.

"HEY SHUTUP!" Douf commanded from the front seat. "NO CUSSING, EITHER!"

Pete and Whitey stayed in the trunk for twenty minutes of the first movie. It got colder and colder. Pete drew the Army blanket over himself and Whitey. Each time they would yell at Douf to get them out of the trunk, Douf would find some reason for not doing it. Most of the time he just said, "I can't, they're watching the back row like a hawk."

"What'd you park in the *back* row for?" Whitey groused. "They *always* watch the back row like hawks."

Pete was looking at the bumper jack. He was thinking of Edna's gap teeth and what it would feel like to stick his tongue there. He just *knew* she would make out.

"DOUFFFFFFFFF!" he screamed, "get us the hell out of HEERRRRRE."

Douf didn't say anything. The girls laughed. "Come on, Douf," Roberta said, "let them out."

"Yeah, Douf, let us out. Pete just cut a fart."

Giggles from inside the car. "Think we can kick the back seat out?" Pete whispered to Whitey. "If you just squinch around a little," Pete said, "I'll put my feet over your head and then we both can kick."

"Okay, you guys," Douf said, "I'll let you out." They heard the front door open. "The attendant's gone," Douf said. They heard his feet crunching the gravel as he walked around to the back of the car. "Oh," Douf said, "he came back."

Douf finally let Whitey and Pete out of the trunk when the girls went to get some cokes at the refreshment stand.

Pete was furious. He stood there stamping on the ground, trying to get some circulation back. He was shivering from the damp cold. A thin ground fog hovered over the cars.

"Some goddamn date, sure, now you don't have to buy us diddley either, you made sure of that, didn't you?" Whitey groused.

"You want a coke or something?" Douf said. He reached in his pocket and took out a quarter and handed it to Whitey.

"Shit, thanks Douf, sure you can spare this?" Whitey said. He wheeled around and left. Pete took out the Army blanket from the trunk.

"What's that for?" Douf said.

"I'm *freezing,*" Pete said. "There's no heater in the trunk, you know."

"Gee, I'm sorry, Pete," Douf said.

"Sure," Pete said. He climbed into the back seat of the car. Douf stuck his head in. "Your girl's okay, huh?"

"Leave me alone," Pete said.

Douf looked back at the refreshment stand. "I'm going back, it's taking them an awfully long time," Douf said.

Pete bundled himself up in the blanket. On the screen Annette Funicello was at a California beach on a blanket talking to Frankie Avalon. She was wearing a single piece swimming suit. All around them the other girls were in bikinis. Pete wondered if the single piece suit meant Annette was a "good" girl. *Good girls don't show their navels,* Pete thought. The sun was shining in the movie. Pete watched it glumly. He was thinking that he had to wait another ten months before he saw any *real* women in swimming suits, let alone *bikinis.* And sunshine, that was gone too.

Edna came back first. "It's really cold tonight, isn't it?" she said. She handed Pete her popcorn carton and Coke. Without being asked, she slipped right underneath the Army blanket with Pete. "There," she said.

"That jerk Douf," Pete said. "I was *freezing* in the trunk."

"Oh here," Edna said. She moved closer and Pete put up his arm and she snuggled under it.

Pete could not believe his good luck. "Is this movie any good?" Pete said, looking in her face.

"Who cares?" she said, looking up at him.

Pete kissed her. She was good. "I guess I don't care, either," Pete said. They kissed again and this time the tip of her tongue slipped across his lips.

"Put the popcorn up the back window ledge," Pete said. Edna lifted the carton off the seat and put it up along with her coke. Pete scooted under her as she did it, so she was sitting on his right leg. "Ooh," she said. Her hip slid off his leg and then she turned and they went into a long french kiss.

Pete slid his left arm along her side. "You see much of Roberta and Jackie?" Pete said.

"No," Edna said, "they're dopes."

Pete sighed. "Yeah," he said, "they sure are."

"Well, you took them out," Edna said.

"Yeah," Pete said. "A guy's gotta try, doesn't he?"

They kissed again and this time Pete had his left hand on her back and drew her breasts into his chest. Her tongue was all around his.

"You getting warmer?" she said.

Pete looked up. "Oh shoot, here they come back. I wonder where Whitey is," Pete said.

Whitey came back fifteen minutes later. Jackie got out of the front seat and got in the back with Whitey. By that time Pete was wishing that Whitey never came back. He and Edna were stretched out over the back seat. They were *almost* lying down together. Pete scrunched up in the corner to give everyone enough room and Edna followed him, squeezing her body next to his. From his spot in the corner Pete had a good view of Whitey and Jackie over the top of Edna's head.

Jackie was ignoring Pete and Edna under the blanket. Roberta had checked them out when she got into the car. She said something dumb about turning up the heat. Jackie had looked down once when Pete was moving his arm across Edna's legs under the blanket but then she didn't look again. She stared straight ahead at the beach blanket movie.

Whitey was acting slaphappy. Douf had said that Whitey had run into Logger Linkhorn at the refreshment stand. That probably meant Whitey had a few drinks with them. Jackie had flirted with him a bit before zeroing in on the movie, but Whitey wasn't going to leave it at that. Whitey tried to put his arm around her and get a little closer. She allowed the arm but not the closer. Pete was in a liplock with Edna when he saw Whitey take a brief one quarter turn of Jackie's head to mean she wanted to kiss him and made a lunge. Jackie saw it coming and bowed her head so that Whitey got a mouthful of hair instead of skin.

Pete enjoyed seeing that. He had much the same luck on his only date with Jackie.

Whitey was pissed off. He clamped his arm down on Jackie's neck and went for her. "Whitey," Jackie hissed, a second before Whitey got the right edge of her lower lip. She wiggled out from under Whitey's arm.

Lots of luck, Pete thought. In the front seat he could see Douf had put his arm up on the back of the seat and was slowly letting it *sag* down on Roberta's neck. Pete turned back to Edna and they went into a long slow kiss. Edna had his left hand in hers and was stroking the skin between his thumb and forefinger. His tongue was finding the gap in her front teeth.

Then Edna let go of his left hand and Pete felt it fall on her bare skin. Her blouse had crept up out of her jeans. Pete let his palm rest there and then lowered his fingers one by one on her side. Her skin was so hot he felt his fingertips burn as each one touched down.

Pete opened his eyes from the kiss in time to see Whitey get shrugged off of Jackie's neck. "Whitey, *don't,*" Jackie said.

Roberta turned to see what had happened. Then she glanced down in time to see Pete's arm going down and then up Edna's leg under the blanket. "It's getting steamy in here," Roberta said.

"Do you have any more popcorn?" Jackie said.

"You want some popcorn, huh?" Whitey said, "I'll get you some popcorn." He jerked open the door, rolled out and slammed it shut.

"Move over," Pete said. "What?" Jackie said. Pete slid his hip under Edna's left thigh and pushed her down the seat so her right leg crowded Jackie. "Move it over," Pete said. He was pleased to see Jackie look down to see what he was doing.

She scooted over by the door. "I don't think you need more room," she said.

"No one asked *you,*" Edna said. She pushed her breasts up on Pete's chest and they went into another long slow kiss.

Pete didn't pay Whitey any attention when he came back with Jackie's popcorn. He had to sit up with Edna to give Whitey some room. A little after that he looked up and he saw Whitey had Jackie in another necklock. But she twisted around so her body was turned away from him. Pete saw that she was avoiding watching what he and Edna were doing. She had her head straight and her eyes on the movie even though her body was toward them, away from Whitey. Pete was pretty sure that Whitey had drunk a little. He began complaining into Jackie's hair. "C'mon," he whispered. "Hey, c'mon."

Pete knew Whitey was getting turned on by what he and Edna were doing. He caught Whitey staring across Jackie's neck at them. The corner of the blanket had slipped out from behind Edna's back and Whitey could see her blouse was riding up and where Pete's hand was. Pete winked at Whitey and Whitey gave him the finger.

When Pete looked up next, the Beach Blanket movie was about to end. Annette Funicello was sitting among a lot of boys in swim suits. Both Jackie and Roberta were engrossed in this scene. Annette was the queen of the beach. She had all the boys eating out of her hand. Without taking her eyes off the screen, Jackie reached over with her left hand for the popcorn, holding her right arm at an angle against Whitey to keep him at a distance.

Pete stared up at the screen and then he felt Edna's lips move up from his neck and fasten on his earlobe. He had *never* had this done to him before. She began to suck. Pete felt himself balloon up in his pants.

"AHHHHHHHHHHHH!" Jackie screamed. Popcorn flew all over the back seat. Jackie recoiled against Pete and Edna, almost causing Edna to tear Pete's earlobe off in the crush. "AHHHHHHHHH," Jackie screamed again. She began hitting at Whitey with both hands. "AWH, AHHHH, YOU, YOU!" Then she let out a long screech and Whitey fell out of the door. He was laughing. He ran off between the cars.

"What was it?" Roberta said.

"AWH, AWH," Jackie was speechless. She opened the door and jumped out of the car. She stood there with her hands both out, fingers spread wide apart.

Roberta scooted across the seat and got out the passenger side of the car. Both Pete and Edna were watching Jackie kick at the ground outside the car. Roberta grabbed her by the shoulders and they both fled toward the refreshment stand.

"Jesus," Pete said. "What was *that* all about?"

Douf was staring back at Pete. "You don't know?" he said suspiciously.

"No, I don't know, I was *busy,"* Pete said. His earlobe was throbbing. Edna was looking up at him. He felt her right hand go down on his leg. "Well, go find out what's the matter, Douf," Pete said.

Douf got out of the car. Then he leaned in the open door. "If Whitey comes back, you tell him Douf is looking for him."

"Oh yeah, sure, Douf," Pete said, "I'm sure he'll be right back for his bruising."

Douf walked off toward the screen. A big white THE END was on it. All around them car doors were opening and closing. The sign for the intermission flashed on the screen. Pete turned down the speaker hanging from the window. "I bet Whitey was drunk," Pete said. "I bet he got some stuff from Logger when he went out for the popcorn."

"What do you think he did?" Edna said.

"I don't know," Pete said.

Edna slid out from under the blanket and leaned across the seat. She rolled down the window. Cold air streamed in. Pete picked up the blanket and fluffed it once. It was getting hot under it. Pete looked at Edna's ass as she stared out between the cars. He scooted over and leaned against her back, pushing himself up under her. Over her shoulder he could see out the window the empty parking space next to them. Then he saw the popcorn carton on the ground with a big hole bored in the bottom.

"Oh no," Pete said, "that *can't* be."

Edna pushed back into Pete's lap and looked to the right. "Uhhh," she said. Then she laughed. "I've *heard* about someone doing that," she said.

"Really?" he said.

"Haven't you?" she said. Then she laughed again, but

louder. "That's *dirty,*" she said, giggling.

Pete laughed too. "That's a first for Jackie, let me tell you."

"I don't know about *that,*" Edna said.

"What?" Pete said, "you're kidding. The ice queen?"

"When she came to Boise, she went out more than I did and I know the guy she went out with. He was *fast.* Her parents weren't there, or Roberta. It's Roberta who keeps tabs on her, you know that, don't you?"

"She keeps tabs on herself," Pete said. "Here, let me out. I better destroy the evidence or Douf is going to make mincemeat out of Whitey."

Edna rose up and Pete slid all the way under her and then she sat down, straddling his left leg, her ass back against his crotch. "Hey, no fair, lemme up," Pete laughed. Edna squirmed. Pete brought both hands up under her blouse and he was amazed how easily his hands slid under her bra. Her nipples stiffened against his fingers. "Edna," he said. "Pete," she said. "Edna," Pete said. He was getting crushed by her squirming. "I gotta get out." She rolled back and forth, her head came back and her hair fell in his face. Then she gave a little shudder. Pete felt her relax in his arms. "You okay?" he said.

"Ah," Edna said. She was almost out of breath. Pete could feel her breath coming fast, her ribs heaving under his hands.

"You sure?" he said. "Edna? Did I hurt you?"

"Um," she said.

Pete lifted her up off his lap and he set her down on the seat. With the pressure off him, he felt suddenly light-headed, as if he were about pass to out. He waited a minute and then he pulled at his pants, giving himself a little more room.

Pete got out of the car and he picked up the carton. He turned back to the car and he held the carton up to his eye and looked through the hole in the bottom at Edna. "Peekaboo," he said.

Edna giggled. "That's dirty, Pete," she said.

Pete put the carton up an inch away from his mouth. "Calling all cars," he said. Then, "I'll be right back." He walked two rows forward and ditched the carton in back of a pickup as he walked past. Then he returned to the Ford.

Edna was under the blanket in back. She had her head back against the window. Pete climbed in and she pulled the blanket off her and Pete lay down on top. She flung the blanket across his back. He felt her legs part a little as his hip rested on her left leg. "Welcome back," she said. "Did you get rid of the evidence?"

They heard Douf and the sisters coming back. Pete started to get up off Edna but she held him close. He could only sit partly up.

"I don't know where he went," Douf said.

"Forget it," Roberta said.

"If you want me to, I'll get him," Douf said.

"No!" Roberta said. All three got in the front seat. Jackie looked over the seat at Edna and Pete once and then looked to the front. No one said anything. *Harum Scarum*'s credits were unrolling on the screen. Douf turned up the sound on the speaker.

Roberta looked back. "Well you two are cozy," she

said. She smiled. "It's all steamed up."

"You don't like to get warm, Roberta?" Edna said.

Roberta turned back around. There was silence in the front seat. Edna whispered in Pete's ear. "They'll leave us alone for the rest of the show, I bet."

"Should I ask Jackie what happened?" Pete whispered back.

Edna giggled. "No."

"You see Whitey?" Douf said to Pete. He turned his head and glanced back. "He come back?"

"Nope," Pete said.

"The car Logger came in was gone," Douf said. "I looked around but I didn't see it." Douf turned back to watch Elvis in his opening scene.

Pete shifted back down on top of Edna's leg. This time she let him rest right between. They made out like that for a bit, and then Pete began to move his hips and she moved back. They both began to breathe more quietly. Pete glanced at the front seat as they got into an easy slow rhythm. Pete had never done this before.

Pete caught Roberta sneaking a look. He winked. Roberta whipped her head back. Pete could see Elvis going into his first production number surrounded by pretty girls.

"Douf," Roberta said, "can you turn on the heat?"

Douf started the Ford and turned on the heat.

You bitch, Pete thought. He was already so hot he was sweating up and down his back. He dug in with his hips and began to urge Edna on.

"What are you two *doing* back there?" Roberta said, without turning around. "You're rocking the boat."

"Watch the movie, Roberta," Pete said, "you might learn something about life."

"Hey!" Douf said. He put his arm on the seat behind Roberta's head. "Knock it off, Dwyser." But he didn't turn his head either.

Edna sat up and Pete rolled off her. She stared at the backs of their heads and then she looked at Pete. She leaned into his arm, and drew the blanket up tight from her shoulder to his shoulders. Then she went for his earlobe again. She sucked and bit on it as Pete sat there with his head exploding. On the big screen in front of him a leering Elvis pronounced isolated bits of babble.

Pete reached up under her blouse and felt her full hard nipple. Her bra had slipped down all the way. Pete felt like he was about to tear his pants apart. He brought his hand down, and he felt her hand riding on the back of his. All he could think of was *do I dare do this?* but he knew that if he didn't, he might hurt himself. He slipped the three middle buttons on his jeans. Her fingers were tracing circles on his hand and then they slipped down. He felt them close around him. She had his ear in her mouth. She was blowing very softly on it and then sucking the wet air back in over it. Pete reached over and squeezed the edge of her hip. She squeezed him back. Pete put his fingers down the side of her pants. Her fingers straightened out and slid down. He felt the top button open and the zipper slide open under the pressure of his hand. Hers cupped him. He had hair now on the tips of his two fingers. He let his fingers ease down. Then he began to rub. She brought her hand up. She began to slip her hand up and down in time to his motion.

Pete opened his eyes. With the blanket up over his shoulder in a straight line from her shoulder, no one could see what they were doing. He arched up off the seat. She pressed hard against his hand and her lips drained the wetness off his ear in a hot suck. He looked up and watched the screen. Elvis was talking to a sheik. Pete tried to concentrate on the screen to make it last but the face of Elvis dissolved.

When Pete's eyes cleared, the face of Elvis was filling up the screen. Elvis was looking serious. Elvis shook his head. *"I'd say,"* Elvis said, *"you got big trouble, your majesty."*

Douf was holding Pete off the ground up against the car. "What did he *do,* Dwyser?"

"I don't *know,"* Pete said. "Jesus, Douf, I was making out with Edna." Pete tried to touch the ground with his toes. "Lemme down, I'm *tired,* damnit, Douf."

Douf lowered Pete enough so his feet were on the ground. "Jackie was upset," Douf said. "She wouldn't say." Douf looked off over the fog-shrouded rows of cars. "You take them home," Douf said. He shook Pete a little. "I'm going to look for Whitey and I'm going to find out what he did to Jackie." Douf let go of Pete and stared off into the thick mist blanketing the cars.

"Douf," Pete said, "how you going to go looking for Whitey without a car?" There was a sudden movement on the screen. Pete looked up. On the screen Elvis had swung out of a window and was sneaking along a rampart.

"I talked to some guys at the stand," Douf said. "They know where Logger went. They're going there. When the girls come back from the john you make sure they get home okay. Here's the keys." Douf gave Pete the car keys.

"Douf, you were dating Roberta tonight," Pete said, "what do you care?"

Douf shook his head. "I think it's really Jackie. I got to do this alone. There are some things a man has got to do alone," Douf said. "For Jackie. I got to show Jackie how I feel." He stalked off into the night.

Douf disappeared in the low ground fog. Pete felt as if his back was wrenched out of place. Pete waited until Douf was out of earshot. *"I wiped myself off on your blanket,"* he screamed.

Pete looked down at the keys in his hand. *Shit,* Pete thought, *Douf lives three miles from my place. After I drop off his dad's car, I'm going to have to walk home.*

Pete sat behind the steering wheel. The three girls were in the front seat, Edna next to him, then Jackie and Roberta. Pete had his arm up on the back seat. Jackie glanced over at Pete. Roberta was watching Elvis dance among the harem girls. "Gee," Jackie said, "we could have a harem right here."

"Jackie," Roberta said, "really."

"You want to get in the back seat with Pete, go ahead," Edna said. "I'm leaving tomorrow."

"You are?" Pete said.

"Edna," Roberta said.

"Really?" Jackie said. She gave out a short little laugh. "I might."

"Honestly, Jackie," Roberta said.

"I'm older than you." Jackie said, "I can do what I want."

"Back to Boise?" Pete said to Edna.

"Yes," Edna said. "Back to Boise."

"You want to get in the back seat with me, Pete?" Jackie said.

Pete looked past Edna at Jackie. "Geez," Pete said, "why does everything always have to be some place else?"

"I thought you two already went out." Edna said.

"That's easy for *you* to say," Jackie said, "all you have to do is confess."

"Jack-eee!" Roberta said.

Jackie turned back to the screen. "I'll come visit you in Boise," Jackie said, "okay, Edna?"

"Sure, Jackie," Edna said.

"Maybe I'll come too," Pete said, "I'd like to see you again." Then, "You're not coming back here again?"

Edna looked at Pete and then at Jackie. Then she shook her head. She didn't say anything.

"Will you guys *shut up,*" Roberta said, "I want to watch the movie." She ducked her head and glanced sideways as a car came down the aisle. Roberta caught her reflection in the wing window and she turned her head to the right and checked on the curl above her temple. There was a couple in the front seat of the passing car. They were sitting so close together their shadow almost had one head. "They're leaving early," Roberta said. "The movie's not even over."

"Maybe it is for them," Jackie said. Then she laughed. "What am I saying?" she said. "I can't say things like that."

Logger Linkhorn's 1928 Buick

Logger Linkhorn's 1928 Buick :: At age seventeen Logger Linkhorn looked old and tough. He had coarse dark hair and a five o'clock shadow. By the time he was a senior in high school, Logger never had any trouble buying beer. People thought he was an old twenty-five. Logger only played one team sport: football, and even then he played split end, out away from everyone. Logger wasn't a joiner. His best sport was wrestling. He competed in the 178-pound class. He was wiry and a little crazy. He went out on the mat and grabbed his opponent and then he didn't let go. There was always that moment when his opponent realized he had just been seized by a hillbilly. All the guys used to wait for that moment. They liked the look in the other wrestler's eyes, especially if the wrestler was from some "sosh" high school, like Clover Park. "LINK HORNS WITH HIM LOGGER!" That's what they used to yell. Logger went to the state wrestling tournament in Pullman, Washington more on guts than skill. He always finished high in the rankings but he never won first place.

Logger got his nickname from his father. His dad was a gypo logger. Independent trucker and independent logger, that was what Logger was going to be, too. No one ever saw his mother. Logger lived in a big old house out by the swamp. The house looked like a Gothic horror house: big wide rotting porch, a peeling tarpaper roof, sagging grey screens. Tall fir trees leaned over it and made the house a mess of shadows and shade.

None of the guys ever went inside. Around the house were pieces of castoff machinery, cables, and broken down cars. Everyone called them rust flowers.

In his senior year, Logger rescued a rust flower from

some barn up by Mount Rainer. It was a 1928 Buick touring car. His dad towed it down the mountain to Tacoma behind his truck. Logger parked the Buick under a canvas tarp strung up between the back porch and a fir tree.

The Buick was a four door touring car. The paint was a faded moss green. The upholstery was a mouse brown. It smelled damp and sour like rotting hay. The wheels had wooden spokes and big round skinny tires. The steering wheel was made of old-fashioned rubber. It felt like a hockey puck. Above the horn in the center of the steering wheel were little flippers that retarded or advanced the spark and the throttle. There wasn't any accelerator pedal on the floor. Under the hood was a big flathead straight eight. It ran, but not very well. The best the Buick could do was 35 miles per hour.

Logger put in hours on the body work. He peeled the leather top off and sanded the roof down. Little by little primer spots began to appear on the fenders and on the body. After he got it so the body looked worked on, Logger used to drive the Buick to football practice in the afternoons. Because the Buick was so big, he would give everyone who lived down his way a ride home. Mainly it was the juniors. They called themselves the guys, mocking the clean-cut senior types who tried to be so straight. Pete and Rob and Ray and Flipper and Hubie all rode with Logger in the Buick. They had their own cars. Rob had his new Pontiac, and Hubie his black and white 54 Ford, but they rode with Logger because the guys had adopted Logger. The other seniors on the team wouldn't have much to do with Logger. Most of the senior football players lived down by the Lutheran college and made it a point to date the Lutheran girls. The juniors regarded them as going "sosh."

That fall Logger would take the Buick putputting down the old highway out to the Air Force base. All the junior guys would stick their heads out of the windows and the hole in the roof and yell and have a good time. That was about it for the Buick. The headlights were little more than yellow saucers and the hole in the roof made it too drafty for the wet Washington autumn nights. But the Buick was fun for the afternoons.

Rob was the leader of the juniors. His family had recently hit it rich, selling strips of worthless prairie to the state for the new freeway. Before that they were hillbilly just like Logger. Pete and Ray and Flipper and Hubie all used to joke about Rob going "sosh" like some of the seniors. "Now that you got a swimming pool and that big brick house," Hubie used to razz him, "you'll be picking nothing but those blonde Scandahoovian hairs out of the water filter, Rob."

"He'll be picking them out of his teeth," Logger put in.

Rob joked about going "sosh" too, but then Rob put a stop to all that talk. He made it plain that the guys were not going to change by inviting Logger over to shoot some pool.

Logger never did look comfortable. "I'm used to shooting pool in taverns," he said.

Rob laughed at that. He got Logger to talk about some of the fights he'd been in at the taverns up by Mount Rainer. Rob made it clear that he wanted Logger to be in on any of the runs that the guys made. The guys felt that was okay since they had their own style of doing things and

Logger fit in. They joked that Logger was their model of a good senior.

After football practice one Thursday afternoon Logger decided to keep on driving down the old highway. They ended up over in Lakewood by Clover Park School. The big game with Clover Park wasn't until later that fall so there was no reason to go over there to their arch rivals other than it was a warm September day and Logger wanted to keep on driving.

Lakewood was one big suburb. The big houses had cars to match their double garages. They had concrete flamingoes on their lawns instead of rust flowers and swimming pools in their backyards instead of swamps. The guys talked about going to the Clover Park hangout but none of them knew where it was. They didn't even know if the Clover Park guys *had* a hangout. They guessed that those guys were so weird, they might do something *else* besides cruise around a drivein. None of them could guess what that might be, though.

Another senior had ridden along with them, Whitey. Whitey was an obnoxious guy who lived just down the road from Logger. The junior guys all liked Logger but they didn't like Whitey. He had a big mouth. He played defensive back and he was always mouthing off during the games. He caused trouble that he could not back up. Logger always took care of any trouble he started.

So Logger drove the Buick around the shopping mall. No one there seemed to think that the old Buick was funny or anything. The people just stared. The guys were all feeling rowdy and they decided to go back to their neck of the woods. But on the way back they passed a Dairy

Diner drivein and Whitey stood out on the running board and started to badmouth a bunch of guys getting hamburgers there. They yelled back and Whitey and Logger and Rob all said a few choice things about Clover Park and then the guys said come back at eight that night. Whitey yelled that they would be there and for them to go fuck themselves. Then they drove back to Rob's house and shot some pool. They took Rob's new Pontiac to get some burgers at the A&W. Rob was talking it up about going back to the Dairy Diner. He wanted to impress Logger and have the guys join in on an adventure with Logger so he would really be part of the gang. "We're going to kick ass tonight, right Logger?" Logger nodded. "Look at Logger," Rob said, "he's ready."

Then Rob told the story about how Logger never shaved the day before his wrestling matches with Clover Park. "Old Logger gets that chin on the guy's back and *scrape, scrape, scrape.* You can hear it all the way back up to the top rows in the gym when Logger gets his chin in the guy's back." Logger smiled. "Whisker burn," Rob hooted, "that's Logger's secret weapon."

At seven-thirty they all piled into the Buick and started down the old highway toward Lakewood. They crossed South Tacoma Way at a little-used road to avoid the police. Logger got on a service road out behind the Rhodes department store and they drove onto the mall that way without taking any main roads in. Logger took it up to top speed. The Dairy Diner seemed to be deserted as they rounded the corner.

"Hey, no one's there," Rob yelled.

"Chickenshits!" Whitey screamed. He climbed out the

hole in the roof and he slid down to the running board and began to yell at the drivein as the Buick went past. There were two people at the service window. They turned to look. "Screw you!" Whitey yelled. The other guys in the car held up their fingers out the roof. "Take another turn," Whitey yelled at Logger.

Logger turned the Buick around and they made another pass. Whitey was ranting and raving at the two people when it happened. The entire back lot of the Dairy Diner lit up with headlights. There were at least eight cars hiding there. "Jesus Christ," Logger said. He hung a U-turn but the way to the service road behind Rhodes was blocked. He headed out across the mall. The cars came out of the back parking lot single-file. They were all newer cars.

Hubie and Flipper and Pete and Ray were in the back seat. They turned and looked out the back window at the line of cars behind the Buick. In the glare of the headlights they could see that some of the cars had three or four guys in them. Whitey was still screaming at them from the running board. "Get the hell in here, you asshole," Logger yelled at him. "How many of them are there?"

"A lot," Hubie said. "Christ, there are a *whole* lot."

The cars followed the Buick back towards South Tacoma Way. "They're just escorting us out," Rob said. He laughed. "At least I hope so. Otherwise we might have to kick their ass, right Logger?"

Logger didn't say anything. He was hunched over the wheel. "Hey Logger," Flipper yelled at him, "step on it."

"He can't step on it, there's no accelerator!" Rob yelled back.

As they passed out of the residential area, the car closest roared up close. "Left, Logger!" Hubie yelled. The Buick swerved over and the car fell back. Then the car roared right up to the back end of the Buick and hit the Buick's back bumper.

"Hey, they're getting rough," Whitey said, *"big deal."*

Hubie looked down into the front seat of the car following them. "They got tire irons," Hubie said.

"What?" All the guys in the back seat turned and looked. Just then the man riding shotgun in the first car leaned out of the window and yelled "Fuck you!" His arm went back and then forward.

A bottle hit the edge of the roof. The glass broke and some glass showered over them. "Hey," Logger yelled, swerving back and forth, "what the hell are those guys doing?"

Pete sniffed his wet sleeve. "Jesus, they're throwing beer. Those aren't Clover Park guys."

"Then who the hell are they?" Logger yelled back. Another beer bottle hit the top of the Buick as Logger swerved out into the left lane to block their pass. Beer and glass flew all over them, only this time it was glass from the right window too. "Shit," Logger yelled.

"Those are Army guys or something," Hubie yelled, "they got crewcuts."

Logger began careening back and forth across the road so no cars could pass and box them off. The cars lunged forward behind them, then back. Another bottle flew into the Buick, then another took out the back window. Everyone was rolled up in a ball, their hands over their heads. "These guys are serious," Rob said.

"Let's ditch the Buick and run," Whitey said. Rob pushed him out of the front seat into the back seat. Another beer bottle burst on the top and showered them.

"We ain't giving them Logger's Buick," Rob screamed at Whitey. "You little shit," Flipper screamed at him, "you and your big mouth."

A beer bottle flew into the Buick and smashed on the back seat, just missing Whitey's head. "Oh, Jesus, Jesus," Whitey moaned, "I'm cut." He curled up and tried to burrow down underneath the other guys' legs. Flipper kicked him.

Hubie peeked out the back window. "They got bats, man," Ray said. "Goddamn, they got baseball bats."

"Go for the base, Logger," Pete said. "Get to the MP gate."

The Buick roared across South Tacoma Way against a red light. "God, I hope a cop sees us," Ray prayed, "please let there be a cop." The cars followed them through the red light.

As the Buick came up to the freeway overpass leading to McCord Air Force Base, they saw that the sandbags that used to close the overpass down to two lanes had been taken away. It was now four lanes. "Oh fuck," Flipper said.

Logger swerved left and right but the car behind them feinted and then roared past on the right. The other car pulled up tight to the Buick. As they came over the overpass rise, the car in front slowed down, swerving this way and that each time Logger tried to squeeze the Buick past. The car behind shot out on the right. The next car closed up the left. The Buick was boxed in. The car in front stopped. Logger put on the brakes. Underneath them the freeway night traffic streamed by. The only sound was the cars passing. Down the road they could see the gates for McCord Air Force Base and the MP shack. They heard the doors opening and slamming around the Buick. "Don't get out of the car," Logger yelled.

A guy came up to the driver's side and slugged Logger in the face as he turned to say something. Blood shot out over the windshield. Everyone in the Buick started yelling. Behind them they heard the taillights being smashed out. A guy appeared in the window on Pete's side and hit him in the face with his fist. Pete doubled over. A bat crashed through the side window. Several guys jumped up on the running boards and began to punch down at them, slugging them on top of their heads. Logger was dragged out of the Buick. Pete held his hand on the door handle and kept slamming it shut as they tried to open it. Two guys threw Logger up against the fender and took turns hitting him. Pete looked up through his tears and saw someone wrench the headlight off the Buick and smash it on the road.

"Hey, these aren't Air Force assholes," one of them said. "These guys are nothing but a bunch of high schoolers."

"Hey, check out the MPs down there," another voice broke in.

"Scatter, huh?" a third voice said, 'let's go. Let's get out of here."

The car doors opened and slammed again. The engines roared. The cars all began to back up and make U-turns. They kept their lights off so no one could get their license plate numbers. In a few minutes they were gone.

The guys began to sit up, one by one. Underneath there was the steady hum of cars passing. Something was creaking on the Buick. Slowly Pete and Hubie and Ray climbed out of the back seat. Logger was sitting on the fender. He had his face in his hands. There was blood all over his hands and pants.

"You okay, Logger? Anybody hurt bad?" Pete said. Ray and Hubie stared down at Pete from the running boards. His nose was bleeding. "Are you okay in there, Rob?" Pete said, turning to the Buick. Flipper was reaching over the front seat and holding Rob's head.

"He's been knocked out," Flipper said.

"I'm okay," Rob said. He sounded dazed. "Logger," he said. "Is Logger okay?"

Pete looked down the road. Two MPs were standing out in front of the guard shack. "We better get out of here before the cops come," Pete said. Blood was running down his throat. He could taste it. He looked at Hubie and Ray. Their hair was wet from the beer. "We'll get busted if we stay. We smell like a brewery."

Logger heaved himself up off the fender. The fender was sagging. He looked down at the smashed headlight on the road. Just then all the guys saw just how bad the Buick looked. The back bumper was loose. There were dents and stains where the beer bottles hit. Two windows were busted out. Logger looked at his car and he looked at them. Then he climbed in the driver's seat.

Ray got in and Hubie and Pete followed. Whitey was still down on the floor of the Buick. He was crying, his face in his hands. "Sit up," Flipper said. Over the back of the front seat he held Rob's head up so Rob could breathe. Rob was staring up, blinking slowly. Flipper kicked Whitey. "You little shit."

"You okay, Logger?" Rob said. He pulled his head forward out of Flipper's hands. "Logger?" he said.

Logger wiped his hand down his pants. There was the sound of gravel falling on the floorboards. He spit. Then he wiped his face. A few more pieces of gravel fell off his face onto the seat. He spit again. Then Logger looked around the Buick. "You all are a bunch of high school kids," he said.

A 50-50 Marriage

A 50-50 Marriage :: Cheri picked Pete up in her car after work. "You'll see," she said. She was wearing her peach business suit with a frilly white blouse. Pete could see that she had on her girdle. "You look nice," he said. "I've always liked that outfit."

"Changing the subject won't get you out of it," she said. She laughed when she looked at his face. "Later," she said, "later for that. You are so transparent sometimes."

Pete didn't look away, he kept looking down at her legs. "Am I?" he said. Then he stared out the window. "I haven't been to a wedding in a long time."

"You don't like them, do you?"

"Did I say that?" Pete said. "It was my brother's wedding, a shotgun wedding." Pete remembered what he could of it. "Everyone was trying to be happy."

Cheri sighed. "Well, they were," Pete said. "I was small but I knew that much. I remember the men out by the corner of the church drinking out of paper bags."

"This isn't a shotgun marriage," Cheri said, "and they won't be drinking out of paper bags in back of the church."

Cheri looked over at Pete. He had his knees up on the dashboard. She giggled. "You look funny all cramped up."

"Short legs driver," he said. He touched her right leg.

"Why don't you drive back?"

Pete tried to make his voice sound steady. "Okay."

"No, this is not a shotgun wedding," Cheri said. "Eva was not going to have one of those. She said that after her last scare that was it. I don't blame her."

"What did Ray say?"

"I thought Ray was your friend."

"I haven't seen him since that weekend out at O'Rourke's cabin before graduation where he got shot in the leg," Pete said.

"He's got a job and there is no reason why they shouldn't get married."

"But what did Ray say?" Pete said. "Did anybody talk to Ray about it?"

"He was for it," Cheri said, "you'll see."

"I will, huh?"

"You'll like it," Cheri said.

After the wedding Pete left the chapel where the photographs were being taken. Ray had not looked at Pete the whole time, even when he walked down the aisle. Pete had thought that he was good friends with Ray. But after the weekend at O'Rourke's cabin where Ray had got a .22 bullet in his leg by accident, Ray had stopped going around with the guys. And none of the guys were at the wedding. Not that they could have come. O'Rourke and Flipper were still up at the cabin, repairing the damages and Hubie had gone into the Marines. Pete wondered if they were even invited. He hadn't been, Cheri had been invited by Eva.

Pete walked down the steps of the church and looked into the hall windows. He saw some women in there carrying things. He walked over to the door and went in. The women were moving into the next room. Pete stood there and thought about weddings again as he looked at the table full of gifts. He had never heard anyone male talk about them, one way or the other. No one he knew who was married even talked about their honeymoon. Pete looked over the stuff on the long table. He was surprised about how much was there. Then he remembered all the business buddies of Ray's dad. And Ray was going into the business with his dad, too.

Pete looked at the toasters and frying pans and pots and silverware and linens and pillowcases and dishes and salad bowls. He felt as if he were in a store all alone and he didn't want to shoplift any of it. That made him feel sad.

He tried to imagine Ray and Eva using it. He saw Eva's face reflected in a mixing bowl's aluminum curve. He saw Ray's face reflected in a Revereware electric skillet top. Pete couldn't imagine all this stuff in a house. This was only good for a store. Pete thought about that. He felt as if he were in a store, a store that was about to go out of business. The last big sale. That made him feel so down Pete turned away and walked back out of the hall.

He wished that there were guys drinking back by the corner of the church. But this was Parkland, this was the Lutheran church. There were no empties in their parking lot. Pete's brother had gotten married in a Baptist church out by the Indian Reservation, out in the boonies. Pete tried to remember where that church was. He must have been nine years old when that happened.

"That's what I want," Cheri said on the ride back to her house, "a 50-50 marriage."

"What's that?" Pete said. He didn't turn off for her house but kept driving down Pacific Avenue, going out toward Rainier Corners. He was thinking of finding the church where his brother got married.

"Where the man and wife go 50-50 on everything."

"How do you do that?"

"Did you like it?" Cheri said. She took his arm and snuggled up to him. Pete could feel that she had taken off her panty girdle. Probably in the church, then put it in her purse.

"Yeah, I like it," he said.

"You don't act like you liked it," Cheri said. She slid away from him and looked at herself in the mirror for a moment.

"How do a man and wife go 50-50 on everything?"

"You'll see," Cheri said. She was teasing him. "Half and half."

"Well, I don't see," Pete said, ignoring the tease. "I really don't know."

"You decide things together," Cheri said.

"Okay," Pete said, "and then what?"

"You didn't like the wedding, did you?"

"Just because I'm trying to find out what you're talking about doesn't mean I didn't like the wedding," Pete said. "And?"

Cheri didn't say anything. She slipped out of her shoes and brought her bare feet up and rested them on the dashboard. As Pete turned off the highway onto a side street he looked at the underside of her knee. He always liked the way it looked. He started to circle the blocks, checking for the church. There were few houses, mostly overgrown summer pastures and rundown sheds. "So, and?" he said. Cheri looked out the window. "Look, I liked the wedding, okay? It just made me sad."

"One of the guys got caught, right?"

"I didn't say that. At the end, *after* the wedding, I

walked into the hall, you know," Pete said, "and that's when I got sad."

Cheri worried the left side of her lip with her teeth. She kept staring ahead.

Pete caught sight of a white barn-like building down the block past a stand of pines. He stopped Cheri's Ford, backed up and drove down the side street toward it. As they got closer, he knew that this was the church. Only it was so small. "Boy," Pete said, "I remember this as huge. I think maybe this is where my brother was married." He drove into the parking lot and pulled around to the side and stopped where they had a good view of the church. He looked up at the roof and saw a tiny bell-tower tacked on top. The wood wasn't even good wood, it was old shiplap. Around Spanaway the chicken houses were built with shiplap.

"We're not parking here, are we?"

"Who said we were going to park?" Pete said. "Just because you let me drive your car, doesn't mean I automatically go park somewhere. I was just looking for this place. My brother got married here."

Pete thought about the big Lutheran church. He tried to imagine if this dinky church could fit inside it. "Look," he said, "I got sad when I saw all that crap after the wedding, that's all."

"What crap?"

"All the junk they got."

"I didn't think it was crap. I thought they got wonderful presents." Cheri shifted around on the seat and put her shoes back on. "You don't like presents either?"

"Hey," Pete said, "Cheri, Jesus, you want to hear what

I've got to say?"

"Sure," she said, "only I know what you're going to say. You don't like seeing one of the guys getting married. That's all you see."

"No, I saw all those toasters and waffle irons and . . . you know. Think about it, coming back from your honeymoon and walking into your front room and seeing all that stuff stacked up there. Christ, I can imagine us having a fight over what to use, what to sell and keep."

Cheri laughed. Pete slid over to her and put his arm around her shoulders. "See what I mean? Like you're starting your life with a store instead of a wife."

"They already got the wife stuff out of the way," Cheri said.

"What?" Pete said. "Hey, I'm not talking about sex. I mean starting your life with, you know, someone by making a list of what you dump and what you keep." Pete could smell the hair spray in Cheri's hair. It was starting to smell flat, chemical. "That's kinda depressing, isn't it?" he said. "You know what I mean?"

"No," she said, "I think you're just trying to be funny again."

"I'm not trying to be funny again," Pete said. "I mean it was like they were supposed to be children at Christmas and those were their toys, or something."

"That doesn't make any sense. It's not Christmas. What's wrong with toys?"

Pete looked at the white church and he tried to think out what he was trying to say. "You know my brother's wife," he said, "you know what she would always say when everyone started talking about marriage. She'd say, *little girls grow up to be women and little boys grow up to be big boys."*

"Eva says that," Cheri laughed. "It's true."

"You really think that?" Pete said.

"No, I'm just teasing," Cheri said. "Can't you see I'm just teasing you? You're so serious today."

"I don't think that," Pete said. He sat up straighter and let his arm drop behind the seat. "I mean, that wasn't for Ray."

"What wasn't?"

"The wedding. They could have put a dummy in his place." Pete eased over a little toward the steering wheel. He traced the curves in it with his left hand. "That's a hell of a way to start a life together," Pete said to the wheel, "playing dummy in a discount store."

Cheri slid over. She put her face on his chest. "Let's get married, Pete. We could do it. I can get a job anywhere. You could still go to school. You could keep your scholarship. I could transfer to another government job by your school."

Pete looked down at Cheri. "Does that make any sense?" he said. He slid back behind the steering wheel. Cheri sat up. "You'll see," she said, "if all the decisions are 50-50, everything will turn out okay. If you don't want to, then don't."

Pete put the Ford into Drive. "The only reason they got married was because she was afraid of getting pregnant. She could do something about that. So could he. They got married instead."

"You just don't like the idea of getting married. You'll see," Cheri said. She patted his leg. "You'll like it."

Pete drove out of the parking lot. He was remembering his brother's wedding. His brother had a 32 Ford coupe, painted purple. It was chopped and channeled and his brother had cut the roof down just right. It had a horn on it that went ougah-ougah. Right after the wedding they sold it and bought a 1950 Chevy so they'd have room for the baby. Pete could remember the white wedding veil of the bride sticking out of the Ford's little window. "I don't want to be a big boy," Pete said, "I don't want to live in a store."

"What are you talking about?" Cheri said. She looked over at Pete. "You need those things," she said. "You're just scared, that's all."

You Can't Miss It

You Can't Miss It :: The bus let Dean off at the restaurant by the freeway overpass. The old highway from Mount Vernon was back a mile from the freeway. He could see the line of trees heading into the mountains. There was a service station with a propane gas business beside the restaurant. He used the rest room. Then he started to walk and he stuck out his thumb. Dean was still wearing his work clothes. That morning he had been on the bus going to downtown Seattle to his construction job when he decided it was Friday, to hell with work. The freeway could build itself on Friday. Dean got off the city bus at his regular stop but walked four blocks to the Greyhound bus station instead of punching in at the laborer's shack. He got some change from the newspaper stand. He called up the construction company and reported in sick. Then he called Elsie. She was surprised. He bought a ticket for the local bus to Bellingham. And twenty minutes later he was on his way.

The Greyhound bus drove past the work site. Dean looked at the exit ramp. He would have been working on that. He imagined the ramp veering off into the hill, making a sudden turn and plowing into the apartment houses.

Dean loved bus rides. He had read books where bus rides were important to the characters. Today he felt like a character in those books. *Get on the Hound and ride. Just go.* He sat with his brown lunch bag in his lap and he was happy to be on his way. "Who knows," he said, "I may not go back." He began to eat his lunch and watch the scenery change from urban to suburban to country.

Only the apple was left from his lunch as he walked along the road toward the old highway. Dean took a bite from time to time, to cool off. He was happier than he could remember being for days. The smell of the alfalfa and the barns and the hot weedy stink of the ditches worked on him. Every now and then he thought about what he would have been doing on the job. Then he smiled. He was happy. "Going to see my girl," he said. He liked the way it sounded.

And not going to work.

That was the part he didn't say, wanting to stay right on what he was doing right then, forget about the rest. It was enough to think of that and be happy. It was nearly 1 o'clock. If he got there soon enough, he'd take her out to an early dinner. She had to work the swing shift at the cannery.

A few hours was all he wanted. He thought about how crazy it must have seemed to her. He was happy about the effect he must have caused. *The hell with work! I'll take the bus up! Let's have lunch! What's money?*

Dean turned and stuck out his thumb as he heard a car coming. The blue Chevrolet slowed and the driver checked the rear view mirror as he pulled over, rolling past Dean.

Dean had the door open before he saw who it was. "How far are you going?" he asked.

"Town," the officer said. "Hop in."

Dean did. "I guess there's no other place to go on this road," he said, "but town."

"Right. Where you from?" the officer said.

"Seattle." He thought about what else he wanted to say. "Going to Uwe."

"I'll take you as far as the edge of town," the officer

said. "Uwe's just down from there. You going to school?"

"Yes, going to the University of Washington."

"What are you going to do when you get out?"

"I don't know yet."

"Well," the officer said, "if you go do your service, you might as well pick what you're getting into."

Dean didn't say anything.

"I suppose you've thought about it?"

"No," he said, "I haven't."

"Well, you can't go to school forever, you must have some plans."

Dean looked over at the officer. He looked at the stripes on his sleeve. Navy men always go over big in farm country. "I've made my plans," Dean said. *One.*

"Good," the officer said. "A lot of young people don't know what they're doing. That's where I step in."

Dean didn't say anything. He looked at the officer's polished shoe as it pressed on the accelerator. He could see the wires under the dashboard reflected in it.

Then he looked at his own boots. They were scuffed and dirty. He thought about how much he hated the words duty and job and work. *And plans.* Dean looked up at the officer. He was watching Dean out of the corner of his eye.

"I'm not interested," Dean said. He wanted to add, *I'm going to see my girl.* But he knew that wouldn't work. It would only lead to more conversation. Dean didn't need plans. He was going to see his girl.

"You can't miss it," the officer said.

He started down the side road, leaving Dean by the green bridge over the river. Along the side of the road were blackberries. Dean walked by them. He looked up through the blackberry vines at the main street of town above him. He saw a dragster parked there on its trailer. It was all shiny. Dean laughed as he thought about telling the Navy recruiting officer about how he always thought of dragsters as giant lawnmowers. He should have said it. He laughed again. He was feeling crazy with the heat and the smell of ripe berries. He was crazy anyway.

Dean stopped on the other side of the bridge. Below in the shallows there were swimmers. Dean smelled the hot green paint on the iron railing and looked at the dusty berry leaves streaked with dark purple juice. He could tell that officer a thing or two. He ate some berries. His fingers turned black and purple. Dean walked on, thinking as clear as he had ever thought before.

He turned and stuck out his thumb as he heard the planks of the bridge rumble with an approaching car. A truck stopped for him. *It's my magic berry black thumb,* Dean thought. "Going to Uwe," he said. He climbed in the back end and sat down and leaned his head against the hot metal of the cab. He closed his eyes to the sun. He felt the trees going past and he opened his eyes halfway so they all became a big green blur.

The car parked in front of the house was a 1958 Chevrolet. Dean stood and looked at it. He never bothered to imagine her house. It was a white one-story house beside the highway, on the damp lower side of the slope. Dean walked up to the door. He could smell the mold, the damp odor of rotting wood. The front door was open. An old woman was sitting on the couch. She was staring at the linoleum floor. She looked up as he knocked on the screen door.

"Yes?"

"Is Elsie here?"

"Yes," the woman said. "I'll get her." She got up off the couch. She moved easily, so she wasn't crippled or sick as Dean had thought for a minute. "Come in," she added, without looking back.

"Elsie," the woman said to the hallway, "your beau is here."

Dean was taken back by that. *Your beau.* He stepped in the house. Inside it was worn and shabby. Somehow he had never thought about what Elsie's house might be like.

"She's getting up," the woman said, coming back out. "I'm her mother. She has to work tonight at the cannery."

"I know," Dean said. But then he didn't know if he should have said that. Her mother sat down on the couch. She resumed staring at the floor. A frizzy old afghan was thrown across the back of the couch. It was grey and white. The couch was brown with white worn stripes. Her mother leaned back.

Dean wanted to say something. But he did not know what. Her mother looked straight ahead for a little, almost resembling Elsie, but more like a faded skinny copy. Dean looked back outside for help. He could say it was hot. Shadows filled the front yard from the poplar trees overhead. It wasn't hot in here, it was damp.

"Dean," Elsie said. She stepped out from the doorway.

She was wearing a pair of pedal pushers and a blouse. She had no makeup on. She looked tired, in a kind of ordinary country way.

"Elsie," Dean said. He moved toward her and stopped, becoming aware again of her mother. He smiled. The pedal pushers made her look like a hick. And he knew that she was anything but a hick. "I got here," he said. "Like I said," he said.

"I've got a few hours before I go to work," Elsie said. "Did you meet my mother?"

Dean looked down at her mother. She was looking up at him with a fierce gleam in her eye. Dean stepped back. "I'm Dean," he said. Her mother looked up at Elsie and her mouth changed for a moment. Then she seemed to fade back into the couch.

"We'll take the car," Elsie said, "down to the river."

In the car things were different. Dean felt happy, he could not stop looking at Elsie. Out of the house she seemed like the beautiful girl from last spring. She looked tired and worn out, but still she was Elsie. Dean tried to drive the image of her mother out of his mind.

Dean wanted to reach over and touch the back of Elsie's neck. Her hair was up and she looked so different that way. Dean decided that was it. That's why things were strange. "I wish you had a piano in back," he said.

Elsie smiled.

"I'd like to hear Summertime," he said. "I had Summertime on my mind all the way here." He waved at the blackberry vines and salmon berries along the highway.

Elsie tilted her head and hummed a little. She was still

smiling but less. Her face had always reminded Dean of a bird's face, small-boned, and angular. But especially when she sang. He looked down at her again. She was always so well-dressed back at college. "I just, uh," he said, looking away as she caught him looking at her, "wanted to get out of work. I wanted to take off. I wanted to feel like summer again. Not be all covered with clay and guck and dirt."

Elsie cleared her throat. "Lucky you," she said.

Dean looked at the back of her neck. She usually wore her long blonde hair down. With her hair up the light blonde hairs on her neck shined in the sun. He wanted to smell them.

"I guess I'm, uh," he said, "taking away your sleep."

She turned and looked at him. She nodded. "I thought we'd go down to the river," she said, "we can talk there,"

The trail was mud. It led through a stand of alder. The trail turned into sand a few feet past the feeder creek and then let out on the river bank. The rocks were hot. There was a breeze coming around the bend. They could hear children down there in the river. Dean followed her to a sandy bank topped by a huge grey log.

She sat down in the shadow under it. He sat next to her. He put his hand on her neck.

"Elsie," he said, "I wanted to see you."

She looked back up the river.

"That's all," he said. He took his hand off her neck.

"I should have called," she said.

"What?"

"It was too early to talk."

Dean leaned against her. "I just got the notion," he smiled. She smiled back. He felt his chest suddenly breathe free. "Did you get my last letter?"

She nodded. "I've been meaning to write."

He kissed her. She tilted back a little and her head came out of the shadow and he felt as if he were kissing sunlight.

"Did you read those books?"

"No, I haven't had time. I've been on swing shift." She looked down at her feet. She dug them into the sand. "Dean," she said, "Dean, there's something I've got to say."

There was a loud rattle as something heavy passed over the bridge downstream. A gush of wind came up the river and the sound of the rumble and the swift wind sound mixed and passed them by. There were some words. Then it was only hot again.

It was hot on the road to the freeway. It was about as hot as it was going to get. Dean sat in the Chevrolet and he thought about the time he met Elsie at the cabin. Then he remembered the weekend in Seattle. And he could not put those two times next to today.

He looked over at Elsie. She was driving in that funny way of hers. She always seemed so much older when she drove. Her arms and her face and her posture all seemed older when she drove a car.

Dean tried to figure out what he could have done. When he met her, it had taken a while for him to get rid of his old girlfriend. Then there was the Jewish girl, but how would she have found out about that? One night?

Dean reviewed everything and there was only one thing to believe and that was what she had told him by the river. And there was nothing he could do about that.

Saliva coated the outside of his lips. His eyes felt burnt. He had tears in them. He licked his lips and looked out at the fields going past. He saw the restaurant and the service station coming up. He wanted to say all the things that he had already said and they would somehow work this time. But he couldn't do it.

Elsie pulled up to the propane tank beside the service station. She put the Chevrolet in Park. Then she looked over at him.

"We could have seen each other on the weekends," he said.

"Yes," she agreed. She licked her lips. She had thin lips but. . . .

And he wanted to do all the things they did one more time. He did not want her to go. He didn't want to go back to Seattle. He didn't want it to be summer but spring when they went down to the lawn for the first time and lay on the blankets and laughed about the party in the house above them on the lawn, what fools were there, and then they rolled into each other's arms. He wanted it all back.

She put her arm up on his back. One wrist touched the back of his neck. He felt the old weak feeling again, and he watched her face move toward his.

She kissed him and pulled back. "Elsie, . . ." he said. But that was all he could say. He put his hand on the door handle. He pulled it up. There was a click.

Dean stood beside the propane tank. He watched the taillights of the Chevrolet. He wished that she had put her hair down. He wanted to see her hair down one more time. The heat was flat and heavy. He was sweating. The sweat was burning at the edges of his eyes.

She had been the most beautiful girl he'd ever known. She was the best lover he'd ever known. She was the one he could talk to about all his books, his plans. She was the one who was always ready to go. To party. To do the things that no one else ever thought about doing. Just like that, no plans, just do it. He never thought about doing things like that unless he was with her. And now she was gone.

He tried to think the whole thing over. How the house was so shabby. Was she ashamed? Did his coming there do it? He hated her mother. That crone on the couch. *"Your beau."*

That hadn't been hard to miss. The way she said that.

He started walking toward the bus stop. Sweat was running down his face. He tasted it. It was salty. He saw the mother's face again. Then he knew. Elsie had never been there. It would have been hard to see Elsie after he saw her. He knew that now. She was one. The old woman. She jinxed him. She was the one who did it. Elsie was never there. She saw him in his work clothes and she changed Elsie into that. Someone else. She did it.

He walked toward the freeway. In the heat the freeway seemed to be lifting off the ground and floating up. It was moving in waves of heat. It was floating off the ground.

When This Van Is Rockin'
Don't Bother Knockin'

When This Van Is Rockin' Don't Bother Knockin' :: On Saturday night they sent over their daughter Teri. That's the way the Burkers worked. She knocked on the door. The wife opened it. "Is your husband home?" I got up off the couch. I was in the middle of an appendicitis attack, only I didn't know that then. I thought that it was my bad back. "Yes?" I said.

"My dad wants to know how much you would charge to cut down the tree."

The tree. See, that's what gets me. In my neighbor's world there was only one tree. *The* tree. In their front yard. "I'm not feeling well," I said. "I came home early from work yesterday." And I point to the city truck parked across the street. "Didn't even get the truck back to the yard."

Their daughter reacted to this. She thought I was putting her and her family down. But I wasn't. "I got bad back pains again," I said, "I can't work now. I'd loan your dad the chainsaw but it's the park department's saw and I can't do that, Teri."

Teri didn't know what to say. She nodded and backed up. Then she turned and went away. I knew that I'd done her a bad turn. Sure enough, I hear Burker and his wife yelling at her next door. The old man sounds drunk. The old lady sounds drunk. The two houses are only ten feet apart, so we can hear. "That poor kid," the wife said.

"Well, they have to offer to pay, they can't ask me as a neighbor," I said. I lay back down.

That evening the pains increased. I realized that I had to see a doctor on Sunday. So I took something to get me through the night. A Darvocette for my back pain, or something like that. But the pain got worse. So I'm on my couch in the front room. The wife was sewing. I begin to think that this could be appendicitis. The pain was real bad. And that's when I heard the chopping.

I got up and went over to the window. I've got an angle on the neighbor's front porch from there. They've put on a few shows for us. Burker was out there with an ax, hacking at his pine tree.

They bought it years ago at a sale. A cute little pine tree. That would have been like them. Planted it and then it turned into a monster. They were doing that with puppies and kittens all the time. *Hunchy* or *Cuddles* they would call them. When the animals got too big, they kicked them out and let them feed off the neighbors until the animals ran away or the SPCA got them.

Anyway, Burker was out there with an ax, whacking at the branches. The moon was up and he was quite a sight. He had himself in a tangle. Branches were bouncing up and hitting him. He fell over a few times when he swung too hard. He made the job interesting. I thought he was going to cut his foot off.

"What are they doing *now?*" the wife said. "What do they want to cut that down for, anyway?"

"Maybe so they can see their camper better," I said. About then Burker stopped slashing at the tree and he disappeared into his camper for a little refreshment.

"When this van is rockin'," I said, "don't bother knockin'."

The wife laughed at that. Burker had that decal and other stuff like it plastered all over his camper. I really don't care for such stuff myself. I figure that it is hard enough to get through this world without people typing you. You don't need to give them any help like that, especially if you're only a working man. Anyway, that's my opinion. I guess it gave Burker a feeling of belonging to something—a club for people who have their love life in the backs of campers.

Burker came back out and started in again. I was about to lie down when I heard the tree go. *Crack.* And over the tree goes. He dropped it right in the middle of his camper. The dummy didn't even look to see where it would drop, if you ask me. So there it was, moonlight, and a pine tree leaning against his camper. That was a real redneck postcard, let me tell you.

"Well I chopped down the fucking tree for you!" he screamed. I looked at his front porch. The curtains were open and then they closed real quick. I heard their front door lock. Burker was standing there on the porch with the ax in one hand, a Bud in the other. He dropped the ax and the Bud and ran back to the tree and began tugging on a limb. The tree didn't budge.

Then he got the ax and whaled away at the limbs for a while, scattering them all over the sidewalk. I thought one of the neighbors might be calling the police by now, but ours is a working class neighborhood. As long as he wasn't dropping trees on their yards, I guess the other neighbors figured a man has the right to get dead drunk in his own front yard on Saturday night. Besides, there was still the question of how the hell he was going to get the pine tree off his camper and that could turn out to be better than anything on TV.

So I heard him muttering. Swear this, cuss that. And then he opened up another beer and began to figure out loud just how he's going to pull that pine tree off his camper. I took a peek and I saw him out in the middle of the road, sorting through his tool kit. Throwing ratchet wrenches all over the street and talking to himself he was. Then he got out a come-along.

That wasn't bad reasoning for a man drunk as he was. Burker hooked the come-along to the pine tree and then went to find something to hook the other end to. I went back and lay down. The pain was getting worse. I must have dozed off. When I woke up, it was to a loud crunch. I got up as the wife came back in the front room. "What's he done now?" she said.

We both stepped out on the porch to look. The fool had got the pine tree off his camper, all right. It was sideways now on the sidewalk. But he'd hooked the other end of the come-along to his front porch and had ripped out the supports from under the porch roof. Half of it was hanging down over the front door, drooping to one side like it was just as drunk as he was.

Burker was in the camper, celebrating his victory.

"How are you feeling?" the wife asked.

"Very bad," I said. We stood there looking at the back end of the camper. The door was open. The light was on. "I guess that's all the rockin' and knockin' for tonight," she said. "Come on in and lie down. You look terrible."

I dozed off. The pill took over, I guess. I was worn out. When I woke up, it must have been past midnight. I had this pain. I'm not sure how to describe it. The pain wasn't hot or cold. It was just there. This isn't going to make any sense but I'm going to say it anyway. The pain was like some big white wall in my right side. But not *in*. That's not right. It was so big I felt I could lean against it.

I woke up and my eyes were open, boom, just like that. I was on the couch and wondering if anything in the world would help me when I heard the shot.

There wasn't any mistaking it. I know a shot when I hear one. I got up off the couch and I opened the front door. The moon was up, a big full moon. The lights were on in the camper. The pine tree was still blocking the sidewalk. I went out and stood on the porch. Nothing else happening up or down the street so I knew it had to come from the camper. I stepped off and started toward my neighbor's camper. I was amazed, really, that I could walk at all.

The back door of the camper was ajar. I could smell the smoke. The camper was rocking, sort of slow, from side to side. I stood there and looked at that damn decal and I decided to hell with it *and* knocking, I would open the door and look. If someone was dead, they wouldn't shoot me, and if someone was going to shoot at me, I would have surprise on my side. So I opened the door.

My neighbor was sitting behind the kitchen nook table. He had a pistol in his hand. He was rocking back and forth and looking down. His foot was bleeding. *"She just don't know,"* he kept saying. *"She just don't know."* He was shaking his head and rocking back and forth and saying that over and over. He didn't seem to notice that there was blood running down the floor all over the ratchet wrenches. He looked up at me. I got the door ready to shut if he brought that pistol up. *"She don't know the pain she causes me,"* he said.

It didn't seem like he was going to use the pistol again,

so I leaned in, funny to think of it now,—I leaned in on my right side just like the pain wasn't there, could have burst that thing and died on his camper steps—and I took the pistol out of his hand. "Do you have a drink?" I asked him.

Burker looked surprised. He wiped back his hair and that's when I saw the round circle, all red, from where he had been pressing the gun barrel against his forehead.

He checked the Budweiser cans on the table, lifted an open one up and shook it, and then he located a pint of Jim Beam. He handed it over. He looked straight at me. There wasn't any shame in his eyes. It was like he was looking right through me.

The pint was about half gone. I drank a good part of that. About then the police car turned the corner. I wasn't the only one who heard the shot go off. I waited there until the police pulled up. Then I noticed that I had the pistol in my hand and I put it down on the pavement and kicked it away from myself.

They were about to draw on me, the police were. They didn't know what had happened. I could have got shot myself. So everything cooled out. They took Burker off to get his foot fixed.

The house lights came on and out came his wife. She acted like she hadn't heard anything. She was about as pie-eyed drunk as usual. The daughter came out and acted proud that her dad had shot himself in the foot. That made me sort of sad, even though I didn't think I had room in me for sadness, what with the pain.

I thought about that feeling when I was in the hospital on Sunday. The staff couldn't give me a shot until a second doctor had come in and given his opinion on whether to operate. So the pain widened out and what was left of me was clear clean through. The wife was there, and a nurse. I felt that I could look at people and tell what they were thinking, I mean, *really* thinking. Nothing was left in me to get in the way. I didn't particularly like what I saw.

I suppose that I had the same idea Burker did then: *if I live through this, I'll never forget what I saw.*

And then we both went back to our regular lives, only things changed. He left his wife and kids. She sold the camper and used the money to dry out. I thought about quitting my job with the parks, to do something I really liked doing—working with wood. But I didn't. I think I could say why I did what I did. Only this is about as close as I want to come.

Back to Nature

Back to Nature :: There was a wet trail across the gravel up to the edge of the grass. Walt saw the trail when he got out of the car. He thought that the radiator had overflowed. Walt opened the trunk of the car and began to throw things out on the ground. Ella and Erin sat in the car. Walt made the car rock as he took out the gear. He got busy pitching the tent behind the car. He wanted to rent a boat and get out there on the lake.

Ella got out of the car. She looked at where the tent was laid out. "It's not like we belong here," Ella said. She looked around the resort grounds at the RVs and campers. "They only have *four* tent sites," Ella said. "This is plastic land."

"Can I just pitch this tent?" Walt said. "There's only a few more hours of light left. That's what we came up here for, isn't it? To get out on the lake?"

"You didn't have to go blasting across the parking lot like that," Ella said.

"I didn't go *blasting* across the parking lot," Walt said. "I went *careening—in reverse*—across the parking lot."

He began to hammer the tent stakes into the ground. Ella watched him. Walt waited for her to say something when the first stake didn't go in. The ground was rocky. Ella had wanted to camp behind the resort lodge. That tent site was next to the lake. Walt had pointed out that it was low and wet there. A bog, in fact. He had pointed out the light over the rear door of the resort, close to the tent site. "Mosquito heaven," Walt had said.

Ella got stubborn. "Well, you want to be close to the lake, don't you?"

Walt had jammed the car in reverse and sent it flying back across the parking lot to the tent site up on the slope.

That site was a good 100 yards away from the lake. Walt thought there might be a chance of a wind up there to keep the mosquitos off them that night.

When he finished pitching the tent, his daughter Erin refused to get out of the car and go out on the lake with them. She said she hated boats. That was the first time Walt had heard anything about that. "You came all this way to a lake and you're not going out on it?" he said.

"I didn't come all this way," Erin said, "you took me all this way."

Walt didn't argue any further. He rented the boat and he and Ella went out. That end of the lake was full of weeds but there were trails through the tules and lily pads. They saw flocks of wild birds. The lake turned out to be a wild bird sanctuary. Signs stuck out of the weeds with pictures and names of the different birds.

Walt skippered the boat out, and Ella brought the boat back. On the ride in he stretched out in the front of the boat. The sun was shining. He trailed his hand in the water. "See," he said, "this makes that drive worth it, now doesn't it?"

Ella agreed. She was smiling. "You were right," she said.

Walt pointed at the long dock sticking out from the back of the resort. "When I was a kid, we had a dock just like that, every summer we'd go swimming. No bathing suits, jeans," Walt said. "A pack of cigarettes and a comb and jeans, that's all I needed. When I smell this lake, I can smell those wet jeans too." He laughed. "It's nice up here, I'm glad we came," he said. "After that drive, this feels good. Doesn't it feel good?"

"Sure," Ella said. She looked down at the water. "But I don't think I'd swim in this. Looks slimy."

"That's the way lakes look this time of year up here," Walt said. "You can't shop around for one any different. They're all like this."

That night they tried to play cards on the picnic table but mosquitos drove them inside the tent. Ella and Erin both wanted to read and they had a fight over the flashlight. Walt had not wanted to go inside the tent at all and that did it for him. "I'm going to the resort and watch the game on TV," he said.

"That's a fine way to get back to nature," Ella said, "watching the game on TV."

He said come and join me. She refused and went back to reading her book by the light of the flashlight. He crawled out of the tent, zipped up the mosquito net after him and went to the resort bar.

As he walked across the parking lot, Walt saw a primered 1955 Chevy parked by the restrooms. He stopped and looked at the hood. It was welded shut. Then he saw that to get at the engine, the whole front end of the Chevy, fenders and all, had to be lifted up. "Christ," Walt said, "looks like someone rescued a stock car and turned it back into a road car." He walked around it. He looked inside. There was no back seat, only the cross braces. The front seat was plain smooth black leather. There were no floor mats. A chrome stickshift with a chrome knob stuck up from the driveline. Walt laughed. Some joker had stuck a Hydromatic in it. The gear selector plate was dangling on the chrome stickshift halfway between the knob and the driveline. Walt laughed again. He stared down at the plate. He couldn't imagine how the plate could ever fit snug into the driveline. "Hell, it's going to hang there forever. What a project," he said. He could remember spending whole summers parked by the lake, sanding down old cars and going for swims.

There was a cable TV in the resort bar. Walt watched the Monday night game. He talked to the bartender. The bartender said that he had come up from California too, only he and his family had stayed, buying the resort. He said they had sold the family business and moved up, lock, stock and barrel. He asked Walt what line of work he was in. "I was in electronics, management," Walt said, "but you know how the economy is. They say it's going to bounce back. My wife's got a regular job." Walt looked out at the lake. He laughed. "So I'm taking a vacation from doing nothing. I come from the Northwest. I spent the first nineteen years of my life around lakes like these."

Walt was on his third drink when Ella came in. He had stopped watching the game and was looking out over the lake. Ella sat down. "Those mosquitos, they see the light and they get in," she said. "We need a new tent." She ordered a brandy. The bartender brought it to her in a warmed glass. Then she said that he was right, the bar was a good place to be on a night like this.

He pointed down to the first camp site that she had wanted to take. The light above the back entrance to the resort about five feet from the tent site had clouds of insects around it. "I told you," he said. He peered down at the site. "It might have flooded too," he said. He thought he could see wet mud in the moonlight. "Any waves would have come right over that."

Ella didn't say anything but drank her brandy and left. Walt stopped watching the lake and looked at the fish photographs above the bar and drank. He talked to the bartender about fishing. "The fish are big this time of year but they don't taste good," the bartender said. "Something in the weeds they eat."

The next morning Walt was hung over. He did not remember drinking that many at the bar, but he did remember getting thirsty and switching to beer some time during the evening. Ella was not talking to him, so he assumed he had been a bit clumsy getting into the tent. He hated the tent anyway. It was a burrow of a tent. He called it the orange gopher hole. Ella said it was designed to save heat. She said that a tent like that put you closer to nature. Walt said okay, it was a designer orange gopher hole. He slept without any clothes on with the sleeping bag unzipped halfway. He woke up drenched with sweat. Ella woke up complaining about the cold. Erin complained too. They looked out the tent opening at him as he made breakfast and talked about how cold they were. He said that he didn't want to rent the boat and a pole to go fishing because the fish didn't taste good. Ella asked him how he knew if he hadn't caught any. He didn't answer her. She said she would just as well leave this camper heaven and go someplace where people really camped out.

Walt was not in a good humor anyway and that remark did it for him. "So you didn't *like* getting your head out of the mosquitos for an hour or two?" he said. "Hard to get your brandy in a warmed glass out in nature, isn't it?"

Ella and Erin both left for the restrooms. Walt had noticed the trail across the gravel again. But he was thinking about how Erin and Ella were taking showers and fixing their hair and putting on their faces for camping out in nature. He had the car warmed up and ready to go by the time they got back from the restrooms. Erin got in the back seat and Ella sat down in front. Ella got the map out and began plotting their next three hundred miles in search of nature. Walt put the car in Drive and pulled out. He saw in the rear view mirror a dark trail behind the car. For a moment he thought that he had forgotten to plug up the ice chest. He had done that once before. But when a burnt smell came in the car and the car lost power completely, he knew that it was the transmission.

Walt got out of the car. "Something wrong?" Ella said. Walt looked under the car and he saw that the two lines to the transmission radiator must have been jarred loose. Big fat violet drops of fluid were hanging from the line. He stood back up. Ella rolled down the window.

"What is it?" Ella said.

"It's the transmission fluid lines. They're loose. We'll have to get some fluid."

"How'd we do that?" Ella said.

Walt shrugged. "I don't know, maybe scraped it on something," he said. "I don't know how it could have happened," Walt said. "I saw some transmission fluid back at the resort in the grocery store. Maybe that will get us back to town."

He hiked back to the resort and bought the last two cans of transmission fluid that the resort store had. He put it in the transmission. The fluid got all over his hands. They started off. They got about a quarter mile down the road before the smell came back and the transmission began slipping. A ragged trail stretched out behind the car. "Shit," Walt said. "I better jack it up and try to fix it. I doubt if I can. You better go back to the resort and call a tow. Even if I get it fixed, there's probably not enough fluid left in the transmission to get back to town."

"Can't you buy some more?" Ella said.

"No, I can't buy any more. I said those were the last two cans."

"You never said that, " Ella said.

"He said that," Erin said.

"I never heard him say that," Ella said.

"He said that when he came back," Erin said. "You weren't listening."

"Will you get out and go get some help?" Walt said. He got out and opened the trunk. He only had a rachet set. Then he found a vise grip plier and a screwdriver. He began to feel better. That might do it.

Ella walked back to the resort with Erin. Walt jacked up the car. He thought he might be able to discover what exactly had come loose. He didn't know if he could fix it. He hated the feel of the transmission fluid on his hands. He did not want to get his hands back in it. Good old 90-weight gear oil, that was different.

Walt was underneath the car when he heard a car pass, slow down and then stop and back up. It sounded like an old pickup truck with its muffler off. He slid back out from under and looked up at the back end of the grey primered Chevy. The driver got out of the car. He was wearing grey-green coveralls. He looked over the top of the roof at Walt.

"The wife said you had something go wrong," he said.

"Transmission," Walt said. He motioned at the ground. "Got a loose line, I think."

The driver walked around to the back of the Chevy. There was no lock on the trunk. It was leaded off, nothing but smooth grey primered trunk. The driver hit the middle of the trunk and the trunk opened up. The only thing in it was a big red tool chest, four shelves with a swing top. The driver opened the top. He reached in the pocket of his coveralls and took out a long white cigarette. He put it in his mouth and then reached in his pocket with his left hand. He lit the cigarette with a fliptop lighter and returned the lighter to his pocket. He found a pair of needlenosed pliers and turned to Walt.

"How much did you lose?"

"All of it," Walt said. "Then I got the last two cans from the resort. I put them in but started losing that."

The driver nodded. He looked at the pliers as he opened them and closed them. Then he knelt down, grabbed the front bumper and slid under the front end of the car.

"Your wife was going to call the tow truck. That's 28 miles," he said from under the car. "At five dollars a mile. I said, don't do that."

Walt stood there. He was trying to remember the name of the brothers. He couldn't believe how much this guy looked like the two greaser brothers who used to hang out at his old drivein when he was sixteen. Carmino brothers, Carmelo brothers, he couldn't remember. C, C, C something, he thought. Then, *Carmody brothers!* Underneath the car he heard the guy say something. "What?" Walt said.

"The lines got jammed up and they popped out," he

said. The car shook and then there was a wrenching sound and a loud click. "That ought to do it."

"I couldn't see where it had worked loose," Walt said. He watched as two hands came out and hooked onto the front bumper. "There was fluid all along both lines."

The driver pulled himself out from under and stood up. His cigarette was still hanging out of his mouth. It had a violet spot halfway down its length. "Now we got to get you some fluid in that."

"I sure appreciate it," Walt said. He put out his hand. "Walt," he said.

"Keeson," the driver said. He put his cigarette back in his left hand, wiped his right on his coveralls and shook hands with Walt. "You want to come along?"

Walt nodded. Keeson leaned over under the raised hood and took out the long transmission dipstick. He put a finger on where the fluid showed. "Yeah," he said. He put it back. "Know what it takes?"

"Oh shit, I forgot all about that," Walt said.

"You can't put just any kind in that," Keeson said.

"Christ, how did I forget about that." Walt was embarrassed. He hurried around to the driver's side. He got out the car care pamphlet. He noticed that his hands were shaking. "I must be getting out of touch with things," he said. "Here, it's a 250 cubic inch." He pointed at the column for transmission fluid.

Keeson leaned over and looked at the numbers. He pointed at one. "That's what I thought, F type," he said.

Walt put the pamphlet back and then followed Keeson back to the Chevy. He went to the other side and opened the door. Walt could smell coffee and cigarettes and doughnuts. Keeson started the Chevy. The whole car shook as the engine caught. Keeson looked down at the gear selector plate dangling from the gear shift. It was vibrating with the engine roar. Keeson put the gear shift down into Drive.

"What is that, an Olds Hydromatic?" Walt shouted at Keeson.

"A 56," Keeson said.

"What you got in it?" Walt nodded at the hood.

Keeson looked in the rear view mirror and then they lurched out onto the road. "A 283," he said. He goosed it and the front end rose up and the sound of the engine flowed back over them. Keeson took the Chevy up to 65. The Chevy went around each corner with a stiff kind of strictness that Walt found strangely exciting. At a Y in the road, Keeson slowed down to 35. "There's a sheriff," he said, a sly smile on his face, "hides out right . . . there." He nodded toward a blank billboard to the right of the Y.

The store was a big square house with two picture windows. It had a gas pump and an ice chest out front. Keeson pulled up to the big oil-stained wooden block that served as the front porch and shut off the engine. Then they went in. "Keeson," the man behind the counter said. He stood up a little straighter.

Keeson nodded. He fished out the pack of Pall Malls from his coveralls. "Got some Type F?" Keeson said. He lit his cigarette and snapped the lighter shut.

"Oh I don't know," the man said.

"I said to get some awhile back," Keeson said.

"Yeah I know," the man said. He hurried in back and looked at a shelf of motor oil and transmission fluid. "No, no got," he said.

Keeson let the smoke ease out his nostrils. His head was tilted back.

"I know you told me," the man said. Keeson stood there. "I thought I ordered some," the man said.

Walt watched as he hurried back behind the counter. "Um," the man said, "I can get some right away."

Keeson looked off to the side. He reached up and took the cigarette out of his mouth. He looked down at his wrist.

"I'm really sorry about that." The man looked at Walt. "This one of your friends?"

Keeson sniffed. He looked up at the ceiling. Then he turned and went for the door. Walt stepped back and let him pass. "I'll have the tanker bring up some in the morning," the man said to Keeson's back. Keeson went out. Walt turned to follow him. "How'd you get hooked up with him?" the man said. Walt didn't answer, he left.

"The Forteons will have it," Keeson said as Walt got in. "It's a little farther but. . . ."

"I used to have a 55," Walt said. "A 265 in it, though. And a Powerglide." Walt shook his head. "That transmission wasn't worth a shit," he said.

"Yeah," Keeson nodded. He backed the Chevy out. He put it in Drive. "Those Powerglides aren't worth much."

The Forteon grocery store and gas station had the right stuff. Keeson pointed at the cans and went back to the Chevy. Walt stayed behind and bought four cans of the F type fluid. "You a friend of his?" the clerk asked. Walt told him the story. "You're lucky," the clerk said, "he's the only mechanic for fifty miles around here. Except for the Indians. But you wouldn't want the Indians. But he's a loner all right. He's working on a friend's 47 Chevy."

Walt asked Keeson about that on the way back to the car. "Putting it in all stock," Keeson said. "I found a brand new stock engine back in Indianapolis. Now I got problems with the driveline."

"My dad had a 47," Walt said, "four door."

"Oh yeah," Keeson said. "This is a coupe."

Back at the car, they put three cans of fluid in. Walt started it up and they checked for leaks. There weren't any they could spot. Walt cleaned the spilled fluid on the fender of the car as Keeson put his tools away in the tool chest in his trunk. Then Walt took out his wallet. "Look," he said, "thanks a lot." He handed Keeson a ten. "This do?" Keeson folded it over and stuck it in his cigarette pocket behind the pack. "I'd like to see that 47," Walt said.

"I'm going up the hill to look at it now," Keeson said.

"I know something about those U joints," Walt said. "We had some problems with ours. I bet that's where you've got some problems, right?"

Keeson nodded. "You aren't wrong," he said. Walt got back in the Chevy. "I'll just take a look," he said.

The 47 Chevy was parked in a garage set up in the hillside above the resort. As Walt walked in, the smell of old oil rose from the blackened floorboards. He walked around to the front of the Chevy. From the garage window Walt could see over the top of the trees to the tip of the resort dock out in the lake. Beyond the dock he could see the swimming float in the lake.

There was an old bay sunk in the center of the garage floor for working under cars. At the bottom bits of metal and washers were stuck in the dirt here and there. The 47 was centered over the bay. Walt slipped down into the bay and Keeson followed. Keeson put a flashlight up on the U-joint. It had been taken apart.

"Oh yeah," Walt said, "now . . . if you've got an old Chevy truck somewhere around here, 49 to 54 will do, this can be fixed. That's where you've got to get those bolts. Any other bolts you put in either got too big of heads or aren't long enough, keep coming loose, right?" Keeson nodded. "And even if you get the right ones, then you've got to get a jack fore and aft so you take the pressure off the driveline and get those bolts in tight." Walt was pleased at how it all came back to him. "Oh yeah," he said, "that's what you need for that job."

"I know a place," Keeson said, "but it's out by the reservation. They got a field full of old Chevys."

It was around four-thirty when Keeson and Walt drove back to the resort. When they came around the curve, Walt's car was gone. Only the trail of transmission fluid was left on the gravel. Walt didn't say anything. Keeson drove to the resort and pulled into the parking lot. Walt looked over at their old tent site up on the slope. No one was there. He looked over at the tent site behind the resort. His car wasn't there either. He went into the resort restaurant with Keeson.

Keeson ordered a hamburger and fries. Walt felt tired and hungry. That was all he felt and that felt good. He had the barbecued ribs, mashed potatoes with two bottles of Blitz. He had a slice of apple pie, too. Keeson stuck with coffee for desert.

"What have you been up to today, Keeson?" the counterman said.

"Fixing the 47," Keeson said. "Rewired about half today."

"Thought you were going to have to send away for someone."

Keeson nodded toward Walt. "Didn't have to."

"You do the job?" The counterman grinned at Walt. "No one up here knows anything about electrical stuff."

"I told him he could work a year, if he wanted," Keeson said. He looked at Walt. "Enough work around here."

"What's your rates?" the counterman said. "I got a Dodge. Never have had the air conditioning. The guy I bought it from said it had it but it didn't."

Keeson smiled into his coffee. "I know that Dodge," Keeson said to Walt. Then he looked at the counterman. "He's working for $20 an hour."

Walt took another bite of his apple pie. The counterman wiped off the countertop. "That so," he said. "How far did you get on the 47?"

"Got the drive in," Keeson said. "And he got the dash working."

The counterman picked up the coffee pot and poured Keeson another cup. "The whole dash in?"

Keeson didn't say anything. Walt had another bite of apple pie. "You going to be around for awhile?" the counterman said. "It's something I need done next," he said. "No hurry." He wiped off the counter in front of Keeson. He looked back at Walt. "You guys could have the whole county to yourselves, if no one wants to call up the Indians."

Later that night Keeson left Walt in the bar. He wasn't drinking anything but coffee anyway, and he left Walt to his brandy. When he came back at around ten, he handed Walt sixty dollars. "What the hell," Walt said. "You saved him a couple hundred," Keeson said, "the owner knows that much. He didn't want me mucking it up. You want to finish it off?"

Walt said sure. He put the sixty dollars in his pocket. He thought about how this was the first money he had earned in three months. He sat around the house when he wasn't out at the employment office, which wasn't very often. Keeson had another cup of coffee and then he left. Walt walked out on the dock. He stood there looking at the float and out over the lake for awhile. Then he went back into the bar and rented a trailer for the night. Before he went to sleep, Walt took thirty dollars and folded it up in a sheet of newspaper. On the blank strip on top he wrote "Ella." The next night he rented the trailer again. On the third day he took the money out of the newspaper and rode into town with Keeson and bought himself a pair of jeans. That night he went out on the dock. He took off the rest of his clothes except for the jeans and dove in. He was surprised how warm the lake was. It seemed warmer than any water he'd been in for years. He walked back to his trailer with the jeans on. He changed. Keeson had loaned him a pair of coveralls and he put them on. Then he took the jeans and his old clothes back to the resort laundromat and washed them. He was happy that he had remembered to buy the jeans a little big.

The next day Keeson picked him up and took him to his

second job, rewiring the interior lights on an Apollo RV. He had fixed Walt up with a small kit of tools. He told Walt to forget about the counterman's Dodge. "I worked on that one," Keeson said, "you don't want to see what I done."

Walt put in eighteen hours of work and got paid for that job on Saturday. He was surprised how good it felt to have his own money in his pocket. Somehow he had never thought about the unemployment checks as being his own money. He put the checks in their checking account and never got cash for them. It surprised him to remember that.

He thought about calling up Ella. He had to do it sometime. So he went over to the resort bar and got some change and made the call. The housesitter answered the phone.

"No," she said, "there's no messages for you. You got a postcard from Oregon. You want me to get it and read it to you?" She started to put down the phone. "I think it's on the bureau. . . ."

"Wait," Walt said, "no."

"What?" she said.

"No," Walt said. "I'll read it when I get home." He hung up.

That night Walt got drunk. The resort bar was full of weekend campers. There was an outdoor barbecue, horseshoe throwing contest with some serious betting on the side. Everyone got a little loose and rowdy. Even Keeson had a couple of beers. Walt watched Keeson pick up one of the women weekenders. She had a friend but Walt left and he went to bed early.

He woke up at 3 a.m. all dried out. He drank a glass of water. Then he decided to take a walk. He put on his clothes and went out. The resort was dark. All the campers were shut down for the night. The moon was up. A wind blew in and died down. The dock was dark, some boards were wet where the waves had lapped up over them. Walt took off his coat and shirt and shoes and socks. He left on his jeans. He slipped into the water.

It was still warm even though it was night. Walt swam out to the float. He pulled himself up and looked in at the resort. He saw Keeson's Chevy parked at the top of the slope leading down to the boat landing. It was backed up to a big cedar stump. Walt stood up. A gust of wind swept over him. His jeans were damp and tight around his hips. Walt looked in at the primer grey 55 Chevy. In the moonlight it was shining.

I Remember The Day James Dean Died

& other stories

by Albert Drake

WHITE EWE PRESS

Acknowledgments:
The stories in this collection have appeared in the following magazines: *Cairn, Chicago Review, Colorado State Review, December, Epoch, The Falcon, Fiction International, Gallimaufry, North American Review, Northwest Review, Redbook, TransPacific, West Coast Review, Wind.*

"The Chicken Which Became a Rat" appeared originally in *Northwest Review*, and was anthologized in *Best American Short Stories 1971* (Houghton, Mifflin), and *Fiction 100* (Macmillan and Co.).

Cover: "35 Most Important Words" first appeared in *December*; reprinted in *Essaying Essays*, R. Kostelanetz, ed. (Out of London Press).

ISBN: 0-917976-17-7
Library of Congress
Cataloging in Publication No.: 82-51027

Published by:
The White Ewe Press
P.O. Box 996
Adelphi, Md. 20783

CONTENTS

I REMEMBER THE DAY JAMES DEAN DIED

"Well jeezus," Hop said, flipping his cigarette ashes out the window, "did he say *why?*"

Chris held the steaming cup tightly between his hands, a defense against the fall air, and over the rim he watched Mary the Car-Hop. The way her weight shifted, the movement of her body against the tight black slacks. She wore a clean white blouse, and in spite of her slightly protruding front teeth, which gave her a weird smile, he thought that she was the most beautiful car-hop Merhar's had ever had.

"No," Chris said. "Just that the job was taken when I got there." He sipped the hot, thin coffee, watching Mary walk sexily toward the kitchen, her money apron jingling, a harvest of coins. She went through the door, startling the final insects of summer which swam dizzily around the light, falling in loops farther and farther from the arc of yellow until they were lost in darkness.

Every night this summer they had sat in Merhar's parking lot, lingering over a cup of thin coffee or slowly sharing a small wax sack of french fries, dipping the slivers of potato one by one in catsup—or if they somehow had any money, they would buy the hamburger deluxe, where two lightly toasted buns were separated by a quarter pound of fresh beef, a slice of onion, tomato, lettuce, a layer of relish. On those nights even after their tray had been removed Chris liked to sit in the car and savor the odor of cooked meat, hot coffee, and the rich cigarette smoke. He did not often drink coffee, and did not smoke at all, but at those moments he could appreciate the heightened sensations of pleasure, and with a groan of contentment he would sit back, utterly happy. And if on those nights they had a couple of bucks for gas the little coupe would nose out into the traffic. Chris would drive with slow determination, heading toward no goal. He felt the restless excitement of moving, being mobile, seeing in the store windows the reflection of his own little coupe singing along the pavement, the white sidewalls flashing.

Then like a revelation he had discovered that they could meet girls—that they could pull alongside a curb and talk and that if they talked a fast, silly line that, why, the two girls would agree to yes they would accept a ride home—that is straight home. The first time he and Hop *had* taken them straight home. But during that summer he soon learned that if Hop quickly jumped in back with the first girl, to sit on the coupe's small, homemade seat, then the other girl had to get in front, her legs tapering to the floor alongside the slim gear-shift lever, and with this easy movement the divisions were made. Then the four would exchange the same question: *What high school?* and this would lead to another, the words rotating around the coupe's small space: *Do you know? Rick Ron Marty Slats Betty Mary Virgie*—Driving slowly he would head the coupe down Foster Road and at the city's limits he would turn up the long incline that was Mt. Scott, toward The Point. Here, under the endless stars, with the city's neon spread before them, he had learned to awkwardly slip the arm which lay on the seat cushion around the girl's slim shoulders and she would slowly begin to lean toward him, until he could smell that strange perfume, and wonder that the flesh of each hand and cheek felt different.

He had learned all this in one summer, in this car.

He loved the car. A 1937 Ford coupe, he had bought it in June for $45 earned picking strawberries. It was painted primer-gray, with a new chrome grill, and '38 DeSoto bumpers; when he cruised the Porter mufflers emitted a mellow roar and the Hollywood hubcaps with the single bar spun frantically. Because he was broke, he had only been able to buy some paint: he painted the sidewalls white, the firewall pink, and the dash and window mouldings a bright blue. But because the body and interior were cherry, he did not need to do more. He loved to sit in the car, to run his hands around the steering wheel, to touch the blue dashboard, to gun the engine. In the coupe's small space he was utterly happy, because this space was all his. The only thing he had wanted this summer was a radio. At The Point, high over the city, as he mustered the courage to slip his arm around a girl's shoulder, songs seemed to ride the air waves into his head, and each was aimed directly at him.

The coupe was fast: with .040 milled from the heads, the flywheel chopped to twenty pounds, it would hit forty-five in low, seventy in second, tires chirping rubber when he shifted, the exhaust growing to a powerful rumble as he wound it tight through the gears. Even in July he had been able to beat newer cars in the drag, but as summer shifted into autumn things happened: the trail of light blue smoke grew behind the car, a frantic metallic knock sounded from one rod. And when the clutch began to slip, he was no longer able to make the long climb up Mt. Scott.

Soon it would be winter, and he wanted a car with a radio *and* a heater.

"Well jeezus," Hop said, "did he say *why?*"

"No. The job was taken when I got there."

"Ain't that the shits," Hop said, flipping his cigarette ashes out the window with a quick, determined gesture. "How about Tracy Chain Saw? Heard that they were hiring."

"Well," Chris said, watching Mary walk inside, scaring the insects which swam around the bulb's heat, "they ain't hiring me I guess."

Headlights flashed off the street and a red '53 Olds convertible rumbled through the drive-in, the pipes trailing a thin lace of exhaust. Lowered, the rear bumper almost touching the pavement, the car conveyed the illusion of speed. A pair of fluffy dice flashed from the mirror. The driver wore a crew-neck sweater, and his face was darkly tanned; he drove with ease toward a parking place.

"Mother look at them wheels," Hop said.

Chris had it all planned: when he got a job he would buy not only a good used car with a radio and heater—something nice to cruise Merhar's, pipes rapping, whitewalls flashing—but he would also start buying clothes. He was tired of wearing the same faded levis and dull shirts, the brogues run-off at the heel, socks with holes, and this was one reason he didn't plan to go back to school for a final year. Instead, as soon as he began making money he intended to buy an article of clothing a week: a good Strad shirt, pegged charcoal slacks, a pair of suede shoes—or even just some socks. In the year that he would have spent in school, he would have a swell car and clothes and he would be all right. If you had those things, it was easy to get girls.

Tires screeched at the curb and a gray DeSoto sedan bounced into the parking lot, the driver leaning out the window; the car rocked sluggishly as the driver popped the clutch, and tires chirped rubber.

"That gawdamn Crazy Grunt," Hop said, laughing, turning to watch the car cut a doughnut at the far end, tires screaming, and he laughed again as the sedan spun into the space beside Chris' coupe.

"Hey you muthers," the driver yelled. He jumped out

and ran around the coupe, followed by his two passengers. Tonight Crazy Grunt was driving Yakima and Buzz around in his father's car, because only one of the three ever had a driver's license at the same time.

"Let's go to a movie," Crazy Grunt said, leaning against the coupe's window, his flaming red hair brilliant under the lights. "What's on at the Bob White?" he asked, turning to the two who stood beside the running-board, hands in pockets.

"A Man Alone," Yakima said. "Audie Murphy, supposed to be pretty good." Yakima, who resembled Audie Murphy, liked western movies. He thought of himself as a cowboy, and standing by the car, thumbs hooked in his belt, he looked like one. He loved horses more than girls, and hunting more than either.

"Yeah, Man Alone," Crazy Grunt said, his face ghostly white under the flaming red hair, "supposed to be good. Well what say?"

"Got any money?" Hop asked.

"Aw sheeut." Crazy Grunt's insane smile faded for only a second, while he stomped heavily in a big circle beside the car, and when he noticed what was parked beside them he laughed again. "Where the Barth brothers at?" he asked, pointing toward their car. "You could borrow a buck from them, get you guys inside, and then you guys could let us in the exit door. What say?"

"They'd already parked there," Hop said, "when we got here. They probably got dates."

"Dates?" Crazy Grunt screamed, his voice rising like the crackle of burning wood. "Dates? With *guuurls?*"

Chris and Hop leaned back in laughter as Crazy Grunt danced madly across the blacktop. Chris looked through the far window to the car parked beside his coupe: it was a 1934 LaFayette sedan, and to make it more sporty the Barth brothers had removed the car's front fenders, running-boards, and hood. They had split the exhaust manifold and had built a flange on the intake manifold for another carburetor, and they had dropped the front springs *under* the axle, which made the car much lower but caused it to steer in strange ways. Chris thought it was a miracle that the car even ran.

Chris didn't care much for the car, nor its owners. The Barth brothers—Randolph and Scott—were twins, and they operated as a team: they traded clothes and dates, so each had two wardrobes and a little black book full of phone numbers. They spent most of their time meeting girls, and since there were two of them they met twice as many. Even in grade school, when Chris had been reading comic books in his backyard or riding his bicycle on the trails at the park, the Barth brothers had been taking girls to the movies or meeting them downtown for lunch or other totally foreign activities. The feeling Chris had was disdain, mixed with envy and astonishment: he did not know how they could be so successful.

"Well now then there," Crazy Grunt said, "let's go burn a barn, what say? Get them old matches, get a little candle."

"Sheeut, yes," Buzz said, and everybody laughed. Crazy Grunt liked to start fires. Buzz shifted his weight against the side of the coupe, wiped his nose on his arm, and grinned crookedly: he liked to promote trouble and then stand back. "Let's go get Betty Crawford, and all burn a barn."

"Betty Crawford?" said Hop, flipping ashes hard against the window moulding. "You know how to get hold of her?"

"Get hold of her?" laughed Crazy Grunt. "Why you just grab her ankles—"

"You dumb butt," Hop said. "You know what the hell I mean—do you have her number? Man I'd like to get a little of that."

"You wouldn't know what to do with it," Crazy Grunt

said.

"Balls!"

"That's what I mean," Crazy Grunt said, giggling, jumping against the car, his hand reaching through the window for Hop's crotch, his elbow knocking off Hop's glasses. "Let me see what you got to work with—"

Chris grabbed the cup off the glove-box's open door before it spilled, and put it on the tray, as Yakima tried to pull Crazy Grunt back. Hop had reached overhead and held Grunt in the circle of his arms, squeezing his head until suddenly the other screamed and raised his hands to show that they were empty.

"You bloody fairy," Hop yelled, checking his glasses to see if they were broken. "I ought to pants you right here and make you walk home bare-ass."

"That's okay with me," Crazy Grunt screamed.

"What we ought to do," Chris said, "is take away his matches."

"What we ought to do for sure," said Buzz, spitting, his eyes shifting away to a distant point across the street, "is to call Betty Crawford, to see what she's doing."

"Whose nickel?"

They began to dig through pockets, coming up with pennies and toothpicks and buttons and keys, and sometimes a shiny coin. "Maybe we ought to pay here first," said Chris, and as the loose change was shoved forward he could see that they had just enough for the coffee and fries, with a small tip. Chris debated about taking that back but Mary was already walking across the pavement, crossing the dull yellow beams of his headlights, and he could see her breasts shifting under the clean white blouse in time to the plaintive beat of the radio down the line—he left the extra pennies on the tray, and she smiled as she took them, walking easily and sexily toward the kitchen.

For a minute Chris had felt lifted on the pronged hook of excitement—the question of what to do had to be answered—but now they did not even have a nickel for the phone, and the awful dismay of being unemployed hit him. Better even than having a radio in the car would be to spend a little time with Betty Crawford, holding her, feeling her up, maybe even laying her, and when he realized that a lousy nickel was keeping him from that erotic vision he felt like hitting the dashboard.

"Why don't we drive over?" Yakima said, breaking his tight-lipped silence. "She's babysitting for that insurance guy."

Talk stopped as they looked at him; then Hop opened the door, flipping his cigarette across the pavement. No one questioned how Yakima could know where Betty Crawford might be; when he had something to say, he said it with a cowboy's soft directness—or at least he was not known to promote bullshit. Someone gave a whoop, and Hop said: "What the hell are we doing here? Let's take your Dad's wheels, Grunt—this thing'll never make it."

All four doors of the sedan opened and the group pushed in, laughing, hollering, grabbing ass. Three doors slammed shut before Crazy Grunt jumped out, ran to the Barth brothers' LaFayette, and hovered over the hoodless engine for an instant; Chris saw him quickly switch two plug wires. "For when they return with their *guuurls*," Crazy Grunt laughed, gunning the sedan out of the lot, rear tires chirping, the car speeding along 82nd.

Chris relaxed as the deep upholstery sank under him. He realized the odor of a father's car—it smelled of paint and newness; there were no rattles at all, and the car eased along on deep springs. Chris leaned back, closed his eyes, and felt as if he was being propelled into a dream. "Turn on the radio, Grunt."

Beyond the window flashed the lights of used car lots and service stations, small stores and taverns—all places where he might find a job—and then the lights faded, they were at the city's edge, beyond it, and entering the darkness. The car angled upward, past the cemetery, toward Mt. Scott's crest. Limp with pleasure, Chris felt tremors of excitement along his legs and back; another night, nothing to do, no money—and then bang! the evening had opened up like a mystery. Every night something—*anything*—was possible, and it was this movement toward the unknown that kept him alive. *Where are you going?* one might ask. *Nowhere. What are you doing? Nothing.* Night after night things happened you couldn't plan or write down; they happened, they were part of the changing times, his changing life.

On the mountain he saw the insurance man's house, lights blazing. He had often looked up from his front steps, Mt. Scott a dark shadow against the night, and had wondered what it would be like to live up there. Now in that house Betty Crawford waited, her legs spread, blouse open, like the girl on the cover of any paperback book.

The road circled the mountain above the house. Crazy Grunt rocked around the sharp curves, the DeSoto's rear wheels kicking up a shower of loose gravel, the car skidding sideways at every turn. He drove like a madman until they came to the radio towers and then, as if his sense of reason had been reached, he drove slowly the rest of the distance, until they could see the driveway and, beyond, the house. He cut the headlights.

"See anybody?" Hop asked.

"Aw it looks okay," Buzz said, rubbing his nose. "Hell, let's go in."

"Wait a minute," Yakima said. "Don't you see?"

They sat leaning forward, their breath rising in small clouds. Below them was the house; below that the city lights spread at their feet, and in the clear sharp air of fall Chris could see the bright neon of downtown: the clock on the newspaper tower, the flashing beer sign, he could even read the print on the utility company's illuminated billboard.

"I thought I saw Betty, crossing by the window," Hop said.

"No," Yakima said, indignant at their blindness, as if his eyes, trained for years to search out distant game, were the only good ones here. "Don't you see? There's a damn car in the driveway."

"So what, maybe they got two."

"But they wouldn't leave it outside," Yakima said. "It'd be in the damn garage."

In silence they sat, eyes straining to see in the windows, to see Betty Crawford in her beautiful nakedness. Chris felt the excited tension stretch within him like a rubber band, threaten to snap. In his mind he saw the brilliant ruby-red lipstick, and the hard plates of her bra through the sweater.

Although Chris had seen her at school often, he did not know her. What he knew of her was by rumor: on Fridays in the parking lot, when the guys skipped pep assemblies and sat in their cars, shooting the shit, he would hear the same stories of who had laid Betty Crawford where and how it was. But he found the stories so erotically incredible—events so bizarre, beyond his wildest sexual fantasies—that he never quite believed them. Nor had he ever talked with anyone who had laid her—the telling was always at least twice removed from the experience. What he did know of her for certain was that she had a drawer of sweaters, all a size too small.

They sat hunched into their own steaming breath, straining to see a figure walk murkily across the room.

"She probably ain't even up here," Buzz said. "Probably getting laid in a car somewhere."

"She's in there," Yakima said.

"How do you know?" Hop asked, lighting a cigarette, the flame reflecting off his fogged glasses.

"I got ways," Yakima said.

Finally Grunt started the engine, and reluctantly the others relaxed their eyes. "We didn't come here for nothing," Buzz said. "Let's go down to the house."

"We can come back later," Crazy Grunt said, turning the car around in the road and heading for the top. "I got to piss." He drove a fast half-mile and pulled the car to the side, cut the engine, and was standing in the ditch, fumbling with his fly.

"Might as well water my lily," Yakima said, getting out.

"Hop," Buzz said, "you want to play with it some?"

"Up your bunny, sonny."

Chris followed Hop, and he stood in the line, the five pissing in the ditch; there was the sound of water against grass, the patient rattle of crickets, and the chafing noise of dry corn stalks in the night wind. The air cleared his head, and as he zipped his fly he looked upward at the stars, near points of light in the thin air.

"Hey!" Crazy Grunt exclaimed, tugging at his fly, looking from the radio towers to a point beyond the horizon. "Hey, there's a barn over there I remember." He began to laugh, his feet drumming the ground. "There's a beautiful barn I want to see."

"C'mon Grunt," Hop said, "let's get to Betty's."

But Grunt was already mounting the fence, his foot over, and in the darkness they could hear the sound of corn stalks being trampled.

"Grunt, at least leave us the car keys," Hop shouted, his voice ringing across the black distance. "Hells bells," he said, "if the cops come by we've had it."

"Think I'll go along," Buzz said, climbing the strands of

barbed wire. "Might be something worth getting. Anybody else?"

No one moved, and then Buzz was gone. Chris shivered in the night air; the tremor moving along his skin carried equal parts of excitement and fear. In the same unconscious way that he had got to this ditch, instead of sitting in Merhar's or being in bed this moment with Betty Crawford, he might easily an hour from now be in jail.

"I'm freezing," Hop said, pounding his hands together. "Damn that Crazy Grunt." He lit another cigarette, the red glow a small heat source in the crisp fall night. Yakima leaned against the car fender, studying the sky, and Chris sat on the ground beside the tire.

"Just what the gawdamn hell are we doing here?" Yakima asked.

No one could answer. In silence they waited, hearing the distant noises of the last summer insects, dying before the killing frost, or perhaps the sound of feet crashing far away. They waited, wishing that they were at the Bob White eating popcorn and watching a 3-D movie, or downtown cruising the streets, or even sitting again in Merhar's.

"You get that job?" Yakima asked.

"No," Chris said, feeling the quick, fleeting panic of unemployment. "It was taken when I got there."

"Well," Yakima said, moving toward the fence, "we might as well get some of that corn while we're waiting."

Chris looked at the bent and falling stalks, leaning like rows of old men against the night. "Corn? What the hell for?"

"Gonna need it," Yakima said, climbing the fence and moving among the broken stalks. "Gonna be a hard winter. Get some jerky, hardtack, stock up on some supplies." Chris could hear him breaking off an armload of ears, talking about how he would be able to withstand the winter, weaving a prescription for survival which he half-believed. He threw them to Hop, who tossed them in the car.

Chris climbed over the fence, giggling: he broke off ears of corn and threw them in wild gestures over to the road where they glanced off the fenders and roof of the DeSoto to ricochet into the night. He might now be in the same room with Betty Crawford, might even be in bed with her; instead he was stumbling across the dark furrows of this field, wildly stealing corn, while Crazy Grunt over the hill was burning a barn. Tomorrow he would head the old coupe into town, searching everywhere for any kind of work, but tonight he was in this field, throwing ears of corn overhead toward the car, feeling his breath rush coldly into his lungs.

"Christ, I'm freezing," Hop said, his voice a sharp whisper from the road. "Don't you think we got enough?"

"Gonna be a tough winter," Yakima said, throwing two more ears in the direction of the voice. "Got to keep our powder dry and our ramrods straight."

Chris heard Hop say to hell with it and at the same time, coming from the other direction, he heard feet running. The wall of corn fell with sharp cracks, like pistol shots. Farther off a dog began to bark, and Chris ran for the car—not panic, not fear, but mirthful excitement drove his feet into a run across the uneven ground. He was laughing when he got to the fence, where the figures that burst from the foliage knocked him down. Laughing, he threw up an arm to protect himself, but then he saw that it was Buzz who was climbing the fence.

"Let's go," Crazy Grunt said, swinging a gunny sack over his head.

Even before the doors were shut Crazy Grunt was accelerating through the gears, heading downhill with his lights off. Chris was looking back to see if the flames from the barn were visible, when he felt something against his leg:

on the floor, on the layer of corn, was the gunny sack, and as he watched the sack moved.

"What's that?"

"Chickens," Buzz said. "He didn't have any matches."

Looking back, Chris could see only the radio station lights, and low in the eastern sky, like a ball of tallow, a huge harvest moon. Then through the rear window he saw the distant lights of farms, mere specks against the darkness. The moon hovered over the serrated ridge of fir trees, covering the fields with a blue haze. Happy Valley was laid out like a miniature landscape, and Chris felt a dreamy sort of power, as if he could push buttons to send model trains steaming through the artificial night.

"Where the hell we going?" Hop asked.

"Indian Rock," Crazy Grunt said. "Gonna build a fire."

"We're going to build a fire," Yakima said, turning from the front seat, "and cook those chickens. It's going to be a hard winter."

"Especially if we spend it in jail," Hop said. "Christ, Grunt, what do you want to set fires for? You're crazy, you know it? They're going to lock you up."

The car sped downhill, moonlight flashing through the trees with hypnotic intensity, blending the landscape to a monochromatic design. Chris breathed deeply the acrid odor of corn husks, the rich smell of paint, upholstery, newness, and as they mixed in his brain he reeled with sensual pleasure.

Buzz kept saying that they ought to go back to the house, but now Yakima wanted to build a fire so he said that maybe she wasn't there, and as the car got to the bottom of Mt. Scott Chris figured that he would never get a chance to see her up close. On the city side of the mountain was a lumber mill, and Crazy Grunt swung to the left, skidding to a stop. He jumped out, and Chris heard the trunk lid open and slam shut; then under the faucet at the curb Grunt was filling a kettle. He had brought a kettle along—did they intend from the start to go clear to the top of Mt. Scott to steal a chicken? he wondered. Was Betty Crawford only a ruse? Had anyone ever laid her? Did Grunt set fire to the barn tonight? And where was the watchman? He peered into the darkness for the watchman's light but saw nothing and heard only the sad, patient croak of bullfrogs in the mill pond. When the kettle was finally full Yakima held it on his lap and Crazy Grunt cut a tight doughnut and headed uphill again.

People said that Indian Rock was an old stone quarry, abandoned years ago. To Chris it was a rugged stand of huge boulders interlaced with trails, small trees, and grassy levels. It was a place where short years before he had hiked often from his house; where he had played all day, investigating the caves and cliffs, and some nights he had even camped here. The DeSoto crawled the rutted road, headlights angled toward the sky, and at each bounce Yakima muttered about the water that slopped onto his pants. In the center of the flat plateau Crazy Grunt jerked on the handbrake, and killed the lights. In a group they stumbled along the steep trail through darkness, Yakima carrying the kettle as if it were the chalice of some ritual. Laughing, they followed the trail until they came to a flat place in the hillside, an indentation hollowed from under a slab of rock.

Crazy Grunt shredded a comic book he found in the car, and piled on sticks. "A match," he said, "somebody give me a match."

Someone gave him a match, and he plunged it into the pile. Flames blossomed, the color of his hair; Crazy Grunt jumped back, giving his mock-insane laugh which was a series of hard grunts. He waved his arms and jumped up and down, staring at the growing flames.

"Christ, Grunt," Hop said, laughing, "why do you have to act so queer about lighting a fire?"

In the flames the short twigs snapped frantically, consuming themselves. Grunt found a limb, broke it against the cliff, and laid the pieces across the flames; he disappeared into the night, and came back with an armload of brush, limbs, broken boards, which he threw on. Yakima pushed three flat rocks up to the fire and when the flames shot skyward he put the kettle on the rocks. Streaks of flame curled around the metal, as the fire's intensity diminished.

"What the hell are you doing?" Grunt screamed, raising his foot to knock the kettle over. "Let it burn."

"Thought you wanted to eat the chickens," Yakima said.

"How are you going to kill them?" Chris asked. "Boil them to death?"

"Eeeeeeeha, eeeeeha," Grunt laughed, looking at the fire. "Kill them? Christ I wouldn't eat those gawdamn chickens."

"What the hell," Yakima said, surprised. "We *got* to eat them."

"You kill them, cowboy," Grunt said, laughing, jumping around the fire. "You got your knife?"

Yakima stood up, threw something hard against the ground, and walked slowly down the trail toward the car; he was a pioneer, a hunter, a camper, and felt that anything caught or killed had to be eaten. Crazy Grunt danced his stiff-legged dance around the fire, Hop sat on a rock and lit a cigarette, Buzz leaned against the cliff and picked his nose.

For a fractional second Chris felt dizzy wondering how they had got here: from Merhar's, to the corn field, to Indian Rock, where the fire blazed red and black shadows against them, and the rocks were washed a stark ghostly white in the harvest moon. This was not where they had set out to go, not where they wanted to be. Betty Crawford was not here, loving and warm: instead he was with a pyromaniac who danced crazily around his fire, a frustrated hunter, a habitual liar and nosepicker, and a skinny chain smoker who was now crawling closer to the fire complaining that he was cold. None had a steady job, none would finish high school; they would meander through life, making false starts, arriving finally at places they did not mean to be and would not know how they got there.

He walked to the edge of the rocks and saw lights glimmering like a rotating galaxy, pulsating with the city's energy—below people were getting ready for bed, planning on tomorrow's work, paying bills; in his own house, whose sixty-watt bulbs were faint glimmers lost in the night, his mother would be worrying about her social security check, his sister worrying about her school clothes, worrying about whether she would have a date for the post-game dance. He stared hard to find that house, but his eyes were carried away along Foster Road, along 82nd, along the spokes of light which radiated from downtown, from the neon excitement of Broadway. There, he knew, even now the chartreuse or purple chopped Fords and Mercs cruised Broadway to the penny arcade and turned to come back down Sixth, a never-ending circle which was a beautiful, mindless activity.

From below he heard the chicken squawk but when Yakima returned he had an armful of corn, and he began to quickly strip off the husks. As each ear was bared he slipped it into the boiling water, which splashed over to sizzle on the hot rocks. When the kettle was full he sat on the ground beside the fire, waiting.

"You going to eat that crap?" Crazy Grunt asked, laughing, saying jeezus, jeezus.

"Hey. Are we going back to the house?" Chris asked. "To see if she's alone?" In his mind he saw her, tucking her sweater into her skirt, pulling the material tight over her womanly breasts. She sucked on a cigarette, and pushed some hair back from her forehead.

"Hey you muther, you're really horny," Crazy Grunt said. "Seems like Hop could help you out, off-hand?"

Crazy Grunt laughed and jumped through the column of smoke, and Hop said, "You queer muther—don't worry about me. I do okay."

"What's the noise?" Buzz asked. "There's lots of others."

In his mind Chris saw her sit, legs draped one over the other; he saw the top leg begin to rock in a growing rhythm—the fleshy calf, the bobby sox rolled into a doughnut around the ankle, the saddle shoe, all swung outward and back with frantic intensity. Her bright lips gathered around her cigarette, sucking the smoke deeply into lungs that filled somewhere behind her full sweater; when she exhaled the smoke streamed slowly straight down from her nostrils and at the same time outward from her bright lips. She was all the women he had wondered about on the covers of paperback books.

But there was hope, he thought, as he returned to squat near the fire: he would see her sometime, at a bus stop, walking along the road, in the drug store, and he knew he would say hello, ask if she would like a ride anywhere?

Yakima jabbed the ear of corn with his pocket-knife, held it in the cool night air for a minute, and passed it to Chris. Even Grunt moved closer, and soon they were in a circle around the glowing rocks, each holding a steaming ear of corn. They had no butter, but Yakima pulled salt and pepper shakers with Merhar's written in red on their sides, from his coat. Around them smoke swirled, like the mist rising from Johnson Creek and the millpond. The huge boulders were white in the moonlight, each plane of rock glowing like kryptonite. Silently they gnawed the ears of corn, hearing only the sound of their own chewing, or the small night animals rustling far back in the trees.

"A man could live like this," Yakima said, spearing another ear of corn with his knife. "You could survive, without working. Pick a little corn, hunt, trap a bit."

Grunt laughed and Buzz farted and Hop reached in his pocket for a cigarette: everyone was content, happy, unconcerned about tomorrow, next year, the job he didn't have, the future which at one minute seemed endless and open, the next totally closed off. The heavy odor of steamed corn hung in the air, and for a long second Chris had the thought that they *could* all live like this together, not changing, not growing up, becoming separate: they could steal corn and chickens, meet girls, raise hell all night. Then he knew it wasn't possible. He had only to look around: Indian Rock, which had always been a really free place and had seemed permanent, had changed. Once anyone could come here and targetshoot into the clay bluffs, or ride motorcycle over the network of trails: now there was a no shooting sign, and the county had taken a bulldozer and cut off the bottom of every climb. All was changing, he knew.

"Christ, I'm freezing," Hop said, holding his arms tightly against his chest.

"Want me to stoke up the fire?" Yakima asked, "and fix a chicken?"

"I gotta get up tomorrow," Chris said, throwing his cob into the darkness. "And go look for a job—again."

"We ain't going back up on the hill?" Buzz asked. "To see Betty?"

"C'mon, pardners," Yakima said, wiping his knife blade against his pants. "Stoke up the fire, I could have some more corn cooked in a few minutes."

"Let's go," Grunt said, tipping the water from the kettle on the fire, which hissed into wet ashes. "I'm tired of this horseshit."

"How about burning a barn?" Buzz asked.

They slid down the trail, loose gravel falling in a small avalanche behind them. At the bottom momentum carried them across the plateau in a run, and they fell sprawling against the sedan. Already an early frost was forming on its metal, the car glowing with a silver sheen under the moon. Looking around, Chris suddenly had the feeling that he had never been here before: the high stone walls, the bare trees moving in an invisible wind, the uneven land falling into bottomless shadows, and every surface was plated with the moonlight.

The spell was broken when Grunt opened the door and the dome light flashed on: the sound from the sack was the cry of terror. Grunt picked up the sack and looked in: he lifted out a chicken, its neck laying across its back. "Sonofabitch suffocated," he said, laughing, throwing the dead chicken into the weeds. "What the hell should we do with this one?"

Yakima wanted to take it home to eat, and Hop thought that they should let it go here, and then Buzz suggested that they toss it out in Merhar's—just to see what might happen?

Crazy Grunt laughed and threw the gunny sack on the floor and they all piled in, laughing, the sedan dragging across the deep ruts as they drove to the road; then they were past the mill, their excitement contagious and submerged, their laughter suppressed as the car raced along the emptiness of Foster Road.

"Wait," Chris said, laughing, "you'll want witnesses." When Crazy Grunt stopped at the curb Chris and Hop got out and walked quickly to the primer-grey coupe. Merhar's was full: radios blared the Hit Parade, disc-jockies wailed the night with their rapid-fire commentary, crying play me, buy me, this is our song honey. The shows were out, their screens dark, ushers gone toward home, and now the lovers huddled in their cars, warm on burgers and fries and coffee-steam and love.

Chris and Hop waited, giggling quietly, their faces near the coupe's windshield.

Soon the gray De-Soto came down the street and turned into the parking lot from the far end, cruising the aisle between the rows of cars. It slowed to a crawl, and two hoods away Crazy Grunt revved the engine, popped the clutch, and tires spinning the sedan leaped ahead. But just before Grunt burned rubber Chris saw Yakima lean out the passenger's window, saw in his hand the bundle of feathers held by its legs, and then Yakima swung the bundle underhand in a high arc. There was a flash of white, the chicken tumbled along its trajectory, rolling like a pigeon until at the apex it became righted, and flapping its wings it attained flight. Head extended far forward, wings flapping, it struggled for altitude, to get clear of traffic. But it fell rapidly and its route described perfectly a half-circle which ended at a point a few feet beyond the Ford's hood tip. It hit the pavement, wings extended, and bounced, as if with a series of huge leaps it could again find that barn.

It hit the pavement as the DeSoto leaped ahead, and Chris had a fleeting vision of Buzz's face against the glass, his mouth distended in a silent laugh. Chicken and tire, traveling at approximately the same speed, intersected: when Crazy Grunt careened around the corner Chris sat looking at that spot of feathers pressed flat on the asphalt, the two wings extended as if flight were still possible in a modified way.

As faces turned in the windows of every car, focusing on that pile of feathers, Chris and Hop broke into uncontrollable laughter. Talk stopped, radios seemed to grow silent; from one car a boy walked cautiously across the pavement, to prod the chicken with his shoe. Chris gripped his ribs tightly, laughter taking his breath away; he looked at Hop, felt the tears come to his eyes, and folding his arms across the steering wheel he laid his head on them, laughter coming in silly spasms.

They were still giggling when Bertha, the other car-hop, came from the kitchen; she hesitated, looked at the disaster, and walked to the car on Chris' side, to take their tray. Chris heard her ask the driver: "What's that?" "A chicken," the man. "A chicken?" she said, "what's a chicken doing in a drive-in?"

"She wants to know—" Chris said, laughing harder, "what's a chicken—" and he began laughing so hard the unfinished sentence was left hanging in the air.

They were still laughing when the Barth brothers came out. Both wore new tweed overcoats, and they hesitated outside the door to pull on black leather gloves. Slowly, as if they expected all eyes were aimed at them, they opened their cigarette cases and each took out a smoke. In the simultaneous glare of their matches Chris could see them clearly: clean-shaven, their hair neatly trimmed, teeth white and even. No doubt they had been on a successful date, a dance somewhere, and an exclusive party afterward. Perhaps they had even had a drink or two. Even though they were the same age as Chris, he realized that they looked much more mature and seemed infinitely more successful; but tonight, as he watched them step off the curb, he could not dislike them. Everything tonight was funny.

If the Barth brothers saw the chicken they ignored it, as they ignored Chris and Hop. They got into their LaFayette and Chris waited: the starter churned, the engine caught—and backfired. The report set off another explosion of laughter, and Chris turned to see two feet of flame blossom from the car's carburetors. Again the starter ground, and the reports were like a pistol being emptied. A door opened, and he saw Randolph get out, heard Scott swearing from behind the wheel. "Try it again," Randolph said, and this time there was a single massive explosion.

Every face had shifted toward the noise, and Chris knew that the brothers were furious at *this* kind of attention. They stood beside the hoodless engine, like two insurance men investigating a wreck.

The sound of laughter turned them toward the coupe.

"Did you pricks mess with this car?" Randolph asked.

"Hell no," Hop said. "Wouldn't touch the damn thing."

Chris gripped the wheel tightly, trying to stifle the spasms that churned within his ribs as he watched Randolph and Scott seriously study the plug wires. They leaned over the open engine, carefully holding their tweed topcoats away from the oil surfaces. Finally, he heard Randolph say: "Okay, try it."

The starter ground harshly, the engine caught, exploded, but continued to run: it was still cross-firing, but somehow the remaining four cylinders kept going. The doors slammed, the transmission scraped into low, and, with great effort, the car bucked and jumped toward the street. Long after it was gone Chris could hear the eccentric explosions which traced its slow progress through the night.

"Oh, jeezus," Chris said, wiping his eyes. He had not laughed so hard in a long time. He knew that tomorrow, when he reviewed these episodes, they would still be funny—he had not got close to Betty Crawford, had not felt her weight against him nor slipped his hand along her soft thighs except in his mind, but it had been a good evening. It had been something to do.

"Hey muther," Hop said, "I'm freezing. Let's cut out."

"Yeah," he said, reaching for his key. It was late, and anyway they had no money for coffee. He unlocked the ignition and turned on the switch. When he pressed the starter button the engine spun easily—too easily, without compression—but did not fire. He tapped the gas pedal a few times, and hit the button again. On the third try the pistons began to slow, dragging against their worn walls. He let up and waited, as if it were simply a case of temporary insanity or some minor illness which, if left alone for a short time, would cure itself. He heard Hop mutter something to the car, and when Chris punched the button again he began to have some doubts: the engine turned over slowly a dozen times and then quit, the solenoid clicking against the pink firewall.

"Battery's dead," Chris said, shutting off the ignition and checking the light switch.

"Hells bells," Hop said. "You mean we have to *walk* home?"

"It'll start if we push it." As Hop opened the door, Chris said: "But wait until some of these cars leave."

He would rather have his mother catch him naked in bed with Betty Crawford than to be seen pushing the Ford across the parking lot: he would wait. Already there were fewer cars; as he watched, a Chev convertible turned on its lights, and Bertha waddled over to take the tray. Slowly, with the easy movements of newness, the car rolled across the parking lot.

He rolled up his window against the cold air. Winter was almost here, and it would be, as Yakima had put it, a hard one. Tomorrow he would again look for work, asking at every service station and garage, asking people he might meet, searching the classified ads for some opening: there were jobs he did not even know by name, nor did he know how one got them, but he would find something—he had to.

Bertha went inside and when she emerged, to take another tray, she wore a purple sweater over her white blouse. She walked heavily, as if her feet hurt, and Chris wished that Mary was still on duty. He wished that they had a dime for coffee. He wished that the car would start.

"Christ, I'm freezing," Hop said. "Whatdya think?"

"Okay," Chris said. There were still a dozen cars in the place, all bright and shiny, and as Chris opened the door he knew that they would be looking at him. He turned on the ignition and, door open, he leaned his weight against the cold metal: he strained, and with Hop pushing on the other side the car began to roll forward. He swung the wheel with one hand, pushed harder, and the car picked up speed.

Straining, he saw only the blacktop moving faster beneath his feet, and with a slow swish of white the pile of feathers went past. For no reason at all he thought of the future: although he now silently cursed this car, he really did love it, but he knew that soon he would trade it for something else, something better he hoped, and he imagined through a long succession of cars some distant day when he would be driving down the street in a big station wagon, his wife beside him, kids in the back, a week's groceries in sacks piled around them, and on such a day he wondered what he would do should he see this car, rising like a mirage, its firewall glowing like a bright pink jewel.

"Jump," Hop said, and Chris, looking up from that long black blur of pavement, jumped.

IN THE TIME OF SURVEYS

When Julia Blume descended to the main apartment to prepare the noon meal, she saw, first, Mr. Blume, nude except for a beach towel emblazoned with Italian motorcycles at speed; second, the bare heel of Rosa flit around the corner with a rapidity rare in so thick an ankle and so lazy a person. Mr. Blume was in the doorway of the shower, a simple, puzzled look on his face as Rosa's coughing laugh trailed back from the kitchen. Undeniable evidence.

John Blume closed the door to a crack and said, as if he didn't quite believe it himself: "She had no key. And of course she rang and rang that infernal bell. I believe she did that to you, last week?"

Then he made two mistakes: one, he continued to talk, and two, he shifted to his poll-taking voice. Which caused Julia to think he did protest too much.

But it *had* happened to her last week. She *had* been in the shower when Rosa returned from the market without her key. Julia had known it could only be Rosa. For even the stupidest peasant would have given up. Soap stinging her eyes, Julia had slipped wet into her clothes to open the door. The maid had smiled and nodded in goofy comprehension when Julia tried to explain, in English, what a bloody bother she'd been.

Now, in the kitchen, as she followed the laughter to its source, she saw the girl's cheeks where coin size marks of cardinal blossomed on the henna skin. And, as she watched the girl lazily knead the *pasta*, Julia actually began to wonder about her husband—after twenty-two years of marriage. Of course, she thought, considering the hot latin air and Giovanni's lewd talk, John has never been in a position of such constant temptation.

The Blumes came to Italy so John could finish a sociological study of war-displaced persons and their re-adaptation, a study carried on by three other professors for the past fifteen years. In the last year, as most of the research material was being processed, the professors had rapidly died: one by illness, two in separate plane crashes. John, a sort of intellectual trustee in the sociology department, was appointed to finish up the study.

The Blumes roomed where their predecessors had, at the house of Count Giovanni Alberghetti Arturo Popolo Babuino di Barberini, now ruler of the block of crumbling masonary where they lived, and the dry land which aproned it, the thin shadow of his ancestors' grandeur. But he had "friends in Washington," he often said—a place he considered both powerful and hateful. Giovanni, a precise, small man, with the same clean profile found impressed on ancient Roman coins; a slick, vibrant man who managed to act, in spite of a world weary sophistication, like a stage Italian. His two professed loves were the land and the grapes. But Julia saw through this: she knew he really loved the women and the wine. When his eyes dilated to two shiny black olive pits, small with conspiracy, then Julia feared him. Or rather she feared the effect he might have on John. For Giovanni also boasted of his ability to corrupt Americans, when they were around.

But Julia, who was incorruptible, disliked most

Giovanni's incessant chatter and despicable laziness. And his white duck jodhpurs, his monocle and riding crop she found somewhat extreme, almost foppish. Especially as he had no riding horses.

John, now two weeks out of New York City, was glad to speak English with anyone. And although Giovanni's dialectics infuriated him, the man's ease with life attracted him. John had arrived burning brighter than the Italian sun with ambition: promotions, tenure, new studies would be his when this project was finished. But day by day his ambition waned. A glass of *vino* placed between the eye and the sun reflected beauty invisibly. Sleep after the middle of the day. Coffee on the balcony. His mouth soon welcomed conversation as it did the soft pulp of fruit. And in these conversations he found himself emulating Giovanni: the sporadic, quick hand gestures, the stylistic lip twisting.

As neither Julia or John quite trusted the *pensione* food, Julia cooked for the two of them. A determined woman, she was thankful Giovanni was a bachelor; it was not necessary to share the small kitchen with a wife or mother. Only Rosa, the maid.

"Rosa," Giovanni said often, "is a beast. A stupid beastly peasant."

This was obvious to Julia. The girl was fifteen, with hips so heavy they bowed her legs. And, although her face was now pretty, Julia could predict exactly what Rosa would look like in ten years: another of the stubborn shrewish women in the market place, fulfilling her heritage. Fat from *pasta*; broad from bearing too many children, as if her pelvic structure were sprung.

"Rosa," Giovanni said again that night, speaking against the thorn he was too tender to dislodge, "will become prostitute, oh yes, of that I am sure. Rosa will become prostitute."

Although this speech had been repeated a dozen times,

tonight Julia saw John's ears redden with blood. He wiped his glasses in round, deliberate motions, to occupy his hands.

"Yes, I am certain. What does she make here?" Giovanni cracked his riding crop against his boot side. "You see, I do my shoes, and I make my food most meals. You know this. Rosa does nothing! What does Rosa do? Nothing! I tell you when Rosa leaves here (and I must discharge her soon) she is unfit to work in the house of a family. Here she cannot make the needs of one, myself. A family will keep her only one day: then—out! I say to you," and he aimed the riding crop at Julia, as if somehow America was to blame, "she will become prostitute and go to Rome. My last five servants, all have become prostitute when they left here."

"That's really not too good for your side, Giovanni," John snickered.

"Oh, no, no. It is because I am *too* good. They are paid and do no one thing."

John continued to wipe his glasses, ignoring the conversation when Giovanni shifted to his second favorite topic: U.S. foreign aid.

"Well, the newspapers say you have given us forty million dollars. Ho ho," he roared, "ho, certainly. Five million into the hands of two, three select families, and thirty-five million in old tanks, guns, trucks for our army. Your scrap metal. And why do we need an army? I don't think Austria will invade."

John ignored the booming mocking laughter, and squinted into the fireplace. The scene this morning in the shower, which Julia had pranced down the staircase to interrupt, was foolish. An American, a university professor, compromising himself with a beastly peasant. For him there was no reason, and certainly no precedent.

He had told the truth: the girl had no key, and he

opened the door only because her stubborn finger remained on the bell. But backed into the narrow geometry of the hall, his body concealed only slightly by the towel with its gay racing motorcycles, his scowl had softened to a grin, matching Rosa's. Suddenly, he had offered her a hundred lire to scrub his back. Struck by what he decided to call her 'primitive beauty,' he was amazed by her stupidity. With simple Italian phrases and blunt sign language, it took a full five minutes for Rosa to understand; when she took the money, laughing, and they were ready to begin, Julia descended to fix lunch.

He had acted badly. Not in approaching Rosa with his pleasurable idea (wasn't that what servants did, scrub backs?), but in his lack of discretion. He had acted on impulse this morning, at a time when Julia was in the house.

And again this business of Rosa becoming a prostitute. His statistics showed less than two per cent of the women hadn't made proper re-adaptation; of those who had 'gone on the turf' (as he unofficially phrased it), almost to a woman they had moved to larger cities. But he couldn't reconcile the pudgy, grinning Rosa with the sleek girls he had seen in Naples: they lined the entranceway to the city, one under each arc light, thirty feet apart for a mile. Or those who sat on the benches in the *Piazza Indipendenza* in Florence: girl-children, whose legs scarcely filled the shape of the nylons which sleeked up under their high skirts. Rosa was pretty enough, in a Tuscan, olive-plump way; but she was destined for the hard work of a peasant's wife, and not for the pleasures of Roman males.

From the corner of her eye, Julia Blume watched her husband watch the wall, while she still affected to listen to the wild rantings of Giovanni. She was well aware that at forty-five a man will plunge, head-first, into a last bit of hanky-panky. Although, somehow, she could not imagine this happening to John. She watched the studious, flat face stare now at the empty fireplace, and she wondered as a faint smile tugged at his cheek.

The girl was in his mind during the next two days. Days spent on the balcony, where the sun appeared as a raisin against the filament of the closed eye-lid. Days in which John drank more wine than he intended, and got less work done, his thoughts boxed in the rhomboid of his private vice. He watched the yard below, where Rosa scrubbed clothes in a copper tub; he followed her movements with eyes that pretended sleep. The copper of the tub blazed, reflecting the damask mantle of the girl's shoulder and arm as she worked the knot of clothes in sexual motions.

And when he did try to work, the paper secretly became covered with words which shocked him. From margin to margin it was in his handwriting: Rosa, rose, rosy, roseate. Ruby lips, rufous breasts. From the red flame of passion to the darkness of his sin: smirçh, smudge, smut. The darkness of the ebon pitchy place, the chiaroscuro between Rosey's thighs, below where her dress hangs out and down, from her tummy tum.

Not that he had a plan of action when, on the third day following the shower scene, he interrupted Rosa in the kitchen. Rather, his orgy remained private, the intimate details piling up in the front of his mind. Rosa stopped her song when he lifted a pot lid and sniffed; she began to grin when John's glasses clouded with steam, and laughed when he removed them to squint at her.

For, to Rosa, the professor was the object of good natured curiosity. He was her weekday amusement, and his antics were better than a walk around the *piazza*. His bulky notebooks would fall open, spilling papers in the trail of his stiff walk. His thick glasses perched on the limpid, peering face; his high, quiet voice—so unlike the voices of the men and boys she knew who, like Giovanni, were booming, boastful, expressive.

Then, on the third or fourth day after the Americans arrived, Rosa made a remarkable discovery. She noticed that when she was bent at her work, the professor's face would turn red. He would enter the kitchen to inspect her cooking, or to ask her questions in stuttering Italian from the phrase book; while his eyes feinted at the window, she knew he was looking into and under the cloth of her blouse. Her eyes would dart up, to catch his shifting away, his transparent cheeks touched with crimson, his ears like red fly wings.

So it was partly the money, partly the joke, that directed her into the shower with the professor that day, just when his wife arrived. And for the same reasons she now accepted the six one-hundred lire pieces he pressed into her dough-covered hands. She took the money, shrugged her shoulders, and tied the coins into her handkerchief.

Now that he had paid, what? The next move, he realized, was his. For after Rosa placed the handkerchief on the shelf above the table, she stood on bowed, squat legs, like a patient animal waiting to be mounted.

"So young and pretty to go to Rome," he said.

The slow curve of Rosa's smooth, oiled shoulder was bare; her grin widened as he placed his hand there, cupped to the complementary anatomy. When his fingers began to tremble, he let them dance toward her hard, corded neck. He tried to relax; his cheeks tightened into a smile of pleasure. The broad, unquestioning face was a few inches from his; the square teeth, the pyramidal sharp nose, the opulence of flesh at his fingertips. Ripe, unpicked fruit; the bursting figs of nipples hard and tight under the thin cloth. He was drunk on the wine-dark sea in each inviting eye. A classical picture, he thought, nymph and satyr; even the strict garlic odor might be a musky perfume.

His hands shot back at a noise in the hall; his knees crumbled, and he could barely walk from the room as he tried to tidy up the interior of his mind. But he had planned this encounter, they couldn't be disturbed. Julia was not due back from town for two hours. Giovanni had gone to cheat a peasant out of some land, to sell to one of his Washington friends. John somehow steadied his knees, and entered the kitchen again.

Nor, he found, did caution matter. This forbidden encounter was driving him to a kind of madness. This was the girl he had wanted in high school, the easy girl others had had under the bleachers during sporting events. She was the bohemian in college who had invited him to her room to discuss literature and had tried to rape him. He had fled, panic-stricken. She was all the girls he had wanted, all the missed opportunities: students of his who sat in the front row, dresses raised to expose fleshy knees; friends of Julia, faculty wives, women on the street, shadowy figures at bus stops, waitresses, nurses. Women who had left him clouded in their musk, but not one had he ever really known. No one but Julia, who could not be called a representative random sample, he was sure.

Rosa had returned to her work. Now, as he stepped beside her again, she grinned and stuck out her hand. John, baffled, then angry, thrust his hand into his pocket and threw coins on the table. As the girl picked up the first one, he grabbed both her shoulders savagely; from movies he tried to remember how this scene progressed.

Like a golfer working into a tee shot, he stepped in half steps until he was behind her and tried to move his hand into a position the wrist wouldn't allow. Her head was thrown back, the wide animal eyes met his; her lower lip, plump, moist, hung like fruit about to fall. Was he to kiss her? He decided against it. Some kitchen passion now, a starter. Tomorrow, perhaps, they could meet somewhere. At the thought of delay, passion became a dancing partner whose hand pressed at the small of his back, forcing air from his lungs. Then his hand went inside the cloth, to collect most of a breast which lunged forward in his grasp.

"Such a young girl to go to Rome."

Either she recognized *Roma*, or his hand tickled, or she found his expression curiously absurd, for her giggling became uncontrollable. His hand loosened inside her blouse; the excess of flesh rocked against his hand with the free laughter. In the heat of the moment, as he reconsidered the bedroom, his hand squeezed her breast tightly and he felt the rockiness.

"What's this?"

Her giggling stopped, and she looked at him, uncertain.

"What's this, girl?" Now he fondled the skin with the objectivity of a medical man, probing harshly at the unyielding flesh with his thumb and forefinger.

Rosa scowled and sucked in her lower lip—it was a bad joke for him to show anger.

"What is thls lump, girl?" he gasped. "Oh, good heavens. . . ."

Passion drained away. By touch he compared the other breast to its mate, but there was no unnaturalness under the skin. The girl watched without understanding the English, but she recognized the display on John's face. Her lips were uncertain whether to laugh or cry; she decided on both as the professor studiously removed his hands, unbuttoned his shirt, and solemnly worked the skin of his own slanting chest, testing it. Rosa scooped the money from the table, laughing; as she ran from the room, blouse open, laughter converted to tears without noticeable change.

John Blume dropped into a straight-back chair, overcome first by the unwilling discovery he had made on the girl's body; then by the realization he must tell someone who would help her. But how, without revealing how he had made the discovery? He dragged himself upstairs to reason things out, and in his study the hills, valleys, and mountains of paper-work laid neatly on his desk were meaningless now. For the knowledge of one girl's discomfort (illness or death he couldn't even consider) far out-weighed the data of displaced and replaced people. And his own discomfort was involved: what would it cost to get out of a situation he should never have promoted.

Logically, he reasoned the possibilities. An anonymous note to Giovanni, or to the local doctor, divulging the writer's intention but not his name? No, he cast this away as it formed. He simply couldn't write Italian well enough (or, if it could be considered to come from a peasant boyfriend, badly enough) to carry the thing off. The doctor might be a fool, but he would realize at once the grammatically bad letter was a foreigner's attempt, not that of an illiterate native.

Giovanni. Surely that man of the world would understand. After all, it was he who had supplied the initiative to John.

That evening, as Julia finished washing their dishes (she didn't believe Rosa would heat water to get them clean), Giovanni and John drank their brandy in the main room. John hedged the wild flow of talk to the subject of Rosa.

"Ah, Giovanni, about Rosa . . . "

"Rosa, she thinks she is very clever. She thinks I am stupid, you are stupid, your wife is stupid. I tell her my shirt is not clean. Is yellow. She wonders, when her father, or her stupid boyfriend with no one lire in his pocket for cigarettes, change their shirts each fifteen days, why should I make clean change every day." Giovanni nodding and spitting with gusto, as his talk became more excited. "Am I better than her stupid boy-friend, or her peasant father, she wonders? I must be very stupid to think so. And I *am* stupid, or I would dismiss her."

"No, that's not what I meant. I mean, does she *look* all right to you?"

"Ah, Rosa is very beautiful." Giovanni cupped his hands, in mockery. "Ask her. She tells me she must not work so hard, or it will spoil her great beauty. And I say: Surely, if your legs were not so thick, and bent so, you would make most beautiful girl, Miss Universe. Now," Giovanni laughed, rocking to a crescendo, "now you are only runner-up."

John silently cursed the man's coarse laughter and his heavy lip smacking—as if he wished the taste of brandy to last forever. He told himself to get to the point. "Do you think she's ill? Looks a bit peaked?"

Giovanni's face thrust forward, masked with the common negative expression: eyes closed, lower lip out and down at the corners. "Ill, you think? Rosa is a beast, an ox. Her parents are oxen. For forty-fifty years, she will work, in her lazy way. Then poof. She will appear an ancient woman for five years more. Then . . . " He sounded the final note by slapping his riding crop smartly across his boot. "That is the way peasants are made. They die quickly because they cannot afford to be ill. They are not rich, like you lucky Americans. I, I am neither rich, like you, nor a peasant, like Rosa. I thank God. I am nobility, but I do my own work. I am strong, a worker . . . "

"But is . . . ?" Too late—Julia had finished her dishes. She strolled into the room and picked up an American magazine, her eyes on John.

"You know, Giovanni, John really should have been a doctor."

John knew she had heard—if not the essence then at least the last of Giovanni's words. Now she flashed a smile which was meant to be wry, but which only further misaligned her narrow, pinched face. "Did he ever discuss with you his early illness?"

It had been a mistake to tell her, so long ago. He had revealed his only secret to her on their honeymoon, when it seemed very easy to lie awake and uncover the past.

"John should have been a doctor, or at least a First Aid man. Because he already knows so much about illness—he's had most of the known diseases, and some unknown ones. Dear me," she laughed, "his mother as head nurse, with that insufferable hypochondriac's medicine chest of hers."

Julia flipped through her magazine, snuffling laughter. John looked at his hands, and considered another brandy; Giovanni, puzzled at the rapid, oblique English, *did* have another.

Of course, John did not deny Julia's charges. But that was long ago, and an entirely different case. Early in life he had one of those experiences which radically forms a man's personality: for five long years he believed himself dying of cancer.

This was Julia's little joke. He had told her in a realxed moment during their honeymoon, glad finally to unload his burden. She had been sympathetic then, but over the years found a delightful viciousness when she alluded to it, lingering on the part about his mother's medicine chest. Simply because his mother, who had instructed John to regard the human body as an object of valid concern, was *both* hypochondriac and collector, and refused to throw away two generations of half-empty bottles of pills, syrups, and tonics.

That night after Julia was asleep, John took Giovanni's huge English-Italian dictionary and wrote his diagnosis, using very simple sentences which he hoped the girl would understand, yet not be alarmed by. Very carefully, he stated she must ask Giovanni to take her to the *medico* and to show that man her left breast. He felt a shame similar to his shame of disease as he hastily added that if his name was not mentioned he would see she was taken care of properly. *That* Rosa would understand. Disguising his handwriting, he wrote a finished, corrected draft. The half-dozen imperfect notes he tore up and watched the fragments burn in the fireplace. The final copy he folded and put in the secret pocket of his sport jacket, a pocket previously unused.

He changed into his pajamas and eased into bed, beside Julia. At any rate, he had done more for Rosa than had been done for him in his dark days, when he had believed the small, hard foreign lumps, strung in chains through his body, ate away life. The moral responsibility lifted from his shoulders.

He turned and kissed Julia's cheek lightly and, almost as an afterthought, slipped his hand into her nightgown; the contact was with a flat bladder of dry skin. Perhaps he pinched too hard as he inspected, because the breathing stopped its cadence.

"John?"

"Yes, Julia." Too late to withdraw his hand. Would it seem overly strange?

"What is wrong?" she asked. "You've been acting like a grad student with false data cards."

"Have I?" He tried to think fast, before she rolled over. "Perhaps the pizza? Mushrooms, salami. Haven't slept well at all the last few nights. My health . . . "

She sat up, letting his hand rattle around in the vacancy of her gown; then she lifted it out and handed it to him. "Really, John. Usually when you can't sleep you try a *book*."

"Yes, dear. I'll be all right." He was awake seven

minutes later when her loud, regular breathing resumed its march, and still awake six hours later when the sun began its dance across the day. A night spent surveying the surface of his own body, comparing it to Rosa's. He pronounced himself cured.

Between breakfast and lunch he shuffled and reshuffled Divorces and Homicides without charting them. Rosa grinned at him as she passed in and out of the room through breakfast, while Giovanni roared about the maid "taking my fortune" (she had hung his white shirts on the balcony, where rust rubbed on them). John, his heart full of pity, ate his American corn flakes in silence, and knew that tomorrow would tell a very different story.

After lunch, with Giovanni asleep and Julia again in town, John crept into the kitchen and startled the girl as she cut vegetables at her usual slow pace. But her amazement passed, followed by the grin as she recognized her benefactor. She reached for the paper he handed her and a third expression, disappointment, crossed her face when it contained no money. She glanced at the paper, at John, and handed it back.

"No! No!" she said, exhausting one-half of her English; her first finger waved in a scolding motion.

"You won't go to the doctor?"

"No, *non capisco!*"

"You can't read?"

His cheeks sagged; he had never considered this. Giovanni was right, the girl was a beastly peasant. But, he weakened, a rather pretty one.

He tried to explain by holding the wadded note against his chest. Then he held it against her breast, where flesh and thin cloth were one; there was no passion this time. Rosa drew back and made a clipping motion with her thumb and forefinger.

Must he pay to save her life?

He dropped a handful of coins into her hot palm and pulled her blouse down with the hope that everything had changed since yesterday. The angry nipples stared back; sweat clung in glossy clusters which broke reflecting light into changing spectrums as the stout curves rose and fell with her patient breathing. She watched John gently lift her left breast and clinically work it over, pressing with trembling fingers; dimpled spots pucked up the resistant skin like watermarks.

It was still there, a deposit of dense hardness between the strata of tissue, just as he'd remembered—though perhaps not quite so large. The girl grinned as he pushed her fat hand to her own breast, and he pressed the wadded note to his chest, in dumb-show demonstration. With wide, square teeth she showed her appreciation for this American game.

John was exasperated. Just as he thought of reading the note to her, he saw the grin fade and die simultaneous with the noise at the doorway behind.

"Good God, John!"

"Julia. Back early, aren't you?" He had not heard the car. She must have cut the engine at the road and coasted down the drive.

"*Too* early, apparently. I suspected it was more than pizza." She held them in the stare fixed through rimless glasses: the dusky girl, half-dressed, preparing vegetables; John with his tie loose, shirt undone, his hand hidden inside as if he were a Napoleon of the kitchen. Rosa began to work faster.

"Now, let me explain." John looked out the window, at the antique landscape which sagged into the far hills. "Rosa must think I'm a doctor of medicine, see. University doctor, you know. Then, well, she asked me to look at her . . . her, right here. You see for yourself." Julia's eyes followed his finger. "At the side, feel the irregular lump."

Julia approached the girl, circled her with cold, exacting eyes and, as a gardener picks the first strawberry of the season, her fingers clutched at the expanse of skin. Her attention was on the patio and the street below, anything except to look into the wary animal eyes of the girl, who now sliced carrots. Her white fingers bit into the brown skin, and finally she turned away.

"I don't feel any abnormality. The usual ducts and nodes found in everyone." Then her brittle lips broke the tension of her face, and she laughed. "A little more prominent, perhaps, but the girl is rather . . . prominent."

"You're certain? Nothing?"

"I don't have the medical certitude of your mother, of course. I'll drive her into town if you think a doctor's approval is necessary. But look at her. Does she *look* sick?"

"You're all right," John shouted, clutching at words to phrase it into Italian.

"What is all right?" Giovanni yelled, stumbling down the hallway, his shirt unbuttoned, his eyes dulled with sleep. "First the swearing of Julia wakes me, the noise, and . . . Christ on a Cross!" His riding crop was aimed at the breast which hung over Rosa's blouse, like a bulbous nose peering over a fence. Then he looked from his maid, now feverishly peeling potatoes, to the conspiracy of two.

"Oh, you tell him," John said, gruffly. "I've finished with this problem." He started for the door, his knees sinking beneath him.

"Wouldn't you like to make a more thorough examination, John? You might make some interesting medical discoveries." Julia's laughter was a spasm of wild humor: in this kitchen burlesque she saw her husband's true innocence. So this was his Mediterranean affair. This was how he emulated Giovanni's conquests. She collapsed into a chair, laughing, and watched the half-nude girl race into her work.

"American corruption," Giovanni shouted, baffled, but glad to find some corruption in these cold blooded people.

John wanted the satisfaction of telling Giovanni to go to hell, but his throat tightened with dryness, and his tongue was putty. In the hallway, he felt dizzy and leaned against the railing. Rubbing his forehead with the tight wad of paper he still held, like a souvenir, he breathed deeply, thinking: Thank God, everything came out okay.

FATHER TO SON

Finally they come to where the sparkling spokes of the Ferris wheel revolve, festive against the night.

His smile crumbling, Martin looks from the wide, laughing mouths of the crowd to the cars that rock upward, their lights like jewels, their shape that of bright evil birds. The wheel is much higher than he remembers it.

Starting from the far end of the midway, they have ridden the bumper cars, danced lightly on the merry-go-round, taken a chance on the ring toss. During one half hour they have toured the Fun House—side-stepped air holes, floundered against gravity in the tilted room, met their own grotesque images in the hall of mirrors. They have even ridden the violent undulations of the Octopus, where screams cut the summer air like flashing knives—and it has all been laughter.

"Let's ride it, Daddy," the boy says, his fingers tugging at Martin's hand, pulling him toward the final ticket booth.

"We'd better get home, Jeff. Daddy's tired."

Martin glances at his wife's face to see if furrows of sarcasm replace the lines of laughter—but no, she understands. She has seen him in elevators with sweat on his face and at those times when someone has suggested a plane trip.

But the boy . . . Martin's eyes follow the square of bulbs

that define a car and watch it rock upward to the stars; at the top, as the lights almost flip away for the descent, the car stops. It hangs in space, rocking, and Martin feels his stomach roll against his belt; from above the flapping canvas of tents, above the midway's laughter, the city's lights stretch to the dark horizon, and the raised arm can touch Orion, the Great Bear, the moon. Thinking this, he feels giddy. Something behind his eyes drops and spins, and he clutches the cold restraining chain. He has known that someday this would happen.

"Why not ride the merry-go-round again?" Martin suggests.

But the boy is six, a product of the Space Age, and thinking of astronauts, nose cones, the countdown; every day he sees photographs on television direct from the weather satellite.

Martin has ridden the Ferris wheel long ago, when he was a boy. He has even flown once, has gone up free in a small plane at an air show. He has ridden elevators, has stood at the edge of cliffs, where the ground crumbled, his knees steady—and then, sometime, somehow, *something has happened.* Now if he even looks at aerial pictures in magazines, he feels himself falling toward that crazy patchwork landscape.

The giant wheel spins, and his wife, understanding, carries the baby under the arcade, toward the merry-go-round.

At his side, Jeff tugs.

Always Martin has known that this day would come. Tonight, when they left the house, he was uneasy. If the carnival should have a Ferris wheel or a roller coaster, the boy would want to go up, and Martin would want to refuse. He is afraid of heights, afraid of himself in high places, and he is afraid of showing the boy that his father is a coward. But more than that, he thinks, his mouth drying, he does not want the boy to be frightened of heights or crowded rooms, or to inherit the throng of phobias that creep under the body's skin; the boy must continue to grow bright, clever, healthy.

The boy insists; therefore Martin sucks in air deeply and he pulls Jeff toward the devilish machinery.

Quickly, so that he will not change his mind, he has the dollar out, is reaching for two tickets and the hot coins. In five fast steps they are up the ramp, and Martin sees their car revolve. Ancient, it stutters, rattles down to meet them, to reveal the flaking gilt that covers baroque filigree; several burned-out bulbs leave dark gaps like missing teeth. Martin thinks it all looks terribly unsafe.

Then Jeff is in the car. The attendant waits, holds back the safety bar. Martin hesitates; he considers offering the man five dollars *not* to stop them at the top, but the words fall foolishly in his mind and would seem foolish even if he were to say, "It is for the boy, doing it all for the boy, first time up, y'know." So Martin coughs and hears the safety bar click shut. His palms fit the cold steel.

In both hands the man grasps the tall lever, and as he pushes it ahead to engage the machinery Martin's eyes close.

The car pitches up.

Martin senses the ground going away, hears the laughter and music dim, feels the darkness on his face when they reach the top.

"Wow! Look at the lights," Jeff says. "Where's our house?"

Martin's hands are frozen on the steel bar; his heart rattles like the machinery below; and he will not open his eyes. He is sorry he did not stay home.

He feels the car pass the wheel's apex and begin the long

descent—and *stop*.

Slowly his eyes open. Their car swings one stop from the bottom, where a young boy and girl are getting on. Martin sees the attendant stare at him, and he forces a smile. He slips an arm around Jeff, holding him close.

The machine rumbles, coming alive; their car dips and then climbs sharply. Jeff waves, his mouth working. Forcing himself to look down, Martin sees his wife and baby diminishing against the midway. He waves once and grips the steel bar. His eyes close; the darkness falls cool against his face. The car moves jerkily toward the top—and past, downward, into the smell of cotton candy.

Near the bottom he is again tempted to signal the attendant, to motion that twice around is plenty, but he does not want to reveal that a terrific fear beats in his chest, flaking away his heart. And then it is too late; they are past the point and moving upward, circling, circling. Lights, darkness, brush his face. The midway noise grows louder and dims. Whenever Martin opens his eyes he sees his wife waving, very proud of him.

Four times the wheel circles continuously, and on the fifth—just when Martin begins to feel some old fears relax—the machinery disengages. Tenuously the chair rocks, and his eyes open to darkness.

The car has stopped at the very top.

Martin clamps his eyes shut and locks both fists on the bar, but the scene is frozen on each retina: blackness sprinkled with distant lights—a picture of death.

Beneath them the car rocks, threatens to pitch out man and boy. Martin's chest slowly charges with the old panic. Again he knows the tightness that has sent him from close rooms and again he does not trust his self-control. *He wants out of here*, and he fears that urge to jump, the desire to dance freely across space. The crazy feeling that he cannot ever explain, that his wife only thinks she understands.

As every nerve end screws tight, Martin tries to concentrate. He steels his mind with statistics, assures himself that sixty-five per cent of all Americans have flown, many more than once, some even making a habit of it. Flying is natural to the century—to all but him. Hanging to the car, which rocks in blackness, he tries to be reasonable; the fear is irrational, foolish.

One leg is almost over the side when Jeff's hand reaches out. "Daddy, I'm scared."

The hand digs into the flesh of his arm until Martin opens his eyes. The horizon tilts and falls away to people sprinkled on the swirling, garish linoleum. Martin looks down the dull white girder, sees spokes stretch into light where the foreshortened attendant walks. He reels back, sorry he looked. But what if the machine has broken a gear—what if they're *stuck* up here!

"Dad. Stop the car!"

Martin sees Jeff's eyes roll, blank with fear. He sees father and son falling, hand in hand, to the waiting earth, and the crazy vision sends his mind spinning.

His arm slips around the boy's narrow shoulders and the tousled head is against him, as if in imitation of the lovers one car below. His other hand holds Jeff's arm, and he says. "Easy, now. Nothing to fear." His own heart pounds; his words come from dry lips. "See there—no, to the left—the high blue neon? That's our shopping center."

He talks gently, for his life has been touched. And suddenly he remembers back twenty-odd years when he sat beside his father in another swaying car near the top. Had he been afraid? Maybe—yes, possibly. Had *his* father? No! His father had had no fears. Martin had been a boy in sneakers and worn blue jeans sitting beside his father, comforted, trusting the man's strength, something steady and eternal, and soon the wheel had moved on, like the wheel of life, from darkness to light.

Perhaps that was when he had learned fear—not at the top of the wheel, but in the dark bedroom, seeing his father falling deeper toward death. His father, fearless, had slipped into shadows, into that terminus which ends all circles.

The wheel jerks into motion; the car pitches frantically, lifting Martin's stomach into his chest. He holds the boy—his boy—as they fall toward bright lights. The car skims upward, but this time Martin's eyes are locked open. Near the top he points out an airplane's running lights, disappearing into the distant, rarefied air of the future, and Jeff nods.

Then they are at the bottom. Martin steps out on legs that threaten to fold beneath him, but he turns to help Jeff from the car, and they walk down the ramp hand in hand to where the woman waits.

"How was it?" Jeff is asked, and the boy, utterly serious, says, "Sometimes I didn't like it. But Dad was there."

Martin smiles, relieved, and his wife understands. Yet, as they walk toward the parking lot he knows that someday the baby too will want to ride that dazzling wheel, and by then Jeff will be insisting on a plane trip—a real plane, cutting tops from dizzying cloud banks.

Knowing this, Martin trembles, asserting himself against that inevitable day.

VOYEURS

Auger entered the drugstore and moved quickly toward the magazine racks. In the air-conditioned coolness he was vulnerable, exposed; rubbing his arm, he felt the tiny cones of skin puckering. He saw two girls at a round, chrome table look at him, look away, then at him again. High school girls, giggling over their sodas, and before he quickly turned away he saw beneath the shiny white fabric of their tennis outfits the hint of breasts. They looked away just before he did and he continued toward the magazine racks, rubbing his arm with his hand, trying to get acclimated.

From the rows of publications he took a general interest magazine and opened it, pretending to read about kidney transplants. Then, sensing by peripheral vision that he was not being watched, he quickly slipped a copy of *Playboy* between the opened pages. The street outside was dark and in the window's reflection he could see the view over his shoulder: the two girls still giggled at the ends of their straws, the breasts jiggling against the table edges were mere nubs; the soda-jerk washed glasses, the pharmacist walked behind his cash register, whistling. At the counter a woman sat on a stool, the ice in her untouched drink melting; the heavy calf of one leg was draped over the other, the red shoe pumped in the air. She looked toward the door, as if expecting someone.

Auger suddenly realized there was a face beyond the reflection—a man's face, pallid, unshaven, dark horn-rimmed glasses, hands cupped to each side to cut out the glare. Shaken, Auger ran to the doorway and onto the sidewalk, but the man was gone. Behind him he heard the soda-jerk yelling and he realized he still had the magazines. Auger dropped them inside, then ran down the deserted sidewalk. The street was empty—no people, no passing cars, no sound except for Auger's padded footsteps. At the corner he stopped, looked in all directions, and wondered why the man had been looking at him, of all people.

From the bushes Willy saw the man run to the corner, then wait under the arc light, briskly rubbing his arms. Willy breathed deeply, got his heartbeat back to normal. The oppressive odor of laurel leaves and the fine road dust almost caused him to sneeze, but he forced his tongue against the roof of his mouth. Only a few minutes more—the man would give up, they always did. Willy had been chased by some of the best, and he had always escaped—there were a million places to hide if a man knew the route beforehand.

Somewhere a dog barked; Willy stiffened, listened, moved to straighten his cramped legs. Dogs, now, were something else. The man was still on the corner. A cruiser came out of the night, eased along the curb, the red roof light dull. Willy saw the man slip into the shadows, and he relaxed. He eased his weight until he was lying on his back, viewing the summer stars; there was something not only restful but secure within the bush, and he was reminded of a tree house he had built long ago, where he could remain until well after the adults were asleep. He had seen a few things in those days.

Now, shifting his weight again, he looked from the stars to the building on his left—the backside of a two story apartment house, cluttered with washpans, laundry, brooms and mops. Near a lighted window he saw a man leaning on the balcony's wooden railing; he was a large man in an undershirt and bib-overalls, and he smoked what seemed to be a cigar for the periodic red glow that burned the night air was the size of a small bulb. How long? Willy wondered. If he'd seen him, why didn't he call out, or point him to the police? Willy broke into a sweat, fearing that he'd been *seen*, and he waited without moving until the pain in his muscles became acute, the nerves sending small needles along every surface.

The light from the window behind the man spread across the side of his face, reflected from the bald skull, the transparent fluffs of hair above the ears. Willy watched as the man watched, unmoving, seeming to bore with his eyes into the very core of the laurel bush. Finally, after what seemed an eternity, Willy heard a door open, saw a woman emerge from the yellow quadrangle of light and call to the man, who slowly turned and entered the room.

Willy slid from the laurel bush before the man's eyes could adjust to the light; he didn't even look to see whether the first man still waited across the street. A hedge connected to the larger bush, and Willy clambered on hands and knees in its shadow until he came to a narrow sidewalk. Flat on the ground, he crawled into the shadow of a tree, reached the front porch, skirted it, and went to the rear of the house; there was only a small fence, which he was easily over, and then he was running softly along the sleeping back street.

As he turned to put the empty beer bottle down, he saw movement in the alley below—heard it, actually, since his head was turned away from the railing. Feet, perhaps—a person, a dog, or only the sound of newspaper blowing along the gutter? But there was no wind. He had sought the coolness of the balcony, a few minutes of escape from the humidity before he slipped into whatever sleep was possible between the damp sheets. He viewed with apprehension the prospect of his and Nora's vast expanses of flesh in sweaty contact all night; perhaps, he thought, he should sleep here.

From the balcony he viewed the alley, bushes, the street. A man stood on the corner under the arc light; perhaps it was his feet he'd heard. Then he saw a light go on in the house across the alley. He saw her come into the room, pass by the window, disappear. The naked light bulb swung from the motion, light gyrating in crazy circles until it slowed, stopped. She came to the bed and sat, kicking off her shoes. He bit the cigar involuntarily, stifled a cough as he saw her slide the dress up over shoulders, shake her hair loose. She stood in the slowing circle of light in her underclothes, then moved out of sight to hang up the dress. When she returned she sat on the bed and slowly, slowly unfurled first the one stocking and then the other, rolling the sheer fabric across full thigh and calf until it slipped over the toe. He waited while she put these somewhere, felt his breath coming harder with the energy of expectation; he shifted in the chair and when she returned she doubled her arms behind her in a quick gesture, unhooked hooks, slipped the bra off. He saw fleeting light catch the upper expanses of her breasts, saw the slow curve of the underside end like a question mark in the nipple; her hair fell forward, a cascade long and dark across her shoulders. He waited, breathless, wondering whether this happened every night, but before she slipped out of panties she put on her nightgown, tying the front shut, and left the room. He felt aroused but when she returned she simply switched off the light. He waited, knowing now that *he* might be seen. That she had not stripped completely left him unsatisfied, and it was almost with relief that he heard Nora call. He picked up his empty bottle and went inside, hot as a dog, aroused by the vision of that girl sleeping almost naked and unprotected in that ground-floor bedroom.

From the window Nora watched her husband stare across space, saw the woman crossing the room beneath the dancing light bulb. A breeze moved the window shade beside her face, fanning a large blue fly into action; her fingers gripped the drainboard, and she was acutely aware of the overpowering odor of old food, soap, stale milk which churned from the sink. He sat without moving, and she too noticed the girl's firm thighs, the flat stomach, and she tried to recall what she had been thinking about in days when her flesh lay close to her bones. Or had it ever? Not about an apartment over an alley, not a husband whose idea of a good time was to sit on the balcony with a beer, gawking at girls undressing. But she waited until the light went out before she opened the door, and called.

Mitch was making his way along the roof when his foot hit the sheet of loose tar paper, sent it skittering toward the edge, and at the same instant he saw the man on the balcony. He dropped flat. The man straightened in his chair, looked across the alley and toward the street. Mitch held his breath, sheltered his face in the sleeve of his black shirt.

Then, shifting slightly, he saw the man across the street looking toward the roof.

Mitch exhaled, swore—he'd thought the place was pretty empty at this hour. A police car cuised beside the curb.

Across the alley a light went on and as he turned he saw a girl cross the room; she sat on the bed, took off her clothes, and began to undress. Mitch smiled, watched the man watch that yellow square of light; he waited, and just when he was about to move back into the darkness the light went out. He heard a voice call to the man. A woman stood in the illuminated doorway, waited, then went back inside; the man got up, tucked in his shirt, and followed.

The man on the corner under the arc light was gone also, Mitch noticed, but as he raised himself to a crouching position he saw something move in the bushes below. With incredible speed a man ducked out of the hedge on hands and knees, and followed the cover of its shadow until he got to the darker shadows beside the porch. Mitch waited, doubting what he had seen; the figure appeared behind the house, running, was over a fence, and disappeared down the alley. Mitch shook his head, waited to see whether anyone else would show up.

When it seemed clear he climbed from the roof to the fire escape. It was a short jump to the balcony where the man had been drinking beer. Through the window he heard voices, saw past the fine mesh curtains to a room, a bed, the bib-overalls hanging from the bedpost. The small night light revealed the pair partly covered by a single sheet; they were incredibly large, their bulk multiplied by the creases which broke the parts into segments. The noise that the bed made covered any sound Mitch might have made as he reached through the open window to unplug the teevee set, the toaster, the waffle iron; he wound up their cords and carried them down the fire escape like a string of fish. The sounds of bulbous love-making could be heard in the alley, echoing against the building, until it merged with his footsteps as he ran for his car.

Willy flattened himself into the recessed doorway as a car sped from the alley, its lights sweeping the dark street; tires squealed at the intersection as the car turned left, tilting, then sped away. Willy wiped his forehead with the back of his hand, peered both ways before stepping out. He heard footsteps before he saw anyone, and ducked back. The steps came closer, and he heard the sound of laughter, like ice in a glass. Two girls ambled along the sidewalk on his side of the street; they laughed, and pushed at each other with tennis rackets. Willy flattened himself against the doorway and watched them slowly walk past, saw the flash of thighs beneath their small dresses, and when they were beyond his hiding place they looked back, their laughter echoing on the dark street. Willy relaxed, exhaled the air he had been holding.

He waited until they were out of sight before continuing on to the corner. The only business still open was the drug store, but it looked deserted. Willy crossed the street, walked to the window and peered at the clock on the far wall; ten minutes before closing.

Suddenly he realized that he was seeing a face in the foreground: a man at the magazine rack, staring in surprise over the top of *Life*, mouth open, as if trying to shout. When the man started for the door Willy began to run, heading for the alley and the dark shrubbery beyond.

Klatz laid the 8 power telescope on the dashboard, and slipped the doe-skin gloves on a finger at a time. He had watched the two girls leave the drug store, considered them, then noticed the man in the shadow of the doorway. The girls disappeared around the corner, and Klatz was reluctant to expose himself to the other man by starting his engine or turning on headlights. He waited, saw the other man go to the window, make a gesture, and saw a second man chase him down the street. Even now he stood, rubbing his arms, under the light.

Eventually the drug store's windows began to dim, and the last customer left. Klatz waited until he was certain of which direction she would take, and then he started his car; he backed to the corner and, lights out, eased the car around the block. There were two houses on this street, both with thick shrubbery, and between them an empty field. Klatz unfolded his heavy wool scarf and hung it loosely around his neck. From the back seat he opened a small leather case, and even in the dim light the row of scalpels glowed. From the glove box he took an aerosol can of ether and a length of rope. He had removed the bulb from the dome light, and so he was able to leave the car in darkness, squatting beside the rear fender. He looked at the sleeping houses, dark shrubbery, and felt safe.

Along the sidewalk the woman walked quickly, her red high heels sounding a note of urgency.

THE HEM OF HARVEST

"Feedel!"

Garry stared across the street at darkness, honeycombed with dim doorways. Now he could not determine into which one the young woman had stepped—a fluid, secret motion—after catching his eye. But she was somewhere in the shadows, or in a room, filled with the lazy scent of olive oil, waiting. At his back the voice of salesmanship called, and while he waited for the lighted window, silhouetting dark curves of love, he pretended to be sightseeing other items of interest: the ant-life which hurried along the evening walks, the archeological mysteries of the street—history spilled from the diggings, paving stones stacked like bread loaves to the left, dirt piled to the right. Several bent black women stopped to stare into the sewer's vitals, to see why their toilet pans weren't flushing, and then hurried on.

Even bad plumbing could be romantic, he thought, and although he was eager to submit to adventure tonight, he was not alone: his wife tugged an arm, and when he turned he saw she was being pulled by the man in American levis, who stood in the shop's light like a husky cowboy. Loose black curls emphasized an air of sweet malice, as he grappled them toward the shop, spewing his insane pitch: "Feedel Castro, hey?" he said, stroking an imaginary beard.

Garry's laughter was hollow as he pulled Avis away, toward Las Ramblas. There they would sit on a bench for two hours, watching the people, before returning to the damp, stifling room in the *pension*. There would be no breeze all night among those watermarked walls—the cheapest room, for transients who took no meals—where the single window opened to an airshaft, an echo chamber for the goat cough of the man across the way. But the room was very *cheap*, and saving money was his own idea, and absolutely necessary—so they would sit on free benches until ten, avoiding the outstretched hands of waiters, guides, cab drivers, vendors of cactus buds, and men who dragged you into shops.

"But you are not Feedel! You are American?"

"Come on, Avis. It's a clip joint." Garry pulled her his way, out of the pool of light. Dull yellow bulbs flickered along the sidewalk, the naked filaments baffled by moths, and all windows in the granite-dark buildings were shuttered—although he could imagine the various positions love assumed behind boards. And standing in darkness, imagine was all he could do: *Somehow, everything was supposed to be different*. Days, years dribbled by like a session of clap. Already he stared at thirty, and he had planned to be here ten years ago. Now they had scootered down from the cold north, over the Low Countries, sliced France from Paris to the Pyrenees, into Spain, sleeping on the ground, eating bread and cheese in the antique landscape, digging everything, as their book of Travelers Checks slowly diminished—but it was incredible how *nothing at all was happening*. Except that right now his wife was being led away by a man resembling a minor devil. "He's a shill."

"I am Luiz. Do you know malaga?" he asked, pulling Avis toward the shop's opening to show her a long wall lined with shoulder-high kegs; from each keg a neoprene hose trailed to a spigot over a thickly lettered sign. When she turned Garry saw her eyes shine with pleasure: the little barrels of wine were so *cute* and *foreign*—and besides, she had never had *two* men fighting over her.

"Nuts, let's go," Garry said. "It's a racket: I'll bet his dad was here forty years ago, pulling his chin and shouting *Lenin*."

Garry jerked her from the shop and they struggled toward the street, until Luiz released his grip. "Stop! You don't like the malaga, *you don't pay*. Okay! No charge."

"One can't hurt," Avis suggested, allowing herself to be led back to the yellow light. "Only one."

Abruptly he surrendered Avis' arm, thinking what the hell—no lights were winking at him, drawing him up the archipelago of stairs, winding and narrow, to where passion trembled like a guitar string. If Luiz didn't get the buck, another hand would. For sure. "Okay. Deua then." Reluctantly he followed Avis over the rubble toward a table but suddenly turned back—remembering the *cactus bud* or whatever it was in his pocket—as if he would only be pushed so far. "Wait. Combien costa?"

"Why, eighteen pesata, For two."

It was not Luiz, but Paco, who brought the malaga.

Paco, descendant of bull-fighters and flamenco dancers. He arched through the hanging smoke with fluid, stylized movements, a series of pirouettes and veronicas. With a flourish the glasses were placed and he spun away, tall and thin in tight levis and a blousy white shirt stained red—a gored fighter, bleeding wine.

For the two English girls, Paco lifted the *boticho* and from the phallic glass stem wine shot deep into his yawning aristocratic mouth; the stream drew back with his hand, a foot-long stream of wine falling perfectly between dark lips. Slowly he moved the vessel up until wine ran from the tip of his nose, off the bridge, and into the tray of his lower lip; the stream climbed to his forehead, washing the scalloped curls—wine flowed across his face, neck, shoulders; it soaked shirt and levis, stained his legs cordovan, filled his shoes.

Then the stream returned to the curled lips, and was broken off neatly with a flick of the wrist. The *boticho* was returned two-thirds empty to those who had paid for it.

" 'e's a thirst, wot?"

Her partner nodded vigorously. Although the evening had cooled considerably they popped out Spanish fans, gay night flowers.

"My God," Garry said. "Aren't they something?" He saw their stools sink into skin somewhere under the flowing homemade dresses. Thick plantegenet legs were rammed downward into "sensible" shoes, the kind the royal family stands in for newspaper photos. Female Falstaffs, the Red and White Queens, fans blazing and roses in their hair. Garry thought: uncross their legs and there'll be English gunboats in the bay, it'd be the Armada all over again. "They're trying like hell to be happy."

"Probably are," Avis said. In her sketchbook she recorded the scene, the characters, with quick, deft lines. "Probably are happy. They're just working girls on vacation."

Garry thought about this, and raised his glass: the malaga was beautiful—a velvety maroon, thick and sweet—it tasted of seasoned casks hidden in a white-washed old building high on the Costa del Sol. That was what he liked to imagine. He dreamed of the *textures* of Eruope—wooden banisters palm-rubbed for centuries, the brittle varnish of great paintings, intricate tapestries, worn marble. A south wind scented with myrrh and frankincense, of strange foodstuffs. Where, he wondered, is the decade-old vision of a man strung with sausages, a wine-skin in one hand, a drum of cheese in the other, and a bundle of French bread loaves under the arm, like bullets. These Stateside myths he clung to, and expected.

Yet, at times, he knew he was no traveler.

There were mornings when the ground shook earthquakes into his back, when he truly felt thirty, and did not want to move along the map's thin blue finger; what he wanted was a chaise lounge and a glass of cold milk, for the stomach. There were days when a crumbling medieval wall, or fluted Gothic columns rising like delicate reeds, did not excite him. On these days, when wine was vinegar and food caught in his throat, he would count again the thin book of Travelers Checks, and actually consider blowing the whole works on one big night at Monte Carlo—fulfillment—then to return to a gray job in the States, at a desk somewhere, chained to payments of a tract house, and the children Avis desired. To this he would not surrender, and on the bad days Avis' enthusiasm carried them the hard miles.

"Capture your true self?"

At his side the photographer stood, preening his mustache, a vintage Graphlex and battery flash slung over his shoulder. Garry shook his head, and the man sank to the bench.

Near the front Paco performed for the praise of thick German laughter: his back sharply arched, wine ran from curlock to chin.

"Wine," Avis said, draining her glass. "More wine."

A signal brought Paco and *vin ordinaire*, as if the boy were able to read Garry's mind. The *boticho* touched the table in salute, then was jerked away and raised to Paco's lips. As the jet entered the black, yawning mouth, Garry grabbed the *boticho* back, smiling.

A lottery agent arrived, tickets pinned in ribbons down his chest, as if his coat had been sliced to gay, fluttering rags. He held a lump of newspaper stiffly before him, like a man in shock. At a corner table he opened the paper and gave half the bread, cheese, and olives to his daughter, a girl of twenty with a dirty dress and bad teeth; his half he set aside and spread the wrapping paper flat, to read it.

Avis began to sketch the girl who smiled behind her hand and, shyly, shifted attention to the heavy metal emblem hung from a chain at her waist, her sole concession to luxury.

"Roma," she said, to indicate travel or religion.

"MEEL RAH-yohs—" the Red Queen screamed. "Oh, wot's it mean, anyhow? We know AH-gwah non pohtable, and—"

The English girls swirled fans, repeating Spanish words in harsh Anglo accents for the dark man, their mentor, who sat in the shadows on an empty wine cask.

Paco, hemorrhaging from a dozen wounds, put two demi-litres on the table and picked up the cigarettes, taking several. "Any American cigarettes? No? S'okay, because you are good friends."

When Paco danced away, Avis said, "Maybe he knows what that *thing* is you bought. Ask him."

Garry felt the burden in his pocket, hard and heavy as a blackjack. "Let's forget all about that," he said, recalling the butt of the naked baby that earlier on the street had flashed past, and the girl who faced them, walking backwards, shouting: *Buy mister buy buy*. A swirl of purple gauze neatly masked her face, to fall to loose, gaudy rags. She clutched a thin brown baby; the other hand offered a green object. Confused, Garry found himself handing the girl a coin and taking the *thing*. It was hard and green and cucumber-shaped, and Garry decided it was a cactus bud, or a seed—or *something*.

Two middle-aged couples in matching Hawaiian shirts and blouses stopped at the entrance, shaking their heads. The lottery man slumped over his coffee, smelling it, warming his hands on the cup, while his daughter studied the drawing Avis had finished. The photographer nodded in sleep, undisturbed by the thunder of German laughter that carried to dark corners of the room.

And later, the *boticho* again empty, when Garry was about to place his hand on the shadow between Avis' hairline and collar, to tell her yes he really did love her and yes they would have that baby she wanted—even a house, where washer hoses would anchor all to basement walls—as he was about to speak, Paco danced past and motioned with his head, to the rear. "For my friends, look see this."

They followed, slipped through shadows to the rear door's crack, and when their eyes grew accustomed to total darkness they saw the hooped outlines. "For my friends, when the boss don't see."

This was the old stuff, Paco said, thirty years maturing in mossy 600-litre barrels; he ran up the narrow aisle thumping each great drum.

The glasses were out.

In this tiny room was a terrific silence, all noise deadened by the barrels towering to the high darkness. A *plink plink* broke near their feet, coins falling from a spigot. The wine dripped like money, and Garry wasted no time fulfilling old dreams: from spigot to drip pan, turn and scoop and drink. They moved barrel to barrel as the dream flowed from wood, from glass, flowed silkily down the throat.

"Drink, Avis my love."

He urged speed not because the wine was *free*, but because he was amazed into acceleration by the hand-worn spigots, the mossy wood, and because this narrow wedge of architecture—cryptic and musty, dark as a monastery vault, filled with the past—should have survived ancient wars. He knew he must sample each hermit cask before the opportunity faded, faded like wine into mouth, aching throat, and stomach. "Drink, drink," he ordered, knowing that whether drunkeness or the boss caught them first the good time must end.

Then Paco was speaking in a loud voice: " . . . ver' fine, thirt' year old, from Malaga on the south coast. . . . " It was the voice of advertising and they were dimly aware of the polished bald head that leaned through the open door.

There was no trouble, but Garry tried to pacify the boss with a Celta, the poorest of cigarettes, while Avis urged Garry to shut up, and Paco trailed behind praising the wine.

At their table a worn man and his girl were kissing; his hand crept along her knee, her hand restrained his. The battle of hands, surging like Latin blood. The dark workman's hand laid like a stain on the faded dress, above an inch of raggèd slip; yet they drank champagne.

Beside the lovers, yet ignoring them, sat a tall, gaunt boy with a crew haircut. It was five minutes before Garry and Avis were noticed.

"*Mucho amour*," the worn man said, removing his hand to pound the table furiously. The woman smiled shyly behind the man's rapid stream of Spanish. "*Non comprendo?*" Then, to clarify, he stood and shouted the words twice as fast. The four shook their heads slowly while the gaunt boy sat silent; but all five glasses were filled with champagne.

"*Allemagne?*" the worn man asked.

"Why no," Garry said, surprised. "Americanos."

"Ahhhhhh," he said, sinking slowly into his chair and turning to the woman. "Ahhhhhhh," she said, smiling at Avis. "Americanos."

"*Mucho amour*," the worn man said, and the couple fell to the death grip of love.

The tall, gaunt boy raised his head and said, in very good English: "He has won a lottery. A small one, but a winning. That is why he drinks champagne."

"That's wonderful," Avis said. "But why are you so sad?"

"Because it was not a bigger winning. And because I did not win it. And because this fool spends money like water."

"Is he your friend?"

"Not my friend, no," the boy said, spreading his hands wide. "The woman is my . . . my, how do you say in English? That is, we live together. It is a word I don't know."

"*Mucho amour*," the worn man screamed.

Without prefacing remarks the tall boy stood and lifted his shirt to the armpits. "Look at this, will you," he said, with neither malice nor anger nor special pride. A large, dished scar ran vertical on the abdomen, from hip to the floating rib; when he turned there was an identical scar on his back. "Two years ago, at Pamplona, we ran the bulls. This is what happened to me." The horn had passed clear through the boy's body but as both scars were equal in length, and both puckered inward, it was impossible to tell if he had stood the bull's charge, or run away.

"My god," Garry said. "That's terrible."

"It was a lesson, all right." The boy pulled down his shirt and lit a cigarette. "I spent six months in hospitals."

Then Garry raised his glass and announced in a mixture of four languages his love for Spain—but really his love for the patient, scarred boy; the dirty lovers; the wine-sodden Paco; the rummy and the ragged in the room. He was shouting, laughing, babbling, to the row of grinning, baffled faces, when the Red Queen hulked over.

"Excuse me. Do you speak English?"

"Oie, a little bit," said in fine, round tones.

"So good to hear one who does." She motioned to the White Queen, who unkinked to full height and easily carried stools, purses, glasses, and the *boticho* to the crowded table.

"Miss Harrington," said the first girl of the second, "and I'm Miss Watson. I say, the wine's not too clean, wot?" She seemed a bit embarrassed by the admission, as if drinking dirty wine was the thing to do away from home.

"Not so good, but good for you," Garry said, beginning the laughter which spread around the table like a parade of klaxons. The mucho amour couple were clamped in silent embrace, staring from the English girls to the Americans and back, with limp slash grins.

Both girls were somewhere over nineteen and under forty. Miss Watson—the Red Queen—was heavily rouged over hard skin; she was big, but seemed small beside Miss Harrington, who rose up from the table like a dense, substantial fog. Miss Harrington had a large matching chin and forehead, hair like waved taffy, and two composition teeth. She rode her stool, legs firmly planted, and fiercely fanned the glistening trickles along her white-powdered chin. "And the men," she said, "I think they're working us."

"Working you?" Garry said.

"Coo, like the gent in Pamplona—remember, Gracie? Said 'e 'ad a fine collection of Russian icons; asked us to see 'is icons. And all because we took the wrong train from the coast."

Miss Watson, lips pursed, added: "I think this is a place to work girls."

Garry thought about this, and drink affected his speech. "Not really. I'd bet a quid every man here hates women: y'know? Except old Paco, who is their Princess. And our friends, I don't know about them."

"*O mucho amour*," the man shouted.

"Princess?" asked Miss Harrington and Miss Watson, holding tightly to their purses.

"Why," Garry said, leaning close, "it's a flit joint; the

teddies, don't y'know?" Avis beside him snickered into her glass as he asked, in fine indignation: "Why, it's all in the guide book. Haven't you one?"

In unison the girls slowly uncrossed their legs, and a cold fog rose. That dark man who taught them Spanish words of dubious meaning: what pornography was tattooed on his chest? Or Luiz, barrel-chested lover of men. Paco, that thin gimlet with his tricks, a devil in the marginal underworld.

And the couple drinking champagne?

"*Mucho amour*," he roared, and then leaned forward to stammer his first fragments of English: "I love so much with her."

"Married but not churched, eh?" asked Miss Harrington.

Red and White faces shattered as the Queens rocked in fog-cold laughter—why if these blokes were teddies, it was all right, wasn't it; everything was all right.

"Oh, excuse me," Miss Watson said, shaking with laughter, "duty calls." She blushed and hurried to the rear, to the room with penciled English on the wall: No good to stand upon the seat, The crabs in Spain can jump ten feet. The tourist's curse in scribbled iambic tetrameter, bridging oceans.

Miss Harrington was holding forth: Why, the brother of a friend of a friend of hers had the *practice*, and it was hard to find a nicer boy. He had inherited it, she said, when his tonsilectomy hemorrhaged and he'd had a transfusion—*it was in his blood*. Now he was a Christian Science convert, and they had accepted him in spite of his *practice*.

And somewhere in merrie olde England, Garry thought, there was a flit who gave his blood and gathered followers. Less painful than a werewolf's bite; probably even got paid a pound a pint.

"Gotta go," Garry said, his kidneys aching; he held his sides, floating along the dark hallway. In the shadows he bumped soft flesh, and heard the gasp in the echo of the toilet's ringing flush. Miss Watson's mouth came open, thin tight lips askew, the face misaligned with surprise. She jumped back, and their hands locked.

"It's I, Miss Watson."

"No," she said. "I'm Miss Watson. Coo, gave me a start."

Keeping her hand, he pulled her toward the door of the cask room. "Miss Watson, I've no icons, but as a special friend of the owner I invite you to visit the wine cellar. No need to make a purchase. And think of the stories you'll tell the girls at work." She followed, drawn by his firm hand. "Step up, easy now."

Enough light came from the door's crack for Garry to fill glasses, and there was enough darkness to shelter Miss Watson in beautiful shadow. Faintly, from far away came the noise of the wine-shop; here was only the rustle of wine caught in cups, and Miss Watson's fan, like restless breathing.

"Don't fret, Miss Watson, everything's above board—haha. Well, here's looking at you—and a finer sight I don't hope to see. As I was telling *my sister* out there."

"Aren't you an American?"

"No talk of nationalities now," he said, squeezing her thick, demanding forearm. "The mission in prospect is a world united—and it's well known how you British feel about we Irish."

"Oh, now," she said.

"No, I know. You don't care a bit about us."

"Not true," she said, her free hand grasping him. "I do care. I've known some fine Irish people. I care!"

"Listen." Silence, cut by a splashing sound. In the dark she was demurely quiet; perhaps, god knows, he thought, even *coy*.

"Tad more of this grand malaga, Miss Watson," Garry asked, moving closer. "You know, at times like this I like to think about Europe, what it *means*, what it's all *about*. Isn't it really experiencing Life in another place. Being able to live, to do what one wants, because one is able to shed the private and public inhibitions of one's own country. Having Experiences." He could almost feel emotions flutter across her face. "It's these times, as I was telling *my sister* out there. Enjoying life, before our skulls are bloody worm cages—"

"Oh yes, really. Reely—LIFE."

"There's more to Europe than art museums, don't you agree?"

"Yes. REELY. Oil say."

A scurry in the hall and a door slammed. Avis looking for him?

"Here, Miss Watson, in the corner." She pulled into the niche behind the last towering barrel and they stood toe to toe, crushed into the blackness. Slowly her breathing eased and she asked, "Wot is it?"

Far away Paco shouted and something banged; another door slammed. Voices rose and fell from the big room and in between Garry heard a familiar sound, like water being made against a wall. From Miss Watson, a pert fart, which both pretended not to notice.

"Cozy?" Garry asked.

"Truly, it's something to tell the girls at the Trust." Earlier cautions about clean wine had vanished; a gurgle into the mouth at Garry's ear, and a cascade down the chasm of her throat.

"Yes, it is," he said. His cup fell, and he steadied himself with a hand on each expansive hip. "It surely is."

"Really, Mr.—?"

"McNectar. But call me Tom, I think we can."

"REELY, Mr. McNectar. But it's not proper."

Her breathing up again, a compressor sucking in the damp air and exhaling stale wine must; Garry getting drunker on the very air. Her cup crashed and she was grappling for his arms, his waist. Towards fulfillment, his head fell on her breast, an island firm as Britain.

Meanwhile, the noise of flat gurgling.

"I know what it is."

"What what is, Miss Watson?"

"Europe. Being here. It's wine and warmth and—"

"Yes?"

"It's—it's LUV!" she cried, and, propelled by her own profoundness, she held him to the wall with her hips, pinned like a prize butterfly, while her immense hands squeezed his head and the thin lips searched his furry bearded cheek to his mouth. Lips touched and four hands probed fitfully, flitting like bats about the dim corner, tearing at each other's clothes.

Her hand found his leg, his groin, pocket, and—*LUV!*

"Mr. McNectar!" Shock cleared her head, her lips pried from his.

"On no, you misunderstand, Miss Watson. It's not really *me*. It's a cactus bud, or *something*."

"Call it what you like." Her knee jabbed his crotch, as she tried to bring up her thick foot. "Coo, it's wet."

Garry wiggled his toes, and heard the wonkey slush of sock and leather. They stood at the sloping end of the room, in two inches of wine.

"You forgot the faucet."

"Bung plug, Miss Watson," Garry said, releasing her and wading to the cask, to wrestle with the wooden spigot.

Reverently on his knees before the barrel he tried to stop 600 litres of thirty-year-old malaga which ran into the catch pan and across the floor, collecting in puddles to feed the reservoir where they had been standing.

"Try it the other way."

"A little quiet, Miss Watson. And stand back." Garry braced a foot against the handle and shoved. With a rifle crack he feared would bring down the house the bung plug gave; the wine, freed, shot across the room, catching Miss Watson at the knees, running down her straight stiff knees into sensible shoes.

"Must have been old, rotten," he said, making for the door. "The trouble with Europe, everything's old."

In the hallway Miss Watson disappeared into the head and Garry entered the crowd: Paco screaming at his boss, the boss shouting *Finish* ('urry up now, it's time); the lottery man fagged on the table and his dirty daughter farting incessantly as she struggled to get him afoot; the lonely photographer staring at the floor's composition of olive pits, fish bones, shrimp casings, bread crusts, and cigarette butts, as the great chrome eye on his chest reflected the room in miniature upside down.

At the table with Avis were the mucho amour couple, still in rapt embrace; Miss Harrington, a stoic Gibraltar, in her cups; and an old man with a seaman's cap and no shoes.

"Garry," Avis said, "come meet a man whose son has been to San Francisco once." And still smiling, she added: "You s.o.b."

"I did nothing to disgrace you, Avis."

"What's that on your shoes and pants? Where's Miss Watson?"

"Let's go, believe me."

"Gawdam," Paco screamed, "tomorra I no come to this house. Tomorra I go on the street. Gawdam this gawdam house."

Although he really wondered why Paco swore in English, Garry asked: "What's wrong?"

For the big table of Germans, Paco said, he had performed with the *boticho*—also sung and danced—and now his boss, who hated Germans, was mad at Paco for accepting a twenty-five pesata tip. "Gawdam, I no like the Germans. But

I no like that bastard too. Tomorra I not stay in this fuckn house, I go on the gawdam street."

"Okay okay," Garry said, in a hurry to be gone. "How many pesatas, Paco?"

"Oh, nineteen," he said, a number off the top of his head. "S'okay. Thanks."

"And one for you, Paco. No, it's nothing." Beneficent Americans. Everyone shaking hands except Paco and his boss, who exchanged insults; the mucho amour couple promised dancing and champagne for tomorrow night; Miss Harrington helping Miss Watson along, the latter wringing out her sad, homemade dress. Garry stumbling in soggy shoes into the night with thoughts of waking the photographer, to capture evidence of this madness.

The street was nearly empty: a block ahead Avis' weaving figure turned the corner, but toward Las Ramblas crowds clutched the cool air. As he watched, the last lights of the street were extinguished, leaving on each block the hump of darkness which was the sleepy night watch.

Behind him, two women left a door and walked in his direction. The old one, in black, blended with the night; the other, younger, wore a shiny flowered print dress which clung tightly at the hips and breasts.

"What time is it, please?" Her smile was pleasant, subtle, the moist lips barely spread and yielding at the corners.

"Why, it's one fifteen."

He was factual, so her hand took his wrist and bent it, until the luminous dial faced her. "Where will you sleep tonight?" The smile did not change; as she released his wrist, he slipped his hand into hers.

"With you, I believe."

Slowly they walked, and where the excavation ended they moved to the middle of the street, the old woman to one side, peering from under her shawl. Glancing up from his book, the block policeman grinned at Garry.

"So," she purred, her eyes straight ahead, "and have you 300 pesatas?"

"I have only 100—there was the hotel bill, and drinks, but I expect more money tomorrow, from America."

"No," she said, without anger, her lips still smiling. The hand unclasped his, the smooth hip against his moved three inches away; the two women came together. But nothing had changed, really.

"You're beautiful," he said, as they walked.

"Thank you."

"Beautiful," he repeated, more distinctly. "Do you know what that word means? Beautiful?"

"Wait here for us. We walk to Las Ramblas and perhaps will return in five minutes."

Darkness covered them, the younger woman with her peasant stride: back straight and hips pivoting easily on sturdy legs, as if she carried a basket of grapes over a steep, tiered vineyard.

So this is how it goes, he thought. He walked up a short alley to the plaza; here, under the arches of what had been the stalls of an old bull arena, he removed his shoe, took all but a hundred pesata note from his billfold, and put the money into the toe of his shoe and replaced it.

And why had he lied? Why not take the woman—would 300 pesatas, less than five dollars, make any difference?

Not for the money then.

He walked back to the alley's mouth and stood in the shadows. Girls and women drifted in the faint light; the block cop reopened his book as two forms crept past to the lip of the street; they watched the man with the walking stick, then felt their pockets and slithered along the opposite side of the wall.

Garry's foot moved against the wad of money and at the same time he felt in his pocket his only weapon, the cactus bud, or *whatever* it was, dangling like a sap.

Two more Celtas were smoked in ten minutes; when he knew the women weren't returning, he walked back to the serrated darkness of the arcade. Only one of the four corners was lit, where a garish sign said: *American Style Jazz.* Two Negroes, with horn cases, climbed the stairwell and hurried away, in four-four time. A girl's laughter blanketed the square and collected under the arches; the girl soon appeared on the arm of an old, old man. They entered a drop-head Lancia and roared off. Once, in the darkness, Garry was certain he saw Paco's face grinning like a tempter; but when he approached the shadows dissolved.

He lit another cigarette and gave one to the bum who immediately appeared. Soon a girl crossed directly to his cigarette's hot eye. Even in the poor light Garry saw that she was very young and fat. Her line was as direct as her route: Did he fuggee?

When he hesitated, she said: "Fuggee, fuggee, you know?"

"Well, I only have a hundred pesatas—there was the hotel bill, and drinks—"

"Okay," she said, impatiently, a hundred then, for one hour (marking time on his watch). And where was his hotel?

"Oh no," he said, pointing to his wedding ring. He thought of Avis in the airless room, her tight slim body against the wet sheets, waking to the goat cough from the airshaft.

Then another 35 pesatas for a room. One hundred and thirty-five pesatas. Did he or didn't he fuggee? And if not, what the fuggee was he doing here?

"Wait now—" The girl reminded him of her sisters, who stood around slot machines and magazine racks in American bus depots. But to *know* he could have her for a buck and a half, that was good enough, wasn't it: the knowledge itself was a fruitful orgasm. "Wait now, let's talk a bit," he said, his elbow nudging her breast. But he was not surprised when another cigarette bored a red hole into the dark two arches away, and she moved toward it, heels slapping.

He paced the arcade restlessly and six Celtas later found he could have had a dozen women: young, pretty, some not so young or pretty, the fat, the lean. Even one in a house-coat, who flicked the garment open to show him she wore nothing underneath.

And all under the knowing eye of the police.

So when a clock struck three, when even Barcelona dropped into sleep, Garry sat on the curb. He smoked one last Celta, not tasting the harshness, tired and mystified, and now completely sober.

A man and a boy clattered up the empty, silent street; when the boy returned and asked Garry in French for a cigarette, he remembered the robbers. He gave the boy the crumpled pack, and in the match's glow he saw the young, whiskered cheek and bloodshot eye. The boy thanked Garry and asked him to come along—they wished to have a farewell drink.

Not just fear restrained Garry, for he was tired and his teeth and tongue ached, and he thought of Avis alone in her room; he refused, the best his limited French would allow.

So the boy remained bent over him, as if an explanation were necessary. "I came from Paris only yesterday to stay two weeks. And now I leave this damn city."

"But, this is a wonderful city."

"Notice this." His hand, bruised and cut, pointed to the purple blotch under his eye. "The damn police. And I did nothing to deserve it."

"But, I don't understand—this is a grand city."

"Come with us, my friend."

He had no fear now, but again he politely refused, explaining he was resting, getting strength to return to his hotel. The boy clutched Garry's head tightly and, with passion, kissed first one cheek and then the other. "You are a good friend. And remember, to the police I did nothing, nothing at all." He turned, and hurried to catch the older man.

Somewhere the clock struck four, and Garry lifted himself from the curb to lurch through streets where light began to filter. Already peddlers had set up their carts and scrubwomen were returning home. On the sunny side of the street cats washed themselves in every doorway.

This preparation for the new day emphasized to him his weightless, elated fatigue. By the time he reached the *pension* a blister had formed on his lower lip, from the strong Celtas; but he walked faster, hardly noticing his aching toe bent back by the money in his shoe, as if it were a huge sum.

PEGGED

Chris walked quickly, his thick-soled shoes clacking against the red tiles flooded by a late September sun; his shirt front tugged at his belt, his pegged pants legs, tight collar, his clothes made him feel slick as he passed seniors in letterman sweaters, girls whose breasts bounced as they hurried, the boomerboys who gathered at the base of the main stairway to watch the girls. The halls were filled with the noise of happy people, everyone moving with a busyness that amazed him, and made him want to work harder. He felt himself part of a long procession whose energy was ceaseless.

People smiled, said hello even though they might have been together only an hour before; in grade school you might not say hello to a person the entire eight years. But Chris has also learned in this first month that *who* you said hello to depended on who *you* were—people who had been your friends might now look away, or give a brief, blank smile.

"Hi, Ron." In high school names changed, and now Ronnie was Ron, Leonard was Len; some teachers even addressed the boys as Mister. Not only names but people had changed during the summer; he however had not. When he passed the seniors who grouped at the base of the main stairs he saw their hairy arms, the scuff mark of beard, tried to imagine looking like that in only four years. He did not even shave.

"Hi, Horace." Horace shuffled past, hardly looking up, his hand raised in limp salutation; Horace hadn't changed either. In fact, Chris noted, he still wore levis with a big cuff, the kind that they had worn in grade school.

The bell rang, the halls began to empty, and he broke into an easy run, his cleats ringing on the tiles.

The biggest difference between grade and high school, he thought, was that clothes had become very important. He had never thought about clothes before, but now he owned a pair of real levis and white cords, two thin-striped dress shirts with cutaway collars, and a narrow oval belt. His parents had objected to his spending money on these clothes when more practical things were available for less, but his mother had bought him an expensive natural brown cashmere sweater from her summer berry-picking money. He loved the sweater but prized even more his shoes, because he would wear them every day. They were high-toed brogues and he had paid more for them than he, or rather his father, had ever paid for any three pairs of shoes. He had taken them directly to a shoe repair shop and had had an extra half-sole and inset heel cleats added. He had carefully dyed them oxblood, coat after coat, working the leather to a high shine.

He had his mother sew down the belt loops so that the belt rode low on his pants, and then had her cut out a section of the leg, sewing it on a bias until the cuff was so narrow he could barely get his foot through; the turned cuff was reduced to a thin lip. He wore a straight pin through the front of his shirt at the neck, and at the bottom a rubber band linked the shirt's lowest button to the pants' top button, pulling the shirt front down. His mother said that this made him walk stooped over, but he insisted on wearing the rubber band because all the boys did it.

His English class was on the third floor and he took the

steps two at a time; the door was shut, and he opened it as quietly as possible. Half the class turned as he entered, breathing hard and feeling sweaty; he walked to his desk and concentrated on the names carved in its surface. Was Joanne looking at him? he wondered.

Someone was reading aloud, a girl whose name he didn't know. Her voice was clear and cool, and from where he sat he could see that she had long auburn hair and a slim figure. Then, as the sunlight shifted slightly it illuminated her blouse and Chris realized that the shadowy nub he saw through the cloth was her breast. He leaned his head against his hands, so that he could watch her while seeming to have his eyes on his book.

Surrounded by women, he became aware of them in a way that was terrifying. He loved to look at them all, but their physical presence confused him. All seemed so developed, like the women in the Sear's catalogue: most wore blue or white skirts that ended a few inches above the ankle, a white blouse or blue sweater, and saddle shoes. Against the cloth he could see the outline of panties and bra. In grade school he had flirted, had even been in love without telling the girl, had thought of sex in a vague way; now sex seemed essential.

The readers were going around the room, each person reading approximately three paragraphs. He quickly calculated that he would not have to read, but even as he counted paragraphs the readers seemed to read faster, the clock's hands moved more slowly. Shakespeare—he had never even heard of him before except as a joke, and now the whole class was reading his play.

There was a lull between readers and Chris, fearing that the teacher had seen him counting paragraphs and students, searched the page for the last word that echoed in his mind. In grade school he always seemed to get behind right away because he couldn't find a sharp pencil or clean piece of paper; the list of spelling words would grow while he looked through the accumulated junk of his desk. Some nights he had bad dreams about falling behind.

The readers read on, and when they got three students from Chris—the clock hovering on the number—the teacher said that she had to go to the office and asked them to read quietly to themselves. The room was quiet for a full minute, and then, from the back of the room, Dick Garfield belched loudly. Some students laughed. A low buzz of conversation began, like clouds of small flies. The tension was broken.

Chris half-turned in his seat, looked out the window, at the back wall, then at Joanne, who sat behind him. "Hi," he said. She was a fleshy girl with a clean outdoors complexion, and he liked the way she wore her plaid Pendelton skirts. He liked the way she laughed too. She struck him as a girl who was more serious than most of the others—for example, she was one of the few girls he had talked with who wasn't interested in the school's social clubs—and yet a girl you could have fun with.

"Hi," she said, closing her book and putting her pen away. "I like your shirt. Those are neat colors."

"Oh. Thanks." He was pleased, and encouraged. He wanted to ask whether she was going to the game tonight.

She looked at the clock which, he noticed, had again begun to move, and then wound her watch carefully. He wished that he had some gum to offer her, or that he could think of something to say. "You know Marie Schweitzer, don't you?" He knew she did; they came to school on the same bus, and he had seen them together in assemblies. He knew Marie from Math, but not very well. "She was telling me about your new horse," he said, "it sounds real neat." Chris hated horses.

"Yes," she said, "I'm raising him for a 4-H project." She

laid her hands on the desk, palms flat, and said: "Why were you discussing me?"

"Oh, you know," Chris said, feeling his face begin to glow, the tremble moving along his fingers. "It just came up." He partly turned toward his desk, not trusting the voice which would come from his dry throat. He sat there, feeling stupid, a roar growing in his ears.

And then the bell rang.

* * *

Chris sat on the floor in the front room, the phone book opened on his lap; he had found her number, but desire and fear were warring in his stomach and not even the cookies and milk he had had could quell that battle. He had to make the decision of whether to call Joanne—soon his mother and sister would be back from the store, then his father would be pulling into the driveway, and they would eat dinner, listen to the radio, and it would be just another Friday night. But he had never before called a girl for a date.

After school he had followed what was now a pattern, almost a routine: he met Horace at the bus stop and they rode together to Loaner's Corner, talking about the things they enjoyed, guns, hunting, the history of warfare, pulp magazines—a discussion which in some ways was more literate and intellectual than anything heard at school. When he was at school he thought about classes, teachers, clothes, but as he moved farther from it he began to think about other things, things that interested him, and at times he felt as though the school did not exist.

In the Rexall they had bought ice cream cones and planted themselves before the magazine rack, reading EC comics, *Tarzan*, working their way through *True, Argosy, Cycle, The Police Gazette*, whatever they could read before the owner told them that this wasn't a public library.

Then they had walked on, kicking stones, looking in alleys, trying to drum up any kind of adventure, until they finally parted, walking in different directions. Horace didn't ask Chris what he was doing tonight—but then he never did; Horace was either very shy or secretive, Chris couldn't be sure. But he was glad that Horace hadn't asked, because he really didn't know what he would be doing.

He took a deep breath and began to dial; he would do it—he had to start somewhere, sometime. The finger beneath her number trembled and he had to stop before dialing the last two digits—he would ask her to the game; no, to a movie. As the phone rang in his ear he closed his eyes tightly, shutting off everything else. "Hello," the voice said, trailing through wire from her own house. "Hello, Joanne?" He was surprised to hear his own voice from the dry throat, a noise like fingernails across a blackboard; his legs felt weak, suddenly it was difficult to breathe. "One moment, I'll call her."

Then after a long wait, during which he saw himself holding hands with Joanne, walking beside her down a pleasant tree-lined street, like two people in a Coke ad over the Rexall's counter, he heard her voice. "Hello?"

"Hi." For the first time he said aloud the words that he had rehearsed in his mind, working to get them letter perfect. "Would you like to go to a movie tonight?"

"Who is this?"

"Uh it's Chris." The hand at his side tightened into a fist; he was so stupid, he should have said who he was and *then* suggested that they go to a movie.

"Who?" she asked.

"Chris—from English One."

"Oh." Pause. "Oh, hi. It's very nice of you to call and ask me to the movie, Chris, but I'm afraid that I have a prior engagement. I'm really very sorry."

"Oh sure," he said, "that's okay." He should have told her his name immediately, should have called a week or two ago—you didn't call a girl the same evening you were asking her out, not a girl like Joanne anyway. He wondered how he could face her Monday in class. He shouldn't have called.

Then, as if the empty feeling was suddenly filled with the sense of relief, he dialed Horace's number, and asked if he'd like to sleep on Indian Rock tonight, which might possibly be the last good night of the year.

* * *

They walked through Dwyer's mill loaded with sleeping bags, knapsacks, canteens, and both wore .22 pistols at their belts and carried .22 rifles. They turned off the road and hiked into Indian Rock at dusk, the late September sun settling beyond the log piles. Indian Rock, once a stone quarry, was a complex of paths which wound around huge boulders and wooded areas. Although it wasn't far from their homes, in the dark night with the rock cliffs reaching toward the stars they might have been in North Africa, in the Sudan Camel Corps—a fighting outfit they both intended to join someday.

It was dark by the time they had collected wood and had a fire built, spreading their sleeping bags beside it. They cut potatoes into a frying pan, then cooked weiners and eggs in the same pan. Chris sat cross-legged on his bag, savoring even those potato slices which were not done. He ate quickly, drank from the canteen, and leaned back, enjoying the odor of burning wood on the chilled air, the smoke which rose to the star-hung sky. He thought of ancient Egypt, the pyramids, the mysteries of time; he imagined himself at the Khyber Pass, or fighting the Fuzzy-Wuzzies, or with T.E. Lawrence. School seemed as remote as those stars. He thought of Joanne, and although he felt a pang of regret, loss, he was glad she had turned him down—how would he have picked her up, with no car or even a driver's license? He must have been berserk as a thug to have called her.

They lay in their bags talking, looking at the stars, listening to the voices from the mill and the high whine of the buzz saw, watching the fire burn to bright embers. It was too early for sleep and he felt restless; although it was good to be here on the mountainside, with a fire and a rifle at hand, there had to be more to the adventure.

"Want to walk to Loaner's Corner?" Horace asked, as if reading his mind. "We could get some weeds."

"Sure," he said. They killed the fire, then put their sleeping bags and guns under a small tree where they wouldn't be seen by anyone—lovers, bums, cops—who might come up here.

It wasn't that either Horace or Chris was crazy about smoking, but rather that smoking fit in with a kind of life they imagined—drawing rooms with heavy leather chairs, the Explorer's Club, rum-soaked cheroots, massive pipes with silver lids, latticed-windows, shutters, a fireplace, rows of books, crossed sabres on the wall, coin collections, a glass of brandy, a suit of armor. Therefore, when they went downtown they would stop at Meier and Frank's and attempt to get some older person—usually a woman—to buy cigars for them, or they would get a pack of cigarettes from a vending machine; but these were stored away, for some obscure event or emergency, and at times like tonight, when they wanted to smoke, they would pick up the longest cigarette butts they could find and reroll the tobacco into a piece of paper.

They walked past the mill, where the night shift worked in the steam-filled room and the headlights of Hysters spilled crazily between the stacks of lumber, crossed Johnson Creek, and went down Foster Road, searching the gutter for a good butt. Chris felt a real sense of excitement; he felt like Alan Ladd without a trenchcoat, or like Holmes and Watson on a case—his own neighborhood approached from the reverse side had the allure of Tangiers or Casablanca.

They walked slowly to Loaner's Corner, and stood in the apron of light from the Rexall's windows. Some toughs were hanging around in front of the Aero theater, and a drunk staggered out of the Rose Lantern. They debated about going inside the Rexall and reading magazines, or whether they should wait until they found someone who would give them a cigarette or maybe buy them a pack. Chris, who was afraid that his father might drive by and see him standing on the corner, thought that they should head back; they had a good pocketful of butts, and by the clock in the drugstore he could see that it was 9:30. They went into the Texaco station, copped a handful of toilet paper, and began to walk back.

The brightness of Loaner's Corner faded into occasional arc lights which dotted Foster Road, and when they got past Dwyer's mill the blackness was total. They stumbled along the rutted trail, unable to see even the trees on each side, the shadows darker than night.

Something brushed Chris's fingers. "Wait, hold it." He stopped, reached upward, his hand clawing the invisible wall.

"What's up?" Horace asked.

Chris felt it again, cutting the air at waist level, and he said, "Come on," moving quickly back to the pavement of the road. Horace, surprised, beginning to fear the darkness, followed close behind; he was chuckling but the soft laughter was edged with terror. "What was it?"

"A string, stretched across the road. It wasn't there when we came down so that means someone's been here—is here."

"A string—what for?"

"I don't know, maybe it's a warning device." Chris imagined that the string led to a bell or was perhaps tied around the toe of the person who had put it there, and anything breaking the tension on the string would warn the man. "We could go around from the west, circle in from behind." They then realized that whoever was up there not only had the sleeping bags and food but also the guns.

They walked back downhill to the security of the mill's lights, wondering what to do—they could talk with the mill guard, or call a policeman, or call their fathers, but they hesitated, reluctant to admit they had got themselves into a fix. They didn't want to admit that they were terrified of whatever was on the hill. If only they hadn't left the guns there, if only they had stayed in camp. . .

"You sure there was a string?"

"Sure I'm sure—I felt it, a cord right across the road. It wasn't a spiderweb, it wasn't anything that was there before."

Because they didn't know what else to do, they walked slowly back to the security of Loaner's Corner, to figure things out. Now it was ten o'clock and the only businesses open were the taverns, who shed little light on the street. The Aero was still open but had turned out its marquee lights to save money. They walked on to 82nd Street, and crossed it to Merhar's, a drive-in which was open all night. They sat at the counter, drinking Cokes, watching the toughs around the pinball machine, the scuffle at the doorway. Merhar's served some rough customers—cyclists, hoods in smoking jalopies without fenders, men with high waves in their slick hair—and Chris wondered what these people did, how they lived, what their strange lives were like. Ann Martin, a girl he had seen at school, left a low Ford convertible and walked through the restaurant to enter the restroom; she wore bright lipstick the color of her maroon skirt, and

Chris watched furtively as she walked past. He liked to imagine what she was up to—would he ever have the guts to call her sometime?

When they looked at the clock they saw the minutes passing too slowly.

With only a quarter between them and the curfew coming, they couldn't stay in Merhar's all night. They left shortly after eleven, walking slowly toward Loaner's Corner; one by one houses went dark, people drifted into bed and the sweetness of sleep. On the road an occasional car passed, tail-lights quickly disappearing into the night.

In Loaner's Corner they went into a doorway and sat on the stairs that led to the apartments and the dentist's office above. To pass the time and buoy their spirits they peeled the paper from a dozen butts, broke the tobacco up, and rolled it into a piece of toilet paper. Horace lit the match, which flared in the dark hallway, and puffed on the ragged cigarette, fanning sparks into the air. "Hmmm," he said, passing it to Chris, who put the wet paper to his lips, puffed hard, felt the harsh smoke rush into his throat—he liked the odd sensations along his mouth, nose, the slightly dizzy feeling in his head. It reminded him of last year, when he had had a paper route and kept a cigarette in the bike's handlebar which he took out and lit from time to time.

Later, afraid that someone would catch them on the narrow staircase, they walked again, slowly, in the direction of Indian Rock and their own houses—it was only a matter of turning one way or the other. They didn't even ask whether they should go home—it would be too difficult to explain the situation, they would be laughed at, kidded.

Chris, worried about his gun, which was a present from his father, thought that they should sneak back again. "Here's what we'll do," he said, "we'll wait a while, until that guy has given up on us and then we'll cut back the other way, from behind."

Horace snuffled, leaned into the night slump-shouldered. "What'll we do until then?"

Although they yearned for the lights of Loaner's Corner they didn't want to walk that way again, but there was nothing in the other direction except the city limits, a few houses whose yards sloped off into pastures. Across the street was a small factory which made concrete blocks, a corrugated tin roof supported by semi-open walls. They went inside and stood by a stack of blocks for a minute; then Horace slumped to a pile of gunny sacks and Chris climbed on the seat of a fork-lift truck—it was soft if not warm, and as he sat down he was suddenly very tired, as if he had been walking for hours. His eyes burned from a lack of sleep and from the odor of limestone which filled the air; he closed them, leaned his head against the steel framework which protected the driver, thought about his guns and Joanne. Probably her prior engagement, as she put it, was with a boomer-boy, a senior with his own car; probably she had gone to the game, then the dance, and perhaps even to a party, and was now home in bed while he leaned against the cold metal of the fork-truck in this brick factory. There were people who made the right moves, and there were others who didn't.

He did not really sleep all night—he would doze for a few minutes, then shake himself awake and look around, heart pounding wildly until he realized where he was. Sometimes he got up, climbed off the fork-lift truck, and stretched his cramped, cold legs; he walked around, talked with Horace, then climbed back on his seat. He had never spent such a bad night, and he had never known such a long one. Each time he opened his eyes the sky looked the same, black beyond the timberwork of the building. Hours later, when he despaired of ever seeing daylight again, he heard the noise of birds—dozens of them, from the sound—and finally, after dozing some more, he opened his eyes to a gray-white sky. Stiffly he climbed down from the machine and stomped his shoes against the floor to shake the blood into his legs; he was cold, cramped, tired, and miserable.

They walked through the mill as the false dawn shifted toward day, and a mist rose as the sun broke through to burn away the dew. Indian Rock was a clump of gray boulders rising from the eerie mist. Leaving the road they walked cautiously along the ruts, searching the ground and trees for anything unusual—but there was no string, nothing. "I know it was here," Chris said, examining the trees for any trace of string or scraped bark or footprints. They moved on through the mist, came over the rise and entered the flat space where they had camped a long night before; under the tree where they had left them were the sleeping bags, knapsacks, their guns. Chris belted on his pistol, examined the cylinder for loads, and looked down the road, wondering what it was he could have felt in the night.

OVERTURES TO MOTION

The horses rattled in the same traces; the wagon still traveled on bent hubs, so the wheels canted a foot sideways for every foot forward. But this fair Benton was three inches taller, and soon he would not need to tilt his head to look directly into his father's eyes, when they spoke.

And, although the same rolling scrub trees and clay banks moved past, Benton felt a year's change: an engine inside drove bones to the skin's limits, extended the taut ropes of tendons.

Thinking this, he was not surprised when the balloon's pink and red bulk did not stir restlessly this year. What he saw, at the last rise, as he squinted along the valley floor to the sprawling gridwork of ridge-poles, canvas, and makeshift shacks, was a cross shaped shadow of red and blue. Benton's eyes did not release the bright cross during the wagon's fretful descent: the gliding curve of fabric and wood, tapering from the three sets of wings to the high, broad tail-fin, and all held together by the framework of struts and wires blazing in the sun. Centered behind the wings was the motor: a bright continuum of baffles and tubing and riveted plates.

Then the wagon settled on the valley floor, and the hunched buildings interfered. As Benton helped his father unload the sides of smoked meat, he swore he would *not* go down that road toward the field and the aeroplane—until after dinner.

He unhitched the team, and watered and picketed them in the shade behind Main street. But energy still pounded at his temples, so he walked up and down the town, seeing nothing, talking to no one; his boots struck the dirt in hard, heavy steps, calculated to tire him. Walked, and shifted his itching shoulders against the hot sun.

Fraaaaaaap. Ahhhh, he heard, a rising and falling sound; a mechanical imitation of energy and pleasure. He looked, for the first time, at the aeroplane. But its propeller, a gleaming, razored log, was still.

Fraaaaap. Ahhhhh, he heard, and the noise turned his head the other way, where a cloud of dust moved up the hill, toward town.

Cyclone, a man yelled. Horses shied, pawing the air.

The cloud mounted, and then Benton made out the dust-brown dot at its head—a motor-car. It passed out of sight, but soon reappeared at the end of the street; its horn warned twice, but the motor-car did not slow for the dogs which ran to meet it.

Fraaaaaaaap, he heard, the high tires speeding at him; and as he jumped to the board sidewalk, a sound of *Ahhhhhhhhh*, when the driver—hunched over the wheel, goggles dull with dust, cap worn backwards—jerked the lever beside the seat. Benton saw the flash of the brass radiator, beaded with dust, like sweat on a golden muscle; the wooden spoked wheels spinning in reverse; he smelled the sharp odor of gasoline and leather. The machine roared past, in the noise of pleasure, and beyond the town spun to a stop beside the aeroplane.

Benton had said he wouldn't go, that he could not be satisfied with anything once he had seen the aeroplane, perhaps touched its varnished fabric; yet he jumped into the crowd of men and boys who ran through the falling, filtering dust.

At the field, the Driver faced the group of angry townsmen. The Sheriff touched his gun handle, but when his hand came back it was only a finger he pointed. The Driver had slid his goggles to the top of his head, and now he spread his legs and the four eyes stared down. "You folks got to get used to this Century," he said. Laughing, he walked to the rear seat of the motor-car, where he lifted out a piece of gleaming wood wider than the machine. Benton saw another man coming out of the aeroplane's motor—raising his legs around pipes and heavy brass tubes—to receive the new propeller. Gently, he laid it on the open strutwork of the fuselage.

"Okay, move back," the Sheriff said, waving people off the field. "Do not want any taxpayers killed."

Benton walked to the wagon, his fingers imitating how the Mechanic had fitted a spanner on a bolt; there was a kind of naturalness in the way such things went together. A union.

And as the family ate dinner beneath the wagon, Benton thought only about how a man could take metal, wood, and fabric, join these with his own hands, and *fly*. He did not hear his father mention that the smoked hams and bacon sides had been sold, nor did he hear his father's plan to buy some mill lumber. Absolutely committed to the machine, what he did hear was the sound of prairie grass brushing the aeroplane's lower wing, and the wind strum and chord through the taut wire-work which held the machine together: a tune he recognized.

As the family walked with the others to the edge of town, Benton decided he would ask his father for a dollar. That was what it cost, he had heard, to go *up*. But when they reached the field, where grass bent like silk in the wind, he did not ask. For his father was laughing, softly, and when Amos walked past, the father said: "Going up again this year, Amos?"

"Nosir," Amos said, his arms pumping at his sides. "I am not. It likely won't get offn the ground."

"That's what I told the boy again," his father said. "It ain't going nowheres." The two men laughed, in agreement.

His father did not believe in these machines, and so it was useless to ask for the dollar. Last year, when the price was twenty-five cents to ride the balloon, when there was an offer of two *free* tickets, Benton had not gone. *We could go, Pop*, he had pleaded. *Nothing's free*, his father had said, *and anyways, it ain't going nowheres*. He had been right, last year.

It was Amos, the blacksmith, and Parsons, the town drunk, who had climbed into the wicker basket, where a crackling, smokeless fire shimmered the field into a mirage. And it was Parsons who, as the warm bag shot skyward, had fallen to one side, tipping the delicate assemblage; when the shower of sparks began to eat away the fabric, Benton had heard three identical noises: his racing heart, his father's laugh, and the ropes which supported the basket burning through—popping sounds, like hickory knots.

In the last twenty feet the burning bag became free, to slowly fold in upon itself, and float south. The basket had plunged its bottom into the hard earth and collapsed, spilling the three men. But before the stunned crowd had reached them, Parsons was on his feet, holding up his pants with one hand and staring at the broken suspender strap in the other, while Amos and the Pilot walked unsteadily away, in separate directions.

Today it was a different Pilot who stood in the back of the open motor-car, buttoning his heavy jacket. The crowd stopped where the Sheriff pulled on one end of a rope, and over the tops of heads Benton saw the Mechanic wipe his hands, and climb into the network of silver wires; with his flashing spanner, he played them like a harp. Over thick black hair the Pilot pulled a chamois helmet, wiped his goggles on his leg, and stepped to the ground. Benton saw the puttees and patent slick boots walk in jerky steps to the aeroplane where, without hesitation, the Pilot's hand shot out and caught a steel bar; he swung up, to perch ahead of the radiator. He raised one finger.

As the Mechanic slowly turned the propeller, someone laughed. Benton tensed, and realized it was his father. The propeller was rotated a half-dozen times. Then the Mechanic teetered on his toes, cupped both hands over the tip of the blade, and spun it by jumping to the ground.

The cloud of white smoke which enveloped the fuselage began to dissolve before Benton heard the staggered roar. The propeller whipped to a shiny blur. Then spun backwards, and stopped.

As if this were a bad sign, the Mechanic kicked the dirt where he stood, and scrambled back into the strutwork. He rotated the blade again, and shouted something to the Pilot. His hands cupped the propeller, and like a suicide he threw himself off.

After a hundred heartbeats, the propeller cleared the white smoke away. The ragged wheezing of pistons smoothed; the grass around was assaulted, the dust below driven up.

Now the Mechanic ran toward the crowd, his fist in the air, thumb raised.

At the other end of the Sheriff's rope, there was a struggle; men ducked under the rope, laughing, pushing one man ahead of them. The Mechanic got the dollar in one hand, while his other held the crowd's volunteer by the elbow, steering him toward the aeroplane; halfway across, the passenger reeled, spun around, and fell to his knees. Benton recognized the absurd, blank face: it was Parsons.

The Mechanic half-carried the unprotesting Parsons to the front of the machine, where the Pilot pulled him up.

The motor raised its tempo of anarchy. Grass flattened.

The sets of wings rocked, the invisible propeller sawed air, and the aeroplane began to move—although at first Benton imagined that he was moving. It bounced down the field, picked up speed, and turned into the wind; under his shirt, Benton felt his shoulders shift. Then the craft skimmed the waist-high grass, and just as Benton felt himself lifted off the ground, he saw the fuselage part—the back half jab the earth, crumple, splinter, and stop; the front half speed along the margins of flight, bumping, moving forward like a pole-axed steer, and then, as he realized the propeller had come loose, to slice the machine neatly in two, the mobile half flipped over and the engine stopped.

The Sheriff's rope gave under the surging crowd. Benton, running from his father's whooping laughter, was halfway across the field when he saw the Pilot rise from the grass, twenty feet past the aeroplane. When Benton got to the wreck, the Pilot was already there, staring at it through broken goggles; he kicked the wing, and walked quickly toward the motor-car.

The Sheriff and two other men began ripping apart the twisted mass of fabric and wood, until they found Parsons, his hands still clutching the sides of the wicker seat.

"Is he dead?" people asked.

"Yeah, dead drunk," the Sheriff said.

Benton was the last to leave. As the Mechanic circled the wreck, picking up pieces, Benton thought: Why, a man could put her together again. For the machine did not seem badly hurt—it was mostly that the bottom wing was on top. A man could right it, and fit the two halves together. And if done properly, she would fly. No doubt.

II

Summer was stasis, and unendurable: the hoe was a propeller, spinning in the sun; later, as the plants went skyward, the wind caressing their leaves was the sound of air over taut fabric. Every day Benton chopped the ground, as if digging himself to another place, but the journey was from the row point and back.

Hoe and bucket handle were hot as summer, and when he stopped to scan the horizon, where low hills shimmered into sky, his impatience turned to fear. Everywhere beyond that line, *things were happening.* While his feet toed the unyielding dirt, men were putting engines into the ground, to move the world ahead and past him; or sending their buildings into the sky, their metal ships to sea, their air-machines to the moon. He staggered with this vision of the world as a complex, mechanical arrangement of pistons and gears, gasoline and smoke, racing into the century.

Here, was stasis. The only change was the cage-work of mill lumber which grew to lean against the house. Benton saw the addition as a cage, but at one point, before the siding went on, the construction had resembled the framework of an aeroplane. The sturdy uprights, the gusseted beams, the windows like a closed cockpit. And inside, piloting this addition to the bedroom, was his father.

And when Benton did see the skeletal geometry of yellow pine and red cedar not as a cage but rather its opposite, he was reminded of the wrecked aeroplane.

He had been right: a man could put the two halves

together, and it would fly. Because the day after the crash, he had heard, twelve men and Amos' biggest wagon had been hired to get the machine to the railroad; there it had been put on a flatcar, and taken to the State Capital.

When they had restrung and paneled and spliced her, no doubt she would fly at the next fair.

Above, the burning sky; below, the land. The wind blew, the leaves hummed like feathers, and the ground before his eyes became a study in motion: the rich alluvial soil lifted, moved downhill, or flung itself skyward in clouds, where it sifted to the grass across the creek. Benton chopped furiously at the ground, to stay it; and as dirt crumbled around his ankles, claiming him, he sank—but drove no roots.

III

Fair day again, Benton had his ear tuned to the wind, should an engine cast its *sccrrruuuuuuub-kkkkk* over the gulleys and washouts. For he had heard it, yesterday. But the sun was a flame, the sky a reflector: he could not have missed seeing the aeroplane pass over. Or aeroplanes. For the faint *sccrrruuuuuub-kkkk*, breaking and shattering on the hard land, seemed to be the noise of several motors.

"Get cash," his father warned.

"Sure, sure," Benton said, edging to the door, listening. He returned, to get his hat and gloves. "Sure, Pop."

Today his father was not laughing: the leg, above the crusted bandage, was blue-green—like water reflecting sky. He would be laid up for Doc did not know how long. Which was why Benton must get cash for the hog.

Lying beside his father—like two plowed furrows—was

Benton's mother. The Doc, who was treating both patients for the price of one, was more certain in her case: it would be just any day now. Anyway, the extra bedroom had been built; the family could grow.

He watched his parents—his father growing more furious on this bed; his mother, gentle in her pregnancy. Benton shuffled his boots, fiddled with his hat, and then—aware of the the contrast his restless strength made—took the sandwiches and water-jug from his sister and strode from the room.

"Cash," his father shouted, "make 'em pay by the pound."

His voice raged as Benton whipped the team across the yard, through the trees and to the road—as if the boy's whip reached to flick the tender leg. The man helpless, another mouth to feed coming, and the family's wealth must be trusted to a boy with no head for practical business.

When the house was a dot behind him, Benton wrapped both reins in one solid fist and stood high on the wagon seat. His whip bit the oily flanks, until the horses hurtled in terror toward the valley, their heads thrown back, eyes rolling, the wagon bucking in pursuit. At each chuck-hole the bent axles screamed a protest, and the hog was pitched on his side.

Benton had never gone so fast: standing on the seat, the wind laying his brim back, tearing at his shirt cuffs, he stood on the world. The scenery blurred past, unrecognized. His body rolled, the wind screamed down his throat, tore at his eyes—until it seemed he must be flying.

Not until the last rise sped to meet him did he release the reins. And when he felt the wagon begin the descent, he opened his stinging eyes to the valley floor. But saw no aeroplane. Or even a balloon, although he could barely remember the one two years before. There was nothing, except a thin plume of dust from the horse track. His heart flaked a beat, and his eyes closed again.

Today, there would have been a chance . . .

Downhill the wagon screeched and groaned, and it was not until he yanked on the brake at the livestock building, and silenced the scream of the wagon's dry hubs, that he heard the report: SCCRRRUUUUUB-KKK. The sound shattered conversation, like summer thunder.

"Why, what is it?" he asked the first man.

"Fool nonsense," the man said, marking in a tally-book.

"But what KIND of fool nonsense?" Benton asked, standing on the seat to locate the noise.

"This particular fool nonsense," the man said, without looking up, "is motor-cars. At the trot-race track."

Dust clouds, brown duplicates of the trees, circled the horse track. As Benton's feet hit the ground in a fast run, he was recalled by the noise at his back—the hog struggled against the rope wrapped tightly around its feet.

Benton came through the slot between buildings and walked to the fence. The motor-cars were in the paddock: two-seaters, with hoods long as a wagon, and tires almost as tall as Benton. The body on each ended at the jutting steering wheel; behind this was a fuel tank, and three spare tires.

And as a plume of dust accelerated from the north turn, Benton heard the sound of anarchy which had carried to him over the baked street and sagging tent tops. A sheet of dirt spewed beside the leaning machine; it straightened, and the back half was lost in lines of speed.

Fraaaaaaap, the crescendo grew as Benton jumped the top rail and dropped into the track, and when it passed he was in the middle of the machines—black, red, green, yellow, they opened like immense, rare prairie flowers—where Mechanics hammered and cussed and crawled into engines. His hand touched the great golden radiator shrouds; his finger traced the name plaques: Ford, Stanley, Bugatti, Peugeot, Daimler-Benz . . .

While he hoed and carried water, men had hammered out their ideas, and carved the oak wheels, and cast these parts: they had given motion to their dreams.

Fraaaaaap, came another down the straight, and Benton jumped when the boot struck his ankle. Two booted feet clawed the ground, followed by legs and a fat body; finally the greased face, divided by a huge mustache, squinted up at him.

The Mechanic got to his feet and for a long minute studied Benton. He wiped his hands, then squeezed the boy's arms, and said: "Harjar like to work on her?"

Benton didn't understand until the Mechanic led him to the other side of the high hood. An angular, knee-high steel block waited in its own oil.

"Transmissin," the Mechanic said. On his haunches beside the motor-car, he regarded the boy, the dark metal, and the bottle in his hand; after a long drink he said: "She's too heavy for one. Harjar like to help?"

When the man's feet disappeared, Benton grabbed the steel—fingers slipping in delicious grease—and budged it. As if he had been waiting for this, with every muscle he directed the heavy metal upward, to the motor-car's floor. Steel edges crossed his palm; grease pushed in to stop the blood. When the world shifted, he laid his head against the warm, lacquered body.

"Harjar like to move it," the voice came up, "to the middle. Don't drop it, for chrissakes."

Benton slid the metal housing to the hole, and lowered it into the Mechanic's waiting hands.

"Holdit," the Mechanic said, "holdit." Through a crack Benton saw the man slipping bolts into holes, and, arms trembling, he realized the motor-car was being assembled, becoming continuous, from front to back.

When Benton's arms were dead, the Mechanic clawed his

way from beneath the machine and sprawled beside the dull brown tire. "Well, harjar like working on her?"

Benton found himself accepting the bottle, and his first hard liquor—it tasted of rubber, smoke, gasoline, and lacquer. He drank again, corked the bottle and passed it back. "Like it fine," he said, and sat on the tire, as if he did this everyday.

The Mechanic burped, got to his feet, and raised the hood. While his fingers made adjustments, Benton stared into the complex of tubes, foundry brass, and riveted plates. His fingers touched the top of the motor, and somehow, as the dark metal pulsed, he knew that this would be called the Head. And the functional, neat bowl with its directed copper lines, nestled in the pocket under the porcelain exhaust pipes, would be called the Carburetor. Yet he had never heard these words.

"On the motor," he asked, touching the efficient, curved bowl, "would this be called the Carburetor?"

"Why yes," the Mechanic said, raising his greasy skull cap in mock salute. " 'Cept it is not 'motor,' but engine. N-JINE. Motors are ee-lectrical; engines, internal combustion."

"Ee-lectrical?" Benton said.

"Ain't never heard of ee-lectricity?" He laughed, and passed the bottle. "M'boy, the world is going right past you."

He woke to the staccato of engines.

First, he felt the barbs of straw under his head; then tasted the metallic whiskey; then realized all the engines in the world raised and lowered their voices beyond the stable door.

And last of all, he remembered: He had paid the Mechanic five dollars of his Daddy's money. To ride in this race.

The starting gun fired at him as he ran out the door and

plunged to the ground, his legs unsure; he was standing when the wall of high, narrow tires and brass radiators charged, engines rising and falling—FRRAAAAP-AAHHHHHH—in mechanical anarchy and pleasure. The Stanley shook itself past him, a tire scraping Benton's knee, and accelerated in a silent burst of steam toward the first turn.

Benton flapped his arms as the Ford, straight and spindly, swung at him; the passenger waved back. Below the chamois cap and goggles, Benton thought he recognized the passenger: Parsons.

And this thought drove him into the lunging motor-cars, where the dust obscured him and the exhaust muffled his cries.

In the final motor-car he saw the Mechanic, grinning beneath his wide mustache. The Driver was a smooth faced young man, whose hand flipped the shifting rod in confident motions. They did not see Benton; as the motor-car passed, his fingers clutched the spare tires on the back, and with long running steps he followed his thoughts, to swing his legs into the high, narrow rubber circles. His body folded, his feet braced, dust and exhaust spun up to blot the world from his sight.

AAHHHHHH, he heard near his ear, the motor-car sliding into the first turn, the clincher rims slicing his shoulder blades—sliding, sliding, and then FFRRAAAAAAP, as the track became a straight line. Benton's only regret was he could not see where he was going, but where he had been: the dust, the brown track unreeling, and, dimly, the continuous white line of the top rail. But he could *feel* the vibrations of movement—of power transmitted from engine to driving wheels—and he could *sense* the motions of speed—the motor-car angled forward to its destiny, the lines of speed blurring back from the great brass radiator shroud.

A long slide through the north turn: the motor-car leaning, tipping, jumping out of its groove toward the oblivious grandstands, then aligning itself toward safety.

Down the straight in a terrible burst of speed and past the crowd, where Benton saw men pointing at him.

In the dust of the south turn, Benton saw tires and a brass shroud six inches away. It was not fear, but whiskey, he tasted, as the big Stanley plowed toward the spare tires. When he could almost read the Non-Skid printed on the tread pursuing, his machine slid beneath him, spun sideways, and as fenceposts flashed a hand's span away, the Stanley steamed past. His Driver accelerated back on the track, and as the north turn neared, the whiskey bottle flew over his head—a familiar, silver glint.

Sliding, bouncing again, and at the grandstand the Sheriff ran alongside the motor-car, his huge hand reaching to pluck Benton from the race. Benton was reminded, for an instant, of his father.

Around and around, the track unreeled. Again at the south curve a machine raced through the dust at him, sliding and weaving, the passenger leaning over the side. When the tire was three inches from Benton's nose, he read Ford on the radiator; now he was certain, in spite of the exhaust smoke and dust, that the passenger was Parsons.

Through the turn the two machines moved as one; side by side they slid, subjects of centrifugal force. The Ford dropped back, its spinning wheel beside Benton's face, and it appeared that Parsons was leaning out to speak to him. At that moment the Ford pulled ahead, passed, and something happened which Benton couldn't see. Perhaps the Driver had to release one hand from the wheel, to pull Parsons back.

At first, there was only the impact.

As his machine glided at an angle to the curve, he saw the Ford dart through the inside rail in a shower of splinters and lumber; when its front wheels collapsed, the motor-car arched and tipped on its slim radiator as Parsons shot from the seat.

Under Benton's machine, the sound of breaking steel. The ground dropped away and the world was quietly upside down for a second; it was corrected with a stunning jar. The rod which held the spare tires to the frame pulled free, and Benton and tires were whirled high into space, spinning higher and higher; the smashed motor-cars, the dust, the grandstand, were left behind as the disc whirled across the flat country. Benton, finally flying, braced his feet and back against the rims as earth and sky and earth merged into a continuous dizzy blur.

When the coupled tires landed, it was precisely on the road. They bounced in progressively gradual arcs, with Benton spread in the center like spokes on a hub. When the leaping stopped, the tires balanced down the wagon ruts, spinning to the south, away from home. The land dropped away and the thin plume of dust traced Benton's accelerated voyage.

Benton had no regrets: he had sold the hog, and all but five dollars of the money was in his pocket. And the new baby would replace him at the table. He must leave, any way he could, before everything had been done and said.

The road unfolded and Benton, utterly committed, watched the new World spin dizzily past toward the hard, uncertain horizon.

PSALMS

I

A covered porch, the long railing supported by posts so crude they must have been hand-carved, and on the porch some furniture—the wicker rocker, slat-back bench, a sturdy deal table. The porch is wide, wood floored, and slightly slanted so that water will run into the ivy that grows along the lattice work that is the house's foundation. Beyond the porch the weather alternates between a heavy, clinging mist and a downpour; the corner drainpipe gurgles, there is the flat persistent sound of big drops from the eaves. From inside the house a radio alternates between music and commercials, both belying the mood of the weather.

The man in the wicker chair tilts back, feet propped against the rail, a toothpick balanced on his lower lip, and studies the rivulets of water that churn toward a drainage ditch. The man sitting on the top step just under the eave's shelter rolls a cigarette; he lights it, watches the cloud curl toward the darkening sky.

The fragment recalled is berry-picking in Gresham, perhaps, or the hop-yards near Independence, or bean fields along the Columbia—no matter, nor does it matter whether the one man is my father, though he may well be. What matters is the infinite patience in their stance, speech, sensibilities—if they are cursing the weather that keeps them from the fields it goes unheard. They accept the rain as they accept a tire patched twenty times going flat or an overloaded trailer breaking a spring or a car that will not start—yes, those things or a child crying, a dog splayed across the road, an early thaw, a late freeze, rules, the law. They exist, sure as death.

II

What I want to remember is half-true, half imagined: that men celebrated a cup of hot coffee, a woman, a good machine; that they lived close to the edge, belts tightened against all hungers; that real pleasures were simple, simple pleasures real; that desire was insistent—a house, new car, a pair of warm socks, drinking whiskey—but failure not a curse. That life, which is all we've got, was lived.

III

I need to remember the two Indians who have lived rent free forever on the lower Umpqua; their houseboats are governed only by the tides. They pay no taxes, and therefore every five years they are evicted by the State, their houseboats sold at public auction. The only bidders are the old men who offer five dollars for the other's house, and without carrying off even a blanket they trade houses, dogs, rowboats, trotlines, coffee pots, woodpiles, floats: each moves into the other's life.

IV

Coffee in a thick white mug; a rented room over a theater, above the noise of traffic; the work line; white Relief gravy on bread; roll-your-own smokes; a racy paperback by Faulkner; a car without windows; the pungent odor of kerosene; boots.

How many people do you know with only one suit of clothes?

V

In Mexico you see a man walking in a killing heat, machette in hand, picking up any scrap of paper, tin, wood; nothing is wasted, except the man's life. Beggars near the market, the boy at the cafe's back door waiting for garbage, shepherds alone in the hills for months. In Greece there was a man whose work was carrying rainwater from the roof to the kitchen. The policeman patrolling in the Pryenees, miles from a human voice.

In Detroit and Lansing and Flint the assembly lines turn out men who sleep badly, dream of some green land; they turn to beer, campers, snowmobiles, and wait eagerly for the pension.

VI

When were you last hungry?

VII

Nearly 50,000 Americans killed in action; four times that many South Vietnamese soldiers killed; twenty times that number of North Vietnamese soldiers killed—900,000. Over a million military deaths, and the radio commentator estimates twice that many civilians have been killed. The U.S. has dropped 7 million tons of bombs on Viet Nam—three times the amount dropped in all of WW II.

An estimated three million dead—or 3,000,000: writing it in figures still does not impress us enough. We need to see each death—the falling, dreams bursting, the subdued panic as a life is released. We need a thumbnail portrait of each casualty; what did the victim think about, aspire to, hope for, dream of, desire? What were his pleasures?

Instead, the camera shows us the survivors, and its objectivity terrifies me as much as does their impassiveness. They pick up pieces of brick or tin, shore together a hovel, sit smoking in its entrance. Terror, yes, but I want to cheer their patience, persistence, their acceptance of life. At the table in my warm kitchen I sit amazed at their tenacity for living—this is what I need to remember, to celebrate.

VIII

I need to remember to be like my children, concerned with living, not life—they ignore lungs blossoming like pink flowers, breathing in and out, the heartbeat, but they know the rhythms of life. They see, hear, and recall everything—words, music, flowers, the wind rattling dead grass, books, the smell of crayon on paper. Their world is at eye level, and near. Curiosity is the blue air they swim through.

I think at these times of other fathers who love their children: bucking the bread lines, the assembly lines, whose hearts ride like stones when dreams diminish. Television deaths are false, but what of the father who looks skyward to see the long gray line of bombs falling, or sees his family trapped behind the shifting borders of war. What persistence to live drives the man who has lost his children, or children who have lost parents?

At night the room breathes with their honest sleep, their faces tanned cameos against pillows. This is when I love them most, and have the greatest fears: war, famine, disease, accident, strangers, but most of all the passage of time. I need to remember that we have to collect each day in hand, each minute—time passes, lives overlap, and already they are growing past my eye level.

THE POSTCARD MYSTERIES

From eaves hang icicles like old men's beards. Like dragon's teeth. Like a rip-saw blade. Like silver bars. Chrome strips. Like icicles. Each apple on the leafless tree has a perfect cap of snow. The apples on the ground grow crisp with frost, harden. In spring I will walk on the dark meat of decay. I call this working the earth.

After lunch I hurry to the mailbox, followed by the crunch of my footsteps. The salt truck roars past, the crystals seeking any metal. Some bounce to the edge, chew at my shoes, gnaw pants legs—tomorrow I will wake and find them ragged to the knee, as if the cloth had been soaked in battery acid.

The mailbox holds another postcard.

> *Dear Friend Dena*
> *We received a big letter from Papa, Anna is going to send hers later on because the envelope would be to heavy. Papa was well all the way over, Anna was sick in the beginning but in the end she did not want to get off the boat.*
> *Lucy*

Jethro stomps through the shiny kitchen, a happy grin

on his otherwise vacant face; if he knows anything he's not telling. Mr. Douglas talks about working his farm. Robb thinks up a new gag while Laura smiles. Gilligan almost tries to get off his island.

We have a lot of weather but no climate.

The dogs come, whiskers drooping under crusts of ice. When the cat claws the screen door I know it is cold. She prefers the snowbanks, leaping on hapless field mice and shrews who have no cover, but when the temperature hovers near zero she wants in, wants a saucer of milk, a pillow to curl on like a question mark. Like any storybook cat she wants warmth and love; her contented purr is my reward.

Albany Feb. 13 1910
Dear Burtha

Have been waiting to hear from you. how
do you like this winter I don't like it to
much snow and cold to suit me what are
you doing these days. I have been sewing some
did you hear about Betsy losing her baby their
has been lots of sickness

Grandpa makes a pitch for his pretty neighbor; Tony becomes a keyboard wizard thanks to Jeanie; Oliver gets involved in the legend of the famed ghost of Hooterville; Robb thinks he sees a flying saucer; Betty Jo feels rotten about having Steve do some apple-polishing; Ann gets a wild and wooly workout in Hollywood; Robb struggles to fix his tv; Gilligan is certain he's turning into a vampire; the Barkley family is shaken; Herman is at the museum, sleeping off a pill; a drab visitor to the island becomes Ginger's lookalike; Lucy and Ethyl challenge the boys to a gossip contest; the Douglasses agree to take care of a pampered pig.

Under my boots the snow creaks, whines. The uncut summer grass is bent, dark slashes against the blank whiteness; the oriental scribbling of nature. Evergreens crowd in the rows where someone, years ago, planted them, hoping for his own Xmas tree farm and the fast buck. From the trees there is an explosion of white dust, releasing a bevy of swallows, juncos, sparrows, wrens, grackles, like a scene from *Bambi*; two fat glowing pheasants lift from the high branches, flap upward, then glide far across the open fields. The perfect inviolate whiteness of sky and ground, which blend without horizon.

Belding
Mon. –

Dear Andrew
Does this make you think of Halloween or Xmas? Suppose you will raise cain about next Thur. night. How's all the folks? Tell your mamma and Sylvia they had better hurry up and write.
Yours,
A.H.

The snow is stasis; nothing grows, moves, loves, rots. It announces death, but denies decay. Leaves lie stiff and formal; they will be found in the spring perfectly impressed on the ground, like fossils.

A discussion of legal rights of the mentally retarded; how to fix pizza; a visit to the Walrus Islands; preventive dentistry; menopause and middle age; a culinary lesson on plurals; all about mailmen and their work; a trip to the library; conceptual art; can other planets have life?; real estate as an investment; talking out problems; the role of social workers in treating mental illness; resolving conflicts and classifying by size.

I walk past my trees, my fences, into open fields, large flakes slanting in a stiff wind. My navy jacket is huge, ugly, and for years has been old, but within the unzipped alpaca liner things are snug. My right hand is bare, however, because the pistol is on my belt; I hope to see the quick grayness of a rabbit, or perhaps a fox. Long ago I said no more hunting—an obsolete activity, the excitement gone—but today I want to feel the coldness of the pistol butt against my palm, the gun's weight, the buck, report, the acrid smell of cordite. That is why my right hand is bare and near my belt.

Last night on tv I watched (yet again!) *Shane*. The first time I saw it was 20 years ago, with the bunch of friends who did everything together, and the following day we were up before dawn, driving east over the mountains, to hunt rabbits. A friend had an H & R .22 Sentinel pistol—one of the first made—and that is the model I now wear, the barrel almost as clean as the day I bought it. Today I am in this field, in a mild snow storm, looking for rabbits, after seeing (yet again!) *Shane*: I can really believe that 20 years have not passed.

> *Hello there: —*
> *We rec'd your letter for which accept your many thanks for Well I am getting along OK We are now thru with harvesting how up there. Will write a letter later on Hope you are all well and feeling fine*
> *Goodbye*

The salt truck roars like a dragon through the night, sparks and snow swirling from the blade. Sparkling blue crystals dice along the road as the driver performs what he considers an errand of mercy. He loves to salt.

From my window I can hear the distant swish of cars,

an endless procession. They carry: salesmen, waitresses, policemen, mailmen, shoppers, crooks, politicians, rapists, poll-takers, used-car salesmen, reporters, plumbers, teachers, real-estate speculators, babies, tax collectors, students, madmen, muggers, the unemployed, welfare cases, bankers, mechanics, tree surgeons, bus drivers, musicians, disc jockies, hitch-hikers, literary gents, terminal cases.

I think: the snow falls faster. It would not be difficult to go over there, in those bushes, place the cold eye of the six-inch barrel to my temple. In this snow storm I would not be found until spring, perfectly preserved, only a small ugly bruise beside my eye. Perhaps a smile on my lips, who knows? It would depend on my thoughts, as I pitched into that long cylindrical second.

Today at dawn the freezing rain has left drops of ice on every branch; they sparkle in the cold sun like jewels. Like stars. Like drops of ice. Each snow-capped apple has an ice beard. A film of ice sheets all surfaces. I am on a Greek headland, looking toward the harsh white mountains of Albania, or climbing the glacier fields of Mt. Hood. Today is my birthday: I am 400 years old.

The wind rattles the drain pipes, shakes the poor trees. There is always some kind of weather beating about our ears.

> *Dear Burtha*
> *Will drop you a line to tell you Dan Kirk was killed yesterday crossing the interurban car lines at Locust station the car which struck him killing him almost instantly. Jack told me last night and I thought would write you. It is awfully warm here now.*
>
> *Lovingly yours,*
> *Myrtle*

The sheet beside me is as white as the snow fields. I slip out of bed and walk the cold floors of the silent house, past the immaculate beds of my children, to the thermostat; soon a dry heat will cough from the registers, blow fine webs of dust across the empty rooms. In the kitchen I turn on the coffee pot, plug in the toaster. The refrigerator is white, cold, and its brilliant light illumes the yellow cube of margarine, the jam, milk, a half bowl of vegetable soup, some frayed lettuce. Somehow there is always enough for one more meal. I turn on the tv; the small white dot pierces the darkness like a laser, grows more intense, then larger and duller, the light diffusing into the gray dot pattern. The static, riding forgotten air waves, hovers in the room like the voices of previous tenants. Mental health, how to run a drill press, city people who have moved to the farm, hillbillies who have moved to the city. There is always something on, a program which tells me how to live and how others live.

> *Loma, N. Dak.*
> *We were one day behind in getting home. We had to lay over in one town 23 hours. There was a fair girl with us from Loma. Well a Merry Xmas & a happy New Year.*
> *Ferdinand Winaker*

As for myself, I, who have done many things, and have the freedom to do anything, find my life has diminished to a pair of trails: I walk the fields, or to the mailbox—hoping for the letter that will tell me what to do—or sit before the tv. Perhaps once a week I go to the store—I can stand hunger as long as the cat can—but the crowds, the closeness, the insistent voice over the public address system, and especially the rows of full shelves shoot a weakness to my knees and tighten my stomach. There is too much of everything; no one needs all that.

The salt looks for any metal, the perfect metaphor for corruption. But no one complains; it's part of our weather.

Sometimes, late at night, my eyes burning, the tv screen falling to a test-pattern, sometimes after I have seen hundreds of people shot, stabbed, beaten, thrown from windows, cars, planes, trains, poisoned, blown up, sometimes on these nights I think how easy it would be to remove the refrigerator trays and climb in, pulling the door shut. I would be perfectly alone.

This morning the re-boiled coffee is bitter, the toast hard, yet the steam and the tv's voice give the chilly room a kind of warmth, and in a way it is even cozy. As I eat I slowly shuffle the stack of postcards as if I might find an answer, a message written in a miniscule hand near the stamp, or a tiny postscript beneath the signature. The mail is what keeps me going, and every noon I walk down the hill hoping for her letter; most days the box is empty, not even an advertising circular, but some days I open the salt-rusted box to find a spot of color within the darkness, the gilt-edged embossed paper warm against my hand. They bear old postmarks, as if they have been floating the mail currents for years; the names and addresses are not mine, and she is in another town. How they get here is a mystery.

Dear Cousin Gladys: —
Come to V.C. & spend Easter with us. We will also be glad to have you bring your friend. I have had my new spring hat for two weeks, I suppose you have all your spring duds by this time.
Love from Lois Wolff

And there are specific questions which puzzle me:

Why didn't Anna want to get off the boat?
What did Anna say that made the letter too heavy?
How did Betsy lose her baby?
Where was Dan Kirk going?
Why will Andrew raise cain?
Who was the fair girl from Loma? What happened during the 23 hour layover?
Did Cousin Gladys have her spring duds?
Did the woman's dreams come true?

> (If so, where did they live? Children? Husband's occupation? Own their home? Own car?
> Number of radio shows heard per week?
> Number of films seen per month?
> Were they happy in the hedge-surrounded, ivy-covered house, the beech tree in the yard, kids playing along the sidewalk, husband on Saturday raking leaves with pipe in mouth, or waxing the auto in the driveway which is straight as their lives, the sun setting at the end of a day longer than any we have known, reflecting against the windows which diffuse light like moth's wings, and inside they sit before the fireplace, reading novels, the radio softly humming.)

In the spring, the last snow running into underground water, moss cushioning damp stones, grass spreading its luxury, I would wake, shake myself, and rise from the bud-spring bushes. Stiffly I would walk into the house, kiss my wife, fill the voids that need filling, and at my desk begin to write. An epic, perhaps, of the brilliant stars of winter nights, the stasis of days, dreaming like a sleeping bear of that landscape where nothing grows, moves, loves, and there is only the long empty sound of the cutting wind, like a man far away, over the hill, perhaps in pain, crying. Or perhaps it is a metaphor. Or perhaps it is the wind, and only that.

A SPANISH PARABLE

Tourists, then.

As Manolo petulantly insists, we cannot know Spain. Not *really* know it. How can we, from a country where chrome flanks stiffen us upright and dollars cushion our fall, understand this Spain of Franco a hundred years behind the calendar. Spain of the grandees who cheer the bull in the old Plaza Mayor; of the Inquisition (which Manolo claims still exists); of Quixote.

Tourists, then. After four weeks in the country we have seen more of Spain than Manolo in his twenty-four years. Yet, I suppose we do not know; nor can we ever really know.

But standing on the Puerta del Sol, bearded, slightly soiled, reeling from the wine, and the bloodless heat which crackles across the plateau, waiting for Manolo to appear from the night class he teaches at the Berlitz school, the scene is not too different from other points on the globe: prosperous neon repeats itself, autos fill the Calle Mayor with darting mischievous noise, substantial buildings bound it. On the street the tourist stands out from the natives only because the latter are usually better dressed. It is the beggars; the lottery sellers, tickets pinned to their clothes like fluttering rags; the sidewalk vendors, who peddle candy and single cigarettes from shoe boxes, who identify the country. Spain desperately poor.

We wait in the hub and crash of the evening crowd; myself, my wife, and Manolo's American wife, Billie Jo. It is she who truly does not understand Spain, for she does not understand Manolo. They met when he was an exchange student at our school; they married when Manolo found himself trapped in Franco's army, earning three cents a day and five loaves of steely bread. Trapped, he remembered the fat girl in the States whose father had a small plane, which intoned money somewhere; a correspondence followed, heavy with Manolo's flowery metaphors, which wooed Billie Jo and, more important, her mother. Manolo, the latin enigma.

But Billie Jo. Manolo insists she stand out against the background, and stand out she does. He has commanded her black hair be dyed a magenta, her heavy butt be tightly encased in his cast off dress slacks. I suggest to Manolo that Billie Jo certainly appears different, and yet common, a differential pun which escapes him.

But the men of Madrid she drives to a hot, fettered madness. It is for this reason, not the smell of American money, the traffic cop by the American Express guides her to the island in the center, then allows traffic to flow while he steadily propositions her in gay, lilting Spanish. Billie Jo, the blushing bride of six months, stands helplessly on the island; she cannot protest or even acquiesce, for she knows no Spanish beyond the fundamental pleasantries. Or the monkeys who follow her miles across town, all the way from the American Embassy where she goes daily to hopefully arrange papers for Manolo's immediate exit; who even enter the house under pretext of selling magazines to the American lady: without shame they pull a shabby *Reader's Digest* from a sack.

The coal sellers are less subtle. From their truck tops,

fist size lumps of coal are slammed at her wide butt, with accuracy.

It is too obvious, to me at least, Manolo has made a marriage of convenience, which would please his ancestors: he stands with one foot in New York. An outrageous asset when he deserts the army, which he plans to do as soon as he can steal enough rubber stamps, and official papers to forge; and when, foremost, the money from Billie Jo's parents arrives.

Finally our boy emerges. One can see he is disturbed: his brow is dark, his lips surly. Without a glance in either direction, he knows the state of affairs here, his world. He rudely leaves the sleek blonde who exited with him, and as we abruptly walk away, he says: "There is one of your kind. She is here to *help* the people. The poor *people*." Caustic words sit on his black tongue as he mimics, stretches the last into a dozen haughty syllables. "I think she's a Franco spy. Jesu crist," he says to me, hands palm up in supplication, "this country will drive me mad. I *swear*, when I desert the army, I will never return to Spain while Franco rules. Jesu crist, I swear. You simply don't know at all. The misery here is excruciating. Informers, spies, homosexuals, the monkeys—utter depravity." The 'monkeys' are the aimless, the unemployed, the unemployable who roam the streets, 'monkeying around' as Manolo puts it. "This is Rome in its final decadence, before the fall. I assure you I have no desire to be caught in the debris."

Etc., etc. But why record more. It would be funny if it were not so familiar. Manolo, in another country, across an ocean. Yet the spew of ideology, impatience, sourness, random hate, falling in clipped English, is the same. Manolo the marxist, the revolutionary, the dissenter, who fights the world's windmills but abhors violence. If I toy with him and suggest the hour of the barricades is at hand, that he must stay and fulfill his destiny, he will peel the pout from his lips, furrow his brow and hotly exclaim: "No, no, you miss the point. Lenin waited in Switzerland for the Russian revolution. Stout leaders must be apart from the blood bath." Actually, non-violent overthrow of the country would suit Manolo; one feels he dreads not only a blood bath, but any sort of bath. This is mild humor which I keep to myself, knowing Manolo's petulant nature; he and Billie Jo are the only people we know in Madrid, and one must stay somewhere. Besides, with Manolo I always have the feeling something funnier is just around the corner.

Yet he is verbally dedicated to his task, and now raves in English, with little chance his dull dialectics will be overheard by the informers he fears. As we walk toward the bus stop, through a night which eases its heat, everyone pauses to stare at young Trotsky, who shouts and waves condemning gestures. Billie Jo's pleasurable butt gets second notice; then my beard. Even Avis, my wife, is not immune, for in our months of travel her skirt has shrunk to above her knees.

"America," Manolo rants, "has at least pretensions of democracy. Which is why I want to return. It is not *too* bad a place."

No, he was very fond of the grand stores. To enter one door of a clothing store and emerge from another, wearing an entirely new wardrobe, stolen. When these clothes were stiff with dirt, they would be thrown away; the cycle repeated. Why didn't he wash them? Simple. Cleanliness is next to godliness, and Manolo prefers to be next to neither. Too, in this way he always dressed in the fashion of the moment. A fastidious exterior over his unbathed body: the impeccable question mark.

Shall I give you other intimate snapshots? Manolo in the back of a car with a girl; both are nude. The policeman's flash plays over Manolo's hairy, brown, unwashed body and he freezes as if the beam of light were ice; barely stammers out: "You mean, in this country you do not do this?"

Or Manolo caught for a spectrum of petty crimes, feigning ignorance of both crime and language. He forges answers in a mawkish, guttural tongue. "What I did? No speak so the English. Chicky chink, see see."

Surprisingly, it works. Every time. If he is a bad criminal, he is a convincing liar. The cop, who understands the frantic passion of this Spaniard, lets him off with a warning, as Manolo blasphemously crosses himself again and again. The others simply give up; communication is impossible. The crimes forgotten. And, I must admit, this side of Manolo harbors a cleverness I rather admire.

"In America, of course, my main protest was the discrimination: besides being dark—*swarthy*, if you prefer—and refused rooms by shit-heel old ladies because they thought I was a negro, I found myself also objectionable as a Marxist, an ex-Catholic, a jew, a foreigner and *God* knows what. *Really*, my dear fellow, I told you about the time the Dean of Men, that fat, hairless pig, called me in for singing *communist songs* in the Student Union. Jesu crist, really, I don't know *any*—not *one*. Those were fascist youth songs."

No doubt. Although I try, I cannot feel sorry. Manolo advertised his beliefs and renunciations through thick lips; he earned his world of terror, mostly imagined. For any bad word of careless expression sent him into a violent persecution depression. No, not violent. Passive depression, for Manolo, that child of war, would bear no violence. It is this contradiction of character which makes him so *terribly* misunderstood, and also so interesting. He is exclusive as a shabby, minor myth. His revolutions will be peaceful coups; dancing in the streets will follow, and the next day an ideal Marxist state will be imposed, without a hitch.

"And here?" I ask, taunting him.

"Here," he says, the suggestion of a dark smile fading, "here is all that too: being *dark* is not Castilian, the noble blood. My records say I am a jew, that I have renounced the Church. But *this* is a police state, Franco, the military, and most of all the utter depravity. I swear, I can't stand it."

"They exploit him," Billie Jo says. Her dime-sized mind has been indoctrinated.

"Let me be graphic." Graphically, Manolo's lax hand becomes a fist. "Today a very stupid, monkey-faced man tells my captain, in utter astonishment: 'You mean that *pig*,' pointing at me, 'speaks *three* languages?' Oh, I tell you, the revolution will come, this country breathes the air of tyranny until the lungs are *filled*."

Pretty metaphors. But Manolo has worked up a frenzy, and he is really not himself. Or perhaps he really *is* himself. For as we wait at the traffic light, Manolo, hands in his pockets, an idiotic grin on his inclined face, turns to the cop who stands there, and none of us are prepared for what follows.

"Look at this fat pig," Manolo says, as if he were asking directions. "This is the stooge who wears the yoke of power." We are amazed. The smile flicks over Manolo's face and disappears as he turns to address the policeman, their stomachs almost touching. "Be careful, pig, that the yoke does not weight you to the earth."

Through all this the policeman, who obviously doesn't understand a word of English, smiles now lazily at the boy who speaks soft phrases to him; then at us. He doesn't understand. Nor do I. As the hairs of my beard stiffen with fear, I grab Avis and we run across the street. My beard would identify me with the opposition, accompanied with Manolo's insults; I have already smelled the jail deep in the bowels of the city.

We run. Billie Jo shakes herself along. Manolo dallies.

We turn off the busy Calle Mayor and into the dark puzzle of cobbled paths, where our steps slam out and echo back, until it seems the sound will wake the Civil Guard. In the arcade of the Plaza Mayor, Billie Jo stops, pants for air, and collapses against the pillar, her breasts heaving. We stop, and soon Manolo saunters up. It is his moment of triumph.

"Why did you *run*?"

"Guess," I say.

"And you, Billie Jo. Why did *you* follow? Why didn't you stick by your husband?"

She followed us for the same reason she follows Manolo's politics and idiotic suggestions; for the same reason she came to Spain, she is a herd by herself, easily led.

"Well," Manolo says, "it is a fine night. The stars throw down their first lances of light. Why don't we walk home. Anyway, I don't have the bus fare."

We travel the edge of the Plaza under the arcade. Two centuries ago this was the bull arena; now it is a vast open area boxed to its edges by three story buildings. Small holes at each end, diagonally opposed, release small cars which honk once before speeding across the space, reach top gear and honk again at the opposite end; their yellow lights float like tallow in the darkness. Past Las Cuevas de Luis Candalas, with its phony eighteenth century bandit, who tries to shill us in; down the wide, slope-worn stairs into the Calle de Cuchilleros.

"Here," Manolo says, "the Casa de Botin, once frequented by Hemingway. The menu is immortalized on the last page of *The Sun Also Rises*. I should like to take you there, but I am only a poor proletariat. But come, let me show you the *one* good thing in this rotten country."

We follow. Down a street where one can visualize Cervantes out for an evening of adultery; all along here, built into the masonry, are small stand-up bars. We enter the first:

they are all pretty much alike: shrimp hulks, olive pits, bread crusts, cigarette butts, toothpicks carpet the floor. There are no chairs, but no one seems to stay that long. The wine is thin but cheap; the glasses dirty. Manolo has tutored Billie Jo to count in Spanish from one to ten, and she orders for us; a trained seal trick carried off with all the pleading and abortive aplomb of a pageant. A tumbler of wine; with each a small plate of sardines or mussels or olives, gratis.

"You don't *mind* buying do you, old man?" Manolo says to me. "Call it your share of the American foreign aid. No? You *don't* mind. Well, in that case let us have an order of mussels. *They* are the only thing worthwhile in this rotten country."

The man busily fills glasses, collects change, splashes vinegar. The small closet is packed; hot bodies rub hot bodies, with electric friction. A family scurries in, the mother passes the row of glasses back to the children, ages about six to twelve; the last glass she drains, sucks up the small plates of food; the glasses are shunted forward, and the family leaves. Bang. A distressed young guitar player comes in, finds he cannot move his arms in the crowd, and leaves, taking with him his unsung sad song.

A can of mussels is opened and drenched in vinegar. Manolo adds more vinegar, and sucks the briny mussel into his thick, black mouth with a pouting sound. A juke-box plays Spanish music, American style. We each take a mussel, and raise our glasses.

"To Spain," I say.

"Batshit," Manolo says, and drinks, although he does not like wine. One feels he could be a food faddist very easily, if he cared at all for his body.

We eat and drink quickly, then leave. Twenty feet away there is another bar; the process is repeated, pretty much the same. Except that I don't buy Manolo a can of mussels this time: nor does he press good fortune to the limits.

When I raise my glass this time, I look into the shifting lights of Manolo's eyes with all the seriousness I can muster. "Just think how lucky you are, Manolo. Wine is cheap; all this delicious seafood. For fifty cents one can get quite drunk. And fed too. You're a very lucky young man."

"Is that *so*?" he asks, his eyes rolling upward. "If that is the case, you may have my place in the army. One can imagine how drunk one can get on three cents a day. As such, you can stay here forever. But frankly, I don't know *why* you ever came to this country. Jesu crist, *why* did you?"

"Why, to see you, Manolo. Came all the way to see you."

His head jerks; lips curl into a sneer which means he is smiling. His heart is touched.

"We're Franco spies," Avis says.

"Castro sent us," I say.

His head swings from one face to the other; for a second it is a dream come true. Then his eyes droop and roll back, retreating under heavy lids. "Batshit."

"It's true," I insist. "Castro sent us to organize the ferment in this moldy country."

"Really, it isn't *right* to joke. Not about *that*."

That being the pin which holds his tattered dreams together.

Into the street which tilts downward to the Manzanares river and the Ponte de Segovia. There is something in the night, the dark secret streets, the wine, which goes to the head. I believe even Manolo feels it. His rich voice bellows across the roof tops in song:

> *Ooowww, I don't want to go in the armee,*
> *I don't want to go to war.*

I just want to stay in Picadilleee,
Living on the earnings of a—high born laydee . . .

The houses shoved shoulder to shoulder are dark except for tiny corrugated slats of light which peek from shutters. Darkness brings into focus the near stars, a universe of cold, intense points and one feels fixed in time and space. But even at the same moment there is a shuttling ambiguity in the air, an evasiveness, which plunges one into the city's collective history, here in the underbelly. That old man over there, slouching as he cradles his maimed hand, is it Miguel de Cervantes Saavedra?

As we stumble down the cobbled street, Avis grabs at her foot. She assumes a curious stork stance, holding a bare foot in one hand and her cheap Japanese thong in the other.

"Oh. The strap broke." Where the straps meet the sole, the yoke has pulled out. There is no remedy; she will have to walk home half-shod.

Then, as if Manolo in his cleverness had planned it, there is a crack in the masonry beside us which turns out to be a cobbler's shop. Only the thinnest yellow light proves its existence. Manolo, who I am certain did not know it was there, takes Avis' thong and leads us over the hump stoned walk, into the niche.

"Here," he shouts proudly, "here is the working class, my people. You see they work late, for the Americans."

I flinch a bit when Manolo assigns the epithet working class to himself. But, who knows, he may have worked once. Besides, I am curious. Everything is painted in shadows, the deepest purple-black, a unity of dark values; into this springs the dull yellow light from a small window, but there is no door. The room is fabricated from some extra space tacked on to the next buildings, a few stones mortared on, where the sidewalk bends. At our voices, the two men look up in surprise; the shallow light plays back the continuation of black, the hundred dark half-tones of leather around them: it is a scene which might have been caught by the brush of some Flemish *genre* painter. The text of their trade is written everywhere: leather dust powders the sweat of their faces; their hands are hard crusts of cordovan hide. Their eyes squint into the poor light, their grimaces are relieved only slightly as Manolo spews his language out, and shows them the broken thong. One man leaves his bench and takes the thong, to study it; finally he shakes his head, picks up a heavy needle and with long, continuous strokes sews. There is an undercurrent of Spanish between the men.

"What does he say?" I ask.

"That it can be fixed temporarily." Then Manolo shrugs, and actually smiles. "Well, you see the working class. They struggle to exist, while over *there*," he points to the palace on the rim of the hill, "the rich pigs are fattened for the slaughter. What do you think *now*?"

"Tell them we are very poor. That we are pilgrims." Although the scene is fantastically picturesque, I cannot reject a chance to puncture Manolo's rhetoric. But there is no stopping him; he is at home with the proletariat.

"*Aleman*?" asks the man who is sewing.

"*Norteamericanos,*" Manolo replies, and turns to us slowly, as if he has done a trick.

"Ahhh, *norteamericanos*," both men repeat, to one another and the air.

The strong stitch finished, the man leans out the window, his black arms merge into the darkness as he stretches to the ground and slips the thong on Avis' bare foot. The other man, with barely enough room to move his elbows, takes from the wall a worn, fat *bota*, like a shiny kidney, and hands it to Billie Jo. With a flare of knowledge she unscrews the horn mouth and tilts it to hers, squeezing.

"No, not like *that*," Manolo roars. He takes it and swings the dark bladder into the air, and the jet of wine slips into his black mouth; slowly he draws the *bota* back, and cuts the stream off with a neat flick of the wrist. "That is how *we* working men drink our wine."

"Bravo, bravo," shout the cobblers.

My turn. I emulate the master; my form is good, but I miscalculate and the stream emerges to strike my cheek, dripping down my neck. Everyone has a good laugh. I shrug and hand the *bota* to Avis, who holds it close to her mouth and avoids my error. She slowly moves the *bota* away, the stream lengthens but in a second her mouth is full, her hand shakes as she tries to swallow; when the wine begins to run from the corners of her lips, she withdraws the *bota*, and the stream collapses in a line down her blouse.

"Bravo, bravo," shout the cobblers.

She hands it through the window, and they take their swigs. One man moves against the wall so the other can hold the skin at arm length, tilt and squeeze; the wine lunges into the mouth, the throat accepts it; for an interminable minute the man drinks and the only sound is his throat working; then he drops the bladder. With considerable shuffling the men exchange places, repeat the scene, and the finale is a caucus of laughter in blackness.

"What do I owe?" I ask.

Manolo says something, then turns to me. "Nothing."

"Oh, but I should pay them something," I insist, fumbling in my pocket. The cobbler gestures no. "Por favor"; there is no charge.

"Keep your money," Manolo says. "This is not the basement of the Hilton-Madrid. This is the working class. These are *my* people, the masses," pointing to the two thin men, cramped in their space. "You Americans," he shouts, with a sweeping gesture which includes Billie Jo, "you think anything can be bought with money. Well, there are things that are not for sale."

It is all so absurd, and yet, as Manolo swells with pride, I see a darkness behind his eyes which surprises me, deeper than the shadows. A glinting black enigma, which is chopped off as he shifts his head to lend us his profile. He preens himself as he heartily shakes hands with the cobblers; this dramatization has bolstered his spirit. He shows us terror, he believes, in a handful of leather dust. Yet there is a new hardness in his expression, an uncertain hardness both fearful and foolish. There is no doubt but he would like to literally sit on the ground and talk of the death of kings, if I suggested it.

We all shake hands and as I turn to go I see Manolo is already partway down the hill, his legs casting out in firm steps. His voice cuts the silence in song, cleaning the cats from the street, striking lights in black windows; he sings in Spanish, some fascist youth song, no doubt.

THE TAKE-HOME TEST

Over and over, as the painters barked, Garry read: He was a strange nigger. He said He say to tell you wood and hay kin burn. I said What? That night my barn burned. He was a strange nigger. He said—

"I worked on a Federal Housing," the loud painter said. "They had a sixty foot flagpole and mostly niggers lived there. Sixty foot—that musta cost—"

Like the workers' voices which assaulted the thin walls, time pounded on; when he had read the same paragraph, Faulkner's, yet again, Garry flipped the book over. Perhaps it was the word *nigger*, or the anarchy striking the room, or the tedious take-home test, which sent him to the door. Or perhaps he really did intend to pass on into the kitchen, for coffee.

"Listen," Garry said. Only one painter was in sight; he was walking into the bushes, toward the front. "If you want to talk don't call them niggers." Then into the yard he said, "Where's my kids?"

"Out back."

"Good. I don't want them to grow up *bigots*." He was already on the steps again when the man said: "Then I'd prefer not to talk 'cause I'll call them what I want."

He returned to the book, shaking: He was a strange

nigger. He said He say—

Now all around the house the slap of brushes had quit for coffee break. That same line, Faulkner's, went around and around and Garry knew he had not been calm in the yard, although at the door, hand on the knob, foot on the porch, he had thought he was. Not nerves, nor fearful violence, he said, but that the kids might hear. The boy, three, picked up every new word—he was a genius, no doubt, as his father was not.

Over the rigid, systematic test questions the foreshortened scene hovered and stretched whole: after that nonsense about a sixty foot flagpole he had not intended to say anything, or to even open the door. The painter, thin, angular, white as a ghost—in white coveralls and hands paint spattered—was passing into the bushes. "Listen, if you want to talk about Negroes," and his heart began to trip, throat tighten, "don't call them niggers. Around here."

The man hesitated, his fingers on the siding, a look of stupid surprise on his harsh angular face.

Garry walked jerkily into the brilliant sunlight. Eyelids slid over dry tissue at all the dead, flat grass. The square of sandbox was empty. "Where's my kids?"

"Out back," the painter said.

Garry now realized that the man was calm, perhaps for him there was nothing wrong. The uneven eyebrows did not shift, nor the slack, cruel mouth tighten. But he had moved closer and was a foot away when Garry snapped: "Good. I don't want them to grow up *bigots*." He had not meant to say that so aggressively. Words were falling, tense.

Silently the man came closer; Garry noticed the paint caulked along each fingernail, and for a long frozen second he expected to feel the hand lash into his face. The brass suspender buttons said Union Made. Glossy black hairs stretched from the open shirt front and sweat ran along his neck. Garry retreated to the top step of the porch, saying: "Watch your language here."

The man was unmoved; hate did not show. "Then I'd prefer not to talk about them 'cause I'll call them any damn thing I please."

"You do that." His throat closed in fear and hate and he could not think of a rational, clinching retort.

Then he was in the cool darkness of the hall, where stiff brooms and mops hung in neat lines. The incident had taken only a minute but relived again and again it spread to include all the things he might have said.

He was a strange nigger, he read. That night my barn burned—

Now brushes slapped the walls outside and ladders scraped eaves. What's a *bigot*? he heard. There were six painters, hired by the school to paint the University house, and two were saying: knock his headin . . . nutim.

They knew he heard, in there over his book. And some dark night a bullet could crash through the window as he sat reading. Or a cross illuminating the neighborhood from his front yard. Wood and hay can burn. Obscene phone calls in the night. Tires slashed.

Even in Oregon, where discrimination was only occasionally whispered, like the wind through sweeping tree lined streets, his father would have called them niggers, and had. And the word had appeared twice this year in Freshman themes—from well-dressed Southern boys, who used the word as Faulkner might. Garry had done nothing except to write *diction* along the margin in his neat hand. For he could not change the two Southern boys, nor the painters. If there was any hope at all it rested with his son's generation, and this, he said, was the reason he had opened the door, surprising himself as he went toward the kitchen for coffee. He could not change the world, alone.

N, a painter said. Yeah, or Lover, was the reply. The tone was flat, like brushes striking the siding. RR, said one, but the voice near the roof could not decipher. RR, the man repeated, Race Riot.

Garry pictured black men in breech-cloths charging with naked razors; dark streets with high leaning houses, their broken windows stuffed with rags. Boogy-man Town. Also a wreck he had seen as a boy: a Lincoln V-12, black as death, its roof resting on the two slick ribbons of railroad track. The sharp smell of gas and oil; blood running into dark, metallic pools; empty beer bottles rattling across the street as the bent back wheel continued spinning, spinning.

He did not trust his legs to go to the door. The odor of paint hung heavy and oppressive, and he knew he could not *reason* with the voices which continued to assault the room. He hoped the kids could not hear. What had he been thinking when he opened the door surprising himself and said, Listen, if you want to talk about Negroes—

But he could do nothing alone and anyway—he tried to focus on the neat rows of print—he was busy. Right now there was the take-home test.

MAKING THE POINT

Because Chris knows every eye watched the Lincoln backed into its parking space, he gives the paper to Mr. Paul and turns, walks directly to the magazine rack. The drugstore holds behind brown cellophane the coolness; holds the smell of milkshakes, magazines, medicine, and harsh forbidden cigarette smoke. Brightness strikes his eye: the chrome napkin-holders, convoluted curves of table tubing, the tiers of magazines, the shifting rolling lights of the juke box.

Chris' feet follow the inlaid tiles, the continuity of gears; he does not even glance at those who sit at tables no larger than the Lincoln's steering wheel, but accelerates directly from the prescription counter to the magazine rack. Laughter bubbles behind chrome, over coke glasses—shrill knives of laughter cut the air above people who are independent, this 4th of July. They smoke in public, as he walks past.

For what can he say to these strangers of classrooms, of the dark halls of high school, of street corners. Their clothes are tight and gay, while his fall into cuffs that cover work shoes. Gasoline fumes rise from his shirt, his sweat-stained armpits. Their talk spins across the room like a brilliant hubcap in the sun. What can he say—of broken machinery, of the mysteries of oil, of death?

Because his father had left the garage in May, the ache

of machinery rolling across his ribs like dry bearings, Chris has quit school. Now grease rides each fingernail in a narrow crescent moon. At home, among sheets, his father waits—the pink bills grow on top of the radio; the cupboard leans, slims. Across the street, seen through the opaque light of July's dusk, the Lincoln waits—boat-shaped and black, spaced on fat whitewalls.

In tiers the magazines wait under his fingers: the pastels of comic books, which last year he would have read; at the other end, the men's magazines, the gaudy display of flesh. His hand drops to *Hot Rod*, for his mind steers over the flanks of machinery night and day. He longs for speed, open exhausts battering the green countryside, the mythology of paint and chrome. Once he had considered travel—the French Foreign Legion, Beau Geste, pyramids, the shape of Mexico—but now travel means California, a bobbed roadster cruising down a wide palm-lined avenue. From the pages he dreams himself owner of a fast, cut-down set of wheels, to tour the drive-ins—it means escape, independence, fulfillment.

Near his thumb he reads: STUDY ELECTRONICS at home—high school diploma not needed. Men, earn money, security. Be free. $$$

LEARN Crime Detection at home—free lapel pin, handbook.

EARN on the job—Hog Butchers needed NOW!

There are many ways to work—somewhere on a list there are jobs and jobs he doesn't know even exist. In the window, against the brown cellophane, under the canted awnings, he sees the drugstore's reflection, and beyond the steering wheel tables the reflected image of Mr. Paul walks white-coated in the last sunlight. He shakes red pills into a clean bottle, pastes on a label. On either side strange brown bottles burn. Beyond the small door Chris imagines a room filled with crystalline: beaker, flask, the fragile phallic test-tubes.

There *are* many ways to work, he thinks, and wonders what it would be like to be a pharmacist. To stand white-coated in the pure smell of milkshakes and geared green tile, shaking out pills to the dying. After only two months in his father's garage, Chris knows it would be better than being a mechanic, where one wore the sifted dirt from fender-wells.

"Hiya Chris." In the window he sees a boy known as The Flynn, and when he turns he sees over the boy's shoulder the girls are laughing in their cokes; they wear tight skirts, and thin, gauzy blouses which show the bra's lines. The Flynn looks over Chris' shoulder, past the magazine rack, to the Lincoln Zephyr across the street. His sleeve is turned up over a pack of Luckies; his hair slicked back like fenders over the ears. "O we saw you park it," The Flynn says, grinning. On each bicep he has a tattoo: the right is an eagle holding a snake; the left is Yokohama 1951. There may be more under the T-shirt, or the swirling pattern may be hair. "Nice wheels you got."

Chris turns, looks again: the Lincoln, boat-shaped and black, sits between two rat-gray sedans. Its paint is faded and chipped, but it *is* impressive in an aging, decadent way. His father thinks the car is *class*—Chris knows this means the twin spotlights, the underseat heaters, the push-button doors. But, to Chris' hot rage, the car has no power. The original V-12 engine gulped gas to produce its own smoke screen, and was replaced with a smaller, more economical V-8. Now, over-weight and under-powered, the Lincoln will barely move; like the father, the family, the car limps along.

"Go for a ride?" says The Flynn, winking, thumbs in his broad leather belt. "O I got a couple of skirts."

Sighting along The Flynn's upswept hair, Chris sees the two girls at the small table: their red lips glow like reflectors, dotting the coke glass rims, the cigarette ends. They sit with crossed legs, laughing. He has seen them at school, but does not know their names.

"What say The Point?" says the Flynn. "Get out of town, watch the fireworks—y'know?"

"I don't think so—I got a urgent delivery."

Beneath his fingers the magazines tremble. He had forgotten it was the 4th, Independence Day, thinking only about cars, and the delivery. For his father was wrapped tightly in the bed he had not left these two months, and by the tone of his mother's voice he knew the medicine was needed. Why ask him? he wonders, not even knowing The Flynn, nor the girls. He has moved down the rack and the covers burst with flesh: Captured by the Commie Lesbos, he reads; What the GI Learns in Tokyo; I was at Pusan Reservoir; Wild Wild Women of the Orient. Nude women carry Bren guns, grenades, and smiling they cut down rows of foolish commies: How the Burma Virgins Fought on Our Side. Each woman's breasts are full, tilt upward. Only an illustration, he knows, but inside are actual photos, women in few clothes or none, their faces marked out with a white bar. He feels embarrassed excitement crawl into his crotch, and replacing the magazine he moves along the rack, walking sideways.

Why ask him? he wonders. He is not of The Flynn's street gang, nor of the school's party crowd, nor of any group—alone, apart, he is interested only in cars. On the juke box Hank Williams speaks of love; Chris wonders how do you ask a girl out, when grease rides permanent in the narrow crescent of each fingernail.

He looks up to see Loaner's Corner fill with dusk. The Lincoln Zephyr is dim across the street, where the white mouths of tires sing. Then Mr. Paul calls, and Chris follows the continuity of green tiles to the prescription counter, where he counts out money painfully.

"Your father feeling better?" Mr. Paul says, smiling, his coins hitting the cash drawer.

"He's okay," Chris says, knowing the man is dying.

"O come again."

Waiting beside the car are The Flynn, the two girls—he hears laughter, sees a cigarette glow beside the Lincoln's fender. His throat is tight as he pushes the button to open the door, pulling at the chrome drawer-knobs his father had screwed to the metal. His father thought that the push-buttons were class, but when the springs began to uncurl he added the cheap dime store knobs—to Chris' disgust. But when Chris had wanted a squirrel-knob on the Lincoln's great wheel, it was the father who had objected, had said a red and chrome knob would look like crap, would cut the wheel's fine ivory finish. The father admires the excellence of the yellowed antique wheel, the twin spotlights, the wide expanse of hood. *That* is class.

"Whadda ya say?" The Flynn asks, leaning in. His tattoos glow blue in the dark. Behind, Chris sees the full sweaters, the skirts swirling around wide hips—he thinks of the Burma virgins, the tilted breasts; of Korea, where he will be next year, no doubt, dying far from home—

"O why not," he says. "Only to The Point, and back. To watch the fireworks."

"Daddy-O," The Flynn says, opening both doors, slapping each bottom as the girls lean in, one in front and one in the backseat. "You said it—the fireworks."

The girl moves close to Chris, cramps the arm which shifts gears to glide the Lincoln slowly out of Loaner's Corner. "Whatcher name? I'm Sally."

In the mirror The Flynn kisses his girl long, rubbing his face back and forth on hers, as seen in the movies. Chris is not sure he will know how to kiss—he has never had to—but he will try, for the pressure of warm lips is escape; independence from the garage's dark grease, the home's sweet medicinal smell. Sally's leg is against his, her perfume chokes the air.

"I'm Chris," he says. The name sounds strange—in the dark countryside they have come to he wonders where he is going, what he is going to be: there are many ways to work. He has seen his father worked to death, and unable to name the job he knows he wants something better—for himself, his children.

"O here's the fireworks," The Flynn says, handing bottles. He has a six-pack wrapped in his pea-jacket. Sally takes two, and slips Chris' between his legs—the cold bottle excites him, although he doesn't want the beer. Her hand on the bottle near his crotch excites him, and he smells the throaty cigarette she lights.

"Yer in school?" Sally asks, exhaling thin streams of smoke from her nose.

"I'm out," he says, as if he had graduated already; as if this long, black Lincoln gliding through the night on fat white-walls were his; as if he were free, had escaped to the girl, the beer, the cigarette.

"Yar," she says. "Me too—I'm car hopping at Merhars."

The road turns, inclines toward the blinking lights of the radio station high on Mt. Scott, and at its base The Point. Chris steps the gas to the floor, hears the carburetor's gasp. Speeding upward, the city unfolds beneath them in a carpet of lights. Far to the north a sky-rocket breaks into an umbrella of sparks, and as the explosion carries to their ears he hears Sally's voice at his shoulder—*Ooooooh*, she says—her breasts against his arm.

In the mirror The Flynn's hand reaches under the girl's sweater—his voice shatters the night, his hair sweeps overhead like fenders. The pedal to the floor the carb sucks, gasps, as the car climbs to thinner air. Headlights clip off the white headstones of the cemetery which lies between them and The Point. "Yer cute, y'know it?" Sally says, moving closer; his arm is draped around her back and waist, and with one hand he guides the Lincoln's great white wheel, steering upward.

Small lights spread to the horizon's dark, the air cools. In the deflected glow from the dashboard he can see Sally's bare knees, the legs opened, the skirt raised.

As the road inclines sharply the car grows weary, slows. Chris reaches with his free hand to shift to second, feels the back end bounce, the fat tires accept the new gear. Under the wide expanse of hood the engine whines, straining.

"O don'tcha just love it up here?" Sally says, leaning back, her breasts catching the high-lights from the dash. She is agreeable to anything, Chris thinks, and as the car begins to buck, slow, he shifts into low and curses. The engine is shrill, screaming above the backseat noises and the explosions from the city.

"This crate gonna make it?" The Flynn wonders.

The beer between his legs has warmed, spills across his pants. The car begins the final mile of hill and halfway up, engine screaming, the speedometer needle drops to the small numbers. Half a mile separates them from the top when the Lincoln bucks to a stop, surrenders.

"Wait," Chris says. "I'll try it again."

He coasts down in reverse, half-turned with his leg firmly against Sally, her eager warmth entering him. He coasts back to the final turn, guns the engine, pops the clutch, and the heavy car lunges into the night. In low gear his foot is on the floor all the way, lights clipping the grave markers with rapid flashes of white. Then the car stutters, and a thin whisper of steam traces from under the broad expanse of hood—and again it bucks, shudders, clicks metallic through the drive train, the rear wheels, and all power dissolves.

"O shit," Sally says.

"Let's walk it," The Flynn says.

"No," Chris says, for it is a matter of pride, this being his very first date with a girl. "I'll try it in reverse."

Again he backs down the hill, and at the curve turns the car around. Engine now cool, he guns it, pops clutch and hanging from the open door he guides the big car through the night in reverse. The giant wheel swings, steering the dancing swaths of red, the taillights an echo of the radio tower high over The Point. It is difficult, speeding in reverse into darkness—he wishes his father had let him clip a red and chrome squirrel-knob on the wide white wheel. Thinking of the knob, he recalls the medicine on the seat. At the corner of his eye he sees stars, a million stars spread across the dark mountain stretching to the city's lights—stars brilliant and turning in color, as rocket follows rocket into the thin dark air, climbing to break even with them. That is all he wants, he knows, guiding the car now slowly uphill, only wants to break even—you never get out of this world alive, his father always said.

The gas pedal mushes underfoot, the carb gasps, balks; all power turns to jello within the chromehard cylinder walls —the rear wheels turn slower, begin to hop against the road in excited convulsions as the grade steepens. In desperation Chris pops the clutch, in and out, the engine racing wide throttle for a second then fading into the driving wheels— then perhaps the hand on the steering swings too far, or the left rear wheel catches in gravel for the car lurches quickly that direction, and before Chris can correct his steering the car pivots, glides backward, the bumper driving into the dirt bank, the rear wheels spinning free over the drainage ditch.

The Flynn and the two girls are laughing as Chris jumps out, into the steam and blood-rust water the radiator pumps across the fender. The Lincoln is not damaged, but his mistake has got it hopelessly stuck, and he chokes back tears to shut off the engine, cut the lights. From The Flynn and girls laughter boils downhill, the ghosts of blue tattoos ascend. Laughter claps against the sporadic explosions from the war below, sounds fired into silence.

Chris removes the car keys, shifts the package to his pocket, and his feet flash, small explosions, downhill toward Loaner's Corner. His race is urgent but he ignores the shortcut which traces a winding path through the cemetery; he sticks to the road, a broad black trampoline, falling, falling into warmer air.

THE SCHRAMS AT WATERLOO

The sixth day the Schrams drove their motorscooter off the smooth Belgian road and onto the dry, dusty plain of Waterloo. Stopping past the sign which invited them to park, they surveyed the dull landscape. Like most memorials or cathedrals or ruins they had seen there was little of real interest, and that exploited by a circus atmosphere. Here the interest was a dirt pyramid four stories high, topped by a statue of a man on a horse (or was it a lion? Mr. Schram couldn't be certain). On the north stairs people climbed like ants. A billboard proclaimed the immense mound was a monument to a general who had been killed (or wounded?— the sign was ambiguous) on this very spot.

Around the base was a pocket of disangled, weather-beaten buildings, and from one came music and cannon fire. Plastered to its walls were posters announcing, in several languages, a chance to see the historic battle re-enacted "in the authentic manner"; a voice narrated in French how the battle was going.

As Mr. Schram turned his back to search the empty flatlands, the echo of small arms' fire flying in his face, he half-expected a platoon of ancient, crippled, bandaged soldiers to charge from behind.

Well, he wouldn't climb the pyramid to see the statue,

nor would he go to the movie to see the battle relived "in the authentic manner," but he would eat lunch.

Mrs. Schram unpacked the basket while Mr. Schram worked the stubborn cork from the wine bottle; as they ate, the cannonade at their backs and the empty plain in front, each cheered silently for Napoleon: they knew what it was to be beaten.

They had been in Europe less than a week and they were sick of it. Sick of lumpy beds, cold water, smart aleck waiters; mostly, sick of hands thrust out to receive their money. Oh, they enjoyed the museums, and the *idea* of being here finally, but so many things had happened to offset this partial happiness they thought at times it would have been better to remain at home, reading *of* Europe rather than being disillusioned by seeing it. Their extensive preparations —the books read, the notes, charts, and itineraries made, the French and German studied—had not prepared them for the daily trivia.

Because they were impatient to see Europe they stayed in Antwerp only the first night and the next noon began to hitch-hike north, in high spirits. They had read that "thumbing it" was the easiest way to travel the continent; not only was it cheap, but one met interesting people. They soon discovered the road north was like leaving NYC for Jersey (except there was no tunnel), or hitch-hiking out of downtown Los Angeles. By three o'clock they had walked ten kilometers and were still in the crowded environs, on a road where cars, too small to carry extra baggage, whizzed past. Behind, on a tree-lined path, bicycles and motorized cycles zoomed north, full speed. Surrounded by motion, they seemed to stand still.

But they concentrated on walking faster. The city eventually fell behind and they soon reached the border; it was as if a tangible dividing line had been crossed: the country unfolded, flat as a plate. A brimming horizon was interrupted only by a few houses, and now and then a windmill (which, expected, seemed to prove a kind of traveler's truth).

It was dark when they reached the first town, Roosendaal, where they roused a man and found a room. Because hunger nagged stronger than fatigue, they were disappointed when the manager said that he did not have dining facilities at this hour. He could however direct them to an excellent restaurant, but, no, could not himself cash a Travelers Check. So the Schrams, who had no Dutch money, walked around and around the dark town, clutching their stomachs, and tried to find a cambio or railroad station or shop where they could get a check cashed.

Finally they stopped at the window of a small greasy shop; the smell of french fries hung in the lard-yellow light.

"Do we have *any* money?" asked Mrs. Schram.

He counted. Some Belgian francs, a dime and two pennies U.S. Jerked along by his wife, he found himself standing before a woman who scooped strips of fried potatoes into newspaper. This woman could not understand him, but the other one spoke reasonable English. Mr. Schram pointed to the balloon-shaped sign, advertising the giant portion, and showed her all his Belgian money. The border was very close.

"No," the woman said, closing his fingers into a fist. "That is nothing."

Everyone watched as he slowly drew back his hand; it returned with a thick book of Travelers Checks. "Then would you kindly cash this?" He removed a twenty.

The woman searched his face; then wiped her hands and took the check, holding it close to her eyes. "This army pay check?" And handed it back.

"No, no," he said, "it's an international form of

currency." But the woman moved to the next customer, and Mr. Schram, embarrassed, slid the paper into his pocket. Then he had an idea: American money was good anywhere. He dug out his twelve cents U.S. and when the woman returned pointed at the smaller cloud-shaped sign, which offered a small portion of potato frites for thirty-five Dutch cents, the equivalent of a dime.

The woman looked at this money and the sign and Mr. Schram. "That's last week's price."

Mr. Schram knew she was lying; yet, in shame and dismay, he pocketed his few poor coins and, supporting his wife, walked back to the hotel where their stomachs rumbled all night.

In the morning Mr. Schram got his passport back, left the luggage for security, and found a bank where he cashed forty dollars into Dutch guilders. He would not be caught penniless again. He was too old for foodless nights.

After the American-sized breakfast which came with the room, the Schrams considered buying bicycles; hitch-hiking was out, regardless of what they had read. But in the shop below the hotel they found an old Lambretta scooter. Mr. Schram, who had also read that the price of anything in Europe could be knocked down by arguing, told the man one hundred and twenty-five American dollars was too much for a machine so old, with worn tires and an oil leak. But the man was firm. He had not read such books. If they were in Italy, which they were not, they could find a good scooter for much less, the man said. But here, no.

They paid the man, listened carefully to driving instructions, strapped on their baggage, and rode to Amsterdam in style. But traffic was thick and fast, and in their desire to stay alive they saw little of the countryside. In Amsterdam, numb with cold, cramped after four hours on the humming scooter, they took the first hotel in sight. It seemed cheap.

For two days they enjoyed the Rijksmuseum and the Stedelijk, the canals and sidewalk cafes. But they shrank at every meal when hands reached to be filled; when they were forced to pay extra for bread, wine, napkins and silverware.

"But our books," said Mrs. Schram, "told us Europe was cheap."

"It is," said Mr. Schram, "in the south. These northern countries are cold-blooded."

So they went south, toward warmth and low costs. It was at the Belgian border, when they stopped to buy insurance, that they found they had been tricked again.

The inn-keeper read from the registration and filled out the forms: "A one hundred and twenty-five centimeter machine . . . "

Mr. Schram, who had been nodding affirmatives, looked up from his beer. "No, it's a hundred and fifty centimeter."

The man shook his head and pointed to the registration.

"But I specifically asked the mechanic if it was a one-fifty." Mr. Schram, who knew a little about motors, felt gypped by one-sixth of what he had paid for. He protested, but the inn-keeper continued to write.

"Let's go over to Roosendaal and see the man," said Mrs. Schram, who knew nothing about motors but who sympathized with her husband. "We'll get our money back."

"It'll be dark," said Mr. Schram, kicking the ancient machine to life. "We'll go on." But in his mind he saw a scooter loaded with baggage being pushed by hand over the Alps.

In Brussels the nightmare began in earnest. The guide book listed a low-priced hotel "for people who do not expect luxuries." Somehow, without a city map, they found the address but not the hotel. As they rested on a corner, to check the book again, a fishy-looking man in a worn suit came up and they showed him the name in the book. But he couldn't read, it seemed, and so they pronounced it twice, slowly, and he motioned for them to follow.

Mr. Schram pushed the scooter along the gutter. The first man found another man, and after a brief conference, the second man pointed across from where the Schrams had originally been standing; a small sign on the building read Hotel du Botanique. Mr. Schram struggled to turn the scooter around as the first man returned to lean against the handlebars and point across the street.

"Yes, yes, thank you. *Merci beaucoup*," said Mr. Schram, struggling against the man, against the traffic, against the weight of the overloaded scooter, as he pushed it across the street to the hotel.

The room had a bed which sloped and wallpaper which sagged; and it cost more than the price the book stated. They had no choice really but to take it. When they returned to the street to get their baggage, the man crossed from the opposite corner and mustered up some English. "I find hotel, no?" he said, defensively.

"Yes, thank you." Mr. Schram reached into his pocket to place the first, and smallest, of several coins in the man's outstretched hand.

When they were settled the Schrams looked for the concierge. They found her in the darkened dining room before the teevee set, in the lap of a young man, a bottle of wine in her lap.

"Ahem, could we get something to eat?"

"Dining room has closed, m'sieur. So sorry," the woman said, and returned to her teevee and boy friend.

Then it was like a bad dream which recurs. They walked down empty streets, crossed the bridge and followed the gaily lit street crowded with restaurants. After checking the prices on the menu in the window of the first, they entered. Then Mr. Schram realized he had lots of Dutch guilders, which were useless, very few Belgian francs, and no American money. And again, unless they had exceptional luck, it was too late to cash a Travelers Check.

As the waiter took their orders and brought silverware, Mr. Schram, uncertain what else to do, went up to the counter and asked the aging, beefy redhead if she could cash a Travelers Check. He was sure she could; this was not a potato frite shop.

Her voice turned every head his way. "Oh, no. On those I must lose money. Better you should lose money." Then, lowering her voice slightly, she added: "You have enough to eat on, don't you?"

Mr. Schram, who had felt embarrassment in the potato frite joint, was mortified in this elegant restaurant, where light shining from every fine furnishing reflected his crime. "Of course," he said loudly. "I happen to have a great deal of money." Trying to look scornful and haughty, he walked away.

At the table the silverware and water waited. Mr. Schram drank half the water, looked at his wife, and they began that long walk out the door, conscious of the loud, deprecatory talk at their backs.

"Not another hungry night," cried Mrs. Schram.

"Easy dear," he said, leading her across the street to the Shakespearean Restaurant. "We'll go in here," he said, after reading the menu. He had fifty-five Belgian francs, just enough for one order of fried chicken. But, he was worried about the extras and the tips; he decided on the sidewalk that the best thing was to be perfectly frank with the waiter.

They took a table near the door, and when the waiter came over Mr. Schram preluded the meal with a brief, but factual, account of the situation. The waiter's smile faded, his eyebrows drooped, and he relaxed from attention to shove a toothpick in his mouth. Mr. Schram finished and the waiter said certainly, he understood their problem; who had not been broke and hungry at one time or another. . . . Now, if he could see their money?

Mr. Schram held all his Belgian francs in the palm of one hand, exactly enough for one order; the waiter scooped them to his pocket and walked away.

"You see, my dear," Mr. Schram said, "a true traveler is able to cope with any disaster." Yet he felt absolutely devastated by the incidents of the night, and those of the days before. Shame, anger, impotent failure grew when the waiter brought the food. For he had not only given them the worst parts of the bird—backs and necks—but he had neglected to put on any accessories: no vegetables, no coffee, no potato frites. Only four poor pieces of chicken and a basket of dry bread. Not even a glass of water. But Mr. Schram could not bring himself to protest; the waiter knew there would be no tip.

The Schrams divided the chicken; picked thin pieces of meat from bone, while the waiter picked his teeth and waited. Mr. Schram's jaws ground in silent wrath, and he vowed tomorrow he would return with plenty of money, order the best on the menu, eat it all very slowly, demand every manner of service possible, and leave without tipping. No, that would still profit the restaurant. He would cash a couple of Travelers Checks and simply drop in, to flash the money at the waiter—then he'd go across the street and do the same to the fat redhead there. If they thought Americans were made of money, well he'd prove it.

As there was little to eat they finished quickly. Mrs. Schram said: "See if he'll bring a glass of water."

"He won't," said Mr. Schram, but he motioned for the man anyway.

"Yes?" asked the waiter, bowing slightly; far back in his eyes he seemed to be laughing. "You enjoyed the dinner?"

"Could we please have a glass of water?" Out of spite he laid two American pennies on the table. "For your trouble."

"No trouble, sir," the waiter said, going to the bar and returning with a single glass of water. He picked up the coins, however, and, as Mrs. Schram drank, examined them carefully. "But," he said, "these are nothing."

"That's just what we got here for our money," said Mr. Schram. "Nothing."

They walked back to the hotel and all night fought gravity in the sloping bed. At dawn, tired and hungry, they went to the dining room where the man who had held the concierge on his lap last night now served the cafe au lait and dry, butterless rolls. They ate quickly, paid their bill without argument, loaded the scooter and drove off. On the opposite corner, like a minor devil, was the man who had directed them to this hotel; his farewell wave was ominous.

Mr. Schram drove fast, as if every mile gained to the south would bring better things.

So now they listened to the racket of gunfire and cheered for Napoleon, puzzled only by the question of why he should want this country. It was as stupid and dull as the people they had met. Mr. Schram beat his knuckles against the half-empty wine bottle, as anger replaced shame. Why had he wanted to be a good tourist? Well, by god from now on their own self-preservation came first. He'd argue about every price, and he'd get proof in writing. He'd refuse to pay for extras. And in the future he'd certainly carry a pocket of very small change, for tipping. He'd remain polite, but stand his ground. He was too old for this sort of thing.

A man ambled into the parking field, watched the two cars near the road for a few minutes, then spied the Schram's scooter. He smiled as he greeted them and, in the face of Mr. Schram's scowl, handed over a plain sheet of paper with the number twenty-five.

Mr. Schram glanced at it, then at the man: his torn shoes, patched pants, faded shirt. There was nothing official about either the man or his paper. Mr. Schram considered this a test case, so he handed the paper back with a vague gesture.

"Sir," the man said, smiling, "for parking here."

Mr. Schram was outraged; the sign intoned this was free parking. "No forestand. No spike so."

The tattered man was puzzled; he walked behind the scooter and looked at the Netherlands' license. Scratching his head, he began to speak very slowly in what Mr. Schram guessed was Walloon.

Mr. Schram gestured in a vage, puzzled way. How could they be expected to pay when communication was impossible? He was beginning to enjoy himself.

The man squatted next to Mr. Schram and held out first two fingers and then five; as his lips moved silently he pointed at the scooter on the ground.

"No, no," said Mr. Schram. "No can sell scooter. Oola chicky chick see. No oola chicky."

"Momento," said the man, deciding they must be Spanish, and disappeared.

Mrs. Schram laughed, and Mr. Schram trembled with nervous excitement. "We played the game and won. This is another racket, but he didn't get us." Nor, Mr. Schram vowed, would anyone else. They would pay only when they desired something done for them. By god from now on it would be different.

Lunch was over and Mr. Schram was dropping the litter in a trash can when the man returned, accompanied by a burly, unshaven fellow with a beret and striped tee-shirt. Mr. Schram felt strong; his eyes did not turn from the second man's hard gaze.

"What's going on here?" The burly man's hands were on his hips and his legs spread apart, as if forming a barrier. "You got to pay to park here."

Because this man seemed more intelligent than the first, Mr. Schram did not try any gibberish; his voice was firm. "The sign says to park here; it doesn't say anything about paying. Besides, anyone can scribble numbers on a piece of paper."

"What d'ya mean?" The man shoved his chin out and glared. "You park, you pay."

"Sorry, not us," said Mr. Schram, loading the lunch basket on the scooter's rack.

The man stepped forward, fists balled. He hesitated, the muscles in his face tightened, and he shouted: "We'll call the police."

"You do that," said Mr. Schram, who now feared nothing. He buttoned up his jacket and pulled goggles over his eyes.

"Okay," said the man, pulling his chin back a little. "Since you're leaving make it twenty francs."

Mr. Schram was amazed; the man had actually backed down. "Not one franc," he said, starting the machine and climbing on.

"Fifteen."

"Nope," he said, feeling the weight of his wife behind him. "Go play your tricks on some tourist."

"Ten," said the man, running behind the machine as Mr. Schram slowly drove off. "C'mon, you Americans can afford it."

Mr. Schram, thinking that the man might grab the handlebars and tip them over, twisted the throttle full speed; all his anger and revenge was expended as gravel spewed from the rear tire. Mr. Schram did not consider this a retreat, but good battle strategy. The vanquished remained in a cloud of dust, ineffectively shaking his fist.

And as the scooter turned into the highway, headed south, from the weatherbeaten shack cannons fired a salute and the music was the victory march.

THE CHICKEN WHICH BECAME A RAT

"He ain't *eating* the eggs," Uncle Boswick said. His voice carried that same amazed indignation as when he had asked my father, "Yer *paid* for the window?" or when he had reported to me, "He did it with the *sam-yer-eye*." His world had its own practical logic, of survival; these were acts which left him confounded. "The Jap ain't eating the eggs and he won't sell them."

"What's he plan to do?" I asked.

"No plans." Uncle Boswick shook the beads of dew from his slacks, and pointed his whangee cane across the tall grass which stretched from our house to the Jap's tarpaper shack: within the wire I could imagine the gaunt, long-necked hens eyeing each other suspiciously. "Nothing—the chickens are getting wild, the eggs are piling up, the garden's full of weeds—I don't get it."

And then, after picking out the grass kernals which jutted from his perforated two-tone shoes, Uncle Boswick was off to the USO club. To build the boys' morale.

I was surprised that his attitude toward the Jap had changed from hatred to amazed indignation. The Jap had disappointed him. Eggs were rationed and Uncle Boswick saw the Jap's reluctance to sell his not as a foreign plot but rather as evidence of the humorless intensity of a backward race: Uncle Boswick would know how to make money here, somehow, if the Jap would only work *with* him.

What surprised me most was the change in the Jap's property: weeds choked the garden, the corn stalks were stunted and brown, the chicken coop was a box of rusty wire, a small concentration camp. If Uncle Boswick was baffled, how could I be expected to understand? But it seemed that after V-E Day the Jap had given up, as if he knew the Allies would win, and now the land was reverting to the desolation it had been a year ago—a wasteland beyond the city's limits, marshy in winter, baked hard in summer. It now resembled the useless landscape of before last spring, when one night the Jap had infiltrated our neighborhood. He had sneaked in without noise or luggage, and the next morning, when I peeked through the gun-slot of venetian blinds, he was on the flatlands, bent to his hoe, against the rising sun.

It was the third year of the war.

His blade flashed like a bayonet into American soil. Silhouetted against the sun which spilled red across the tips of furrows, his insect shape reminded me of something I had seen or read—something thin, creepy, and utterly evil.

Then I recalled the source. On the coffee table was the current issue of *Liberty*: on the cover Hitler assumed the body of a jackass, his hoofs kicking Europe; beside him Mussolini was a baboon, dangling mindlessly from a war-wrecked tree; and in the upper-right corner Tojo was a furry, menacing spider whose web, like the land around our Jap, was stained blood-red.

The pavement ended at our house, and Home Front defenses honey-combed the neighborhood's perimeter. The day after the sneak attack on Pearl Harbor we had marched into this wasteland and each boy had dug a foxhole, a hiding place against the bombing raids which seemed imminent. The only bombs to fall were random fire-balloons which fizzled out in the wet forests west of Portland: but as weeks turned to months into years, all our young muscle was directed at the War Effort. We dug a gridwork of slit trenches, pillboxes, and tunnels, and for armament we had stacks of dirt clods, stones, bags of smoke dust, apples drilled to accept a firecracker, and of course our B-B guns. Uncle Boswick had often said that we could expect a Presidential E. flag.

Into these trenches we crawled—Piggy, Slats, Mike, The MacGregor, and myself—soot streaked across our faces, like Commandos in movies; and we moved out, sinking low until the last observation post, where smooth throwing rocks and solid dirt clods were piled. For we were children of war, and had been taught to hate.

"I can smell him," The MacGregor said.

I crawled to the rim and partly turned, one eye on the Jap and the other on The MacGregor, who braced a foot against the dirt wall, his arm cocked. When I raised my finger he fired a distance round. It sailed across the broken landscape and dropped so far behind the Jap did not pause in his stroke.

"Correct elevation," I whispered.

The MacGregor sent off another stone, which arced white against the blue, until falling, it became a black speck lost in the weeds. Still the enemy hoed on.

I realized that if The MacGregor, our strongest gunner, couldn't make the distance, none of us could. But I whispered, "Harrassment rounds," and raised two fingers, which meant fire at will.

Our hate spun five clods upward, where they teetered against the sky, to fall in uneven arcs on the dull ground. The Jap, untouched, continued his insidious ground work, chopping treacherously at this piece of the United States, knocking crystals of dew from the weeds as he enlarged his claim.

Over our heads a whistle pierced the sky.

The black speck seemed to travel forever in its swift, guided flight, diminishing until it reached an invisible peak; with a flash of white, the gesture of a wingtip, it peeled off, screaming earthward, to crash through the window of the Jap's shanty. The enemy jumped, dropped his hoe, and ran, flapping his wings like a chicken attempting flight.

We cheered, and as I turned to see who our supporting artillery might be, a volley of laughter strafed the field. At the edge of the pavement Uncle Boswick flipped a heavy stone from hand to hand; he looked more than ever like the posters of Uncle Sam.

It was toward the Jap that he pointed: I want you.

I could not understand why my father, when he learned of our victory, carefully folded the evening paper, hitched up his pants, and strode down the street, off the pavement and across the field.

He was gone a long time, and dinner was halfway through before he returned. In fact, Uncle Boswick was well into seconds, his mouth so full he could barely exclaim: "Yer *paid* for the window?"

"But why?" I asked. Was he a traitor? Aiding the enemy. I almost believed this in spite of the signs on our front door glass: We Bought Our Quota. We Have A Boy in the NAVY; the blue cloth with the gold star. V for Victory . . .

"Because your Uncle broke it," he said, spreading white margarine on his bread, digging into the Relief gravy over cereal-laden hamburger. "And because what that Jap does on that gawdforsaken land is none of your business."

Now I could not believe it. I felt sick, confused, as shattered as the Jap's window. I looked to Uncle Boswick, but he was smiling as he snubbed out his cigarette—smoked as usual to the middle. Another wasteful habit which aggravated my mother.

"Just leave him alone," my father said quietly, always chewing. "Stay away from his place."

Uncle Boswick could not tolerate the sight of my father calmly eating supper, asking us to leave the Jap alone. "But he's the ENEMY!" he shouted, fists clenched on the table.

"How do you know?" my father asked.

"Well . . . he's a gawdamn Jap, ain't he?"

"There," I said, jumping up, pointing to the wall. "There." On the kitchen wall were two pages my mother had torn from *Life* magazine: *How to Tell Japs From The Chinese*. The photos had an overlay to show that Chinese have long, fine-boned faces, parchment yellow complexion, and never have rosy cheeks; Japs have squat faces with the nose a flat blob, earthy yellow complexion, and sometimes rosy cheeks. I read: *An often sounder clue is facial expression, shaped by cultural not anthropological factors. Chinese wear rational calm of tolerant realists. Japs, like General Tojo, show humorless intensity of ruthless mystics.* The other page showed Tall Chinese brothers and Short Japanese admirals—our allies and our enemies.

"He looked just like the Short Japanese admirals, and..."

"Did he have rosy cheeks?" my father asked, smiling.

"Yes," I said, although I really wasn't sure. I hadn't been able to see my enemy's face.

"I don't like that Jap any better than you do," my father said, looking at me, Uncle Boswick, and my mother. "But he's had a rough row to hoe." As he cleaned his plate with a final slice of bread, he repeated the story the Jap had told him: there had been a large farm near Gresham, where the fields sloped off toward the sun, and where seeds would not stay in the ground—in spring the strawberries grew big as a boy's fist, and in fall the corn was so large and tender that a single ear would make a meal. My father told the story in the dreamy, tragic tone of a man who has not owned anything himself—saying that in only two more years the farm would have been paid off, but after Pearl Harbor it was confiscated by the government and sold at auction, and the Jap—a Nisei, who had been born on the farm, and was therefore an American citizen—had spent the past two and a half years in an internment camp near Pendleton. Now released, he had no family, no farm, no money. "So I think you—everybody—ought to lay off him."

"Whadda think the Nips're doing to our boys?" Uncle Boswick shouted. "Wake Island, Bataan, the Death March. And don't forget Pearl Harbor: those jokers didn't pay us for any broken windows there. I wish. . . . "

My mother got up and began to clear the table. No doubt she was thinking of Grant on the *USS Plymouth*, now a month out of Hawaii. My father rolled Bugler into tan, wheat-straw paper, touched his tongue to the edge and flattened the ends. He always enjoyed one of Uncle Boswick's real cigarettes after dinner, but he would not ask; nor was one offered tonight.

The last thing I heard as I got up and went to sit on the front porch was Uncle Boswick finishing his sentence: " . . . I could get my licks in."

Uncle Boswick was our hero. The Declaration of War was being read over a million radio speakers when Uncle Boswick's foot missed a tailgate at Fort Ord; he lay screaming in pain as Roosevelt's voice called for unlimited sacrifices from our fighting men. The truck had been barely moving, but something had happened to Uncle Boswick's back. He was given a medical discharge and a fifty per cent disability pension, which meant he did not need to work even if he could. In the confusion of that December the papers officially honoring him as the first casualty of the war were lost in channels, but Uncle Boswick got the pension, a Purple Heart, and freedom from rationing: he had unlimited supplies at the airbase PX. It was unfortunate, my mother often said, that the PX did not stock eggs and meat, but only cigarettes and liquor.

With my father it was different: he was 4-F.

At times I felt that he was letting us down by not being in uniform. Oh sure, building Liberty Ships was pretty important work, but I could not get too excited about it—not even on those days when we would go to Swan Island for a launching, when after the speeches and free lunch he would show us the whirly crane he drove, a tiny cab sitting a hundred feet high on delicate girder legs. But seeing it sail down the tracks, with a bulkhead dangling from the long cables, just wasn't the same as seeing those thin, censored V-letters that The MacGregor's father sent from North Africa.

So I could not understand why he had paid for the Jap's window. Although we were not so poor as we had been before the war, there was no money to spend foolishly. Oh, perhaps I had a vague idea why my father had paid off: because he believed that every man should own a piece of ground and a house, and that all others should respect the limits of ownership—even if it was a house no better than ours, where the wind whipped through the ivy-covered latticework which was its foundation.

As I looked through dusk across the field I could see the Jap, his hoe flashing in the dim light. The sight made me furious. How were we to leave him alone? He was the enemy: newspapers, magazines, our teachers, had taught us to hate him. And we learned well to hate. Oh, how we hated him—deeply, intensely. He was the grinning monkey-pilot who gleefully leaned into his gunsight to machinegun parachutists. He was the spidery Nip who saved bullets by using his bayonet on the wounded. We knew too well of his exquisite tortures—bamboo splinters ignited under toenails, fingernails removed by pliers, the eye-lid lifted off by the knife's thin whisper.

These thoughts were bothering me when Uncle Boswick came out to sit on the porch. "What I'd like to know is how he got *released*. With a war on."

"Maybe he escaped," I suggested.

"He's up to something," Uncle Boswick whispered. "Keep your eye on him, kid. That slant-eyed devil is a spy or a saboteur."

Our eyes were on him all right. Every day after breakfast Piggy, Slats, Mike, The MacGregor, and I gathered in the farthest observation post. We pushed Uncle Boswick's binoculars over the rim of the hole until the lenses were full of yellow skin—earthy yellow, I was sure. We harrassed the Jap with random shots. We saluted him with raised middle-fingers and screamed *Banzai*, and asked how the hell Tojo was.

But the Jap refused to notice us, and anyway, we saw nothing suspicious. Just the hoe striking the ground and weeds flung from the tiny green shoots which were beginning to appear. This went on for a week, and suddenly the eighth day was Summer. By ten o'clock it was seventy, the flatlands shimmered, and the Jap, slashing with his hoe or carrying buckets of water, looked like a movie mirage.

The OP was an oven. When Piggy refused to drink brackish canteen water, he went home. Then Mike remembered the bandoliers of ice in his mother's refrigerator. Soon only The MacGregor and myself sweated in the hole, pouring water over our heads, swearing, hating the Jap for keeping us there.

And at noon, when the sun was straight up, erasing any shade, we went swimming.

But the war, glorious and dreadful, near and distant, continued to touch us in many ways. Every day my mother scanned the paper fearfully:

TODAY'S
ARMY-NAVY
CASUALTY LIST
Washington—Following are the
latest casualties in the military
services, including next of kin.
ARMY-NAVY DEAD

Her finger would tremble through the list to where Grant's last name, first name, rank, might be; then the newspaper would collapse in her folded hands and she would cry or pray or both. Sometimes, in the afternoon when the house was empty, I would burst in from play to find her at the writing desk, sobbing over a stack of tissue-thin V-letters; they were all postmarked San Francisco's Censor's Office, and she was wondering, no doubt, where in the wide Pacific her oldest boy might be.

Elsewhere, Captain America turned bullets off his shield, the Green Lantern sought truth, and even the Submariner turned to the side of good: another ring of filthy rotten Nazi spies and saboteurs was broken. The Axis shed their animal skins in defeat. In our comics we fought the war, and in the papers we read of its progress: June 6th was D-Day; during that month V-1 bombs, a terrible undreamed of weapon, began to fall on England; the Marianas Campaign pushed ahead. The pleasant summer advanced, and so did our boys: troops landed at Saipan, and during July the big drive began through Normandy; Guam and Paris were liberated in August.

At home the war controlled us. Our battles were fought every day: we could buy comic books, but few fireworks and no bubblegum. The B-B's for our guns turned to lead. The currency of conversation was ration discs and coupon books. In our driveway my father's 1934 Terraplane sat without tires, graded by the C sticker on its windshield. Now he drove only the sedan, a 1930 Hudson; it was an immense, magnificent car, dark and square; and when he placed an ironing board across the jump seats he was able to haul nine people every day to the shipyard. However essential this was to the war effort, he could not get the red and white B sticker changed to the coveted grade A—so the coupe rested on its rims and the sedan eased around town at 35 mph on ancient patched rubber and there was not enough extra gas that summer to even go to the beach.

But we fought on: we flattened tons of tin cans for tanks and salvaged kitchen fat for munitions and bundled high stacks of newspapers and magazines for who knows what. We bought a twenty-five cent savings stamp a week, and when the book was full it became a War Bond. On walks and walls we chalked our beliefs—*Hitler is a Heel*—and assertions of evolution—*Tojo is a Monkey's Uncle*. We said prayers, pledged allegiance, saluted the flag; and a thousand times our razored hate cheered John Wayne's single-handed assault against the Japs on Friday nights.

One bright morning when even the haze of war could not hide the sun, I came from behind the humped, tireless coupe in the driveway and suddenly noticed the marshland had become a profuse garden. The corn was a screen, thick as any bamboo grove, and below the tomatoes glowed red: tiny suns of nippon. Bayonets of onion greens stabbed upward, potatoes, peppers, lettuce, carrots camouflaged the ground. Even the tarpaper shack seemed to stand a little straighter in the chaos of flowers, and its shutters and front door were painted bright yellow.

Sneaking through the foliage was the Jap: he was building tripods, small tent skeletons, for the beans.

Behind me Uncle Boswick came out, stretched, and surveyed the changed, technicolor landscape. He sported a new panama hat and two-tone perforated shoes, and I guessed that he was on his way to the USO club, although it was pretty early.

"Poppies," he said. "And not the kind the Legion sells."

I admired Uncle Boswick—I would never have thought of *opium*—and so I said yes, when he asked me to reconnoiter the area and to get some fresh vegetables, to be sent to his friends in Washington, D.C., for analysis. In spite of my father's order that the Jap be left alone, I wanted to get in on the fight. Our fight. The rest of the day was spent with the Gang mapping out a plan of action. It was only after the details were settled that Slats mentioned it didn't get dark until nine, his bedtime. Our hoots and jeers at Slats were suddenly silenced when we realized that there wasn't one of us could stay out that late.

Therefore, at nine, as the sun fell beyond the muted, blacked out neon of Portland, I crawled from my bedroom window and slipped into the high grass. In the near-darkness I groped along the trench-work, and at the farthest OP I began to inch toward that garden on my stomach, a hunting knife clenched between my teeth. Near my face the *chiirrruup* of the crickets was deafening, and at every shift of my body the gas-mask bag slipped noisily; I paused to look back, and through the summer mists I saw the dull yellow cracks around black-out curtains in our front room, far away.

Crickets chirped nearby, an echo of bullfrogs farther out in the marsh, and along Johnson Creek the Galloping Goose cried into the night. A veil of wind blew a pungent, acrid green and then I saw the oiled, metallic sides of vegetables: cucumbers lay like small surface mines, aimed in every direction.

I waited, staring into the blackness at the tarpaper shack. Then the knife blade slipped across prickly stalks and three large specimens were in the bag. I crouched among the corrugated sides of squash, knife slashing, and moved quickly into the bayonets of green onions. Beyond were tomato plants, the hard black balls swimming in metallic greenness. Among the wide, sharp leaves of corn I was shielded, and it was not until the fourth ear had been split from its stalk that I felt a pang of fear. In the terror of silence leaf rasped on leaf. The knife was in my hand when I stood to stare into the silent, black night.

Not three plants away the Jap waited, arms folded, hat tipped to conceal his inscrutable face.

Even as I jumped I knew it must be a *scarecrow*—but I threw the knife overhand and flung away the gas-mask bag and ran across the misty, deep grass, the uneven ground falling away under my racing feet. Only when I was again in bed, rubbing my legs to stop their trembling, did I realize that the Jap had my knife—that he was now *armed*.

I slept with this fear and in a dream I heard voices at the back steps: *well they are lovely* and *let me pay* and *I may keep the bag?*

I heard the screen door open and my mother say *Thankew*—it was a trick no doubt—but then the door slammed shut and a figure passed outside my window. It shuffled under that same loose, flowing shirt and broad hat I had seen last night—but again *I could not see any feature of the face*.

"Well, you're awake," my mother said. She was running water into a dishpan at the sink, and on the table, the gas-mask bag spilled vegetables like a horn of plenty. "The Jap man *gave* us these," she said. "He wouldn't take any money, but I asked him to bring us some every week and I said I'd pay him a quarter—does that sound fair? He said he wants to buy some chickens."

Once a week until November the Jap came with a bag of produce, to accept my mother's money (as if there was no war on!) and to pass so close beneath the window that he must have felt the glow of my hatred.

He never did return my knife, either.

In what seemed the middle of summer, school began again. No matter that Paris and Guam and Palau had been liberated, or that bombs were falling on Manila, Luzon, and Okinawa, we marched into dull classrooms, carrying new notebooks already marked A.A.F.: we were all destined to become pilots, wearing white scarfs, chamois helmets, and leather jackets with the Flying Tiger patch on the back, like Errol Flynn. School for us was the twice-weekly War Communique film, where in the fluttering light we saw Patton tanks smash hedgerows, and bombs tumble like eggs toward the ultimate explosion. We squirmed with excitement as infantry charged across beaches strewn with dead and debris, as a flame-thrower sucked burning Japanese from caves, ending their ruthless mysticism. When the narrator's voice and the marching music ground to a halt and the projector stopped and the olive drab blinds were raised, the boys would turn to look at one another and even Ellie Chombrake, the skinniest kid in the class, wore a sense of purpose on his face. The war was a common bond, holding us together; we all knew our role in this struggle for freedom.

Besides Christmas, only two things happened that school year.

One night in December, shortly before vacation, I was doing homework when I heard shouting in the field: it was The MacGregor.

From my front porch I heard him shouting crazily at the Jap and there was a distant crash of glass. I ran across the field, leaping trenches, until I saw the blurred outline of The MacGregor lobbing rock after rock at the tarpaper shanty; through the mist came the report of splintering boards. He was screaming and falling forward with every rock he threw, and I waited a minute before placing a hand on his shoulder. The face that turned was distorted into a crazy mask, and I stepped back, but not quickly enough—his throwing fist, clutching a rock, came from the night to smash into my face.

It was father who helped us both home, and when he returned from The MacGregor's house, to hold an icepack against my bleeding cheek, he told us that Mr. MacGregor had been killed in what the newspapers celebrated as the Battle of the Bulge—where General McAuliffe said "nuts" to the Nazis. The telegram from the War Department assured Mrs. MacGregor that her husband had died a Hero.

My cheek no longer hurt: I felt good, and I wanted to shake The MacGregor's hand. But it was too late that night, my father said, and for the rest of the week The MacGregor's desk at school was empty, and by Saturday the mother and son had moved to Seattle, leaving a dark, lifeless house.

The next week, as if to replace our loss, Piggy's uncle sent home a large, olive drab box from the Pacific. Piggy was certain that it was a Christmas present for him but Gussie, his aunt, who was staying for the duration, said the box contained souvenirs, and that she had been instructed *not* to open it until Jed came home.

And within five minutes she had a crowbar against the lid, splintering wood; inside lay three long, dark rifles, a pistol wrapped in tan, oil-slick paper, and two Jap officer swords. Everything was coated with a thick rancid grease, but the guns were beautiful and the swords were works of art: they had scabbards crafted with inlaid wood and pearl, into which the delicate blade whispered. Gussie, who no doubt expected silks, hammered the lid back and from then on the basement was kept locked.

But for us, knowing those weapons were there, the war

seemed much closer.

School was a huge wheel, grinding toward Spring. Its monotonous progress was interrupted only by the excitement of paper drives and tin can collections, practice blackouts and marches to the basement, which was now called the Air Raid Shelter. Here we huddled until the All Clear bell, discussing how we would fight the war when called, even though we could not see how it would last another eight years: the newspaper maps showed wide arrows, and by April the Americans and Russians were shaking hands in a defeated Berlin, while most of Europe was occupied by our boys. Although the Japanese were using *kamikazes* and Baka bombs, Iwo Jima and Okinawa had been captured and it was only a matter of time before we would invade Japan itself.

Our winter had been mild and the spring rains turned the ground an energetic green. The trenches were hip-high in water, but from my bedroom window I watched the Jap at work seeding and hoeing. I wondered what he thought—surely he knew now that his country was defeated. A hundred short Japanese admirals were no match for one tall John Wayne marine. Why had he come here? What did he want? What was he working so hard for? No matter if he should again transform that wasteland into a blooming paradise, the whole neighborhood blotted him out with hate. Yet he foolishly worked on: feet bare, pants rolled to the knee, he dashed along the furrows in a lurching, forward-slanting crouch under the wide straw hat. When he was not working the land he was building the chicken coop. He had scrounged fragments of wood and wire; and the coop, a temporary, tottering structure, made the tarpaper shack seem a palace. Apparently he had sold enough vegetables the previous summer, because one morning the fenced area was filled with small puffs of yellow, like frantic flowers. His dream was coming true, and I wanted to cross that field to make sure he understood that this could only happen in America—this was free enterprise, democracy.

The Jap had his chicks, V-E Day was celebrated, my dad was talking about the new car he would buy when this war was over, the neighborhood grew green, and school would soon end. It was into this spirit of optimism that Piggy's uncle returned.

If I had not seen him in uniform for a fleeting minute, as he walked from the car to the house that first day, I would not have believed that he had been in battle: all day, every day, he sat on the front porch in a rocking chair, wearing faded bib overalls and a brown shirt, and bearing no visible wound. He was a strange man with small, dull eyes and skin which became red without tanning; when he spoke his voice faded through short sentences, and he refused to talk about the war, even to Uncle Boswick.

"All he wants," said Uncle Boswick, "is to get back to that Alabama dirt farm, and sit."

"That's okay," my father said. "A man ought to own a bit of land."

"Gussie, now she's cut from a different bolt," Uncle Boswick said, winking. "I know her pretty well. She likes it here—plenty of ocean and forests. Bet you five dollars she don't leave with him."

"Oh, now," my mother said, but her protest was weak for she had the gossip about Gussie straight form Piggy's mother: how Gussie had worked at Oregon Shipyard for two weeks after Jed had been shipped overseas. She had been back only for launchings, when the company gave out free beer and food, and we were told that any Saturday night she could be found along Harbor Drive, where ships on the Willamette tied up. Gussie, my mother said, was "wild" and "needed a baby to keep her home." Now that Jed was back she was sure that Gussie would "straighten out." Uncle Boswick, who seemed to know an awful lot about Gussie, said he wasn't so sure.

But rain or shine Jed remained in his rocking chair on the front porch, surveying the neighborhood with dull eyes. His uniform remained in the closet, and Piggy reported that Jed had gone into the basement only once to check the heavy box of souvenirs.

So we were surprised to see Gussie with the big samurai sword.

That late June sun was already an explosion of fire, burning life from the grass, but Piggy, Slats, Mike, and I worked in the trenches anyway; we felt needed, for after V-E Day the war focused on the Pacific, our ocean. We repaired trench walls where the rains had worn them away, and filled sandbags, piled our rocks, and sometimes lobbed an occasional missile at the Jap's chicken coop—but half-heartedly, for now that we knew Tojo was finished our Jap seemed more like a docile intruder: unwanted, but harmless. Uncle Boswick had even taken to crossing the field two or three times a week, to "interrogate" the Jap about when the hens would start laying. For eggs were still rationed.

I trained Uncle Boswick's binoculars on the Jap's shack, then slowly swept them across the chicken coop, the vast garden—for I wanted to see my enemy's face, to see if in these last days of the war that face could maintain its humorless intensity—when at my elbow Slats said: "What's that noise?"

All I heard was Gussie's radio. Whenever she was sunbathing her radio blared hot hillbilly music into the quiet neighborhood. But today she was not sunbathing. When I swung the binoculars past our house to Piggy's backyard, I saw Gussie in the far corner wearing tiny shorts and halter.

The noise that Slats heard was the blackberry vines

being chopped, and what Gussie was using was the big Jap sword.

She was working, and I recalled what my mother had said about Gussie "straightening out" with Jed home. It was the first time I had ever seen her do work of any kind. Like Uncle Boswick, she did not need to work.

We charged from the trench, knowing that long wooden box of war souvenirs was lying open in an unlocked basement. But Piggy said: "If we wait for Jed, *he'll* show them to us."

Under the hot sun we waited while on that porch Jed rocked, his eyes focused on something above the rooftops, and in the far corner of the yard the sword flashed like a mirror. We waited, wondering how many American boys' heads that long blade had lopped off. We shuddered, for the courageous blood spilled on Bataan, Corregidor, Wake Island, and for the blade each time that Gussie hit a rock. Through the binoculars I watched Jed's face, dull and impassive, and finally I saw the lips tighten slowly, pulling his eyes narrow. Suddenly the field of vision was filled with his striped bib-overalls. I lowered the glasses to see Jed stand up; he spit once over the porch rail, scratched his seat, and started down the steps as we charged from the trench.

Jed walked slowly past the basement door, down the driveway, and was blotted from sight by our house. We were halfway to the road when Jed reappeared, to take the sword from Gussie.

Later I was unsure exactly what I saw—we were still a good distance away, and it happened very fast. She had the sword raised overhead in both hands, to assault the tenacious blackberry vines, when Jed stepped from behind and grabbed the blade. The surprise of his movement sent her spinning off balance, and she fell among the daggers of the vines. We heard her cry once—a single, abrupt noise—and saw the blade flash, an arc of sunlight across our eyes, forever impressed. An irregular, stunned line of boys watched in horror as Jed came from behind the trees and the obstructing house; he lurched toward that cool dark basement.

We retreated to the trench, where I exchanged one nervous glance with Piggy: Gussie lay in the vines, pumping her blood out, and beyond that dark, recessed doorway Jed had the guns. We gripped the lip of the turf, not even pretending to arm ourselves with throwing stones, until we heard the thin siren droning from Loaner's Corner, an insect in the hot afternoon; and at the same instant a muffled explosion churned up from that basement, growing like a cloud to envelope the neighborhood.

A few minutes after Uncle Boswick jumped the fence which separated Piggy's yard from mine, the police car raced to the curb. As the officers moved up the driveway, guns thrust into the yard's calm, we raced to the road and saw Uncle Boswick point to that far corner. Blood smudged his shirt, and his eyes slanted against tears—at the time, it was my impression that he had cut himself coming over the fence.

And before the policemen came back from viewing Gussie's slim, decapitated body, and before Uncle Boswick chased us into the street, we gathered at the small, dirt spattered basement window: Jed was sitting in the corner, propped against the dirt wall by the Jap rifle. The big toe of his right foot was hooked into the trigger guard; the barrel pointed into the darkness where half his head was missing. Behind him a fan-shaped stain drew flies.

The deaths were not mentioned that evening at supper, a meal eaten in silence; but later, on the front steps, Uncle Boswick announced, as if I did not already know: "He did it with the *sam-yer-eye* sword. Can you believe that? Ahhhh, she was a beautiful girl." He went on, in a voice charged with amazed indignation, to tell how he had seen the blade flash once across the sun from the chaise lounge in our back yard; he thought it was a dream. From that moment his world was one of missing pieces, of edges that never did quite meet, and when I asked him again what *really* had happened all he could say was: "He did it with the *sam-yer-eye*."

But that was not what I wanted to know.

Nor did the Jap make any sense to him. A few days after the deaths Uncle Boswick crossed that wasteland to "interrogate" the Jap, and when he returned his voice was charged with amazed fury. "The hens are finally laying, but *he ain't eating the eggs*. The Jap ain't eating the eggs and he won't sell them. I'm telling you the whole world's gone nuts."

After Uncle Boswick left for the USO club, I got out his binoculars and my plane spotter's manual—for four years I had been searching the skies for a Zero or Mitsubitsi bomber. From the blue skies I lowered the glasses to focus on the Jap's shack, and for the first time I noticed that the profusion of flowers had shrunk back into the mud. The shack leaned to its own shadow; a yellowed newspaper fluttered from the window broken long ago by The MacGregor's stone. I shifted to the garden out back, and saw corn burned by the sun fold into stiff stalks, diminishing like candle wax.

The glasses focused on the slanting assemblage of wood and wire, and although the nests were concealed I could see the clumps of dirty white which flashed from corners: the hens had begun to lay their eggs in any depression. I slowly swung the glasses across the Jap's property—scanning every inch of peeling paint, broken glass, and browned foliage—but I saw no sign of the Jap. The chickens milled about the dusty arena, without food or water, eyeing each other suspiciously. The eggs began to pile up, dropped from the starving, wiry hens, and I knew this was another fiendish, exquisite eastern torture. I pictured the Jap hiding in a corner of the shack, drunk on sake, giggling his sharp-toothed, rat-faced fanaticism.

The eggs piled up, delicate and white, and every day Uncle Boswick crossed that wasteland to beg, plead, argue the Jap into selling him some eggs. I would watch Uncle Boswick cross the field and stand by the bottom step of the porch; I could see his mouth moving, hands flying—*but I never saw the Jap*. Only a shadow across the broken window, a faint movement which might have been the curtain blowing. On any day during the past year he would have been running on short admiral legs across the tilled soil, a water bucket in each hand, or he would have been leaning on his shovel, or kneeling over seeds, as if in prayer. Now he did not come out of the tarpaper shack, not even to feed the chickens.

It was not until two weeks later, when the heat of summer shifted into August, that Uncle Boswick was able to learn *why* the Jap refused to part with his eggs.

Uncle Boswick was trying to talk my mother into going across that field to plead with the Jap. "You've got to go—the egg route is all sewn up, I've got customers. We've got to make some money soon, before this war is over. Gawd knows every businessman has lined *his* nest: the junkyards selling gas stamps and tires from wrecks at black market prices, the gas stations, the meat markets—they're getting rich!"

We had never had any money, and he was trying to appeal to her only fear: poverty. But apparently she feared the Jap even more, for she would not go—not even when he told her what he had learned.

"Do you know *why* he won't do anything with them?" Uncle Boswick asked. "He bought the chickens so he could have some eggs—and now he tells me he can't eat the eggs of hens he knows personally. That he has fed with his own hands. *Hens he knows personally!*"

For Uncle Boswick this was the ultimate puzzle, and he abandoned his attempt to collaborate with the enemy. Other afternoons would be spent in the chaise lounge, warming his war wounds against the sun, clipping money-making advertisements from magazines.

But I continued to watch the drama of torture with a strange fascination: every morning I went to the foxhole and focused binoculars on the chicken coop, where lean hens milled, eyeing each other suspiciously. Their high wiry bodies bobbed and crowded as they rotated in an endless circle under the blazing sun. I saw those near the fence stretch through the wire, their hysterical beaks reaching for any green leaf.

One day toward noon, just as I was about to return home for lunch, I saw a hen squat in the dust and when it rose, the quizzical eye aimed at the sun, its dusty, hoarse clucking was suddenly strangled. The hen's head darted like a wedge; the sharp beak smashed the shell, and the hen began to devour her own egg.

From the side another hen kicked high into the air, wings flapping, mad with the smell of food. A cloud of feathers exploded over the oily yolk as the two fought—others jumped in, and mass hysteria spread like the rising dust cloud. I watched with excited horror, for I had been waiting for something like this—the dust, torn feathers, the savage choked cries. From behind the wire a gas cloud rose, and the smell of rotten eggs drifted on the wind, an ominous yellow cloud which would stain every house, touch every life.

Fifteen minutes later, when the air was fairly clear, I could see that every egg had been pecked open.

Again the tide rotated wing to wing, hungry for food, space, the freedom of flight. They pressed together tightly, accelerating in a small circle within the confines of the wire until motion became a brown blur. Their movement held no hope for escape, but the smell of food had driven them mad and this was a kind of direct action—in desperation their yellow feet raced across the baked earth, the head at the end of the arched neck in pursuit of something. I waited, watching with that same sense of excited horror I had known the day Jed walked off the porch and the morning the Jap had first appeared on our horizon.

Then, near the wire, one stumbled with exhaustion. Her wings fanned the dust, but before she could rise the beak of her neighbor slashed out. She struggled, her chalky cluuuk filled with urgency and alarm, but from the circle's momentum a dozen hens peeled off and were on her, necks extended, beaks chopping at her eyes.

When two of the attackers drew back, their dusty feathers were speckled with blood. Through binoculars I could see the stained hens lift their wings, crane their necks at a difficult angle to drink off the beads of blood. Behind them the circle began to disintegrate, and the smell of blood carried to my foxhole as hens surrounded to attack the attackers.

Originally there were perhaps thirty chickens, and the next day when I returned there were half that number. On the third day there were ten, and then five walked among the debris of feathers and bones. These five had grown heavy, nourished by the fallen, and they waddled grotesque and wary. One stayed in each corner of the coop, and one paced a small circle in the center.

Later there were only two left, and these had been changed until they looked more like buzzards—their necks were plucked bare, and what lower feathers remained had turned black from the blood and dust. Seen through the binoculars the birds looked arrogant, fierce, and utterly mad. Their feet were claws and their heads like hatchets, topped by the blood-filled comb. Each preened and arched in her space, proud that she had survived. I wondered whether inside the shack the Jap was giggling or filled with revulsion—after all, these were hens he had known personally.

And suddenly the war was over.

On our small street people spilled from houses, cheering and shouting, touching one another. My mother, after saying a prayer to God, even smoked a cigarette in her excitement, and there was cold beer on the table. The cloud of war had lifted. Relief and happiness passed through our house like a seismic wave.

From the radio came the official details: *At 12:01 The Great Artiste dropped the second bomb . . . a pillar of fire, 10,000 feet high, shot skyward with enormous speed, moving to become a mushroom shaped cloud which eventually attained a height of 60,000 feet . . . officials estimate that the blast caused extensive damage . . .*

The war had ended. In that room I sensed a curious mixture of gladness and despair, as if we were suddenly released from what had held us together. I could not recall a time before Pearl Harbor, I could only remember a world at war, and all my energy for four years had been consumed by the war effort—I'd spent hundreds of hours digging the home defenses, scanning the sky for enemy aircraft, watching war communique films at school. I had collected tons of waste paper, tin cans, old cooking fat. I had grown Victory gardens, stayed up nights watching for tire thieves, helped my mother to keep the OPA Consumer's Pledge.

"Jesus." Uncle Boswick heard the news and his hand reached for another cold beer.

My father had his bank book out, and was searching the columns with a scowl. The war had killed the Depression, moving him into the only prosperity he'd ever known. He wet the pencil tip against his tongue and began to figure on an old envelope, moving into peace half-heartedly.

I walked to the street's edge and looked both ways, as if I might see that cresting mushroom cloud, or be touched by its gigantic shadow. For the war *had* touched us all: I thought of The MacGregor, Gussie, and Jed—in the dark enigma of that basement, that stained wall, I later realized we had viewed every casualty.

And in the field where we had labored hard and well, grass already grew in our trenches.

Perhaps because the Jap was no longer my enemy, but more likely because I was curious of the face I had never seen, I walked slowly through the yielding high grass toward the leaning tarpaper shack. Against the broken window the old newspaper floated, the type erased by sun and wind. Closer, I saw that the shutters threatened to fall from rusty hinges, and that their bright yellow paint had now curdled into rivulets. My knock was timid, and unanswered, but the door was ajar and I could see through the single room to the backyard.

The house was empty. Any furniture the Jap might have had was gone, and so was he. There was not even the smell of soy sauce, nor the odor of yellow; not even a grain of rice captured in the floor's parallel cracks remained as evidence. I stood in the tiny room, where dust motes drifted like dandelion fuzz across the sun's scorching shafts, and I wondered where he had gone. I wanted him to see my triumph—we had won, Japan was conquered. Also, I wanted to see his face—just once, up close, to see if he wasn't an exact copy of the grinning monkey the magazines had shown us. Where was he? Had he committed hari-kari in the garden?

The only evidence that the empty room had been lived in recently were the newspapers covering one wall. Bold headlines jumped from the yellow paper; the print faded into blurred words, columns of statistics, tracing the war's progress—down to the two day old newspaper taped at a crazy angle in the corner, its ink still firm.

Under the low ceiling the August heat collected; thick blue flies hummed furiously in the hot air, and as I walked out the back door it occurred to me that the Jap's departure would *really* baffle Uncle Boswick.

The garden was leveled; except for the small, open dirt mound, a row of scabs where the corn had been, all traces of the Jap's industry were sucked into the baked earth. A few loose feathers drifted across the space where last year cucumbers had lain in profusion, like surface mines, and the night air had been green with the metallic darkness of hard, fist-sized tomatoes. The feathers drifted from the rotting pile within the chicken coop, mute testimony to the destruction. The ground within the wire was perforated with the puck marks of claws, littered with bleached, dry bones. From inside the shed came a brittle noise, and I wondered if there could be a survivor—I had imagined those last two hens fighting by moonlight until each had driven a slashing, crescent beak into the other. The noise—a chewing, tearing sound—continued, and I searched the baked earth for a handful of grass, to throw over the wire fence.

As the grass drifted down, each blade flashing like a knife, the burlap cover at the small doorway moved. Then the single remaining chicken emerged. She dashed across the enclosure on thick legs to where the blades were still falling; cautiously, she sniffed at my offering but did not touch it—she had acquired a taste for blood.

The angular, massive head turned and behind deep folds her fierce eyes were fixed on me; with a crouching run she accelerated, to crash heavily into the wire. Her thick, short neck absorbed the impact, and she moved back, grunting, to try again. Her rush had carried the terrific odor of fowl, blood, dung, dust; and with this stink in my nose I now saw that she had lost all of her feathers and the skin was a silky black, broken only by the white scars. Grown short and fat, the crescent beak hooked like a primitive tooth, she had metamorphosed into a kind of rat.

Of the flock, this was the Victor.

Photograph by Robert Turney.

Albert Drake was born and raised in Portland, Oregon, and currently lives in Michigan where he is Professor of English at Michigan State University. During the past twenty years his fiction and poetry have appeared in over 300 magazines and anthologies; he has published two novels, *One Summer* and *Beyond the Pavement*. Recent non-fiction books are *The Big Little GTO Book* and *Street Was Fun in '51*.

In his spare time Drake works on old cars.

SE 22 '96	DATE DUE		
DEC 19 1996			
MR 11 '03			

Controversy and Courage

To Coleen and Tony,
With love,
Mary Kahl

Controversy and Courage

Upper Hudson Planned Parenthood from 1934 to 2004

Mary C. Kahl

iUniverse, Inc.
New York Lincoln Shanghai

Controversy and Courage
Upper Hudson Planned Parenthood from 1934 to 2004

iUniverse, Inc.

For information address:
iUniverse, Inc.
2021 Pine Lake Road, Suite 100
Lincoln, NE 68512
www.iuniverse.com

ISBN: 0-595-33235-8

Printed in the United States of America

To Bill

Contents

ACKNOWLEDGMENTS

This is a story of controversy and courage, and all the players in the history of Upper Hudson Planned Parenthood—volunteers, staff and patients—deserve gratitude. A few are mentioned in the text; an appendix lists the board presidents and executive directors, but there are too many heroes in this story to list every name. To all of who have worked to advance the mission of Planned Parenthood, my profound thanks.

I have had the pleasure and privilege to have worked closely with two Executive Directors, Ruth Klepper and Pat McGeown. I have learned a great deal from them and admired their strength and courage under fire. Both have been immensely helpful to me in the preparation of this book. Along with them, my thanks to the many members of UHPP's staff who are always willing and helpful. In particular, Blue Carreker has sorted through files to find appropriate photographs, and Jeff Lewis has rescued me from computer disaster.

In another area of technology, I am deeply grateful to Libby Post for her generous help in scanning images.

Two executive directors of Family Planning Advocates, Shirley Gordon and JoAnn Smith, have been invaluable mentors in understanding both public policy issues and the intricacies of New York State politics.

Space does not allow me to list all those players in the fabric of UHPP's history who spent time talking with me about their experiences and recollections. The story could not have been told without them. A listing of those interviewed is in the bibliography.

At the time of UHPP's 50th anniversary, several people, especially Shirley Brand and Elsa ("Bunny") deBeer, gathered important documentation for an earlier version of the history. To them and to others who have written their own version of the history, especially former staff member, Robert Pacenza, I offer thanks.

All the existing records of UHPP up through 1986 are housed in the New York State Library's Special Collections and Manuscripts. The staff there has been most helpful in making them available to me.

Before starting work on this book, two institutions supported my research on the issue of population growth and its relevance to family planning: the University at Albany's Center for Women in Government and Civil Society, which through its fellowship program gave me access to the University's library and other resources, and the Rockefeller Archives, which awarded me a grant to study the records of John D. Rockefeller III's role in bringing public attention to population issues. Title X, providing federal funding for family planning, might never have been enacted without the work of Rockefeller.

I have been fortunate in having many models of community volunteers and activists who showed me the possibilities of volunteer involvement. I would like to single out two of them in particular for recognition for their leadership roles with UHPP: Esther Lewis and Phoebe Bender.

Finally, my editor, Marion Roach Smith, has helped me tell the story clearly and concisely, and kept me moving when my spirit lagged. I thank her for her editorial guidance, for her encouragement, for her wit and wisdom, and for her many useful suggestions about the complex process of writing a book.

My close friend, Carolyn Oxtoby, has played the role of cheerleader as she read early versions of the work. Constantly supportive and enthusiastic, she has known when to make useful suggestions, and when simply to exhort me to keep going. I thank her for those gifts.

Finally, my anchor has been my husband, Bill Kahl. He has protected my time for writing, he has been my first reader and editor, he has offered important insights, and his unwavering support has made this endeavor possible. I dedicate this book to him with my love.

INTRODUCTION

Women's struggle for reproductive independence and autonomy was one of the defining social issues of the 20th century, and the struggle promises to continue well into the 21st. It began as a battle over birth control and moved on to abortion. Perhaps no other issue since slavery has been as strident and divisive. Its history is marked by bitter controversy, but also by extraordinary courage. The story of the first 70 years of Upper Hudson Planned Parenthood is a microcosm of the larger national history of the family planning movement, with its own healthy share of both controversy and courage.

Two factors in Albany, however, make its history exceptional. The population of the area is predominantly Catholic and the resulting conflicts with the Roman Catholic Church have been frequent and often dramatic. In addition Albany has had high visibility as the seat of state government. Local citizens watch the action in the halls of the Capitol and have a lively interest in affairs of state. Since New York has a progressive track record on family planning legislation, Albanians have experienced the consequences directly. When birth control clinics were closed down in Massachusetts and Connecticut, women found their way to Albany to seek help. When New York legalized abortion three years before *Roe v. Wade*, women flocked here from many surrounding states.

Women have always wanted control over their own fertility, but the reasons society has put forward to promote family planning have changed and evolved. In the 1930s, the cause of "family limitation," to use a phrase coined by Margaret Sanger, was espoused by many affluent women to provide charitable care for the poor. Later, in the 1950s and '60s, alarm over the rapid expansion of world population along with fears of outgrowing natural resources led to demands for population control. Title X, providing federal funding for family planning clinics, was sponsored by then-Representative George H.W. Bush and signed into law by President Nixon, not for the purpose of empowering women, but rather to control the growth of population. Undoubtedly the policy makers who framed this legislation had some specific populations in mind, and in fact several coercive strategies targeting either women on welfare or the mentally disabled were discussed. Fortunately, however, contraceptive services remained purely voluntary. Not until the civil rights and feminist movements of the 1970s did family planning find the language of "reproductive rights" and claim empowerment of all women as its rationale. *Our Bodies, Ourselves*, a landmark book with a landmark title, first published in 1970, typified the declaration of independence when women finally took ownership of their own reproductive autonomy, recognizing that control of their bodies was a necessary prerequisite to control of their lives, and that this was not a problem of the poor alone, but of all women.

History is instructive. There are patterns in the life of an organization just as there are in the life of an individual. The controversies of the past can shed light on the present, although it sometimes takes a long-distance view to discern trends and patterns. It is my hope that this historical account of the first 70 years of Upper Hudson Planned Parenthood will help give perspective to the contemporary assault on women and reproductive freedom, and will give us hope that the same courage and commitment that has seen us through a stormy past will again prevail.

The Early Years
1934–1964

The Founding

The event credited with marking the beginning of Upper Hudson Planned Parenthood was a meeting of eleven men and women of the Albany County Birth Control Committee on November 8, 1934. "The following were members: Mr. Winchester, Mr. Humphrey, Mrs. Frank McNamee, Mrs. Robert Wheeler, Mrs. Cherry, Mr. Sprenger, Mrs. Cogswell, Mrs. Freund and these who include volunteer workers, Dr. Vosburgh, Mrs. Henry Wright, Mrs. Truman Brown, Mrs. McIntosh." The meeting was probably held in Channing Hall of the Unitarian Church, one of the few places in Albany that welcomed so suspect a group as the Birth Control Committee. Although no direct account of the meeting survives, the topic of discussion was the establishment of an independent birth control clinic to be housed initially in the offices of Dr. Frances Vosburgh at 214 State Street in Albany. (This building no longer exists. It was between South Hawk and Swan Streets, where the Empire State Plaza now stands.)

In fact, Dr. Vosburgh already had been holding weekly birth control clinics in her office supported in part by contributions from the Albany Birth Control Committee, since March 4, 1934, seeing poor women who were referred to her by social agencies, doctors or individuals who knew of the clinic. Thus in a sense the November meeting simply formalized the financial and volunteer support expected from the Committee and established a board of directors for the governance of the project. A constitution was drawn up in January of 1935 providing for four officers and eleven board members. The precursor of Upper Hudson Planned Parenthood was born.

Who were these seven women and three men, and what motivated them to embark on a project still viewed as scandalous by much of the country, and disapproved by the Catholic church in a predominantly Catholic city? Most of the members of the Albany Birth Control Committee were affluent and successful citizens of Albany. Many were listed in *The Blue Book*, the annually-published social directory for Albany. Many lived in the fashionable suburb of Loudonville, in houses that were named Highfield House, or Blue Skies, or Town's End. The only mailing address need to reach them was the name of the house, followed by Loudonville. A few Protestant and Jewish clergymen also served on the committee. Mr. William Sprenger, for instance, was the pastor at the Trinity Protestant Episcopal Church in the South End. Before the founding of the clinic, the committee members had worked together on legislative remedies to make contraception more accessible to all married women.

In the Albany of 1934, the Depression continued and unemployment was high. President Franklin D. Roosevelt's New Deal was not yet enacted. Without any federal welfare system, there were only meager relief funds from the city or private agencies. People on full relief were estimated to receive between $5 and $14 a week, and if anyone in a household was employed, the family was eligible for only a fraction of that amount. The South End of Albany and Arbor Hill, where many Irish, German and Jewish immigrant families lived, had few medical services for the poor, and certainly no access to information about contraception and prevention of unwanted pregnancies. Dr. Vosburgh's office was not far from these two neighborhoods.

A report written by Dr. Vosburgh in January, 1935, about the patients she had seen since March of the previous year, gives a flavor of the poverty and suffering she had encountered. Six typical cases are described:

No. 1 Age 39, referred by church organization for health reasons, unemployed, on city relief—$9.00 per week. 3 living children. Pulmonary tuberculosis.

No. 2 Age 39, referred by Jewish Social Service, wife of bankrupt storekeeper, married 19 years, 24 reported pregnancies, 3 living children, 1 dead at birth (toxemia) 10 induced abortions, 10 spontaneous.

No. 3 Age 22, referred by Doctor, husband irregularly employed truck driver. Wife telephone operator at $17.00 per week. Chief support of family. 1 child. Out of work for long period due to hysterical laryngitis from fear of pregnancy. Withdrawal method of birth control contributing factor.

No. 4 Age 49, referred by Doctor because poor health, husband poor farmer. 8 living children, 2 abortions. Had suffered severe toxemia during last 3 pregnancies.

No. 5 Age 29, referred by Doctor for health and economic reasons. 2 living children, 1 dead (not right at birth). Husband has had anti-syphilitic treatment.

No. 6 Age 29, referred by Public Health Nurse (Rensselaer) husband unemployed, family on relief, 2 children, 2 miscarriages. Sent for economic reasons but of obviously low I.Q., ignorant and superstitious.

Dr. Vosburgh described the "mean case" in this way:

Woman between 20 and 30 with 3 children, having had 1 abortion or miscarriage, husband irregularly employed receiving help from public agency. Feeling insecure and frightened, looking forward to 15 to 20 years more of fertility. Has come to hate her sex life, and is continually hopeless and unhappy.

Only 38% of the women she had seen were from families with regular employment, with 58% on whole or part relief or living on the bounty of their own relatives. The pregnancy rate averaged 3.97 for each woman, with a high rate of induced and spontaneous abortions. She reported religious affiliation as 56% Protestant, 27% Catholic, 13% Jewish, and 3% unreported. She also added, cautiously, that Catholic patients were advised that the one method approved by the church was the "safe period", but that most of her patients had already found this unsatisfactory and were depending upon induced abortions or some unsatisfactory method of contraception like withdrawal.

Several prominent people in Albany had taken notice of the nascent birth control movement taking shape in New York City, Connecticut and other places. They had formed their own Albany County Birth Control Association, affiliated with the American Birth Control League founded by Margaret Sanger in New York, and were ready to rise to the challenge.

Sanger had worked as a maternity nurse in the Lower East Side of New York early in the 1900s. There she had seen many poor immigrant women who had no idea how to control their fertility and who were unable to support all their children. The repressive Comstock laws prevented poor women from even learning about birth control methods to which more affluent women had access from their private doctors.

The Comstock laws were named for Anthony Comstock, an avid anti-vice crusader from New York, who in the 1870s had shepherded through Congress a stringent anti-obscenity statute forbidding the distribution of both supplies and information about contraception and who was zealous in the enforcement of these laws. Many state legislatures followed suit with similar statutes, and some remained in effect until 1965, when the U.S. Supreme Court case, *Griswold v. Connecticut,* finally enabled married women in that state to get contraceptive services. In New York State, the federal Comstock law was challenged in 1935-36 in a federal district court in a case with the unlikely name of *U.S. v. One Package of Japanese Pessaries,* which arose when Sanger tried to import a new contraceptive device from Japan and the shipment was seized and confiscated. The decision was applicable only within the appellate court's jurisdiction, which included all of New York State. It held that the Comstock law had been inappropriately applied and that there was both medical and socioeconomic value to contraception. That ruling, combined with the endorsement of contraception by the American Medical Association the same year, gave legitimacy and courage to the growing birth control movement.

Margaret Sanger outside the courthouse in Brooklyn, 1917

Sanger studied available forms of contraception in this country and in Europe. (The principal method was the pessary, a barrier method that was the forerunner of the diaphragm.) She then began publishing a newspaper called *The Woman Rebel*, and also a pamphlet, "Family Limitation," explaining the importance of proper spacing between children to create a healthy family. She had declared war on the Comstock laws, and never wavered despite fierce opposition, heckling, and imprisonment.

We should not imagine, however, despite the inspiration from Sanger, that the founding members of the Albany Birth Control Association were radical rebels. They insisted that Dr. Vosburgh give birth control information or supplies only to married women, and preferably women who already had at least one child. In her monthly account dated April 1, 1934, Dr. Vosburgh reports having seen nine women during the previous month. "Of this number all had satisfactory reasons for being given information on contraception," she wrote. Later that year Dr.Vosburgh reported having apprehended a man selling contraceptives illegally. In light of the repressive Comstock laws, prevailing puritanical attitudes and critical public opinion, the respectable members of the Birth Control Association were not anxious to rock the boat or to give any impression that their activities might encourage promiscuity.

The Mothers Health Center, as the clinic was first called, consisted of a two-hour session once a week in Dr. Vosburgh's office, for which she volunteered her time. The level of activity was minimal for the first few years. The Treasurer's report for the month of December, 1934, shows total receipts of $28.25, only $6.75 of which came from patients who could pay something. With disbursements of $20 that month, the balance on hand by January 1, 1935, was $8.25. From March 1934 to May 1, 1935, 198 patients were cared for at the Center, which at that time had an annual budget of $652. All staff, including physicians, worked as volunteers. Patients were referred by such organizations as the City Mission, the Guild for Public Health Nursing, Family Welfare, the Trinity Institute, Protestant Welfare, and by doctors or individuals who knew of the service Dr. Vosburgh was providing. It did not take long before word of mouth became the primary referral system, swelling clinic attendance.

In the first year by-laws were drawn up, officers elected, a medical advisory board was established, and sponsors recruited to underwrite the clinic's expenses. The first birth control clinic in Albany was launched.

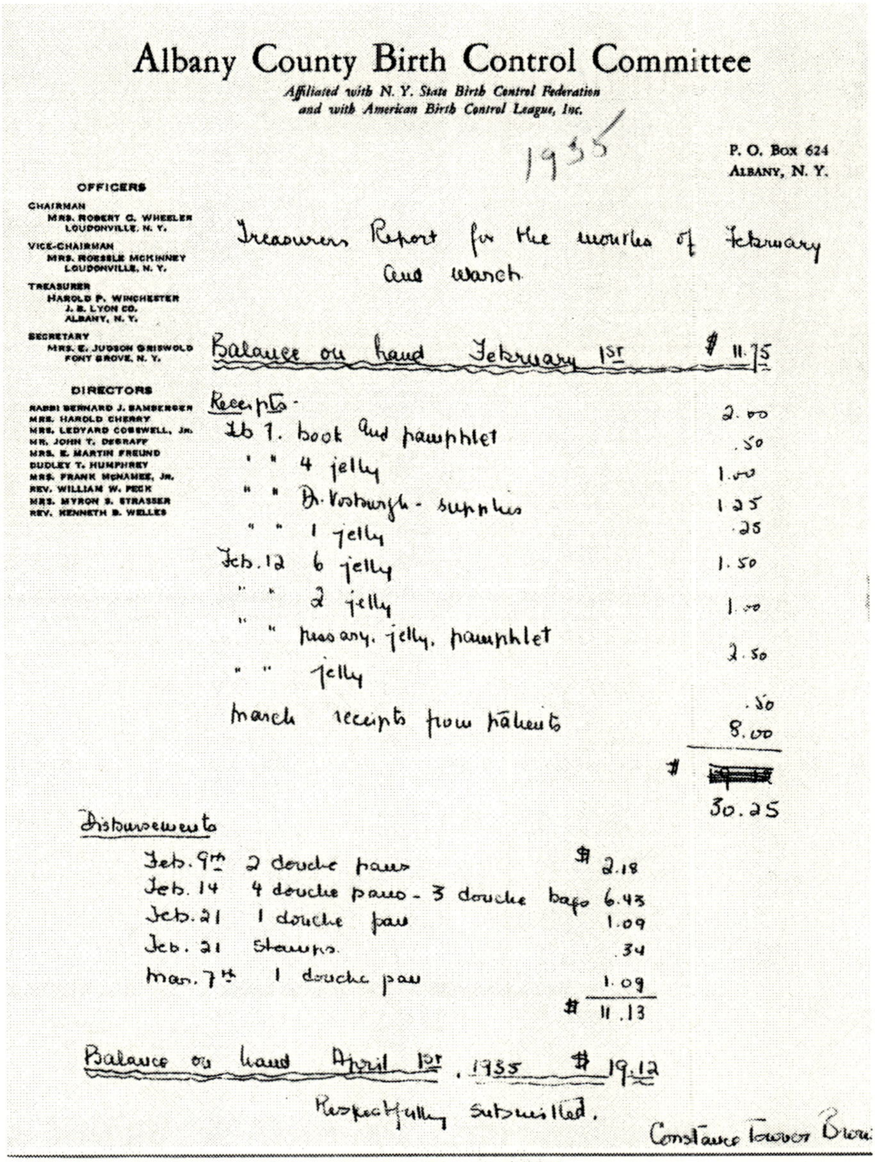

Albany County Birth Control Committee

Affiliated with N. Y. State Birth Control Federation
and with American Birth Control League, Inc.

1935

P. O. Box 624
Albany, N. Y.

OFFICERS

CHAIRMAN
MRS. ROBERT C. WHEELER
LOUDONVILLE, N. Y.

VICE-CHAIRMAN
MRS. ROESSLE MCKINNEY
LOUDONVILLE, N. Y.

TREASURER
HAROLD P. WINCHESTER
J. B. LYON CO.
ALBANY, N. Y.

SECRETARY
MRS. E. JUDSON GRISWOLD
FONT GROVE, N. Y.

DIRECTORS

RABBI BERNARD J. BAMBERGER
MRS. HAROLD CHERRY
MRS. LEDYARD COGSWELL, JR.
MR. JOHN T. DEGRAFF
MRS. E. MARTIN FREUND
DUDLEY T. HUMPHREY
MRS. FRANK MCNAMEE, JR.
REV. WILLIAM W. PECK
MRS. MYRON S. STRASSER
REV. KENNETH B. WELLES

Treasurers Report for the months of February and March.

Balance on hand February 1st $ 11.75

Receipts - 2.00
Fb 1. book and pamphlet .50
" " 4 jelly 1.00
" " Dr. Vosburgh - supplies 1.25
" " 1 jelly .25
Feb. 12 6 jelly 1.50
" " 2 jelly 1.00
" " pessary, jelly, pamphlet 2.50
" " jelly .50
March receipts from patients 8.00

$ 30.25

Disbursements

Feb. 9th 2 douche pans $ 2.18
Feb. 14 4 douche pans - 3 douche bags 6.43
Feb. 21 1 douche pan 1.09
Feb. 21 Stamps. .34
Mar. 7th 1 douche pan 1.09
$ 11.13

Balance on hand April 1st, 1935 $ 19.12

Respectfully submitted.

Constance Tower Brown

Treasurer's Report, February and March 1935

Docky

Dr. Frances Vosburgh

The person at the center of the new enterprise and without whom it could not have taken place was Dr. Frances Vosburgh, or "Docky," as she was known to her patients. Like the traditional small town family doctor, she cared personally about every one of her patients. She was friendly but firm, compassionate and principled. She was a family practice doctor, treating the whole family and the whole person, as interested in a patient's family and circumstances as in the ailment to be treated. At Christmastime when she was flooded with greeting cards from all her current and past patients, she could remember all the details of each person's family and life, just as they remembered her competent and healing care.

Born in 1897 in Voorheesville, she attended the Milne School in Albany, went on to Vassar College and graduated in 1918. Her choice of medicine as a career came naturally considering her heritage. Her maternal grandfather was a Civil War surgeon, and her aunt in Michigan was also a physician. For a few years she worked as a bacteriologist in Lakewood, New Jersey, an experience that confirmed her decision to pursue a career in medicine at a time when few women were accepted into the profession, and then went to the Cornell Medical School where she was one of 13 women in a class of 56, graduating in 1925.

Returning to Albany, she did her residency at the Albany Hospital (now the Albany Medical Center Hospital) and set up practice as a family practice physician at 214 State Street (where the Justice Building now stands in the Empire State Plaza) with two other doctors. They shared a secretary and a waiting room. It was there that she began holding a special clinic for poor women who needed birth control advice and supplies. And it was there that the Albany County Birth Control Committee found her and recruited her to play the central role in what we would call today a family planning clinic.

In the early days of the movement begun by Margaret Sanger, the language used to designate the purpose of clinics changed almost daily. Sanger had tried "family limitation" at first, then moved on to "birth control." During the era of Comstock laws and public controversy, the term "birth control" must have sounded too explicit for the Albany organizers, so the first clinic in Dr. Vosburgh's office was called the Mother's Health Clinic. Soon afterwards the name was changed to Maternal Guidance Association, a name that strikes us today as condescending and paternalistic. The Planned Parenthood designation did not surface until 1947 in Albany, and the term "family planning" was not commonly used until the 1960s.

Although her principal medical practice was that of a general practitioner, perhaps Dr. Vosburgh's greatest love was delivering babies, and before her long career was over she had delivered 2,755 babies, many of them children of mothers she had also delivered. Speaking of the first baby she had delivered, she said, "It was a great thrill. Every one of them since has been just as great a thrill. To me, the birth of a live, healthy baby is still a miracle."

In the early years of her practice she bought a 100 acre farm on Krumkill Road in Voorheesville, and a few years later she renovated what had been a chicken house on the property to be her office, with a large window facing the Normanskill. For the next four decades she lived and served patients from this setting. As a complement to her work in birth control she took a number of unwed mothers into her home and would keep them there for several weeks, or even months, until they delivered and she could help them place the baby for adoption if that was what they wanted. Other doctors would sometimes refer patients who needed some rest and relaxation to her, and she let them come to spend a few weeks on the farm.

For years all the work she did for the birth control clinic precursor to Planned Parenthood was done on a volunteer basis. "Docky" was so unfailingly generous with her time and home that she needed to supplement her private practice income, and did so by working as a physician for the New York Telephone Company for 32 years. Those patients joined the growing ranks of her grateful private practice patients.

Dr. Vosburgh never married. She said when asked, "I am wedded to my profession," but she did love children, and in fact adopted two daughters, one a distant relative and one whose mother was referred to her by an Episcopalian clergyman in New York City. One of these daughters, Marjorie, still lives in the Krumkill Road house; the other, Suzanne, lives in Connecticut.

Her reputation spread outside the area, and when restrictive laws in Connecticut and Massachusetts prevented women from getting contraceptive information or supplies in those states, they would travel to Albany to see Dr. Vosburgh.

She received considerable recognition in her long lifetime. She was elected the first woman President of the Albany County Medical Society in 1959, having served as Vice President, and as Treasurer of the organization in the 1930s. She was chosen Woman of the Year in 1974 by the Women's Medical Society of New York State, and won the Planned Parenthood Federation of America Margaret Sanger Award in 1979. Even after her death in 1989 at the age of 91, she was honored again posthumously by the Albany-Colonie Regional Chamber of Commerce in 2000 as one of the century's 100 Women of Excellence.

The reason she was loved and trusted by all who knew her, however, was for her extraordinary ability to relate to people. "She was so compassionate and understanding and you could talk to her, couldn't you, just talk," said her cousin Phoebe Ziehm.Her patients were devoted, and often women whom she had delivered at birth returned to her when they had babies. Dr. Grace Jorgensen, who worked closely with her at Bellevue Hospital for 30 years, spoke about Dr. Vosburgh's spirit of compassion and caring for women and of the respect she showed to all her patients, offering each one her full attention and the benefit of her considerable medical skills.

The story of this serene and patient woman belies the controversy swirling around her. Her straight-forward manner and good common sense seem to have protected her from the worst of the conflicts. Early in her career she did her obstetrical work at the Brady Maternity Hospital, associated with the Roman Catholic-sponsored St. Peter's Hospital. On one occasion a patient of hers who had gone into labor arrived at Brady Hospital only to be told that there was no such doctor on their list as Dr. Frances Vosburgh. Apparently when the hospital had learned of Dr. Vosburgh's work in birth control, they simply removed her privileges. Unfazed, Dr. Vosburgh contacted Bellevue Maternity Hospital in Schenectady, which admitted the woman, and from then on, Dr. Vosburgh did most of her obstetrical work at Bellevue.When asked what she thought of opponents to birth control in a 1979 interview she replied, "I wouldn't for a minute criticize people who believe that birth control is wrong. People have a right to their own opinions."The same holds true for abortion: "I think it should be the decision of the people who are concerned with having or not having a child," she said. "Leave it up to the parents to decide."Dr. Vosburgh never performed an abortion, but she did say that she had occasionally referred some women to people who could do them safely and properly.

When she died at the age of 91 in 1989, a number of tributes were quoted in the eulogy given by Dr. Grace Jorgensen. (The service was held at the First Unitarian Church of Albany, where she had long been an active member.) Doctor Harry Wood wrote of her, "Dr. Vosburgh exemplified everything the public admires and imagines about the mythical old-time country doctor. As a clinician who cared for and about her patients, she was outstanding. Her colleagues liked, admired and respected her. If you were looking for a candidate for either woman or doctor of the year, she was that woman."The Director of Patient Services at Belleview Hospital, Susan Fraley, wrote, "Dr. Vosburgh was a pioneer for other women in the health care field and served as an inspiring role model for us all. She took great risks to ensure quality care for women and children. Through it all she was selfless and never wanted to take credit for her wonderful work."

And finally, Dr. Jorgensen added her own summary: "Fran cared for a broad cross-section of humanity. She knew first-hand how hard life could be for some of her patients. She was never a prude, but always a lady. In her sweet, knowledgeable way, she helped educate thousands of patients to the need to practice preventative medicine."

The tradition of respectful, compassionate, high quality care for women that has been the hallmark of Upper Hudson Planned Parenthood for 70 years was firmly established by its remarkable founder.

Finding a Home

Controversy has been a constant companion of Upper Hudson Planned Parenthood throughout its history, but never was the clinic's survival as threatened as in its early search for a home.

In the first few years the number of patients remained very modest, but work progressed smoothly. Within a year of its founding, the Albany Birth Control Committee was successful in arranging to place the clinic in the Albany Hospital (now the Albany Medical Center Hospital) where they felt it would have more stability and legitimacy, to say nothing of greater capacity than Dr. Vosburgh's office. On August 1, 1935, the clinic was transferred to the Albany Hospital under the new name of the Maternal Guidance Clinic. The Albany Birth Control Committee, also renamed the Albany Maternal Guidance Association, cooperated with the hospital in raising sufficient funds to pay for medical supplies; the doctors for the clinics continued to serve as volunteers until 1941, when the first modest honorarium for a doctor was paid. A social worker was engaged to work one day a week for a salary of $25 a month. By 1940 the clinic's annual budget had reached $1,500 and its caseload 500. There was sufficient demand for the clinic that a second one opened in May, 1937 at the Trinity Institution in the South End.

Some segments of the community continued to resist the formation of contraceptive clinics, however. The trustees of Memorial Hospital denied a request to establish a clinic there despite the support for it by the medical staff. And in 1941 the Albany Council of Social Agencies refused to accept the Albany Maternal Guidance Association as a member.

Then, in early 1937, the other shoe dropped. The story is best told by the acting President of the Association, Katharine McKinney, writing to the Chairman of the Eastern Region of the New York State Federation for Planned Parenthood:

March 24, 1942

My dear Mrs. McCagg:

A very serious thing has happened which threatens the whole future of our maternal guidance work in Albany, and as Chairman of the Eastern Region, I think you should be the first to know about it. We are going to need the advice and support of the whole state federation and perhaps of the National and we are going to need it soon.

Bishop Gibbons, the same Catholic Bishop who was responsible for the closing of our exhibit at the State Fair has called a meeting of the representatives of the Community Chest and of the Albany Hospital where our clinics are held and has informed them that unless our clinics are closed down he will require all the Catholic agencies to withdraw from the Community Chest. He has said, furthermore, that if we open a clinic outside the hospital anywhere in Albany, that no doctor or nurse or employee of the hospital can have anything to do with such clinic or can refer any patient to it, or else he will see that all the doctors on the staff of the hospital who are Catholics no longer take their patients there or have anything to do with the hospital.

It is difficult in a letter to go into the details of the whole situation but I have given you the substance of it, and I think it is so serious that it must be taken up at the next Executive Committee meeting. I feel fairly sure that because of the large Catholic population in Albany the Chest officials will give in and will have us thrown out of the hospital and also out of Trinity Institute, which is also a Chest agency and where our other clinic is held. The question is, what is the best thing for us to do next?

It so happens that the President of the hospital board is away, ill, and will not be back till the middle of April, and the Bishop has reluctantly consented to wait till he comes back to bring the matter before the Chest. Which gives us about a month in which to work. Also we are having our Annual Meeting on the Eighth of April, a luncheon at which Dr. Bossard is going to speak. It may be that the luncheon should be the rallying point of our efforts, but I am not sure. It also happens that our new county chairman, Mrs. Dwight is in Georgia until the fourth of April which is the reason that I seem to be taking over. Mrs. Ingalls and I are consulting our Medical Advisory Board, most of whom are Albany Hospital doctors on Thursday, to get their reactions, and we will both be at the Executive Meeting on the sixth of April, if that is when it is. I certainly hope that is the date for our time is short.

Will you take this whole thing up with Mrs. Workum and with Mrs. Jessup because I feel that it is the most serious thing that has happened to the Birth Control movement in New York state since the Federation was organized. Apparently what we were told was true. The Catholics wiped up Massachusetts and Connecticut and New York is to be the focus of their next attack. I only wish that I wasn't leaving Albany so soon, because I think we've got to fight and to fight hard this time.

Yours,
Katharine McKinney

Both the Albany Hospital and the Trinity Institution were recipients of Community Chest funds and were unlikely to fight for the survival of contraceptive clinics which would jeopardize not only their own funding but that of other community service organizations as well.

From then on, letters flew, telephone lines buzzed, and dinner table conversations around Albany were consumed with talk of the crisis. Mrs. Dwight, then the President of the Albany committee, got word of the threatened eviction during her Georgia vacation, and replied by mail immediately to the Federation, "I've never been quite so fighting mad in my life.... I do feel that this ought to be brought out in the open now. I cannot see that such blackmail methods should be allowed in a free country."

After appropriate consultation, the Maternal Guidance ladies decided to rally support around the issue of protest against religious interference in medical practice. In a letter to the Medical Board of the Albany Hospital, Mrs. Dwight, now back in Albany and filled with patriotic fervor and high principles, wrote:

> Not only is it an effort of one religious group to dictate what medical practices may be carried on by a non-denominational hospital, but also to control the health services of a non-sectarian neighborhood center.
>
> Contraceptive advice in our clinic is given under medical supervision for health reasons and to married persons only. Our supporters are sincerely devoted to a cause which they believe to be a fundamental social need. We aim to see to it that there shall be no interference with the advised healthful planning of families, and that this right, formerly the sole possession of the privileged and the informed...shall be shared by the poor, the defective, the ill and the underprivileged.
>
> We have no wish to impose our beliefs and standards upon others; but not to defend our civil rights would be not to deserve them. The issue has been raised. If the public condones or ignores encroachments upon the civil rights of others, it will do well to ask itself where this kind of thing will end. The Maternal Guidance Association has warm friends among those of Roman Catholic faith, and we are sorry to be obliged to make this statement. But these things must be said. For the Birth Control clinics in Massachusetts and Connecticut have been closed!
>
> This country is at war. It is the general impression that religious freedom, freedom of speech and freedom to act under the State and federal laws, are some of the freedoms we seek to defend.
>
> The Bishop's insistence on the removal of the clinics has restricted these freedoms!

(There is a notation with this letter indicating that it was never sent because, in the absence of any concrete evidence that Bishop Gibbons had delivered his letter, Mrs. Dwight did not want to risk being the first to put something in writing. No doubt she communicated the passion of her letter in other ways.)

The Community Chest, understandably, saw itself as an innocent pawn in the power play between the Bishop, the birth control clinic, and the Albany Hospital. However, the birth control ladies did have some leverage with the Chest in the person of Mrs. Frederick Townsend, an influential member of the Chest board, and also a sponsor of the birth control clinic. Mrs. Townsend first threatened to resign from the Community Chest board if the Bishop were allowed to get his way in closing the clinic, and subsequently did resign in protest.

The Chairman of the Albany Hospital board, Mr. Alfred Renshaw, perhaps gave false hope to the birth control ladies only shortly before the hospital board met to reach its decision, by telling them that coercion would not be tolerated. However, another member of the hospital board, Mr. Frederick McDonald of the State Bank, had his own clever idea about how to avoid the appearance of giving in to coercion. He suggested that the Bishop be asked to withdraw his demand and instead send a polite request that the clinics be withdrawn. The Bishop agreed, and with this accomplished, the hospital board proceeded to vote for the removal of the clinic. Trinity Institution's board (with overlapping membership with the Albany Hospital) met the same day and reached the same conclusion.

Mr. Renshaw's letter to Mrs. Dwight informing her of the decision made no apologies for the hospital's actions:

> At a meeting of the Board of Governors of this Hospital held on May 12th, it was voted to discontinue as promptly as possible the Maternal Guidance Clinics of the Albany Hospital. The Board of Governors in reaching this decision considered the best interests of this community, of the Chest, and of the Albany Hospital, and believes that the primary responsibility of the Hospital can best be carried out by eliminating its birth control clinics, which are considered objectionable by a considerable sector of the population, particularly when these clinics can be conducted equally well under other auspices. The Board also took into consideration the fact that these clinics have presented continual difficulty in securing suitable personnel to conduct them and to provide professional guidance.
>
> The foregoing action of the Board does not imply any adverse criticism of the practice of contraception for medical reasons, which the Board considers a purely professional matter.

Not surprisingly, a similar letter using very similar language was written on the same day by Lewis Greenleaf, Chairman of the Trinity Institution board.

The fledgling birth control movement in Albany was facing eviction from both of its clinics, opposed by not only the Catholic Church but by two institutions that had appeared until this moment to be supportive. The Maternal Guidance ladies (the term is used advisedly; these women most certainly thought of themselves as ladies) were indignant and determined to fight back. They first replied directly to the two institutions questioning how depriving the community of an established and essential medical service served its best interests. The American Medical Association had in 1937 recognized birth control as a legitimate part of medical practice, and a recent Gallup poll showed 77 percent of the American people approved birth control.

As for Renshaw's comment about problems in securing suitable personnel to staff the clinic, they pointed out that it was probably because the clinic was not included as part of the hospital's obstetrical and gynecological services, where it should have been, because the head of the department was a member of the Roman Catholic Church and opposed such services on religious rather than health grounds. They concluded their letter of protest with an appeal to the patriotic fervor of those early days of World War II:

> Surely, we have learned that the fruits of appeasement are temporary, apparent gains, but the ultimate destruction of all liberties. Democracy thrives on open action and debate, not on threats made behind closed doors. Our Country is fighting on a broad front for democratic freedoms, but let us not forget that democracy begins at home.

Newspaper coverage of the evictions was so bland as to completely misrepresent the situation, presumably out of reluctance to offend the Bishop. Both the *Knickerbocker News* and the *Times Union* published articles on Wednesday, May 27, 1942, under titles like "Birth Control Clinics Close at Two Agencies" with absolutely no reference to the role of the Catholic Bishop nor any explanation of what precipitated the closures.

The Maternal Guidance Association sought legal remedy with help from the Planned Parenthood Federation in New York City, but were told that although the situation raised social and public relations problems of the gravest character, there were no valid legal grounds for recourse. The ladies then undertook a vast letter-writing campaign, explaining the situation from their perspective, and here they received considerable support. Members of the medical staff at the Albany Hospital wrote to express anger that medical decisions at the hospital had been reached by a board of lay men without consultation. Mr. Maynard, rector of St. Peter's Episcopal Church, wrote to report that the Albany Ministerial Council (a forerunner of the Council of Churches) had passed a resolution condemning the Catholic coercion. He also discussed the situation at a meeting of the vestrymen of his church, who expressed indignation, and with the Red Cross sewing group at the church, who felt the same way. The Women's Board of the Trinity Institution wrote a letter of support, first acknowledging the fact that it was an auxiliary group only and without authority to speak for the organization, but then expressing its regret at the discontinuance of a service which had proved its worth and was greatly needed in Trinity's work for the underprivileged. The board members also acknowledged their annoyance, as workers and contributors, at not having been consulted.

Former donors to the Community Chest wrote to divert at least a portion of their gifts directly to the Maternal Guidance Association. A June 22 letter of protest from Arthur J. Harvey, attorney-at-law, to Mr. Renshaw stated baldly:

> Such tactics are familiar in the news, but only when practiced by the Germans, Italians and Japanese Governments, and not in a democracy. I thought that the time for appeasement and for cowardness (sic) was past in our democracy. Surely the example in Europe should convince one that such tactics encourage the aggressor.

For all their indignation, however, the ladies realized they needed to move on and find a new home for the clinic. It was a difficult search since few landlords wanted to rent space for the purpose of establishing a birth control clinic. Just in the nick of time, in early June, before a July 1 deadline for vacating the former clinic spaces, they had success. Alice Dwight reported in a June 10 letter to the Planned Parenthood Federation:

> We have found the perfect place, right across the street from Trinity owned by a Mrs. Oblinski, Russian, who is all for having us in her house. She owns it, no mortgage and her husband is a junk dealer. The place is so clean we wouldn't have to do a thing to it. It will be necessary to get some one to live there by fall to keep a stove going and keep it clean, but we can get along for a while. Price $28.50 a month. We will need to buy some furnishings I suppose but we have

> quite a bit which we put into Trinity which we shall take with us, and a bill which Mr. Greenleaf says he will pay for French blinds $19.50 and a sink, which we once gave Trinity.

The new space at 20 Trinity Place, small, simple and inadequate as it was, was to be home to the clinic until 1965. The ladies' resolve had been tested and they had risen to the occasion. The crisis might even have been a blessing in disguise, because in the long run having an independent clinic with greater community support built the foundation for the healthy agency we know today.

To the modern ear, the "Lady Bountiful" character of the early founders is reflected in ways such as the "Maternal Guidance Association" name they gave to the clinic. The leaders of the birth control movement in Albany were well-to-do, responsible citizens, mostly women, concerned about a serious humanitarian situation, as was the case with many other important movements of the time. Dr. Richard Beebe, former Chairman of the Department of Medicine at the Albany Medical Center, admitted that even at the time there were a certain number of people who joked about their "debutante friends"who might have better spent their time at home having children than battling the community to help other women avoid having children. Writing some years later about her involvement with the early years of the birth control movement, Alice Dwight gave an account of her decision to involve herself in the birth control movement. She recalled that:

> In about 1935 I was trying to make up my mind (after four children and resigning from the Junior League) what I would be interested in when it came to volunteer work. I finally picked two subjects—'Peace' and 'Birth control' as it was then called. I decided that the organization working for peace needed first and foremost: money. I felt I could not do much in the monetary department, so I picked birth control.

However the founders may have reached a decision about involvement in the birth control movement, their seriousness of purpose cannot be doubted. Their dogged perseverance saved the day when the very existence of the clinic was threatened.

20 Trinity Place

The second floor apartment at 20 Trinity Place was to be the home of the clinic for 23 years. By all accounts it was small and shabby, with primitive heating and electrical systems, but its location in the South End neighborhood and directly across the street from the Trinity Institution where other social services were available made it convenient for many needy women who lived within walking distance. One anonymous patient in 1946 wrote, "I am only 25 years old yet I have had six children. The seventh is on the way. Two were born dead." Surrounded by women with situations like this, there was much work to be done.

20 Trinity Place. Photo taken in 1999.

The clinic opened in July, 1942, and with many referrals from both doctors and social workers, it had sufficient attendance that in May, 1943, the daytime clinic was supplemented with evening sessions on the first and third Tuesday of each month. A motor corps was organized for those who needed transportation, but the effort had to be abandoned when the war necessitated gas rationing. Fundraising efforts were so successful that a reserve fund was establishing in a savings bank, which later paid for a two and a half percent Treasury bond. The clinic budget for 1943 was $2,400, considered a comfortable funding level since staffing was almost entirely voluntary, including the services of Dr. Vosburgh. The first education programs were also started in 1943 with group meetings for patients on such topics as Physical Care of Infants, Emotional Development of Children, Problems of Adolescence, and Marital Problems.

Over the next years, the organization reached out to many community groups—including the Visiting Nurse Association, the Red Cross, church groups, and heads of social agencies—to better explain the clinic's mission and goals. By 1945 a Clergymen's Advisory Board was formed, the beginning of a long and successful relationship between the organization and supportive clergy in the Albany area.

Dr. Janet Hood, a clinician during the early years at Trinity Place, remembers both the public pressure against birth control in those days, and the work conditions at Trinity Place:

> In 1942 when I came to live in Albany, individuals who were interested in, supported, or, God forbid, actually participated in providing services to Planned Parenthood were suspect—sort of inferior and doubtless evil. Nevertheless, those of us dedicated to the concept that "every child should be a wanted child" struggled on. We climbed the shaky stairs to the second floor clinic in the rickety old tenement fire trap in the South End, dispensing diaphragms, advice, and moral support as best we could. Services were provided not only to Albanians but also to people who came from surrounding states where such help was unavailable. As I recall, I used to get $2.00 a night for a long clinic which ran as many hours as necessary to accommodate everybody there.

The physical set up of the clinic was primitive. A gas hot water tank had to be lit to provide water for hand washing. A 1949 clinic manual of procedures explains how to manage the electricity. If the ceiling lights and the gooseneck lamp and the electric heater were all in use, the sterilizer must have only one burner on low. If, on the other hand, both burners of the sterilizer were needed on full heat, then the electric heater must be turned off.

Volunteers signed patients in and assisted the doctor; their procedures were also outlined in the clinic manual. The only paid staff was a part-time "Executive Secretary" on minimal salary.

The policy manual also explained the sliding fee schedule. The services of the clinic were not meant for the general public, so if a family of two earned more than $40 a week, they were ineligible for the services of the clinic except under undefined "unusual circumstances." Private donors wanted to make contraceptive services available to those unable to afford them on their own. Eligible patients paid a fee of $2.50 or $3.00 plus the cost of supplies. A diaphragm cost $.75 and jelly $.50.

The end of World War II brought changes to the organization. In 1947 the agency was renamed Planned Parenthood Association of Albany and became an affiliate of Planned Parenthood Federation of America. According to clinic notes, cancer detection and fertility services were added in the same year, although the fertility services were probably more window dressing than reality, and the Pap smear had not yet been introduced. A prior test for cervical cancer, much less accurate, did exist. In the case of fertility services, aside from telling patients to take their temperature to determine the timing of their cycle, not much other advice was available. Alice Dwight remembered how the end of the war helped the recruitment of volunteers:

> Up to and during the war, our board members worked like fury. It was hard to get new board members at that time. However, by the end of the war, we began to find that we could get volunteers for fund raising as well as for the clinic....At a meeting...before our drive around 1946, we had over 100 volunteers. Times were changing a bit.

While the organization may have garnered more community support, the opposition to birth control continued to flourish. In 1947 Dr. Wallingford, a community gynecologist, speaking to a Catholic gathering on "Birth Control and the Catholic Family" delivered a vehement diatribe against birth control. "Unprofessional people are disseminating incorrect information and immoral practices among the illiterate," he stated. He went on to say that the birth control movement is "supported and financed by the rubber goods contraceptive groups of the country...a five million dollar business." Further, he stated, "Use of mechanical and chemical means on the market today are injurious to users. Injury differs only in degree...more efficient as a contraceptive, the more harmful." He asserted that cancer can and does result from the use of contraceptives, and he claimed that when birth control is used, "dissatisfaction, disappointment and disgust" result. "The use of contraceptives by married couples is nothing more than mutual masturbation." With opinions like these coming from a physician to a receptive audience, the challenges facing Planned Parenthood were daunting.

Troy

Sometime in the 1930s in Troy a number of concerned citizens organized their own birth control clinic. Betty Pattison chaired the board, and her husband Edward ("Ebbie") Pattison served as legal counsel and board member. As the founding partner of a major Troy law firm, Ebbie Pattison was widely known and highly respected. Betty Pattison remembered that the make-up of the board was a mixed socioeconomic group, including a couple of African-American women, which was unusual for that time. Although no documents have been found to record the work of this group, both Betty Pattison and Hortense Mintzer, another active board member, have shared some of their recollections. Satie August was another person involved with the Troy clinic.

It was located in a basement office at the corner of State and Second Streets, where the space was shared with two other doctors. There were two rooms, one for interviewing and one for examination. Board meetings were held in the same space. Hortense Mintzer remembers pulling down the window shades so that passers-by could not look in to see who was present. Their medical services were provided by Dr. Catherine Cook, a Troy physician. The founding group first became aware of the need for the clinic because of some contact with students from Rensselaer Polytechnic Institute and the realization that these students knew nothing about their sexuality and needed both services and education.

The major clientele, however, were the poor women of Troy who wanted to limit the size of their families. Many of them were Roman Catholic, married, and with one or more children already. It soon became clear that a network of observers would report to the Catholic priests the identities of those who entered the birth control clinic. "The people who came to our organization who were Roman Catholics...felt the pressure very much," reported Betty Pattison. "They got to feeling very scared to be seen coming in the place. We heard stories about how they were admonished by their priests, sometimes right in open congregation."

The Troy board had trouble raising money because of community disapproval, and also could not persuade newspapers to give them any coverage. "The idea of contraception was very remote in those days. At the time the pressure was very great. You felt there was a lot of pressure against that sort of freedom," recalled Pattison.

Sometime in the late 1940s with both dwindling numbers of patients who were brave enough to come to the clinic and diminishing funds, the clinic was closed and its supplies and records turned over to the Albany Planned Parenthood. Some board members, including Ruth Sampson and Diane Goodman, sat on the Albany clinic's board as representatives from Troy.

Reality outside the Clinic

In its early years the Albany Planned Parenthood was extremely careful to explain in all its communications with the public that they served married women exclusively. We know from Dr. Vosburgh's early records that many of the women she saw had either self-induced abortions or had found someone to do an abortion. The term "spontaneous abortion" also appears in her notes, probably meaning miscarriages, which may also have been induced. The record does not tell us what happened to those women who became pregnant and could not face delivery of yet another child.

A letter to the Editor of the *Knickerbocker News* on March 27, 1979, tells one part of the grim story. Written six years after *Roe*, it addresses the growing opposition to abortion from Right to Life groups:

> In the 1930s, I drove a cab in Albany. At that time there were three major abortionists in the city. Of course, there were many lesser lights and midwives who serviced the poor women who could not afford the $50 the big boys charged.
>
> One of the three was on Columbia Street across from the Albany County Courthouse. Another operated a block from the Cathedral of Immaculate Conception. The third, who had a six-bed wing on his house, was in business a half block from St. Peter's Hospital and the Convent.
>
> Nearly 50 years later I find I cannot forget the muffled sobs from the poor girls—for some reason they almost always went alone—riding to or from the abortionist.
>
> The Right to Life people cannot understand this. It is not a question of abortion or no abortion. Abortion we are going to have. The question is: Will we have legal or illegal abortions? If every legislator would take a minute or two to think this over he would be able to cast an intelligent vote.
>
> DARWIN SKINNER
> Menands

Mr. Skinner, of course, was correct about the frequency of abortion before and after *Roe v. Wade*, as evidenced by the fact that the birth rate nationally did not change after the Supreme Court decision made abortion legal.

Dr. Richard Beebe, former Chairman of the Department of Medicine at the Albany Medical Center, recalled the "awful days before abortions were allowed in hospitals," and made it clear that this problem was not restricted to the poor alone. Because pregnancy outside of marriage was considered a disgrace, girls "would go anywhere to have an abortion to protect their families, so their families wouldn't know they were ever pregnant and to avoid having an illegitimate child when they were still in school or college." He called abortionists—by which he meant those who were untrained and practiced only for the money to be made in it—the lowest type of medical practitioner, and said of them:

> They were not trained in anything. They would do an abortion with any old instrument they had and the poor girls would have an abortion, usually complicated by either severe hemorrhage and death, or infection and a long period of serious illness. So many lovely and wonderful girls from wonderful families as well as from poorer families would die from the results of these untrained abortionists.

Dr. Beebe and many other doctors saw the results of illegal, botched abortions when the victims showed up at the hospital after the fact, bleeding and infected, often too late to save their lives.

On the thirteenth anniversary of *Roe*, January 22, 1986, the *Times Union* carried an interview with Dr. Donald Swartz, who had been chairman of the Department of Obstetrics and Gynecology at Harlem Hospital from 1962 to 1972, and then was chairman of Obstetrics and Gynecology at Albany Medical Center. He subsequently served as a board member of Upper Hudson Planned Parenthood as well as a member of its Medical Committee. He commented on the situation at Harlem Hospital before abortion became legal in New York State:

> So from 1962 to 1970, we watched the problem, and had to cope with the disasters that took place. For $10, you could buy a catheter with a steel insert on the street, and for $50 you could find someone to do it for you in the restroom of a bar, or maybe if you were lucky you could find somebody who knew a little more.
>
> It became clear to me that women who do not wish to bear children, will not do so, no matter what the risk. We had 1,500 patients a year in the emergency room who were pregnant and bleeding, with what we would call an incomplete

> abortion. We knew 1,000 of these were induced, and so by law, criminal. We would lose half a dozen lives annually from that kind of sequel. It was really pretty discouraging medicine to have to practice.
>
> And all that changed completely in 1970. We went from 40 citywide deaths annually to none.
>
> It also became clear to me that by the time a woman presents herself (for an abortion) she has clearly thought through the issues. Almost no women make that decision lightly.

Citing what he called the criticism of the uninformed, Swartz said it is not enough to say, "If people would just be careful." He continued, "This would be valid if we had perfect contraception, but we don't. People are mature, conscientious, use the available methods, and still, some get pregnant. Our contraceptive technology is not that perfect; as people, we are not that perfect."

The records do not reveal what the doctors at the Albany Planned Parenthood clinic did when faced with one of these desperate women. Dr. Vosburgh, of course, helped place many unplanned and unwanted babies for adoption. Later in her life she said that she never performed an abortion, but she did on occasion refer a patient. The options available to women in the pre-*Roe* days were very limited and the toll in personal suffering was immeasurable.

The Fifties

With veterans back from the war and peace and prosperity at home, the fifties was a decade of conformity, conservatism and family values. The nuclear family centered on the bread-earning husband, and controversial subjects like birth control were not discussed in public. Rosie the Riveter may have gone off to work in a factory during the war, but she had returned home to her family and had put on her apron. Before the decade was out, however, both scientific advances in contraception and growing concerns about population growth would rock the boat.

Albany Planned Parenthood brochure

An undated brochure entitled "Is This What You Want To Know?" in the Albany Planned Parenthood records has all the earmarks of the early fifties. The picture on the cover illustrates the ideal American family, a husband reading to his two clean and well-dressed children while the adoring wife looks over his shoulder. The statement of mission it contains sets its place in the history of Planned Parenthood as clearly as the picture:

1. To help married couples plan AS LARGE FAMILIES as their physical, economic, and emotional ability can support.
2. To advise with and treat for infertility the many childless couples wanting families.
3. To encourage education for marriage and parenthood as a safeguard against the ignorance that wrecks so many marriages. Also to further adequate teaching of professional groups and of the public on the health and social importance of properly spaced families.
4. To promote research, conducted through grants to established universities and laboratories, to investigate the physiology of human reproduction, the causes and cures of childlessness, and discovery of a simple and inexpensive method of child spacing.

No longer was this a service to the poor; the message was aimed at the middle class family. The large, healthy and happy family was the goal, and no attention was paid to special concerns of women. The emphasis on fertility services undoubtedly overstated the capacity of the staff as no specialists were available at that time, but reinforced the central message of support for the family unit. The final goal of promoting research was pure wishful thinking. As a Planned Parenthood affiliate, the board may have endorsed national research into new contraceptive methods, but there is no record of any research initiatives taking place in Albany or at the initiative of this clinic. Above all, this was a mission statement designed to be respectable, responsible, and mainstream.

The listing in the brochure of the services provided by Planned Parenthood Center of Albany is equally interesting, as much for the omissions as for the inclusions. Aside from the "consultation...on family planning" there is no reference to prevention of unwanted pregnancies:

1. Consultation service for the entire community on family planning.
2. Information about the latest medical developments in the field of infertility to those who have been unable to have children.
3. An office for doctors specially trained in methods of contraception.
4. Lending library of books, presentation of films, and pamphlets pertaining to preparation for marriage, sex education, and family relationships.

Information regarding Planned Parenthood services in other communities are also available.

5. A teaching service for groups of nurses, physicians and medical students.
6. Provision of speakers for groups desiring educational lectures.

The emphasis on marriage and families continues in the section "Who Comes to the Center?":

> Married women who seek the advice of a doctor about the spacing of their children, in the interest of healthier, happier families.
>
> Childless couples who come to discuss their desire for children.
>
> Young people who come for information in preparation for marriage.
>
> Men and women who feel the need of help in meeting problems related to the physical aspects of marriage.
>
> All these come to the Center directly or are referred by ministers, physicians, hospitals, or social agencies.

Finally, the brochure states that the Center was supported by contributions from "men who are civic and business leaders, and women who are recognized for their interest in the health and welfare of the community," with no apologies to those women sponsors who were independently wealthy or who might have earned their own resources. No longer was there any mention of excluding anyone who could afford to see a private physician. Patients were charged according to their ability to pay, but those who were unable to make any payment were also accepted, and no charge was made for consultation services. The flyer also notes the endorsement of a large group of Albany physicians and the religious approval of many Protestant and Jewish clergymen.

One element that strikes a new note in the flyer is the emphasis on education. In the 1930s and '40s, the only educational programs mentioned were directed at parenting skills. Now there was talk of a lending library, of preparing young people for marriage, and even of "sex education," perhaps the most daring phrase in this highly cautious publication.

If any unmarried women with an unwanted pregnancy paid a visit to this bastion of middle class respectability, it is most certainly not recorded in the historic record. There are anecdotes of young women passing a single wedding ring around among themselves in the waiting room as they awaited their appointment, and doctors may well have turned a blind eye. The public stance, however, was proper, even Victorian, and a far cry from what Margaret Sanger had fought for.

Dr. Janet Hood, who worked in the Planned Parenthood clinic and taught at the State College for Teachers (later known as SUNY), expressed her alarm at the conservatism of the community when she shared her recollections of her Planned Parenthood experiences in 1983. "Even in 1955 I was considered sort of a 'dirty old lady' when I would try to bring up conception control for discussion with my colleagues here at SUNY. Any discussion of making the termination of pregnancy legal was completely taboo."

Despite community pressures, the number of patients served and services offered continued to grow (700 patients were seen at the clinic in 1950), and more clinic hours and more staff were needed. In 1952 Dr. Charles L. Poskanzer began assisting Dr. Vosburgh. Dr. Hood later described him:

> Charlie Poskanzer was a brick...He was wonderful...He did give a lot of time and energy to it...to the clinic and the actual hands on...He was just jovial and fun...Planned Parenthood has always had competent doctors working on staff and Charles certainly was one of them.

Dr. Poskanzer later remembered, "There were two of us. Dr. Vosburgh and myself. She covered the afternoon clinics and I the evenings...In the early days, patients were few and diaphragms were the principal service."

Feeling that positive information about the agency was not getting out in an effective way into the community, the board of directors in 1956 distributed a comic book that it hoped would be both appealing and educational to prospective clients. Board members left them on doorsteps. In 1957 members of the board and volunteers left matchbooks emblazoned with Planned Parenthood's name on them wherever they went.

Many local clergy continued their important support and involvement. Dr. Laman H. Bruner, rector of St. Peter's Episcopal Church, remembered that in the mid-'50s "young men and women would come to our cheerful office...and receive literature and information that at that time they found great difficulty in securing in other places."

One board member in particular had a profound influence on the organization in the 1950s. Catherine Campbell, twice President of the Board and subsequently an officer of the national Planned Parenthood Federation, was a tall, imposing woman and a courageous and a committed advocate for the cause of family planning. She was a frequent speaker to student and community groups, and, when she and her husband traveled, to groups outside the country. She later remembered the advice given to her at the time. "When I was first asked to join the board, my husband (an orthopedic surgeon)...was pleased and proud. Colleagues said, 'Don't let her. It's the kiss of death.'"

A note in the records written by board member Esther Lewis tells of Kay Campbell's importance:

> Kay was the person that held the whole thing together in the '50s and the '60s. She was the one who stood up in the community; was willing to speak to anyone; was willing to move outside the PP group and approach others; willing to ask her friends for money. She was the most outspoken person in the area; she also got involved in the state and national level.... Kay never wavered. She had an enthusiasm and a medical approach. She lent a respect to the agency.

An article in the November 23, 1959 *Knickerbocker News* under the headlines "Loudonville Mother of 4 Backs Planned Parenthood," and "Area Woman Gets National Office" quotes Campbell:

> My interest in PPFA began several years ago when somebody rapped on the door and left a pamphlet by Mrs. Sanger. After reading it, and talking with many people, I decided that perhaps the most important single factor in coping with the global population explosion is a planned parenthood organization giving sensitive and professional advice to parents. The era of greatest challenge for birth control, as the key to voluntary parenthood and population limitation, has just begun.

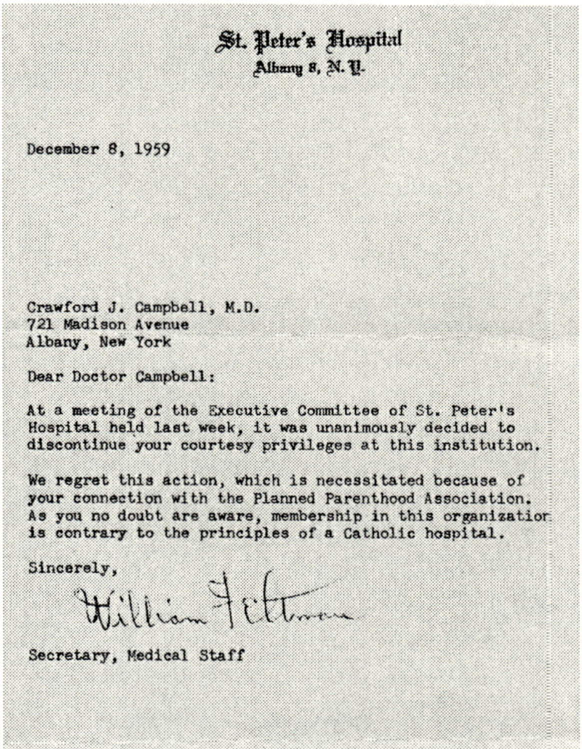

St. Peter's Hospital
Albany 8, N.Y.

December 8, 1959

Crawford J. Campbell, M.D.
721 Madison Avenue
Albany, New York

Dear Doctor Campbell:

At a meeting of the Executive Committee of St. Peter's Hospital held last week, it was unanimously decided to discontinue your courtesy privileges at this institution.

We regret this action, which is necessitated because of your connection with the Planned Parenthood Association. As you no doubt are aware, membership in this organization is contrary to the principles of a Catholic hospital.

Sincerely,

Secretary, Medical Staff

Letter from St. Peter's Hospital to Dr. Crawford Campbell

The article also contained the announcement that Mrs. Campbell was the new secretary of the Planned Parenthood Federation of America. That announcement was to have serious repercussions. In a letter from St. Peter's Hospital dated December 8, 1959, her husband, Dr. Crawford J. Campbell, a highly respected orthopedic surgeon, was notified that his privileges at that Catholic institution had been discontinued. The letter made it clear that his dismissal was caused by his connection with Planned Parenthood.

Albany Planned Parenthood issued a statement making it emphatically clear that the withdrawal of Dr. Campbell's privileges was another incident of Roman Catholic interference into beliefs and practices of non-Catholics. The issue was particularly sensitive since John F. Kennedy, a Roman Catholic, was about to make his bid for the Presidency of the United States.

The news spread quickly. Stories appeared in *Life Magazine*, *The New York Times* and the *Seattle Times*, among others. In the end, the episode worked to the advantage of both Dr. Campbell and Planned Parenthood. His practice grew quickly, and the publicity gained many new friends for family planning. Many years later St. Peter's Hospital again offered privileges to Dr. Campbell, but he politely refused.

Two national developments that would have a profound effect in Albany and in the entire country were contraceptive research and concerns about population growth.

In the 1950s the contraceptive methods available to women had not changed perceptibly since the 1920s. There were diaphragms and jelly, condoms, or contraceptive foam. Margaret Sanger encouraged contraceptive research, and in the 1950s found an enthusiastic supporter in the person of Katharine Dexter McCormick, heir to the International Harvester fortune. She offered extensive financial support to the work of Gregory Pincus at the Worcester Foundation in Massachusetts, who was attempting to produce an oral contraceptive based on synthetic progesterone. She also funded the first clinical trials of the pill which were conducted by Dr. John Rock, a Catholic gynecologist, who came to be known as the co-developer of the pill. He argued courageously, although unsuccessfully, with the Catholic Church for acceptance of the oral contraceptive. The birth control pill was eventually approved by the Food and Drug Administration in 1960 and would have an enormous impact on women and on the social *mores* of the coming decades.

Dr. Rock played a role in another controversial episode in Albany in 1952 when he was invited to speak in Albany jointly by Planned Parenthood and the Albany Medical College. After the invitations had been mailed, the Director of the Albany Hospital, Dr. Hale, and the Chairman of the Hospital Board, Mr. McCabe, made the decision that Planned Parenthood could not make use of any hospital facilities, including the amphitheater where the lecture was scheduled. According to Dr. John J. Gamble's account, "Dr. Hale quite frankly stated that the Roman Catholic bishop of Albany was bringing pressure to bear, and that since the hospital needed financial support from that religious denomination, the hospital could not offend it at this time." (Dr. Gamble, an Obstetrics and Gynecology specialist at the Albany Hospital, was serving at that time as the Chairman of the Planned Parenthood Medical Advisory Board.) Dr. Hale also made reference to the hospital's previous position regarding contraceptive clinics. Fortunately, the dean of the Albany Law School, just across the street, gave Planned Parenthood permission to use the Law School auditorium for Dr. Rock's address on "Recent Advances in the Diagnosis and Treatment of Infertility."

Meanwhile, scholars and leaders were becoming aware of the rapid growth in world population and its impact on living standards and human welfare in developing countries. 1952 was a watershed year in bringing public attention to the problems of "overpopulation" with the creation of both the Population Council and International Planned Parenthood Federation (IPPF), the latter being a worldwide league of autonomous family planning organizations. Despite some misgivings based on Margaret Sanger's early and tentative alliance with eugenicists, the birth control movement and the population control movement quickly identified their common interests and joined forces.

Years of Expansion 1965–1984

The Pill

The 1960s were years of great turmoil and unrest, marked by demands for social justice from African-Americans, by protest against the war in Vietnam, and by women's demands for equality following the publication in 1963 of Betty Friedan's *The Feminine Mystique.* All of these factors, along with growing concerns about population growth, slowly began to change national attitudes about women's role in society and about family planning.

The Food and Drug Administration approval of the Enovid contraceptive pill in 1960 brought a sea change to the family planning movement and a flood of new patients to the Albany Planned Parenthood. The early pill was not perfect, but for millions of women it gave effective and simple control over reproduction and relieved their fears about unwanted pregnancies. Within a few years, the intrauterine device (IUD) was also introduced, finally giving women wider choice in contraceptive methods. Nationally the number of Planned Parenthood contraceptive patients tripled by the end of the decade, and 90 percent of them were choosing either the pill or the IUD. In Albany, by 1965 six different oral contraceptives and the IUD were available to patients.

The Albany Planned Parenthood story is one of astounding growth in patient numbers and in services provided. The clinic had hired a first part-time Executive Director, Vera Schaefer, in 1959. She was followed by Carolyn Garvin in 1962. Garvin's Annual Report for that year recorded a 44 percent increase in new patients over the previous year, and the total of all patient visits, including old and new patients, jumped from 958 in 1961 to 2,223 in 1962. Of the 417 new patients that year, 63 percent earned less than $74 a week.

Garvin's comments in the report help make the statistics come alive:

> Many of these women already have more children than their emotional and financial resources can cope with by the time they hear of us, and come in feeling quite desperate. I recall a 20 year old girl who had recently undergone a series of shock treatments. She was sent to us by her psychiatrist who believed that another pregnancy would endanger her mental health. She chose the diaphragm. Another patient was a Roman Catholic, 36 years old, who had been pregnant most of her married life. She had given birth to 7 children and had at least 6 miscarriages. Two of these abortions were self-induced. If each one of you could sit in the interview room, as I do each clinic session, and listen to these women, and sometimes men, you could not help but have a renewed sense of urgency about making family planning services available to ever-increasing numbers of people.

By the time the 1964 annual tally was done, it reported 720 new patients during the year, and total patient visits of 4,497. Among the patient load were many women who traveled from Massachusetts and Connecticut, escaping the strict birth control laws still operative in those states. A *Knickerbocker News* article on February 17, 1965 carried the headline "Parenthood Clinic Aids Out-of-State Women; 130 Travel to Albany to Obtain Information." The article contains this account:

> "My doctor told me about this place," says a woman from Dalton, Mass. "He told me the address and made me write it out in my own handwriting so he wouldn't get in trouble."
>
> She is typical of the Massachusetts and Connecticut women who come to the clinic. She and her husband have five children ages 18, 16, 7, 3 and 7 months. They do not want any more children for a while, but they cannot get any advice or help in Massachusetts for their problems.
>
> Massachusetts state law prescribes severe penalties for anyone who gives advice or material on birth control to women.
>
> Mrs. Robert Garvin, executive director of the Albany clinic, said the clinic has about 125 active patients in its lists from Massachusetts and another four or five from Connecticut, which also has strict birth control regulations.

Extra clinic sessions were added to accommodate the new patients, making a total of three sessions each week (every Tuesday and Wednesday evening and Thursday afternoon), and separate hours were scheduled when patients could get their pill prescriptions filled. New staff had to be hired. Dr. Frances Vosburgh had retired in 1962 because of poor health, after having worked in the clinic for over 27 years. Dr. Charles Poskanzer, who had been Medical Director since joining the staff in 1952, continued in that capacity, and was joined by Dr. Manuel Pearl, Dr. Corinne Snow, and Dr. Fred DeAngelo of Schenectady. Dr. Arthur Hengerer also staffed clinics at Trinity Place. He recalls that his pay for working one evening clinic a week for a full year was a $25 savings bond. Clearly money was not the motivating force for these doctors. Clinic work did, however, allow young doctors to build their experience by seeing a large number of patients, while at the same time serving a worthy cause.

In addition to the doctors and the Executive Director, there was a part-time secretary who doubled as bookkeeper, a nurse, and a long roster of volunteers. In those small rooms, when clinics were not in session, volunteers would come to do their fundraising and community outreach work. Former board member Herta Krahmer remembered:

> We did a lot of work in that little office: typed, stuffed envelopes and got the campaign literature out. One of the board members protested to envelope stuffing, but we did not want to spend too much money.

The space was so inadequate that Former Board President Marion Raymond recalled:

> It was very small quarters at Trinity Place. We used to have patients waiting down the stairway out the door and all the way up the block waiting to get their contraception, their pills. It was a real struggle. There was a little space at the top of the stairs and we used to sell pills there, and an examining room and a little waiting room, very small.

As Grace Bair Fishell, a nurse at Trinity Place put it:

> I helped down there. We were just mobbed. All of a sudden the pill had come in. We were so completely overwhelmed with people, it was difficult to find a place to go.

So a search for new quarters began. Once more, as in 1942, many property owners were not eager to open their doors to Planned Parenthood. It was important to the organization to remain accessible to the low-income groups of the South End and Arbor Hill who constituted the major part of their patient base, yet they wanted a safe and central location. Finally they found a small house for rent on Lark Street, owned by the Trinity Methodist Church, still close to the neighborhoods they served and easily accessible by bus. Even the church hesitated, knowing the history of the clinic's eviction in 1942 from the Albany Hospital. By the spring of 1965, however, it did agree to lease two floors of the building to Planned Parenthood, spacious quarters by comparison with the cramped five small rooms at Trinity Place.

Into the Mainstream

The 1965 move from Trinity Place to 225 Lark Street accomplished much more than providing additional space. It situated the clinic in the mainstream of the life of the city, on a trendy street near many shops and restaurants, easily reached by bus or car, not far from the commercial center of the city, but no longer in a low-income neighborhood. The new setting sent a message to the community that this was no longer a clinic exclusively for the poor, that it welcomed any and all who wished to visit it and use its services. Combined with the widespread popularity of the pill, the new location opened up the clinic to a much broader-based group of patients.

225 Lark Street

Board member Herta Krahmer had helped find the new quarters and later remembered the move and "that sweet old house" at 225 Lark Street:

> We rented two floors. In the basement were some seamstresses. After some time we rented the basement too. A charming old retired school teacher, Miss Kelly, took over the little garden with the old fashioned roses...After a while we bought the whole thing.
>
> I remember how we furnished the whole house, how we had things given to us. For instance Rosie (Board President Rosamond Plowden-Wardlaw) gave us a big, elegant table for our board meetings. I suggested to my gynecologist that we could use new scales. He thought that his were still quite good. An hour later I got a telephone message that the scales were on their way. One extra examining table arrived the same way.

Marion Raymond, who was Board President from 1964 to 1969, played a critical role in the transition from Trinity Place to Lark Street. A trained nurse, wife of a doctor, she well understood the need for more trained and professional medical staffing with appropriate space for clinics, and also the need to establish better community relationships. She contributed countless hours and her considerable organizational skills to the search for the new building, to community outreach, and to organizing board and staff. The role of Board President in this period carried much more weight than that of the part-time Executive Director, who was in fact more of an office manager, and Raymond fully utilized the influence of her position to move the organization to a new level of professionalism.

With more patients, more revenue, and more medical services to offer patients (Pap smears were added to the roster of services in 1965) the professional staff grew. Although volunteers continued to provide support, they gradually relinquished their central staffing role. By 1966, the clinic had a full-time director, Grace Houghtaling, a secretary, a clinic nurse supervisor, some additional clerical help, and a corps of physician clinicians who rotated to staff the clinics. Dr. Poskanzer continued as Medical Director, Dr. Robert Friedlander began staffing clinics in 1965, along with Drs. Pearl, Snow, DeAngelo and others. Grace Bair (later Grace Fishell) who had begun work at Trinity Place as a volunteer, was the first registered nurse employed by Planned Parenthood of Albany (PPA). She brought a high level of professional competence to the job, and her organization and efficiency were appreciated by the doctors. According to Friedlander, "the clinic hummed" when she was in charge. Later, when Albany Medical Center established its own Family Planning Center, Bair moved on to direct it.

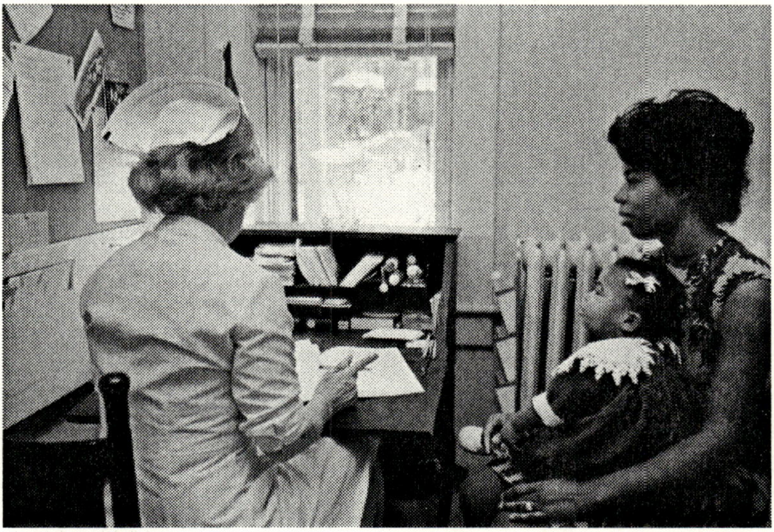

Lark Street Clinic

The 1965 Supreme Court landmark *Griswold v. Connecticut* decision further improved the political climate for Albany Planned Parenthood. In Connecticut, unlike New York, the 1879 Comstock statute had prevented women from legally obtaining or using birth control. Estelle Griswold, the executive director of Planned Parenthood League of Connecticut, brought a direct and successful challenge to this law. Justice William O. Douglas wrote eloquently in the majority opinion:

> We deal with a right of privacy older than the Bill of Rights—older than our political parties, older than our school system. Marriage is a coming together, for better or for worse, hopefully enduring and intimate to the degree of being sacred.

To be sure, the *Griswold* decision applied only to married women; not until the Supreme Court's *Eisenstadt v. Baird* decision in 1972 were unmarried people granted the same right. However, by establishing a constitutional right to privacy it protected access to birth control for all states. Even more importantly, it laid the groundwork for affirming the right to safe and legal abortion, the next battleground for Planned Parenthood.

The impact on women's lives of access to birth control is well expressed by Helen Schnitzer, a personal friend and a patient of Dr. Vosburgh. The oldest of nine children, Schnitzer well understood the difference between her life and her mother's:

> From my experience...just the fact that you could easily get a means of birth control made it possible for you to do things you wanted to do because you weren't going to be pregnant every year and you weren't going to have 10 or 12 children. In that sense it changed the world for you. It changed life.

Community outreach was a particular focus of attention for Planned Parenthood of Albany during the late '60s. Board President Marion Raymond, anxious to send a message of inclusion to the community, held the 1965 kick-off for the annual fund campaign at the Albany Institute of History and Art rather than at a private residence, and included members of the black community for the first time. She also took steps to include consumers of services on the board.

It took several years of persistent effort on the part of both the board and the Clergy Advisory Committee before PPA was finally accepted to membership in the Council of Community Services in 1967. The strong support of many of the Protestant and Jewish clergy of the community was indispensable on this occasion, and continues to be a major strength of the organization. An active Speakers Bureau reached out with presentations to school and college groups, and training in family planning was provided for members of the Department of Social Services, nurses, and other groups. In 1969, at the invitation of PPA, Dr. Alan Guttmacher, chairman of the Planned Parenthood Federation of America (PPFA) and distinguished gynecologist, came to Albany for a day, speaking at the annual meeting, but also meeting with the New York State Commissioner of Health and with doctors at the Albany Medical Center. His message emphasized the great need for New York State to change the law so that medically safe abortion could be legally performed.

Two issues of public concern contributed to the acceptance of birth control by the general public: population growth and poverty. The population issue was stressed in many years of PPA's annual fund campaigns, and in fact surpassed the older theme of humanitarian help to the poor as the dominant rationale for supporting the family planning cause. When President Johnson in 1964 declared his War on Poverty, the clear message was finally sent out from Washington that only through programs of family planning could poverty and overpopulation be addressed. PPA joined with other Albany community groups in forming an anti-poverty program called Albany Citizens against Poverty, helping to further the extension of birth control services to low-income families.

The population issue did have broad appeal to men, and the record of the '60s and '70s does show more men participating on the board and with financial support. One such friend of PPA, Laurence McKinney, wrote facetiously to a colleague about his reaction to seeing a family with 11 or 12 children:

> All I do actually is to multiply them by $600, which is deductible from their income tax and realize that I, with only 3 children, am paying for them. The McKinney suggestion, which has and will get nowhere is: 1) give everybody a tax reduction for 4 children and after that make them pay $600 for every other child. The only trouble with my system is that since most of the explosive families are on relief anyway, there is nothing to deduct from or to tax with.

Distasteful as his suggestion may be, it does convey some of the serious concerns that made businessmen and public policy makers sympathetic to family planning advocates.

A new executive director, Lyndon Schendel, arrived in 1969. A Presbyterian minister by training, he wanted to try his hand at something different. Clearly for him the issue of population explosion was the major motivating interest, as evidenced in his first annual report to the board in 1970:

> It has become increasingly clear to me that Planned Parenthood's main thrust in the 70s ought to be toward the motivation of families to desire fewer children for their own good as well as the good of society. After all, 'Family planning is the best bet for family happiness' and we do have a population explosion! This task of motivating people, especially those in the middle and upper income groups, to want fewer children will be even more difficult and costly and unpopular than providing services but not less important.

In an effort to take the services of PPA more directly to the people of the city, two satellite clinics were set up in 1969, one on Catherine Street in the quarters of the Albany Methodist Society in the South End, and the other in the Sheridan Hollow Community Center on Orange Street on the north side of Albany. After a year or two of operation, it became clear that patients preferred to come to the Lark Street clinic, and the satellite clinic experiment came to an end.

PPA also collaborated with the Albany Medical Center in establishing a Family Planning clinic there. Not only did PPA's nurse, Grace Bair, head the Albany Medical Center clinic, but PPA regularly referred patients there, following through on the predominant national thinking of the time that in order to ensure universal access to contraception, Planned Parenthood should make every effort to integrate these services into those of mainstream providers. Once more, however, patients voted with their feet, preferring the more intimate clinic environment to the large hospital setting.

Throughout the 1960s, no major source of public funding was available, and PPA depended heavily on private fund raising to augment revenues from patients. Innovative approaches planned and executed by volunteers, including an art auction, contributed to growing support from the public. For the year of 1968, for instance, $20,500 was raised from the public on a budget of about $55,000. The first signs of some federal funding did surface in this period in the form of some small grants from the Office on Economic Opportunity and through the Maternal and Child Health federal program. More help would soon be on its way.

A New Era

In the early 1970s state and federal legislation and court decisions dramatically altered the Planned Parenthood landscape. In 1970 in Washington, Congress voted to fund family planning through Title X of the Public Health Service Act. In the same year, the New York State Legislature repealed the 19th century anti-abortion statute still on the books, making abortion legal and available in the state. By 1973, with the Supreme Court's *Roe v. Wade* decision, the legalization of abortion became national. The net effect of all these events was to lay one battle to rest, as the use and access to birth control gained the endorsement of public policy. These same events, however, laid the groundwork for a new battle over abortion, and that continues to rage fiercely today.

The national debate about the dangers of population explosion, national and international, had begun in the 1950s and had finally gained legislative attention by the mid-60s with a series of legislative hearings and special studies. Changing national attitudes toward family planning had made that subject more politically palatable than in earlier years. President Eisenhower, for instance, had made it clear that he considered family planning a private matter and not the business of government. President Kennedy was cautiously more receptive, but not until President Johnson's administration in the mid-1960s did some early grants from the Office of Economic Opportunity became available for family planning agencies. Johnson's War on Poverty built on the clear relationship between poverty and family planning and laid the groundwork for a more active federal role. In 1968 he appointed the Committee on Population and Family Planning, cochaired by John D. Rockefeller III, who had earlier founded the Population Council to conduct research on population related issues, and who subsequently from 1970 to 1972 headed the Nixon-appointed Commission on Population Growth and the American Future.

Population debate brought together a coalition of interest groups, often with very different motivations, including economists, environmentalists, demographers, and family planners among others. Some of the suggestions that surfaced in the discussions betrayed the fundamental concerns of each group. Family planners were primarily concerned with women's health and the ability of all women to make their own decisions about childbearing. Those who wished simply to lower the birthrate, particularly among poorer populations, proposed measures such as tax incentives for smaller families or tax penalties for larger families, and some policy makers suggested even more coercive measures such as forced sterilization for the mentally retarded. The wish to reduce welfare rolls, although not actively stated, was most certainly in many minds. Fortunately, the final legislation kept all family planning services purely voluntary, following the recommendations that grew out of Rockefeller's committee. Nevertheless, the primary rationale for the legislation was population control rather than women's health and welfare. That helps explain why then-Representative George H.W. Bush was a sponsor of the legislation, although subsequently as President he adopted an anti-choice position.

In 1969 President Nixon made the first major Presidential speech addressing population growth and proposed legislation that would enable all American women to have access to birth control information and services. By the end of 1970 the Family Planning Services and Research Act, Title X of the Public Health Service Act, was passed with strong bipartisan support by Congress and signed into law. It proposed a vision of universal access to family planning services, increased support for research into human reproduction and into new contraceptive technology, and created an Office of Population Affairs to guide and coordinate the government's population programs. It barred the use of any Title X funds for abortion.

According to information from PPFA, Title X contributed to a tripling of contraceptive patients nationally over the decade from 1969 to 1979, from 345,000 to 1,165,000. "One out of every six of those patients had an income below the federal poverty level—twice the proportion as at the beginning of the decade. One out of three was under 20."

The benefits of Title X funding were not felt immediately in Albany, but by the 1977 PPA budget, money had begun to flow through the New York State Department of Health to the Albany clinic. Title X funds were combined with the Maternal and Child Health block grant and social services block grant, as well as state funding designated for family planning and allotted to New York's family planning clinics. This funding, combined with Medicaid reimbursements, contributed heavily to the rapid growth of the organization in the 1970s. (Although Medicaid had been created in 1965, reimbursements to the Albany clinic did not begin until 1970.)

Meanwhile in the late 1960s the New York State Legislature had begun discussing abortion reform. Once the *Griswold v. Connecticut* decision had established the right of privacy there had been active consideration of extending this concept to abortion. The Clergy Consultation Service, which began in New York City and spread across the country, attempted to locate reputable doctors who would perform safe abortions and refer women to them through a national network, but that was only a stopgap measure. When the Legislature began talking about how to address the issue, the question in New York as in other states was whether to seek to reform the old 19th century antiabortion statutes on the books to allow for "therapeutic exceptions" to the law, or to seek to repeal the law completely.

Even Planned Parenthood Federation chairman Alan Guttmacher believed, as late as 1968, that a repeal attempt was doomed to failure, and that rather than risk an all-or-nothing proposal, it was more politically expedient to begin with reform. In late 1969 sentiment in the Legislature began to change, however, and a repeal bill was proposed in Albany. About a dozen other states had passed reform legislation, but the only repeal bill was Hawaii, where it passed with several restrictions. Two months later, on April 9, 1969, the New York bill came to a vote.

The story of its passage is dramatic. In the Assembly, where the vote was expected to be very close, the difference was made by one upstate Assemblyman from Utica, George M. Michaels, who came from a conservative and heavily

Catholic district. Michaels' son, a social worker, had witnessed some of the horrors of illegal abortion first hand and had persuaded his father of the importance of the repeal bill. When the roll was called, Michaels first voted against the bill, following the sentiment of his constituency, but as the tally made it clear that his negative vote would cause defeat, he stood. In an admirable act of political courage, he addressed the chamber Speaker. "I realize, Mr. Speaker, that I am terminating my political career, but I cannot in good conscience sit here and allow my vote to be the one that defeats this bill," he said. "I ask that my vote be changed from 'no' to 'yes'." When Speaker Perry Duryea then cast his own affirmative vote to carry the Assembly, and the Senate soon followed suit, New York passed the most progressive abortion law in the nation. It permitted abortion for residents and non-residents of the state for any reason through the 24th week of pregnancy, provided it was performed by a licensed physician. Michaels was never reelected to office after that defining vote.

As anticipated, not only was there a rush of demand from New York State residents, but women from across the country flooded the state seeking legal abortions. The Syracuse Planned Parenthood was the first affiliate in the state to perform abortion, starting as soon as the law came into effect, on July 1, 1970, and the New York City affiliate followed soon after. The Albany Planned Parenthood needed another 15 years to build its resources before it was able to provide the service itself, but it was immediately deluged with requests for pregnancy tests and referrals. According to staff nurse Elizabeth Hull:

> When abortion became legalized nationally, and as sexual attitudes became more liberal, our clients started to include more single women, especially those in the colleges, and later, the high schools. It was at that point that we added educators, who began to be more welcome in the area schools.

In 1971, PPA was averaging about 125 pregnancy tests a month; by 1976 that number had grown to almost 400 a month. Many abortion referrals had to be made out of the area since private doctors and the Albany Medical Center Hospital were the only local providers and they could not adequately satisfy the demand.

The *Roe v. Wade* case that had been working its way through the courts from Texas for several years finally came to a decision by the Supreme Court on January 22, 1973. In a 7 to 2 decision written by Justice Harry A. Blackmun, the Court overruled all state laws that had prohibited or restricted a woman's right to obtain an abortion during her first three months of pregnancy, and said that only in the last 10 weeks of pregnancy, the period during which the fetus is judged to be capable of surviving if born, does the state have a compelling interest in the life of the fetus. A new era had arrived. Legal abortion during the first two trimesters of pregnancy was now the law of the land.

Growth

If ever there was a golden age for Planned Parenthood, it was in the 1970s. Supported by nearly unanimous public acceptance of birth control and public funding, the Albany agency, like its counterparts across the country, grew dynamically. Although population control was still a motivating factor, the feminist movement and the drive for an Equal Rights Amendment built support for a different rationale for family planning, namely the assertion that women's control over their own reproductive lives was a fundamental human right. Despite broader acceptance of contraception, however, opposition to abortion began to grow. In 1973 the National Right to Life Committee was organized in opposition to *Roe v. Wade*, and by the mid-1970s the impact of anti-abortion organizing began to be felt in public policy. Congress passed the first version of the Hyde Amendment in 1976, barring any government support for abortions for indigent women. The amendment was introduced by then first-term Republican Representative from Illinois, Henry J. Hyde, who still sits in Congress today, now serving his 15th term. Throughout his career he has been one of the most vocal and persistent Congressional opponents of abortion.

Planned Parenthood of Albany experienced an intense flurry of activity and growth in the 1970s. The period might well be called the Decade of the Teens as the number of younger patients increased rapidly. To the distress of their parents and other caring adults, teenagers eagerly adopted the increasing acceptance of women's sexuality and equality and became sexually active much earlier than in the past, with the unfortunate outcome of an increase of epidemic proportions of both venereal disease and pregnancies among adolescents. By 1973 PPA found that some 80 percent of its patients were teenagers, and many were coming to the clinic for pregnancy tests.

The specific public health news that gave the PPA board a convenient reason to take aggressive action was the Health Department's announcement of the increased incidence of sexually transmitted diseases among teenagers. The board immediately developed a policy on Service to Minors, endorsing the delivery of confidential services to all who sought them regardless of age. A committee on

Human Sexuality was formed, bringing together professionals and laymen in the fields of medicine, social work, law, theology, pharmacology and family planning to develop and implement programs for young people. This group subsequently became an independent regional Council on Human Sexuality sponsored by the Health Services of the State University at Albany, the Albany Medical Center, the YWCA, the Schenectady Planned Parenthood and PPA. Over the years this group presented a number of public forums on topics such as Male Sexuality and Sexuality and the Disabled.

To address the concern about teens, the PPA board decided to focus initially on sex education for teachers, parents and professionals working with teens. Aided by funds donated to PPA, the Rosamond Plowden-Wardlaw Library of resource materials was established and dedicated in the fall of 1972. Containing audio-visuals as well as books, pamphlets and articles, it was publicized as a resource for parents, students, and professionals such as guidance counselors, libraries, agencies and schools of nursing. The library collection continued to grow and supported an ever-increasing public education program about sexuality and reproduction.

In the direct service area, PPA recognized the period of adolescence as one of great sexual anxiety, meaning PPA needed to meet the social and emotional needs of its younger patients. In the early 1970s it therefore hired a social worker, added counseling services and scheduled special teen clinics. PPA staff were particularly sensitive to the needs of younger patients, knowing they had to establish a relationship of trust with teens, and that confidentiality was a critical consideration for them. In one case in 1974, a PPA staff member was subpoenaed by the parents of a 16-year-old patient, demanding release of the patient's records, but the Court ruled that PPA did not have to give them up.

Today we think of the mission of Planned Parenthood as comprising the three-pronged aspects of patient care, education and advocacy, but it was really only in the 1970s that this broader mission took form. In Albany the position of Education Coordinator was first created in 1973, and the first Public Affairs Committee to monitor family planning and abortion legislation was created the same year.

When Ruth Klepper was appointed the new Executive Director in early 1974, the transition of PPA from a small agency largely run by volunteers to a modern, efficient, and professionally managed and staffed organization was assured. She had administrative and long-range planning skills that allowed PPA to build its patient base, increase revenues, add new patient services, expand to a larger geographic area, and acquire new buildings. During her 20-year tenure PPA grew steadily and gained community recognition.

During the 1970s, Planned Parenthood Federation took the national lead in developing advanced training for nurses, a precursor of what would become the Nurse Practitioner program, preparing nurses to perform more clinical activities under standing orders from a physician, but without the doctor necessarily being present. Several PPA staff nurses pursued the training, allowing the clinic to serve more patients and stay open longer hours. The gradual transition from reliance on physicians to the use of nurse practitioners gave a new flexibility to all Planned Parenthood affiliates.

A number of new patient services were introduced in the 1970s, including comprehensive services for the mentally retarded, where PPA provided group education, individual counseling, staff training, and contraception. As teen pregnancies continued to rise, PPA developed special education programs and clinic services on a completely confidential basis to meet their needs. By 1975 it initiated the first weekly walk-in cancer screening program in the area, with breast examinations and Pap smears. And in 1978 PPA joined with the Health Services of the State University at Albany to open a once-a-week satellite clinic on the University campus. Dr. Janet Hood, who had worked with Dr. Vosburgh at the Albany Planned Parenthood clinic in the 1940s and '50s, had become the Director of the University's Student Health Services. She later recalled:

> I decided that we definitely needed a unit at the University, and of course this went against everyone's philosophy, not only because I saw a tremendous need with the new sexual *mores* that were coming along, but also because I thought it was an educational thing...population growth and how to prevent it, what to do about it....I wanted it on the campus. Between Ruth Klepper and me we did finally pull it off and we got a little clinic there.

Early in 1979 specialized services for men including clinical, counseling and community services were added to the growing roster at PPA. By 1981 these services included on-site vasectomies.

In the early 1970s in the Capital District, all federal Title X funds for family planning were channeled through an independent corporation called the Capital Area Family Resources, Inc. (CAFRI) which served as a grantee for Health, Education and Welfare funds. Klepper soon was seated on the CAFRI board, and when the Rensselaer County family planning clinic was closed in 1975, she seized the opportunity for PPA to expand into that contiguous county and to gain a grant of federal dollars to support the move. In March of 1976 a Troy clinic was opened at 5 Broadway, and by the year's end 1,800 patients had been served there. To reflect its new geographic turf, the organization's name was changed the next year to Planned Parenthood of Albany and Rensselaer Counties (PPARC). Eventually CAFRI closed and public funding, combining both Title X and New York State funds, were distributed by the Department of Health's Bureau of Family Planning to family planning clinics across the state, including PPA.

Until that time, virtually all funds supporting PPA's program had come from patient fees, sales of supplies, and voluntary contributions. Now Title X federal dollars required that there be a sliding fee scale, thereby subsidizing services for the most needy. Uninsured younger patients were the largest group benefiting from these new public monies. A few vital statistics illustrate the dramatic growth over a decade. The annual budget for 1970 was $80,432; by 1979 it had grown to $540,000, of which $196,000 was grant money. During this same period the patient base grew from under 2000 in 1970 to over 10,000 by the end of the decade.

Despite renovations and its expansion to include the basement space, the Albany clinic at 225 Lark Street was far too small to accommodate the growing patient load and expanded staff. By 1970 the mortgage on the building had been paid off, and soon a decision was made to search for a larger location. When 259 Lark Street became available, only a few doors down the street, it was purchased and renovated, and the clinic moved there in 1977. A moving-day anecdote illustrates the commitment and entrepreneurial spirit of the staff. The nurses set up a table on the sidewalk so that patients who came to fill prescriptions that day would not be turned away empty-handed. The new building provided a spacious waiting area, separate rooms for interviews to protect patients' privacy, a fully equipped clinic area designed specifically to meet the needs of expanding services, and a parking lot for the convenience of staff and patients. The expansion in space and equipment increased the range of laboratory tests that could be done internally, and medical services were expanded to include primary treatment of minor problems experienced by contraceptive users.

Staffing and organizational innovations supported PPARC's growth. An Assistant Director was hired to develop grant proposals and to help with budgeting and related administrative work. The Nurse Administrator position was expanded to Director of Patient Services with responsibility for all medical and counseling services, assuring consistent quality in all areas of patient contact. And a Fundraising Coordinator joined the staff to maintain old contacts, to develop new ones, and to devise creative fundraising ideas to attract community support. To support the growing community education program, a Teen Educator position was added, and a Teen Advisory Committee created to make recommendations about serving our younger patients. Education staff also trained professionals of several human service agencies, and worked with schools, individual parents and groups.

In 1980, continuing the expansion, PPARC was invited by the Department of Health to take over what had been a county health clinic in Hudson to serve both Columbia and Greene Counties. In 1981 it changed its name to Upper Hudson Planned Parenthood (UHPP) to reflect its broader geographic scope.

Continuing its focus on teen pregnancy, and with funding provided by the Department of Social Services, the Albany Teen Consortium, a group of six local agencies brought together by UHPP, was formed to develop a network of services for teens at high risk of pregnancy. When in 1981 Albany County's teen pregnancy rate actually dropped below that of upstate New York as a whole for the first time ever, UHPP was gratified that its efforts were beginning to show results. The following year the Columbia County rate leveled off, reflecting an expanded education program made possible through a grant from the Columbia County Youth Bureau. Despite improvement, there was still much to be done as the teen pregnancy rate remained at about 65 pregnancies per 1,000 teens.

A note in the files about two teenage cases illustrates the increasing complexity of the issues facing UHPP:

---

1. A 16 year old is picked up for petty larceny and probation refers her to us for a pregnancy test. The test is positive. The court wants her remanded to the custody of her parents. The parents insist she have an abortion, otherwise they will not accept custody and she can go to jail. She refuses to have an abortion. We provide a pre-natal referral. Outcome unknown to this date.

2. A 14 year old comes in for a pregnancy test (with a full contingent of friends.) She had sex once, last September. She has very irregular and infrequent menses so she couldn't possibly be pregnant. She is very small in stature and dressed there is no evidence, but she is approximately 28 weeks. There has been no pre-natal care, but she eats well and only goes to beer drinking parties on weekends. She does not want to be pregnant and becomes hysterical. With her friends she leaves to tell her parents.

UHPP's commitment to serving teens went beyond its role as medical provider and educator. Early in 1982 it created an Alert Network and joined with thousands of others across the nation to protest the Reagan administration's proposed "Squeal Rule" intended to mandate parental notification whenever teens received prescription services, a regulation that would have compromised Planned Parenthood's long standing commitment to confidentiality for all patients. The outpouring of letters into the Department of Health and Human Services delayed and eventually prevented the promulgation of the regulations. To increase public awareness of this insidious political attack on reproductive freedom, UHPP staff appeared on many radio and television programs, feature stories were offered and background information was provided to local newspapers.

The "New Right" continued its attack on women's right to choose abortion when in the summer of 1982 the U.S. Senate debated the Human Life Amendment, which would have outlawed abortion. Once more UHPP, in concert with Planned Parenthoods across the country, fought back with letters to Congress, full page advertisements in local papers, and encouragement of public support for women's choice.

An innovative program was introduced in 1983. Services to Teens at Risk (STAR), supported by a grant, identified a group of adolescents who were at high risk of pregnancy, and used counseling and individualized support to help them avoid, or at least postpone pregnancy. PPA also developed a comprehensive sexuality curriculum for the fifth and sixth grades which was used successfully in the Berlin School system. The following year introduced another grant-supported project called "Mother and Daughters: Growing Together", strengthening communication skills so as to encourage mothers to discuss sexual information and behavior with their daughters. This project was so successful that a different version called Parent/Child was later introduced so that fathers and sons could be included.

When UHPP celebrated its 50th anniversary at a dinner on June 4, 1984, Mayor of Albany Thomas M. Whalen proclaimed it Planned Parenthood Golden Anniversary Day in the city of Albany. Over 400 friends and supporters marked the half century of community service with a gala dinner. Dr. Frances Vosburgh and Catherine Campbell were special honorees. Long-time board member and supporter Shirley Brand paid tribute to them:

Dr. Vosburgh was a heroine not only in the 1930s and 1940s, but for many years thereafter...Her medical skills, her warmth and big heart endeared her to all patients who affectionately called her 'Doc'...You are a remarkable person

> Dr. Vosburgh, you have practiced your profession with dignity, warmth and generosity.
>
> Catherine Campbell stands out as the personification of Planned Parenthood volunteers. Kay Campbell never wavered. She was as knowledgeable as she was outspoken. Her enthusiasm and reputation lent respect to the agency. She was the person who held us together in the 1950s and 1960s. She was the one who stood up in the community, was willing to move outside the Planned Parenthood group and approach others. The ground work that she provided decades ago is evidenced by the continuing support of more than 400 people who are here tonight.

The guest speaker, Jacqueline Grennan Wexler, president of the National Conference of Christians and Jews, talked about "The Dignity of Life." In that year the UHPP budget surpassed one million dollars for the first time. There were 12,220 women and 450 men who received care at UHPP clinics that year, and the community education staff gave 223 presentations on a variety of human sexuality topics to a total audience of more than 4,000, and films and library materials reached another 2,400.

Upper Hudson appeared to be in top form, but the anniversary celebrations masked a growing controversy. Since President Reagan's election in 1980 the New Right had gained strength in the country, and the threats to Planned Parenthood services and funding were increasing. In Albany, before the anniversary year was out, UHPP faced one of the most serious challenges in its history.

Reproductive Rights 1984–2004

Abortion Wars

By the 1980s concerns about overpopulation had quieted and in its place the language shifted to reproductive rights. Violence against abortion providers had erupted across the country, and pro-choice women were angry. They had learned their lessons from the civil rights and from the feminist movements, and they saw reproductive freedom being eroded under the Reagan administration. Chances for an Equal Rights Amendment, opposed by the New Right, had expired with its ratification deadline in 1982, and issues like the Human Life Amendment threatened hard-won rights. They believed that control over one's reproductive life was a fundamental human right, constitutionally guaranteed by the privacy principle first articulated in *Griswold v. Connecticut* and further established in *Roe v. Wade*, and should not be dictated by Congress. To illustrate the inappropriate intrusion of government into private matters, a famous Planned Parenthood poster of the time showed a husband and wife in bed together with a Congressman squarely in the center between them.

Against this background, Upper Hudson Planned Parenthood had for several years been quietly planning to introduce first trimester abortion services. Aside from more costly hospitals and private medical practices, there was no other provider in the area, and the agency was regularly referring its patients outside the area. The board also believed that the spectrum of services offered by UHPP would not be complete without this option. The clinic had grown sufficiently in financial and staff resources to be able to support the new service, and the board of directors favored the move and endorsed it in a Long Range Plan. When, in 1977, UHPP moved from the small Lark Street clinic to larger quarters at 259 Lark Street, the new clinic space was designed to meet all New York State Department of Health regulations as to size and configuration of space needed for abortion. The Hudson UHPP clinic had moved from its original small location to a new site in 1982, and it too had been configured to provide pregnancy termination services. Klepper and her board President had conferred with the Planned Parenthood Federation about protocols, internal systems, and other procedures and done the extensive internal work of preparation.

The New York State Department of Health required that the clinic go through a Certificate of Need (CON) application to add any new service, which required a careful analysis of the need for the service, financial feasibility, and the character and competency of the agency. A strategic decision was made to apply for the service at two locations, the Albany and the Hudson clinics, so that even if one site was turned down, the agency could still carry out its plans at the other.

Once the application was completed and reviewed by the Department of Health, it was given preliminary "administrative review" approval in December 1983. This expedited approval was intended for projects that had minimal (under $100,000) financial impact, and since UHPP had already done all of the architectural work needed to comply with Health Department guidelines, the cost of adding the new service was under $25,000 and easily eligible. The application was then forwarded to the Health Systems Agency of Northeastern New York (HSA/NENY) which reviewed all new CON requests in order to eliminate duplication of services in an attempt to control health care spending. (In a curious twist of fate, Patricia McGeown, who would ten years later succeed Ruth Klepper as the next Executive Director of UHPP, was at that time the Deputy Executive Director of HSA/NENY. She held firm when the Health Department subsequently asked HSA to re-open the UHPP case, insisting that it had been properly handled in the first place.) The HSA in turn submitted all applications to Subarea Councils and a Review Advisory Group where volunteers reviewed all proposals, including the list of projects that had been approved through the administrative review process. The list of applications circulated before the review boards throughout the summer of 1984, and UHPP was fully prepared to attract some public attention from that process. At that point no public announcement of UHPP's intentions had been made, and aside from the board, there was no public awareness of its intention to start providing abortions. Miraculously, no one on the HSA review panels seemed to notice the UHPP proposal.

By late summer UHPP began quietly informing public officials and finishing the final steps needed to acquire final approval from the Department of Health. The first visit was to the Albany County Executive James Coyne, who was personally pro-choice and raised no concerns or publicity. The next was just after Labor Day when a delegation went to visit the Mayor of Albany, Thomas Whalen. The delegation included Executive Director Ruth Klepper, former UHPP Board President Phoebe Bender and Rabbi Martin Silverman, a current member of the board. As then-President of the Board, I was also part of the delegation. We knew that the Mayor was opposed to abortion and that he would not welcome our announcement, but we were there only to pay him the professional courtesy of giving him advance notice, not to ask his permission.

The City Corporation Counsel, Paul Collins, was with the Mayor, and it appeared that word of our announcement had already reached them. (We learned a few days later that someone who knew UHPP's plans had informed a member of the Right-to-Life Party, who in turn had probably notified the Mayor's office. The informer was never identified.) Indeed the Mayor was not at all happy with the news we delivered, and expressed his strong opposition to having an abortion clinic "in my city." We thought, but did not say, that it was our city too, and pointed out that abortion was a constitutionally-protected service, and that we had gone through all the proper Department of Health applications and reviews and were awaiting only a final site visit by the Health Department before gaining our operating license and initiating the service. We parted on formal but polite terms, sure there would be some repercussions from the visit.

Ruth Klepper hurried right back to the clinic after the meeting, and in an act of valuable foresight, told her staff to tidy everything up and make the clinic "white glove clean" as quickly as possible. Within about an hour, the Fire Department inspectors were at the door, clearly seeking every possible code violation. They alleged nine fire code violations.

Within a day or two, Paul Collins introduced to the Albany County Legislature an ordinance that would require physicians to notify the parent or guardian of an unemancipated minor at least 24 hours before performing an abortion. Since confidentiality about medical records of all patients, and specifically of minors, was a passionately endorsed value for Planned Parenthood, such a measure was unacceptable to UHPP and contrary to New York State law. Leaders of both the Democratic majority and the Republican minority in the county legislature, however, expressed support for the proposed measure, and it was to be introduced at a meeting the following Monday. UHPP's counsel, Miriam Netter, quickly responded that such legislation would be illegal since only the state, not local government, has jurisdiction over such matters. Over the next few days, with prominent attention to the controversy in the newspapers, some quiet behind-the-scenes conversations took place with the Albany County attorney about the legal implications of the proposed law, with the result that at the Monday evening meeting of the county legislature, Paul Collins backed off on his legislation, and instead proposed a resolution memorializing the State Legislature about the need for parental notification. UHPP had won the first round, but the battle had only just begun.

The Roman Catholic Bishop of Albany, Bishop Howard Hubbard, added his voice to the debate in a Saturday press conference, reported in the *Times Union* on September 9, 1984, the day before the meeting of the county legislature. Hubbard was highly admired and respected in Albany. A former street priest, he had been the youngest priest, at the age of 38, ever made a bishop in this country. In a city with a high concentration of Catholics, his voice carried great weight. He condemned the plans for an abortion clinic in Albany, calling it "an affront to the Catholic community and to the community at large" and promised to "pursue every means possible" to prevent the clinic's opening. "Right now we're sitting down to strategize what actions we can take to stop this," he continued, and said that the first step would be to press for Health Department hearings at which community opponents of the clinic could voice their concerns.

It came as no surprise, then, that the Health Department soon afterwards announced that there would be a public hearing to allow all voices in the community to be heard. What was not clear was what impact such a hearing would have on the Health Department's final decision.

The hearing was called for November 9, 1984 at the Legislative Office Building. Any interested party was invited to testify, but those who wished to speak were asked to register with the Health Department in advance, and to restrict their remarks to three minutes. So many people asked to speak that the hearing, which began at 9:30 a.m., lasted more than eight hours. It was decided that, as the President of the UHPP board, I would speak first on behalf of the agency, and that my remarks would be followed by those of Bishop Howard Hubbard. The meeting room was packed to capacity, and we learned later that our opponents had brought in busloads of their supporters from surrounding communities to testify; they outnumbered the pro-choice attendees by about two to one.

I was called to the podium as the first speaker of the day promptly at 9:30. I began by reaffirming our commitment to "professional, safe, legal and confidential care for all women whatever their financial means or personal situation...We are not here today to debate the legality or morality of abortion...We stand by our fundamental belief that every woman has the right to reach her own decision in privacy about whether to continue or terminate a pregnancy." After commenting on the tragic outcomes of unwanted pregnancies, I reviewed the major arguments supporting our proposal.

The Bishop spoke next and harshly criticized the Health Department for failing to notify the public before granting approval to UHPP's application. He questioned the need for the service, and expressed his vehement opposition to it.

Among the 99 speakers of the day, UHPP's position was defended by people such as The Reverend Dr. Laman H. Bruner, rector of St. Peter's Episcopal Church, other clergy members, representatives from the National Organization for Women and from Family Planning Advocates of New York State, from the Capital District Chapter of the Coalition of Nurse Practitioners, and many others. The opposition was represented by members of the Roman Catholic Diocese of Albany, Catholic Charities, the Knights of Columbus, clergy and members from many conservative Protestant churches, and members of Right-to-Life groups. Presiding Health Department officials had to repeatedly remind people not to boo or jeer while testimony was being given. The hearing was rowdy, contentious, and lengthy, and received extensive coverage by the media.

The New York Times

NEW YORK, SUNDAY, JANUARY 13, 1985

CATHOLIC BISHOP SUES ON ABORTIONS

Wins Temporary Court Ban in Albany Against 2 Clinics

By JOSEPH BERGER

Continued on Page 22, Column 1

Bishop Howard J. Hubbard

BISHOP HALTS PLAN TO GIVE ABORTIONS

Continued From Page 1

Increasing Protests

Need for Clinics Questioned

New York Times, January 13, 1985

We then waited to see what decision the Health Department would reach, meanwhile finishing the last preparations so that we could begin as soon as the license was issued. That moment came in mid-January 1985, but Bishop Hubbard was a step ahead of us. Only hours after the Health Department reaffirmed its approval, attorneys for the Bishop obtained a temporary court order barring the Department from issuing a final operating license. The Bishop accused the Health Department of failing to follow correct procedures, but he also noted the church's theological rejection of abortion. It was the first time a Catholic official had used a court order to block abortions, and so revolutionary was the approach that the Sunday *New York Times* of January 13, 1985, carried the story prominently at the top of its front page. Over the next several weeks copies of newspaper articles from local papers were sent to us by friends across the nation.

The legal issue went first to the New York State Supreme Court, which later in January ruled in favor of the Catholic Diocese, saying that the Health Department had processed the application incorrectly. The Health Department officials, represented by Attorney General Robert Abrams, and in consultation with UHPP, came to the decision to appeal the case to the Appellate Division of the State Supreme Court, and asked that court to accept the case as soon as briefs could be prepared.

The Appellate Division heard the case on April 15, 1985. The arguments in both courts centered on two points: did the petitioners, who including The Roman Catholic Diocese of Albany, Community Maternity Services, and two individuals, have "standing" or the right to plead their case; and did the Department of Health incorrectly use an unpublished and informal guideline known as the "50% rule" (that a public need for non-hospital-based abortion services exists whenever less than 50% of all abortion services are available on an out-of-hospital basis). The Appellate Division sent down its decision on June 20, and in a split decision upheld the lower court's ruling.

The one remaining recourse was an appeal to the Court of Appeals, the highest court in New York State, and that was undertaken. Finally, after what seemed an interminable wait, word came through on a Friday afternoon, December 17, 1985. The court reversed the decisions of the two lower courts and found in favor of the Department of Health, and of Upper Hudson Planned Parenthood.

That afternoon Ruth Klepper and I sat in the UHPP offices, fielding phone calls from reporters, barely able to comprehend our victory after almost a year and a half of delays, disappointments, suspense and high emotions. The one silver lining throughout all those months was the support we had received from our friends and supporters in the community. We had started a Legal Defense Fund to which people contributed generously. Four area congregations had spoken out publicly on our behalf. Trinity United Methodist Church, First Unitarian Society of Albany, First Presbyterian Church of Albany and Congregation Beth Emeth had all passed resolutions supporting UHPP and expressing confidence in our work and objectives. The pro-choice community realized how fragile were our reproductive rights, too often taken for granted, and helped us rise to the challenge.

The operating certificate for the Albany clinic was issued immediately, and the abortion service began in January. It seemed an anti-climax after the tumult of the previous 15 months.

Pickets and Protests

Picketing outside the Lark Street clinic and the Columbia County clinic began even before the Health Department had issued the operating license for abortion services. It was not in the Capital District alone that such demonstrations were frequent. The entire country had taken an abrupt turn to the right in the late 70s and early 80s, and the election of President Reagan in 1980 confirmed this trend in both social and economic agendas. Abortion was a highly emotional lightning rod that played a pivotal role in the national debate.

The conservative forces that exerted enormous influence over the Republican party coalesced around a number of social issues such as abortion, homosexuality, drugs, opposition to the Equal Rights Amendment and school prayer. The right-to-life movement had become a political party, and was joined by a growing number of evangelical Christian leaders. Preachers such as Jim Bakker and Pat Robertson flooded the television networks with messages about the moral decadence that had overwhelmed our society. Turning their backs on the constitutional separation of church and state, they vowed to elect candidates for every position from the White House to the local water commissions who measured up to their standards of biblical morality. A pronounced theme of misogyny ran through all their messages. Women should not be out in the workplace, competing with men; they belong at home, taking care of their children and husbands.

Pickets in front of 259 Lark Street, Albany

The Reverend Jerry Falwell's Moral Majority, founded in the late 1970s, preached the same message in a political campaign for a "clean, God-fearing America." On November 14, 1980, riding high on the conservative political sweep in the national elections only a week earlier, he came to Albany to lead a

"God and Country" rally to a crowd of about 1,000 people in the Palace Theater. He called for a return to traditional American family values, which in his message meant positions against abortion, the Equal Rights Amendment, gay rights, sex education and pornography, and positions in favor of free enterprise, a balanced budget and voluntary prayer in the public schools. A group of about 200 community activists, including Ruth Klepper, students and religious leaders from Albany protested outside the Palace Theater that evening.

Starting in 1986, picketing became a regular occurrence. The first picketing took place on a cold February 2 of that year with a group of about 125 members of an organization called Citizens Concerned for Human Life. This group returned periodically for several years, usually in smaller numbers. Sometimes they would simply march outside the clinic, carrying signs or pictures of fetuses, chanting slogans or praying. On other occasions they would try to take pictures of patients as they entered the clinic, or would write down license plates of cars entering the parking lot.

UHPP developed a number of strategies for dealing with them. First, it established a corps of "escorts," volunteers who would escort patients from the parking lot into the clinic. When necessary, the escort would hold an umbrella between the patient and a camera to protect the patient's privacy. Instead of setting a specific day of the week for doing abortions, the schedule was scrambled each week at both Albany and the Hudson clinics to keep protesters confused. Clinic staff would photograph the picketers and were able to identify some of them. A few were regulars; others came and went depending on the weather. A great many were older men.

One successful strategy was to ask Planned Parenthood supporters to "pledge-a-picket." Using a newspaper ad with a coupon, donors were asked to pledge a certain amount for every picketer demonstrating during a given time period, thereby turning protesters into fund raisers for UHPP.

The religious right was equally inventive about finding ways to disrupt business at family planning clinics. Operation Rescue was a civil disobedience movement, inspired by Joseph Scheidler, director of the Pro-Life Action League and author of a book on how to harass and intimidate abortion providers and clinic patients. The titular head of Operation Rescue was Randall Terry, based in Binghamton, NY, who took his band of anti-choice extremists from one part of the country to another. In each city they visited, they gathered other anti-choice demonstrators and tried to blockade clinics, either with their cars or their bodies, forming a human barricade to prevent patients from entering clinics. Since this was a clear act of civil disobedience, many of them were arrested and went to jail, a penalty they were happy to accept in the interest of "doing God's work."

Pickets in front of Hudson clinic

On December 8, 1988 more than 300 anti-choice demonstrators from Operation Rescue arrived at the Columbia County UHPP clinic in Hudson before dawn where they linked arms and prevented staff and patients from entering the office until mid-afternoon. The two police officers on the scene made no arrests, in part because the demonstrators had been instructed in advance to go limp if arrested, thereby requiring at least four officers for each person, one for each limb. But the passive response of the Hudson police did raise suspicions that they were more sympathetic with the demonstrators than with the legal rights of the clinic.

The following March, on Good Friday 1989, another such Operation Rescue attack was planned in Albany, but clinic staff had learned some preventive measures from the earlier experience. In preparation for such an attack, each evening a staff member would take home telephone numbers for all the scheduled patients for the following day, so that they could be called and warned not to come for their appointments. Actually the staff had been tipped off about the March 24 Operation Rescue plans in advance, and came into the office before the demonstrators arrived at dawn. Patients were called to reschedule appointments, and the Albany police were immediately summoned. The police worked efficiently to clear the parking lot and made 145 arrests. About a dozen of those arrested refused to give their names or to pay a fine, and they remained in jail and were charged. The police remained to maintain surveillance until 5:00 p.m., but in fact most of the demonstrators had left by mid-afternoon when the weather turned stormy.

The local group of picketers had been moderately quiet and orderly for the first year or two of picketing, but as time went on they became more loud, hostile and intense. Two violent incidents, in particular, made the staff feel threatened and under siege. On May 8, 1986 the Lark Street clinic received a bomb threat by telephone. The building was evacuated for a short time while police searched for explosives. No bomb was found, and the incident was written off as a crank call. Then, two years later, on Monday, May 23, 1988 at 8:00 p.m., a right-to-lifer threw bricks at the Lark Street office, causing $2,900 damage in broken doors and windows. After the attack, he continued yelling and sat under a tree until police arrived. All four swinging glass front doors were smashed and the frames twisted. The glass was replaced the same night. Bricks and flying glass from waiting room windows posed serious risk to staff and clients inside, although there were no injuries. Witnesses reported that the attacker yelled, "Abortion is murder," and attempted to engage the gathering crowd in discussion after he emptied his knapsack of bricks.

Only a few weeks earlier, the newly-opened part-time clinic in Ravena had been picketed by an anti-abortion fundamentalist group led by a minister.

Against this backdrop of growing antagonism and violence, the Planned Parenthood affiliates of New York State commissioned a poll in 1986 about attitudes toward family planning programs, with results broken down by geographic area. The poll was done by Penn & Schoen Associates, an independent polling firm in New York City. As anticipated, it confirmed general public support for accessible family planning services and for safe and legal abortion. In a press conference in March 1986, Ruth Klepper announced that in the Albany area, 73 percent of those polled favored state funding for clinics that provide family planning advice; 74 percent said the state should provide contraceptive services to women who cannot afford them; and 71 percent opposed picketing, with 79 percent opposed to confronting patients outside clinics to persuade them not to have an abortion. The poll made clear that the picketers and right-to-life demonstrators represented a small but vocal minority. It did not, however, succeed in reassuring staff or patients of the clinic.

To show the strength of public support for family planning services, the Planned Parenthood Federation of America organized marches in Washington. The first was in March 1986, and UHPP was well represented by staff, board members and many supporters from the community. Three years later, in April 1989 another March for Women's Lives/Women's Equality brought half a million people to Washington, including a large contingent from the Capital District.

Nationally the Planned Parenthood family always stuck together, providing some moments of unexpected altruism in the threatening environment. In 1985, when the Albany court case over introduction of abortion services was receiving coverage in the national press, UHPP one day received a $200 contribution to its Legal Defense Fund from the Planned Parenthood affiliate in Washington, D.C. That affiliate did not perform abortions, but it had been bombed the previous fall, and wanted to pass on to Albany some of the support they had received from others. In turn, when the Kalamazoo, Michigan affiliate was burned to the ground the following year, the Albany board voted to send a financial contribution on to them.

It took courage, conviction and commitment to stay the course during those oppressive years. One detective hired by UHPP to help track down some of the protesters advised Executive Director Klepper that she should look under her car each evening before going home. She never shared that story until years later.

More Hurdles

Ruth Klepper remained as Executive Director until the summer of 1994, and the years from 1980 on presented her and the agency with a series of hurdles, some coming from Washington, others from the home front. The presidencies of Ronald Reagan and George H.W. Bush, 1980 to 1992, were heavily influenced by the religious right. Despite public opinion polls that showed the majority of Americans supportive of accessible family planning services and sex education, the administration made repeated efforts to limit government funding for those services and to outlaw abortion. Planned Parenthood affiliates across the country had to learn to live defensively as legislation, regulations, judicial appointments and other governmental agency appointments all threatened hard-won advances for women's equity and reproductive rights.

The "squeal rule," an attempt to mandate parental notification when teens received prescription services from Title X-funded clinics, was proposed in 1982, but intense grassroots lobbying from Albany along with affiliates across the country opposed the measure, and two federal courts threw it out. Then in 1984 the administration did succeed in exporting its anti-abortion policies in the form of the "Mexico City policy" named after the international conference at which it was announced. The policy barred any foreign family planning agency from receiving U.S. government funding if it performed, advocated, referred or counseled women about abortion, even when those programs were locally funded with private funds. This policy, in effect throughout the Reagan-Bush years, and reinstated by George W. Bush in 2000, has severely impacted overseas family planning, and ironically led many more women to have abortions because of lack of funds for prevention of unwanted pregnancy.

In Albany, there was a different problem to contend with. UHPP had begun its abortion services in Albany, and was required by the New York State Department of Health to file a fetal death certificate for each procedure. The form carried the name, address and other demographic information about the patient, and one copy of this went to a county clerk's office. Since this practice compromised the UHPP policy of strict confidentiality, Klepper made a decision, supported by her board, to hold the forms in her office until the conflict could be resolved with the Department of Health. She meanwhile devised a coding system that would give the Health Department all the information they needed for research or statistics while still protecting the identity of the woman.

UHPP then asked the help of Family Planning Advocates of New York State, for a legislative resolution to the problem of breaching women's confidentiality. Such legislation was drafted and passed in late 1987, to be effective the beginning of 1988. Under this legislation, a compromise solution was enacted whereby the patient's name would appear only on the copy that went to the State, and would no longer be included on the forms filed with the county. The compromise did not satisfy the UHPP board which was still concerned about the privacy of the records and saw no valid reason for including the names. UHPP did send its coded forms to the Health Department, along with a full explanation for deletion of the names, but did not send them to the county offices. After a year's delay, UHPP was notified that the matter had been sent to the Attorney General for legal action against the agency. However, with the help of Family Planning Advocates' Executive Director Shirley Gordon, an agreement with the Health Department was finally reached. The coding system was accepted, no names were filed with the certificates, the State Legislature finally enacted a Women's Confidentiality bill, and the fight to protect the identity of women seeking abortions in New York State was successfully concluded.

Introducing abortion services in Troy was the next hurdle. The clinic had been remodeled, the need for the service in Rensselaer County was evident, and the board decided in 1989 to apply for a Certificate of Need from the Health Department for that purpose. The application for an administrative review by the Department of Health was filed in June of 1990, and courtesy calls were paid on Troy and Rensselaer County political leaders to inform them of UHPP's plans.

Soon afterwards, UHPP received notice that the Commissioner of the Department of Health was using his discretion to consider the application under full review, a much more lengthy and burdensome process, and contrary to the Department's own procedures. Not only would full review pose delays to UHPP, it would set a discriminatory precedent for other Planned Parenthood affiliates within the state. On the advice of counsel, and on the grounds that this represented an arbitrary change in Health Department regulations and that it unfairly singled out abortion from all other medical services, the UHPP board decided to bring suit against the Department of Health.

Meanwhile, the application had already been presented to the Subarea Council of the Health Systems Agency where a large and hostile group of observers made every effort to prevent abortion services from being established in Troy. A few weeks later, however, the Executive Committee of the HSA met and voted favorably.

UHPP rallied its Troy supporters. A group of Troy area clergy held a press conference and voiced their support in August. About 100 supporters gathered on the grounds of Rensselaer Polytechnic Institute for a photograph to demonstrate pro-choice support, and this group photo appeared in a UHPP ad in local newspapers in early August.

At the end of August 1990 the UHPP case against the Department of Health was argued before the New York State Supreme Court, with a decision expected within two months. During this period the Troy property had changed hands and the new owner tried to evict UHPP, but was thwarted by the terms of the lease. Despite an unexpected last minute appeal from an individual member of the Right to Life Party which was thrown out, the Supreme Court decision was favorable to UHPP, and the Department of Health approval to proceed came through in early January 1991. As was the case in Albany, the services were implemented with no public announcement and no difficulty, but only after UHPP had been aggressive in asserting its legal rights.

Picketing and harassment escalated at Albany, Troy and Hudson, and in October 1990 UHPP brought an action in federal court against a group of individuals who had been guilty of trespass and conspiracy to deprive patients of their rights to access for medical care. A negotiated settlement giving the clinic some protection was not finally reached until 1995.

Of all the assaults on reproductive rights, the regulations known as the "gag rule" proposed by the Reagan administration in 1987 were the most profound. The new regulations would have prohibited doctors and other health care professionals working in Title X-funded clinics from providing any abortion-related information or referrals. Abortion services were never covered by Title X funds, but under the gag rule, a clinic that offered them would have to be housed in an entirely separate facility from the family planning clinic, with separate staffing and accounting. The regulations not only contradicted the medical practice of informed consent which requires doctors to inform patients of all options available to them, but they also would have imposed extreme financial burden on any family planning clinic offering abortion services.

The gag rule regulations were immediately challenged, and UHPP joined a national lobbying effort to defeat them, using the Alert Network of pro-choice activists it had organized. When George H.W. Bush was elected in 1988, he too endorsed the proposed regulations. The Supreme Court, stacked with conservative judges appointed by Reagan, had already shown its willingness to limit access to abortion. The 1989 *Webster v. Reproductive Health Services* allowed states to place increased restrictions on women's access to abortion, and in two other cases in 1990 (*Hodgson v. Minnesota* and *Ohio v. Akron Center for Reproductive Health*) the Court further restricted access to abortion for teenagers. The pattern continued in the 1992 *Planned Parenthood of Southeastern Pennsylvania v. Casey* decision which allowed restrictions to abortion unless they constituted an "undue burden" to the woman. "Undue burden" has never been clearly defined.

In the *Rust v. Sullivan* decision of 1992, a 5-4 majority of the Court upheld the gag rule, barring any employees of federally financed family planning clinics from any discussion of abortion with their patients. In the aftermath, Congress voted overwhelmingly to overturn the gag rule, but was unable to override President Bush's veto.

The UHPP board, after lengthy and substantive discussion, made the difficult decision to refuse Title X funds attached to any restrictions on informed consent and counseling of patients. Fortunately a series of last-minute court orders blocked the regulations' enforcement. The election of President Clinton in 1992 saved the day. Very early in his administration, on the January 22 anniversary of *Roe v. Wade*, he withdrew the gag rule regulations by executive order and also reversed the Mexico City policy or global gag rule, to the great relief and appreciation of the pro-choice community.

Amazingly, against this background of attacks, threats, and bureaucratic and ideological obstacles, UHPP did continue to move forward on a positive agenda with new services, new programs, and new clinics. In 1985 UHPP introduced the Smart Start program to help patients begin a healthy pregnancy. The project was an early intervention program providing a medical evaluation, education and counseling, and referrals to physicians for prenatal care. The following year colposcopy services were begun to evaluate abnormal Pap smears, to identify precancerous conditions of the cervix, and to plan with the patient for further treatment.

The medical services at UHPP's clinics were strengthened when Dr. Fred C. Storm joined the staff as Medical Director to oversee medical activities in all health centers. Formerly a member of a highly regarded local private practice Obstetrics and Gynecology group, he began to practice at UHPP on a part time basis before accepting the offer to become the full time Medical Director in the summer of 1987. His presence made it possible for UHPP to offer more comprehensive reproductive health services.

When asked why he made the change from private practice to UHPP, Dr. Storm immediately spoke about the satisfaction he gets from his UHPP role. He explained that he knows every day that he is doing something of great importance to the patients he sees, something that will have a positive impact on their lives, whether it is a student who will now be able to continue her studies, or a mother who cannot afford to support another child, or a woman who has broken off a relationship with the man involved. He enjoys the expressions of gratitude he receives from these women.

That satisfaction far outweighs the harassment to which he is regularly subjected. He recounted one incident when a group of picketers with their usual graphic and confrontational signs assembled at his home in an Albany suburb. He drove out his long driveway one morning to find a group protesting at the mouth of the driveway. As he approached, one of the picketers aimed a camera at the car and took his picture. Unfazed, Dr. Storm immediately backed his car back down the driveway to his house, got his own camera, and back at the road, rolled down his window and took a picture of the picketer. That calm, understated and non-confrontational response is typical of this gentle and committed man.

He also reported that on more than one occasion he has performed abortions on women who have been part of the anti-choice protesters at UHPP. In one case, the young woman told Storm that before she became pregnant herself, she had never realized what difficult decisions women are forced to make, and promised never again to picket against the clinic. Not everyone is so easily converted. Other anti-choice protesters have had an abortion, believing their case is unique, and have afterwards returned to the picketing lines.

Responding to increased concerns about AIDS and the HIV virus, UHPP initiated HIV testing and counseling in August 1988. Even more than most new services, this required special training of medical and counseling staff. As new contraceptive methods became available and approved, they were added to UHPP's offerings, so during the late 1980s and early 1990s options such as the cervical cap, new IUDs, Depo-Provera (an injectable contraceptive lasting about three months), the "morning-after pill" or Emergency Contraception, and Norplant (an implantable and reversible option) all were added to the choices offered to patients. Mid-life services were also added to UHPP's offerings. By the early 1990s, moving towards becoming a comprehensive gynecological surgery center, female sterilization also became available.

It was in the area of community education and public affairs that UHPP made some of its most notable contributions. It developed a series of 12 television programs aimed at a teenage audience, called "The Edge." Featuring a troupe of teen actors, each program presented a specific issue related to real problems in teens' lives in dramatized format, followed by discussion and a question and answer session with an expert. These were shown first to a PPFA group where they were highly praised, and several Planned Parenthood affiliates subsequently purchased the series. They were aired on Public Access cable television with considerable success, and were also used by the UHPP education staff in group presentations. The same production group also developed a series of pro-choice television ads aired on commercial channels in early 1990 as part of the national Campaign to Keep Abortion Safe and Legal, with excellent feedback. In recognition of these and other programs, UHPP was given an Excellence Award for Media and Public Relations by PPFA in 1991.

In 1989, at the height of opposition to the proposed gag rule, UHPP sponsored a two page signature ad expressing support for its mission, and using the tag line "It's time to go public for privacy." The two-page ad was published on November 2, 1989 and contained about 2,000 names of individual supporters and 15 organizations. Widely covered by the media, it captured the attention of the community, and of legislators. Donations both before and after publication more than covered the cost of the ad. Another ad listing names of local clergy who supported UHPP was also run in 1990.

In 1992 an automated telephone message service was installed, called the Facts of Life Line. By dialing a Facts telephone number and entering the number of the message one wanted to hear, more than 90 messages related to human sexuality and reproduction could be heard. Although designed for a teenage audience, the system provided callers of all ages with clear and complete information. The 24 hour service was free and confidential and available to anyone with a touch tone telephone.

Hy Rosen cartoon, *Times Union,* December 30, 1987

The problem of teen pregnancies was one that would not go away, and UHPP continued its efforts to educate and to prevent unwanted pregnancies. Often the most successful approaches were accomplished by working with a consortium of organizations. The Albany Teen Community Services Project was a case management project in which UHPP worked with the Center for Counseling and the Whitney M. Young Health Center to provide comprehensive services to at-risk, pregnant and parenting teens in inner city census tracts with the highest rates of teen pregnancies and was funded as part of Governor Cuomo's Teen Pregnancy Initiative. A second Albany project, Project Options, paired UHPP with the Albany Girl's Club and the YWCA to provide educational programs for families eligible for Medicaid. In Columbia and Greene counties, UHPP received another grant to participate in a Teen Pregnancy Network to educate and train about pregnancy prevention.

With growing numbers of patients, additional clinics and office space were needed. In 1986 a part time clinic was opened in Latham. That clinic subsequently moved to a second Latham site where it was expanded and became a full time clinic. In 1988, realizing that the southern part of Albany County had no easy access to family planning, a clinic was opened in Ravena. That clinic later moved to East Greenbush. The Troy clinic was renovated in 1986. And in the early 1990s, when the building next door to the Albany clinic became available, UHPP purchased it, did extensive renovations, and moved its administrative and public and community affairs offices into that building.

Just behind the new building and part of the same property was a small former garage building. Initially it was used for the UHPP library, but when a former board member, Judy Grunberg, suggested opening an upscale re-sale clothing shop in it to benefit UHPP, it was transformed into a shop called Options.

The silver lining to all the opposition UHPP faced in the 1980s and 1990s was an increase in financial contributions to the agency. In addition to the Annual Fund, which grew substantially over those years, UHPP also established an Endowment Fund. A number of bequests had been left to the agency, including a major bequest in 1987 of almost $400,000 from the estate of Mildred Tucker, a childless widow with an interest in Planned Parenthood. Although the gift came without restrictions, the board felt it would not be prudent to simply add it to the general operating funds and instead put it into an endowment fund. As the 55th anniversary of UHPP approached in 1989, that fund was just short of a half million dollars, and the board decided not to use any income from it until after the half million dollar figure had been reached. A campaign to raise $55,000 for the 55th anniversary was successful, and the new gifts were added to the endowment as part of a board-designated fund.

The defeat of George H.W. Bush by Bill Clinton in 1992 marked an abrupt change in many things including health care in America. As the nation moved toward a managed care environment, Planned Parenthood affiliates had to make some strategic decisions about how they could best continue to serve their patients. In New York State, a Medicaid waiver placed many Medicaid recipients into Health Maintenance Organizations, with the possible implication for Planned Parenthood clinics that those patients would seek their family planning services elsewhere. UHPP made the decision that by integrating primary care into the rest of its services, it could position itself to be a Preferred Provider Organization, and began the planning and implementation process to accomplish that goal.

Ruth Klepper

In the spring of 1994, Ruth Klepper announced that she would retire in July of that year. She had served the clinic for 20 years as a courageous advocate, a wise administrator and planner and an able business manager. She led UHPP with intelligence and good humor through a remarkably tumultuous period. After her departure her Associate Director, Wendy Durand, was named Interim Executive Director and a Search Committee was formed to look for a new Executive Director.

A New Leader

Patricia McGeown

The search for a new Executive Director concluded in late 1994 with the selection of Patricia A. McGeown. With a background in health systems and public policy and administration combined with a strong commitment to the mission of Planned Parenthood, the Search Committee and Board of Directors agreed she was a perfect match for the needs of the agency. She had the talents and experience to guide UHPP through the complexities of the era of managed care and to build coalitions with other community organizations. She would take office in January, 1995.

As she prepared to take on her new duties, incidents of attacks on choice and violence against reproductive health centers were increasing nationally. Recognizing a growing problem, Congress enacted the Freedom of Access to Clinic Entrances Act (FACE) making it a federal crime to use force or physical obstructions to injure, intimidate, or interfere with providers of reproductive health care services or their patients. Nevertheless, on March 10, 1994, Dr. David Gunn, an abortion provider in Pensacola, Florida was shot and killed by an anti-abortion protester outside the clinic where he worked.

After the election of a pro-choice President, Bill Clinton, in 1992, the right-wing anti-choice forces stepped up their onslaught and by the 1994 elections they gained control of Congress, immediately producing their "Contract with America," an agenda that among other things promised to discourage "illegitimacy" and teen pregnancy by prohibiting welfare to minor mothers.

Anti-choice violence escalated throughout the year. Two more men associated with reproductive health care clinics were assassinated in Pensacola, Florida, and stalking, death threats, bombings, arson, invasions, blockades and butyric acid attacks took place with increased frequency. Then on December 30, 1994, only one week before Pat McGeown took office at UHPP, violence struck much closer to home when two receptionists in Brookline, Massachusetts health centers, one a Planned Parenthood clinic and the other a private family planning clinic, were shot and killed.

Pat McGeown was riding in a car with her nine-year-old son when the report of the killings was broadcast on the radio. When he heard the Planned Parenthood name, he said to her in alarm, "Mom, that's what you're going to do." By the time she arrived home there were nine messages already on her answering machine, eight from reporters, but the first from her mother in Boston saying, "What are you thinking? You can't take this job."

But take it she did, and instead of turning her attention immediately to the issues of public health that most interested her, she had to concentrate on clinic security and on staff morale. The first move was to hire armed guards for the three abortion-providing clinics in Albany, Troy and Hudson. Their presence was uncomfortable for everyone involved, but they remained until bullet-resistant glass enclosures were installed around the reception area in those clinics. A number of other security measures were taken at considerable expense and a special fundraising campaign was undertaken to cover these costs. Amazingly, only one staff member left UHPP after the Brookline scare. In fact for many staff, the incident seemed to be energizing and uniting. Good internal communication was an essential ingredient to maintaining a positive attitude among all.

In the months and years following the Brookline shootings, UHPP experienced several acts of petty vandalism: locks were glued shut, the door to the administrative building was shattered with a BB gun, and a dead kitten wrapped in a blanket was left at the door of the clinic. In December 2001 during the national anthrax scare, the Troy clinic received a Federal Express letter containing a white powder, which forced staff to close the clinic and to go through a decontamination process. After testing, the powder was found to be harmless. Some 200 Planned Parenthood affiliates across the country received similar letters.

In 1995 the UHPP suit against a group of picketers that had been left unresolved since 1992 was finally resolved by a court settlement that limited where the picketers could walk and what pictures they could take. New York State followed the federal government in passing a Clinic Entrance Act, providing another level of security. Albany has been fortunate in escaping the extreme forms of violence that have occurred elsewhere, and in enjoying a good working relationship with the Albany police. Then, in 1988, Dr. Barnett Slepian, an abortion provider, was murdered while standing in the kitchen of his home with his wife and children in Amherst, New York, one more shocking reminder that some anti-choice zealots will stop at nothing less than murder to interrupt the work of family planning clinics.

By the fall of 1995, UHPP announced the opening of its Primary Care and Prenatal care services. The decision to add these services had been carefully discussed since UHPP did not want to lose its focus on reproductive health. Three factors had contributed to the positive decision. UHPP wanted to position itself to be a player in a managed care environment, and the primary and prenatal services served that purpose. In addition, the clinical staff had noted that patients were coming in with other health problems beyond family planning, and that they would benefit from the expanded services. Finally, from a public relations perspective, UHPP wanted to make perfectly clear to the public that just because it provided birth control and abortion, it was definitely not anti-child. As the bumper sticker says, UHPP is and always has been "Pro-Woman, Pro-Family, and Pro-Choice."

Preparations for this expansion of services had been in the pipeline for over a year, but implementation required a great deal of work from every part of the organization. Development and approval of new protocols, acquisition of equipment and supplies, staff development and training, hiring of new staff, the development of a contract and working relationship with the Albany Medical Center Family Practice Group, new computer systems, new insurance requirements, marketing and public relations, all were necessary for the successful kick-off.

Finally, on September 17, 1995 the new services began, and at a press conference with Mayor Gerald Jennings of Albany on October 3 in front of the Lark Street clinic, the new sign for "The Albany Center for Women's Health" was unveiled. For the staff, this was a particularly positive moment, following as it did on the heels of months of concern with security issues. The prenatal service was an instant success. By the end of 1996, 48 "Planned Parenthood" babies had been delivered.

Opening of the Albany Center for Women's Health

As had been anticipated, managed care did reduce the number of patients seen by UHPP. From a high point of 15,000 patients in 1991, there was a gradual but steady erosion over the following years until patient numbers leveled off at about 10,000 a year. As Medicaid patients were enrolled in health maintenance organizations, many did not make use of the by-pass that made it possible for them to go anywhere, including UHPP, for their family planning needs. Since roughly two-thirds of UHPP's income comes from patient fees and third-party reimbursements, careful financial management was needed to weather the declining patient numbers. During the same period, UHPP needed to adjust its systems to be able to accept all major health insurance plans.

In 1996 UHPP began preparations for another new service. The Planned Parenthood Federation of America sponsored a study of methotrexate, an injectable form of medical abortion, and needed carefully controlled clinical trials done at several Planned Parenthood affiliates across the country, to be reported to the Food and Drug Administration. With Medical Director Dr. Storm as the research director of the study, the UHPP board voted to participate. When the study was completed the following year and the FDA had approved the drug's use for medical abortion, UHPP was well positioned to continue that service. Subsequently, when mifepristone (formerly known as RU-486, or the "abortion pill") was approved for use in 2000, UHPP was able to make an easy transition to that drug. At present, over half of its abortion patients use the medical rather than surgical abortion method, and UHPP has one of the highest proportions of medical abortion in the country. In this clinic's experience, the medical method is both successful and easier for the patient.

Throughout the past decade, UHPP has placed a very high priority on educational projects. Especially in the years of the Bush administration when millions of dollars are being poured into abstinence-only education, UHPP has continued to endorse comprehensive, medically accurate, age-appropriate sexuality education. Abstinence is only one aspect of the program; considerable research has shown that by itself, it is not successful.

S.T.A.R.S. from Columbia County

Among the educational offerings, the S.T.A.R.S. program shines the most brightly. Not to be confused with an earlier STARS program (see **Growth**), although both of them were designed to address the high rate of teen pregnancy within the city of Albany, the new program carries an acronym that stands for Seriously Talking About Responsible Sex. Begun in 1996, it is a comprehensive pregnancy prevention program funded through the Albany Community-Based Adolescent Pregnancy Prevention grant from the New York State Department of Health, and is the result of coordinated efforts of the Council of Community Services, UHPP, Albany City School District and Whitney M. Young Health Center. Teens are recruited and trained to be peer educators who serve as resources for their friends and classmates, offering honest and factual information related to sexual health and adolescent issues. In the Albany High School a S.T.A.R.S. presentation on sexual decision-making is a part of the ninth grade physical education curriculum. The S.T.A.R.S. peer educators also present skits to school and other audiences, illustrating typical teenage situations and how to deal with them. The S.T.A.R.S. members get a number of discounted services and other perks from the participating sponsoring organizations. Since the program's inception, over 4,000 young people have signed up to be members.

S.T.A.R.S. was such a success in Albany that in 1998 it was funded for Columbia County where it has met equal success. Not only have teenage pregnancy rates declined, but it has also been a popular program to showcase to various community groups. And when the S.T.A.R.S. members accompany Planned Parenthood board members or volunteers in lobbying visits to legislators, they are a powerful voice because they can tell a first-hand, accurate story about what teenage relationships and dilemmas really are. Few can resist a testimonial such as this one from Jules Hawkins, one of the peer educators, in 2002:

> My aunt was a recovering drug addict. She was my father's sister and she came to live with us when she came out of rehab...I was really close to her. We shared a lot of likes and dislikes. She liked to dance and sing. I liked music and I could talk to her...She died of an AIDS-related infection a week before my thirteenth birthday. I miss her. Having experienced this is one reason why I joined S.T.A.R.S. I think that being a peer educator is a good way of living and talking prevention. If people know about AIDS and how to prevent it, maybe others won't die...because knowledge is truly power.

Another teen education program is called Teen Choices, an after-school program for 7th and 8th grade girls where an engaging and informative curriculum teaches girls about sexuality, puberty, hygiene, pregnancy and disease prevention, communication and decision-making skills. A long-standing program in the Rensselaer Middle High School for students in grades 6–8 focuses on these same issues.

A completely different audience benefits from yet another educational activity. Starting in 1995, UHPP was invited to design and facilitate a series of training seminars for third-year Albany Medical College medical students. Through a series of seminars, future physicians learn about the history of reproductive rights, problems affecting access to reproductive health care in the current political environment, education and counseling for the family planning patient, and methods of recognizing the special needs of adolescents. This clerkship training is only one of several ways in which UHPP and the Albany Medical Center work closely together. The Albany Medical Center Hospital is the back-up hospital for UHPP, and its Department of Family Practice helps staff UHPP's primary and prenatal care clinic.

In an increasingly hostile political environment, advocacy activities have also increased in recent years. UHPP has long had an Action Network which is very effective in stimulating grassroots responses to legislative issues, and membership in the network has increased dramatically in the past four years. The use of the UHPP web site has made it possible to engage a large group of activists for a quick response. Planned Parenthood nationally has created another network called VOX to engage college students in issues of reproductive health. Locally, UHPP helped establish a chapter of VOX at the University at Albany and other local colleges. The Pro-Choice Volunteers of Faith is made up of volunteers from area churches and synagogues who speak out about issues of reproductive health and rights, especially the need for comprehensive sex education for youth.

A few changes have been made in clinic locations. The East Greenbush clinic was closed in 1998. After years of problems with the Troy clinic site, a new setting in the Hendrick Hudson Building was identified, beautifully renovated, and opened in 2000. At the present time the four clinic sites are Albany, Troy, Hudson and Latham.

In the 2003 UHPP Annual Report, Pat McGeown summed up some of the major accomplishments of the agency:

UHPP is now considered the leading provider of abortion services in the region and one of the leading providers of medical abortion in the country. Our medical and patient education programs are in constant demand, establishing us as one of the region's chief experts for education regarding human sexuality, family planning and abortion. Our services are increasingly customer-driven and customer-friendly and, through coalition building and the use of new technologies, we have dramatically expanded our grassroots activism.

> Also, more and more, we are seeing the emergence of new, young leadership. These young staff members and volunteers are the key to a new and bolder UHPP image—one that says loudly, with no hesitation: "We are here to educate, to heal and to fight for reproductive rights. We are proud of our history. We do make a positive difference in the lives of women and families. And we are not going away!"

The March

The March for Women's Lives brought over a million women, men and children to Washington, D.C. on April 25, 2004. Some 350 supporters of choice came from Albany, including eight busloads organized by UHPP. The march was certainly the largest ever held for reproductive rights, and probably the largest demonstration of any kind ever held in Washington. The excitement and energy generated by participating in so vast a gathering was palpable.

Nationally the march was sponsored by the Planned Parenthood Federation of America in conjunction with NARAL, the A.C.L.U., the Feminist Majority, the National Organization for Women, the National Latina Institute for Reproductive Health and the Black Women's Health Imperative. UHPP also worked with a coalition of local organizations including NOW, NARAL, Pro-Choice New York, the Center for Black Women's Wellness of Northeastern New York, the Feminist Majority, Campus Action, and the Capital District Gay and Lesbian Community Council, Inc. These groups may each have a different focus in their missions, but for that day everyone was united in the fight to protect reproductive freedom and to protest the Bush administration's insidious attack on choice, the attack that Gloria Feldt, President of PPFA, calls Bush's War on Women.

The morning of the March, hundreds of thousands of people began arriving at the Mall. There were young women with children in strollers, there were gray-haired grandmothers, there were men of all ages. Some young men wore shirts with the message "This is what a feminist looks like," or others that said "Cute Guys for Women's Lives." About a third of the crowd were under 25 years old, a very promising sign for the old-timers who fear that the younger generation does not adequately understand the degree to which reproductive rights are in jeopardy. People came from all across the country, and many from other countries.

Some had arrived by overnight bus (a seven hour trip from Albany), others by car, train or air, but all converged on the Mall, dressed in hot pink or deep purple or white in honor of the suffragist movement. I was there with the Albany contingent, one lone voice that was magnified by over a million others that day. We were greeted at the Mall by organizers who directed us to the area where other participants from our own city and state were gathering. Volunteers in charge of counting the crowd asked each of us as we arrived at the Mall to sign in and get a green "Count Me In" sticker. This counting mechanism registered 1.15 million marchers, a far more accurate count than any Police or Park Service estimates.

As the crowds gathered, we watched the huge video screens above the Mall and listened to many speakers supporting the reproductive rights agenda and exhorting us to be activists in the struggle. In addition to all the organizers of the March like Gloria Feldt of PPFA, Kate Michaelman of NARAL, Eleanor Smeal of The Feminist Majority, there were politicians (House Minority Leader Nancy Pelosi, Senator Hillary Clinton, former Secretary of State and United Nations Ambassador Madeleine Albright,) celebrities like Gloria Steinem, Kathleen Turner, Cybill Shepherd and Whoopi Goldberg. A choir from Pittsburgh kicked off the event with a rendition of "If Men Could Get Pregnant, What Changes We Would See."

Finally, about noon the actual march began, and we shuffled more than walked (a million people is not an easy crowd to move) over to Pennsylvania Avenue where the pace picked up, talking with anyone who happened to be near, chanting, and simply absorbing the energizing vitality of the crowd.

Reading signs was a favorite activity. There were "My Body, My Choice," "Grandmothers Nostalgic for Choice", "Keep Your Rosaries out of My Ovaries," and "Keep Your Laws off My Body," or the frankly political "Abort Bush in the First Term." A giant red uterus marched down Pennsylvania Avenue. The crowds chanted, "Not the church, not the state, women will decide their fate," or "We're here, we're loud, we're from New York, we're pro-choice proud," or simply "Ho ho, hey hey, abortion rights are here to stay."

It is hard to imagine just how big a crowd of over a million people is. About half way down Pennsylvania Avenue we saw a young woman who had hoisted herself up a lamppost as a good vantage point for taking pictures. We asked if she could see the end of the march, and she replied that she had been up there for an hour, and that she could not yet see the end in sight. Considering the effort and expense that every one of the marchers had taken on to be there, we knew that they represented a vastly larger group of Americans who feel equally passionate about the cause.

People turned out for the March because in the more than 30 years since *Roe v. Wade*, reproductive rights have never been so threatened. The anti-choice conservative wing of the Republican party has captured the political establishment including the presidency and both houses of Congress. But instead of the frontal attack on choice of the Reagan administration, the George W. Bush administration has attacked by stealth. Appointments to regulatory agencies or to the federal courts often go unnoticed by the general public. Similarly, few people are aware of the hundreds of millions of dollars being spent on abstinence-only education, despite clear evidence that it doesn't work, while no increase in family planning funding has been allocated. The Center for Disease Control removed fact sheets on condom effectiveness from its web site in 2002, while also removing the medically accurate findings of the National Cancer Institute that, contrary to anti-choice propaganda, abortions do not increase the risk of breast cancer. Embryonic stem cell research is at a standstill in this country because of this administration's misguided ideology. Legislation like the "Unborn Victims of Violence Act" disguises the fact that by giving the fetus the legal status of personhood, it lays the groundwork for abolishing legal abortion. The attacks on choice today are just below the radar screen, happening without alarming the vast pro-choice majority of this country.

Then in November 2003 the President signed a bill banning so-called partial-birth abortion, the first federal restriction on abortion for 30 years. In that case a picture of the signing featured in many newspapers showed the President surrounded by a group of white-haired white men, not one of whom had ever experienced an unwanted pregnancy, and many observers took note.

The March sent notice that we are aware of the stealth campaign, and that we will not allow our hard-won reproductive rights to be taken away. In 1920 in her first book, *Women and the New Race* (New York, 1920), Margaret Sanger wrote, "No woman can call herself free who does not own and control her body. No woman can call herself free until she can choose consciously whether she will or will not be a mother."

On the occasion of his retirement from the Supreme Court in 1994, Justice Harry Blackmun, the author of *Roe*, said of that decision, "It's a step that had to be taken as we go down the road toward the full emancipation of women."

Both Sanger and Blackmun understood that women cannot be truly free and equal without the fundamental human right to control their own reproductive destiny. The women and men marching together on April 25 were there to protect more than just decision-making rights. They were there to defend a very basic human right to freedom and equality, and they were determined.

The first 70 years of UHPP's history have been filled with controversies and obstacles, but we have prevailed. As part of the national Planned Parenthood family, we have gained legal status for birth control and abortion, we have developed better methods of contraception, we have brought medically accurate education about sexuality and reproduction to hundreds of thousands of people, and we have created a national network of health services. We have brought accessible, low-cost health services to women and men, many of whom have no other source of medical care, and we have emphasized prevention—prevention of unwanted pregnancies, prevention of cervical and breast cancer, prevention of sexually transmitted infections. We have always treated our patients with respect and dignity and confidentiality. Without the progress we have made towards reproductive self-determination and sexual autonomy, women would never have gained the power and status we enjoy today. We draw our inspiration from the many examples of courage documented in this book and many more throughout our country. And we shall prevail.

Appendix

PRESIDENTS OF THE BOARD

1935	Mrs. Robert Wheeler
1936-38	Mrs. Frank Hughson
1938-40	Mrs. Truman Brown
1940-42	Mrs. Roessle McKinney
1942-46	Mrs. Theodore Dwight
1946-48	Mrs. Richard Reiner
1949-50	Mrs. Eldridge Campbell
1951-52	Mrs. Marshall S. Hannock
1952-53	Mrs. Crawford Campbell
1954-55	Mrs. Seth Wheeler
1955-56	Mrs. Crawford Campbell
1957-58	Mrs. Malcolm Davis
1959-64	Mrs. Thomas Plowden-Wardlaw
1964-68	Marion Raymond
1968-70	Elizabeth Thomas
1970-72	Esther Lewis
1972-74	Shirley Gordon
1974	Julia Van Cleve
1974-75	Philip R. Johnston
1975-76	Jean T. Rich
1976-78	Suzanne C. Bollinger
1978-80	Joseph P. Richardson
1980-82	Phoebe Bender
1982-83	Edward B. Fisher
1983-86	Mary C. Kahl
1986-88	Nancy Pollard
1988-90	Sherry Putney
1990-92	Mollie Lampi
1992-94	Mary C. Kahl
1994-96	Margery Whiteman
1996-97	Jeannie Cross
1997-2000	Mollie Lampi
2000-2003	Katherine P. Henrikson
2003-	Mary C. Kahl

EXECUTIVE DIRECTORS/CEOs

1959-60	Vera Schaefer
1962-65	Carolyn Garvin
1966-68	Grace Houghtaling
1968-69	Clara Brownell (Interim)
1969-73	Lyndon Schendel
1974-94	Ruth Klepper
1994	Wendy Durand (Interim)
1995-	Patricia McGeown

NOTES

Chapter I: The Early Years

The major source of information about UHPP from 1934 to1986 is the archive housed in Special Collections and Manuscripts at the New York State Library. Most early history records are in Box 5 of 14 boxes of records. Unless a different source of information is cited, all quotations and factual citations are drawn from these records.

The Founding

Page 2 — The Channing Hall location of the November 8, 1938 meeting was identified in an interview with Phoebe Ziehm, relative of Frances Vosburgh.

Page 2 — *The Blue Book*, 1934 edition.

Docky

In addition to material in the New York State Library, Eva Gemmill of the First Unitarian Church of Albany generously shared with me a file of information about Dr. Vosburgh. Dr. Grace Jorgensen was also an invaluable help in her interview, sharing many recollections and insights about this remarkable woman.

Page 10 — "She was compassionate..." Interview with Dr.Vosburgh's cousin, Phoebe Ziehm.

Page 11 — The incident at Brady Hospital was recounted by Phoebe Ziehm in her interview.

Page 11 — Quotations from the eulogy come from material loaned to me by Dr. Grace Jorgensen.

Finding a Home

Page 13 — Mrs. Workum and Mrs. Jessup were other Federation officials.

Page 18 — Dr. Beebe's reference to "debutante friends" was made in his December 7, 1993 interview.

20 Trinity Place

Pages 20-21 — The letters of Dr. Janet Hood and of Alice Dwight were written in 1983 when UHPP was collecting historical information for the celebration of its 50th anniversary.

Troy

The information about the Troy clinic comes from the 1993 interview with Betty Pattison and conversations with Hortense Mintzer.

Reality outside the Clinic

Page 24 — Dr. Beebe's comments come from his 1993 interview.

The Fifties

Page 29 — Dr. Hood's,Dr. Poskanzer's and Laman Bruner's comments are drawn from recollections gathered in 1983 for UHPP's 50th anniversary.

Page 32 — The account of Dr. Rock's lecture being moved to the Law School was confirmed by both Dr. Friedlander and Dr. Hengerer.

Chapter II: Years of Expansion

Most of the material for this chapter is also drawn from the UHPP records in the New York State Library, Special Collections and Manuscripts, Boxes 5 and 6. Material from other sources will be noted below. Materials that were gathered for UHPP's 50th anniversary are in Box 5.

The Pill

Page 36 — "Nationally the number of Planned Parenthood contraceptive patients..." The national statistics are cited in PPFA's *A Tradition of Choice.*

Page 37 — "Dr. Hengerer also staffed..." Interview with Dr. Hengerer.

Page 38	"Herta Krahmer remembered..." Drawn from material gathered for UHPP's 50th anniversary.
Page 38	"It was very small quarters..." Interview with Marion Raymond.
Page 38	"I helped down there..." Interview with Grace Bair Fishell.

Into the Mainstream

Page 40	"We rented two floors..." From 50th anniversary material.
Pages 40-41	"the clinic hummed." Interview with Dr. Friedlander.
Page 41	Justice William O. Douglas quotation taken from *A Tradition of Choice.*
Page 42	Helen Schnitzer quotation from interview with her and her mother.
Page 43	Laurence McKinney quotation from his personal papers made available to me after his death.

A New Era

Page 46	"One out of every six of those patients..." From PPFA's *A Tradition of Choice.*
Pages 46-47	The story of the passage of the legislation legalizing abortion in New York State is drawn from Garrow's *Liberty and Sexuality*, page 420.
Page 47	"When abortion became legalized..." 50th anniversary material.

Growth

Records of the 1970s are in Boxes 7 and 8 in the New York State Library Special Collections and Manuscripts.

Page 50	"I decided that we definitely needed..." 50th anniversary material.
Page 51	A moving day anecdote...Interview with Ruth Klepper.

Chapter III: Reproductive Rights

Abortion Wars

In addition to material in Boxes 10, 11, 12 and 14 in the New York State Library, clippings and documents from Ruth Klepper and my own files were used.

Page 58 — Ruth Klepper hurried back...Interview with Ruth Klepper.

Pickets and Protests

Box 12 in the New York State Library is the principal source of information.

Page 66 — One detective hired by UHPP...Interview with Ruth Klepper.

More Hurdles

The UHPP papers in the New York State Library end in 1986. Records subsequent to that date are held at UHPP's Lark Street offices.

Page 70 — When asked why he made the change...Interview with Dr. Fred Storm.

A New Leader

Page 76 — Pat McGeown was riding in a car...Interview with Pat McGeown.

Page 80 — "My aunt was a recovering drug addict..." Quoted in the UHPP Annual Report for 2002.

The March

Page 84 — "No woman can call herself free..." Quoted by Ellen Chesler in *Woman of Valor*, page 192.

Page 84 — "It's a step that had to be taken..." *The New York Times*, April 7, 1994.

BIBLIOGRAPHY

BOOKS

The Blue Books Company. *The Albany, Troy and Schenectady Blue Book,* 1934. Springfield Gardens, 1934

Bowers, Virginia B. *The Texture of a Neighborhood; Albany's South End, 1880-1940.* This work was submitted as a thesis to the faculty of the Graduate School of The College of St. Rose in partial fulfillment of the requirements for the degree of Master of Arts as of May 11, 1991 at Albany, New York.

Chesler, Ellen. *Woman of Valor: Margaret Sanger and the Birth Control Movement in America.* New York: Simon & Schuster, 1992.

Feldt, Gloria. *The War on Choice; The Right-Wing Attack on Women's Rights and How to Fight Back.* New York: Bantam Books, 2004.

Garrow, David J. *Liberty and Sexuality; The Right to Privacy and the Making of Roe v. Wade.* New York: Macmillan, 1994.

Gordon, Linda. *Woman's Body, Woman's Right: A Social History of Birth Control in America.* Penguin Books, 1977

Melich, Tanya. *The Republican War Against Women.* New York: Bantam Books, 1996.

Planned Parenthood Federation of America. *A Tradition of Choice: Planned Parenthood at 75.* New York, 1991.

INTERVIEWS

Richard Bebee, M.D., interviewed by Bruce R. Buckley for UHPP, September 7, 1993.

Grace Bair Fishell, interviewed by Gretchen Sullivan Sorin for UHPP, October 5, 1993

Robert L. Friedlander, M.D., interviewed by Mary C. Kahl, January 19, 2004

Shirley G. Gordon, interviewed by Mary C. Kahl, March 15, 2004.

Arthur D. Hengerer, M.D., interviewed by Mary C. Kahl, January 20, 2004.

Janet Hood, M.D., interviewed by Bruce R. Buckley for UHPP, October 5, 1993

Grace Jorgensen, M.D., interviewed by Gretchen Sullivan Sorin for UHPP, October 5, 1993. Interviewed by Mary C. Kahl, November 7, 2003.

Ruth Klepper, interviewed by Mary C. Kahl, May 5, 2004 and May 18, 2004.

Esther Lewis, interviewed by Bruce R. Buckley for UHPP, September 22, 1993. Interviewed by Mary C. Kahl, March 15. 2004.

Patricia McGeown, interviewed by Mary C. Kahl, July 16, 2004.

Betty Pattison, interviewed by Bruce R. Buckley for UHPP, September 22, 1993.

Charles S. Poskanzer, M.D., interviewed by Mary C. Kahl, March 22, 2001.

Marion Raymond, interviewed by Bruce R. Buckley for UHPP, September 22, 1993.

Fred Storm, M.D., interviewed by Mary C. Kahl, July 29, 2004

Helen Schnitzer and Mabel Carcia, interviewed by Bruce R. Buckley for UHPP, September 22, 1993.

Stevi Swire, interviewed by Bruce R. Buckley for UHPP, September 7, 1993.

Phoebe Ziehm, interviewed by Bruce R. Buckley for UHPP, September 7, 1993.

NEWSPAPERS

The Knickerbocker News

The New York Times

The Times Union

UNPUBLISHED SOURCES

New York State Library, Manuscripts and Special Collections. All the historical records of Upper Hudson Planned Parenthood up to 1986 are archived in Manuscripts and Special Collections.

Upper Hudson Planned Parenthood. All records from 1987 to the present, including Board Minutes, Executive Director Reports, Annual Reports, photographs and public relations materials are held in the UHPP offices at 259 Lark Street, Albany, NY.

0-595-33235-8

Printed in the United States
31456LVS00006B/1-102

9 780595 332359